PROFESSIONAL WCF 4

W9-BFF-876

PROFESSIONAL
WCF 4

PROFESSIONAL

WCF 4

WINDOWS COMMUNICATION FOUNDATION WITH .NET 4

Pablo Cibraro
Kurt Claeys
Fabio Cozzolino
Johann Grabner

Wiley Publishing, Inc.

Professional WCF 4: Windows Communication Foundation with .NET 4

Published by
Wiley Publishing, Inc.
10475 Crosspoint Boulevard
Indianapolis, IN 46256
www.wiley.com

Published simultaneously in Canada

ISBN: 978-0-470-56314-4
ISBN: 978-0-470-25924-5 (ebk)
ISBN: 978-0-470-90235-6 (ebk)
ISBN: 978-0-470-16846-2 (ebk)

Manufactured in the United States of America

10 9 8 7 6 5 4 3 2 1

For general information on our other products and services please contact our Customer Care Department within the United States at (877) 762-2974, outside the United States at (317) 572-3993 or fax (317) 572-4002.

Wiley also publishes its books in a variety of electronic formats. Some content that appears in print may not be available in electronic books.

Library of Congress Control Number: 2010926597

ABOUT THE AUTHORS

PABLO CIBRARO is a regional CTO at Tellago Inc. and is an internationally recognized expert with more than 10 years of experience in architecting and implementing large distributed systems with Microsoft technologies. He has spent the past few years working directly with various Microsoft teams on building sample applications and writing guidance for building service-oriented applications with Web Services, Web Services Enhancements (WSE), and Windows Communication Foundation (WCF). He also focuses on technologies that enable developers to build large-scale systems such as WCF, WF, Dublin, OSLO, and Windows Azure.

KURT CLAEYS is a .NET Solution Architect and trainer with more than 15 years practical experience in software development in many different areas. He was born and works in Belgium, where he is currently focused on service-oriented architectures and enterprise application integration implementations based on Windows Communication Foundation, BizTalk, and Azure AppFabric. After working in VB and ASP since 1995, he started working with .NET in general in 2002 and he got hooked to WCF in 2005. Kurt is now working for multiple financial companies and governmental institutes in Brussels as an architect, lead developer, and/or coach. As an MCT and MCSD, he's delivering both public and in-house training on .NET 3.5/4.0 and Azure, and he was Technical Learning Guide and Instructor Led Lab presenter at TechEd North America and TechEd Europe. His passion for technology is also expressed by speaking at numerous community and Microsoft events worldwide in the area of WCF and Azure. He's been awarded MVP Connected System Developer in 2008 for his community work. Kurt is also the competence leader for a unit of 150 .NET developers at ORDINA Belgium, where he's responsible for internal mentoring of co-workers on the implementation of WCF, BizTalk, and Azure AppFabric. When not behind a PC running Visual Studio 2010 or in front of a classroom, he enjoys spending time with wife and kids at home or traveling around the world. You can reach Kurt on www.devitect.net.

FABIO COZZOLINO is a Software Architect, Analyst and Developer, currently working at FimeSan, a CompuGroup Company, with a special involvement in the development of e-health platforms and solutions. He frequently participates as a speaker at events and user group meetings in the south of Italy, typically focusing his talks on topics like WCF and Windows Azure. He is also active in the community as the leader of DotNetSide, an Italian .NET User Group. Fabio currently writes numerous articles for the most popular Italian programming magazine and has published the Italian *Windows Communication Foundation* handbook, based on the first version of WCF. Thanks to his sustained and high quality activities within the communities, in 2010 he was awarded MVP for the Connected System Developer category. In 2004 Fabio achieved the MCAD (Microsoft Certified Application Developer) certification on .NET. Fabio has two blogs: http://dotnetside.org/blogs/fabio (Italian) and http://weblogs.asp.net/fabio (English). You can also follow Fabio on Twitter: http://twitter.com/fabiocozzolino.

JOHANN GRABNER lives in Graz, Austria, and has been in the software development and database business for almost fifteen years. Starting as a student of economics in 1991, he also began developing database applications. After these early experiences he enthusiastically started working as a Microsoft certified freelance trainer in the software development and database programming field in 1997, achieving all the necessary certifications like MCPD, MCITP, MCDBA, MCAD, MCSD, MCSD.Net, MCT, MCSE, OCP, and SCJP. Johann carried out several large software development and education projects for Austrian and international companies from different fields of business using Microsoft .NET technologies. He delivers consulting, coaching, and implementation services in the areas of service-oriented software development and database and SharePoint programming. Johann has been an MVP Connected System Developer since 2008. He has been a speaker and technical learning guide at various conferences, including Austria.NET, TechEd North America, and TechEd Europe, in addition to being the ASP.NET and VB.NET Proctor and Webcast presenter for several European countries. Johann also is regular speaker at the .NET Usergroup South Austria.

CREDITS

CONTRIBUTING WRITER
Owen Davies

EXECUTIVE EDITOR
Robert Elliott

PROJECT EDITOR
Kelly Talbot

DEVELOPMENT EDITOR
Jeff Riley

TECHNICAL EDITOR
Doug Holland

PRODUCTION EDITOR
Eric Charbonneau

COPY EDITOR
Tricia Liebig

EDITORIAL DIRECTOR
Robyn B. Siesky

EDITORIAL MANAGER
Mary Beth Wakefield

PRODUCTION MANAGER
Tim Tate

VICE PRESIDENT AND EXECUTIVE GROUP PUBLISHER
Richard Swadley

VICE PRESIDENT AND EXECUTIVE PUBLISHER
Barry Pruett

ASSOCIATE PUBLISHER
Jim Minatel

PROJECT COORDINATOR, COVER
Lynsey Stanford

PROOFREADER
Jen Larsen, Word One

INDEXER
Jack Lewis

COVER PHOTO
© technotr/istockphoto

ACKNOWLEDGMENTS

I WOULD LIKE TO THANK MY WIFE, ROMINA for all the patience she has had with me while I worked on this book. Also a special thanks to my good friend and Tellago CTO, Jesus Rodriguez, whose encouragement and support from the initial to the final stages enabled me to write this book. Finally, very many thanks to the people at Wiley and Kurt Claeys for giving me this opportunity to write a book on one my favorite subjects, WCF.

—Pablo Cibraro

I'D LIKE TO ACKNOWLEDGE ALL THE PEOPLE who helped support me in writing my share of this book. Without their support this would not have been realized. I'd like to thank my close family, my wife Marijke for letting me spend night after night locked away behind a computer and my kids Milan and Timon for giving me the needed pleasure being together with them between writing sessions. You're making my life a joy. Although the kids are still young, I feel they knew what I was doing all the time: working hard to succeed in a dream. I would also like to thank my parents for believing in me, years ago, when I had the idea of doing something with computers and wanted to study informatics. Special thanks to Robert (Bob) Elliott for giving me the opportunity to write this book and setting up the team. He's a great person and can really motivate people in rough times. I would also like to thank my co-workers at Ordina; they helped me a lot and supported me with useful feedback. Of course, the biggest credit goes to my co-authors Pablo Cibraro, Fabio Cozzolino, and Johann Grabner. After all, they did the hard work in this book. At last I want to thank all the great people working for Microsoft Belgium for their friendship.

—Kurt Claeys

I SHOULD LIKE FIRST TO THANK THE OTHER THREE AUTHORS, KURT, PABLO, AND JOHANN, who allowed me to work with them. A special thanks to Pablo who believed in me and in my work. Thanks go out to the DotNetSide User Group team, Tiziana, Vito, Mario, Leo, and Andrea, who always encourage me in each of my community activities, and to all my colleagues, especially Alessandro, Benedetto, Mimmo, and Vincenzo, who give me great moral support. Also many thanks to Claudio, my Research & Development Manager, for his encouragement, support, and attention in my activities.

Really many thanks to the people at Wiley. Robert Elliot and Kelly Talbot with whom there was a huge exchange of mail for the organization and coordination of my work. Tricia Liebig, Jeff Riley, and Doug Holland for their hard work in reviewing the contents of the chapters. Their feedback has been important for the success of the book.

Working on this book has required some sleepless nights spent writing, thanks to my parents and my sister for putting up with me.

Finally, I would like to thanks my wife, Tiziana, for her encouragement and support toward working on this book while we were preparing for our wedding. Words cannot express what I feel about her. Without her I can't do all of this, and my life would never be the same.

—Fabio Cozzolino

FIRST OF ALL, I WOULD LIKE TO THANK MY FAMILY AND MY FRIENDS for their sympathy and also for the enormous support, trust, and the motivation they gave me. Without the pleasant hours and days when my family spoiled me with good food and my friends came around with good beer to give me renewed energy, I fear I would have given up writing and working on the chapters after no more than a few weeks.

In my capacity as a co-founder of the .NET Usergroup South Austria, I must also thank the community members and Microsoft colleagues for their constructive suggestions and lively discussions.

Of course, I also owe thanks to Kelly and Bob, who coordinated the target times and checked that work was on schedule, and above all to Kurt Claeys and Pablo Cibraro for their excellent cooperation.

I hope that this book offers the readers a lot of useful knowledge that they are able to apply in real life. It should provide an ideal starting point for a multi-faceted and insightful introduction of WCF.

—Johann Grabner

CONTENTS

INTRODUCTION

THIS BOOK IS ABOUT Windows Communication Foundation in .NET 4.0. WCF is the technology in .NET that you use to build service-oriented applications, to exchange messages in various communication scenarios, and to run workflows built from service operations. With this new book you'll understand the principles of service orientation, learn patterns in communication, and discover how to declaratively define business processes. You'll learn the different parts of the technology to support these scenarios and gain a clear understanding of how the pieces of WCF 4.0 build upon each other to provide a comprehensive framework to support many aspects of distributed enterprise applications. Besides explaining the technical aspects of the WCF 4.0 stack, this book takes also a practical approach by showing three cases (service orientation, communication, and business processes) and implementing them step by step. The authors guide you in the practical aspects of developing with WCF and Visual Studio.

As you build your knowledge of the WCF 4.0 platform, you'll also learn how to effectively use Visual Studio 2010 to build solutions that maximize the new WCF 4.0 capabilities.

This book describes how to build (as a developer and as an architect) applications that integrate into the new programming paradigm in WCF 4.0. You'll also see how to set up a solution in this new architectural form based on WCF 4.0 as technology and .NET Services. You will learn how to solve actual real-world problems that you might experience when implementing WCF/WF 3.5 and the new programming paradigm and the new architectural styles needed for realizing WCF 4.0 projects. The examples shown in the book go beyond the "hello world" examples and guide you to an architecturally correct solution and provide a best practices–based coding guideline.

The authors are experienced in implementing the technology in real-world projects. They are faced with the problems in their daily jobs and come up with usable solutions combined with best practices and guidelines. They have applied this experience from real life to these chapters.

WHO THIS BOOK IS FOR

This book is for intermediate-level .NET developers and solution architects who are interested in using WCF 4.0 to build service-oriented applications, implement solid communications, host business processes, and enable secure and scalable integrations running in the cloud.

WHAT THIS BOOK COVERS

What you will learn in this book:

- ➤ Designing services and using communication and workflow patterns in a correct and solid architecture.
- ➤ Implementing the different WCF Bindings.

➤ The benefits of the WCF 4.0 messaging enhancements.

➤ How to instantiate services and work with proxies.

➤ Different ways to secure the access to service operations.

➤ How to implement WCF in a Service Oriented Approach.

➤ Working with workflow services to organize business processes and create long running orchestrations.

➤ How to build cloud-based integrations based on .NET Services.

➤ How to create RESTful services and use them with lightweight clients.

HOW THIS BOOK IS STRUCTURED

You can start reading any chapter depending on your current knowledge of WCF 4.0, but we advise you to read them sequentially if you are new to the technology. Either way, Chapter 2 establishes the Car Rental Service implementation example. This is the foundation for many examples throughout the book, so it would be a good idea to familiarize yourself with Chapter 2 before diving too deeply into the other chapters.

Chapter 1 describes a number of principles and patterns on service orientation, integration and business processes and shows how they are related to WCF. It also discusses how you can use WCF to implement the patterns. This chapter is aimed at providing you with a more architectural background in the areas where WCF is intended for use.

Chapters 2 through 10 are about the technology itself, the APIs for developing applications, and ways to configure them. These nine chapters discuss different aspects of the WCF stack: Bindings, Clients, Instancing, workflow processes, security, and .NET Services. These chapters are aimed at providing the developer with the needed knowledge to start programming in WCF 4.0.

Chapters 11 through 13 show you step-by-step how to implement a complete solution in Visual Studio 2010. These chapters have a more practical approach and describe the way to develop complete solutions based on the knowledge you gained in Chapters 1 through 10. In these chapters you need to work with Visual Studio to complete a project as a solution for a given scenario. The code for these solutions is also available for download from www.wrox.com.

Each of these chapters deals with one case:

➤ A SOA Case (Chapter 11)

➤ A Communication and Integration Case (Chapter 12)

➤ A Business Process Case (Chapter 13)

The final chapter of this book has a chapter about hosting. This chapter covers hosting in IIS/WAS and Cloud-based hosting. It also discusses how to track and manage endpoints with Windows Server AppFabric. This chapter also explains the routing service.

WHAT YOU NEED TO USE THIS BOOK

You'll need Visual Studio 2010 Professional and .NET 4.0 to learn WCF 4 and work through the examples in this book. You can run Visual Studio 2010 on Windows XP Service Pack 3 (except the Starter Edition), Windows Vista Service Pack 1 (except the Starter Edition), Windows 7, Windows Server 2003 SP2, Windows Server 2003 R2, Windows Server 2008 SP2, Windows Server 2008 R2. Your machine should have at least 1024MB RAM, preferably more.

CONVENTIONS

To help you get the most from the text and keep track of what's happening, we've used a number of conventions throughout the book.

> *Boxes with a warning icon like this one hold important, not-to-be-forgotten information that is directly relevant to the surrounding text.*

> *The pencil icon indicates notes, tips, hints, tricks, or asides to the current discussion.*

As for styles in the text:

➤ We *highlight* new terms and important words when we introduce them.

➤ We show keyboard strokes like this: Ctrl+A.

➤ We present code in two different ways:

```
We use a monofont type with no highlighting for most code examples.
```

```
We use bold to emphasize code that is particularly important in the present context
or to show changes from a previous code snippet.
```

SOURCE CODE

As you work through the examples in this book, you may choose either to type in all the code manually, or to use the source code files that accompany the book. All the source code used in this book is available for download at http://www.wrox.com. When at the site, simply locate the book's title (use the Search box or one of the title lists) and click the Download Code link on the book's detail page to obtain all the source code for the book. Code that is included on the Web site is highlighted by the following icon:

Available for download on Wrox.com

Listings include the filename in the title. If it is just a code snippet, you'll find the filename in a code note such as this:

Code snippet filename

 Because many books have similar titles, you may find it easiest to search by ISBN; this book's ISBN is 978-0-470-56314-4.

Once you download the code, just decompress it with your favorite compression tool. Alternately, you can go to the main Wrox code download page at http://www.wrox.com/dynamic/books/download.aspx to see the code available for this book and all other Wrox books.

ERRATA

We make every effort to ensure that there are no errors in the text or in the code. However, no one is perfect, and mistakes do occur. If you find an error in one of our books, like a spelling mistake or faulty piece of code, we would be very grateful for your feedback. By sending in errata, you may save another reader hours of frustration, and at the same time, you will be helping us provide even higher quality information.

To find the errata page for this book, go to http://www.wrox.com and locate the title using the Search box or one of the title lists. Then, on the book details page, click the Book Errata link. On this page, you can view all errata that has been submitted for this book and posted by Wrox editors. A complete book list, including links to each book's errata, is also available at www.wrox.com/misc-pages/booklist.shtml.

If you don't spot "your" error on the Book Errata page, go to www.wrox.com/contact/techsupport.shtml and complete the form there to send us the error you have found. We'll check the information and, if appropriate, post a message to the book's errata page and fix the problem in subsequent editions of the book.

P2P.WROX.COM

For author and peer discussion, join the P2P forums at p2p.wrox.com. The forums are a Web-based system for you to post messages relating to Wrox books and related technologies and interact with other readers and technology users. The forums offer a subscription feature to e-mail you topics of interest of your choosing when new posts are made to the forums. Wrox authors, editors, other industry experts, and your fellow readers are present on these forums.

At http://p2p.wrox.com, you will find a number of different forums that will help you, not only as you read this book, but also as you develop your own applications. To join the forums, just follow these steps:

1. Go to p2p.wrox.com and click the Register link.

2. Read the terms of use and click Agree.

3. Complete the required information to join, as well as any optional information you wish to provide, and click Submit.

4. You will receive an e-mail with information describing how to verify your account and complete the joining process.

> *You can read messages in the forums without joining P2P, but in order to post your own messages, you must join.*

Once you join, you can post new messages and respond to messages other users post. You can read messages at any time on the Web. If you would like to have new messages from a particular forum e-mailed to you, click the Subscribe to this Forum icon by the forum name in the forum listing.

For more information about how to use the Wrox P2P, be sure to read the P2P FAQs for answers to questions about how the forum software works, as well as many common questions specific to P2P and Wrox books. To read the FAQs, click the FAQ link on any P2P page.

1

Design Principles and Patterns

WHAT'S IN THIS CHAPTER?

➤ Exploring services and SOA

➤ Understanding communication and integration patterns

➤ Working with business process patterns

This chapter describes a number of principles and patterns regarding Service Orientation, Integration, and Business Processes. You will see how these principles are related to WCF and how you can use WCF to implement the patterns.

WHAT IS SOA?

SOA or service-oriented architecture is a style of programming, an architectural approach in software development, where an application is organized in functional units of code with a given behavior called services.

Services are a group of methods that share a common set of requirements and functional goals. They are called by other parts that need to execute its logic, depending on the outcome (such as data, results of calculations, and so on). The functions have a clearly defined and public signature which is published so other code (service clients) can use the functions in the service as a black box. The service operations are invisible — there is no direct interaction with a user and the work is executed as instructed by the given input parameters. SOA allows distributed applications to be organized. This means that the service consumers are running on different machines than the services. This allows the business logic and run user interfaces to be centralized or other consumers to be decentralized across the network. To make this happen in SOA, structured messages are sent between machines containing data.

The main idea behind SOA is to create a loosely coupled system where the only element a consumer of a service and the implementation of the services have in common is the list of public service operations and the definition of the structures of the parameters.

The client only knows the signatures describing the name, names and types of input parameters, and return type of the functions of the service. There's no other dependency. The application platform and programming language can be different on both client and service.

It's clear that this dependency is a functional one and is not based on technical infrastructure. This makes it possible to interact easily from different platforms with a service. A technical cornerstone in the SOA paradigm is the use of the SOAP standard. SOAP is the XML language that defines the content of messages sent to and received by a service operation.

Messages are formed out of the value of the parameters or return values and the data is formatted by SOAP. Every development platform has a SOAP stack, so working with service is supported in many environments. Supporting multiple environments is the goal of working in a SOA style.

This approach makes it possible to create systems that are built out of services. The services make up the building blocks for the application which can be composed out of the service operations. Either an end user application or another service can make use of these building blocks. SOA makes it possible to define a workflow of a business process in which they make calls to service operations.

Implementing an application in this architecture is the way to make code and the functional behavior of it reusable for unknown uses in the future. As the business logic is not coupled to some kind of user interface technology, it's possible to access these functions from clients that use newer technologies for creating user interfaces.

Separation of concerns is also an advantage. When structuring a development team for a project, different sub teams or individual members can be assigned to both sides of the service boundaries.

One team concentrates on building only the user interaction experience without concern about the code dealing with the business logic and data access. The UI team receives the service interface and can start coding against this interface. Meanwhile, another team works out the implementation of the defined service interface without the need to build a user interface. This means a developer is no longer responsible for the code end-to-end, including user interface, business logic, and data access for a given requirement. This results in assigning developers which can focus their knowledge of technology for one layer of the complete application.

Separation of concerns also means that the development of UI and services can be started at the same time directly after the publication of the agreed service interfaces. This is a huge advantage that allows the creation of the UI to be outsourced and keeps the creation of the real business logic in-house.

SOA is a way to build distributed systems where autonomous logic is called using loosely coupled messages via a well-defined interface.

Having a stable definition of a service interface is absolutely needed. The advantages of SOA are only present when the service contract is agreed on by multiple parties and is not subjected to changes during development. It's the business, defining the requirements, that has to have a clear view of the needed functionality. This is done in combination with a functional architect that defines the interface on a technical level. Of course this is not always easy or even possible as business requirements tend to change a lot in most environments. To solve this contradiction, it's wise to have an iterative development process that typically lasts 1 to 4 weeks. The service interface is not changed and the modifications to the interface are clearly discussed and reported to the development teams at every new iteration.

As application and software systems get bigger and more complex, a strict development architecture is needed that supports a great maintainability with a reusability of components. In the more distributed environments we see today — with applications implemented on different platforms — the need for a simple development approach that supports interconnectivity is a big value.

Implementing a SOA architecture is needed to solve problems that object orientation alone cannot solve for very large systems with integration between multiple parts. Integration of existing components needs a well-thought-out and industry-wide paradigm in the form of SOA.

FOUR TENETS OF SOA

To have a good and deeper definition of SOA, some principles need to be described in more detail. Tenets in the software industry are the way to do this. In SOA, the four tenets of service orientation are discussed.

These tenets include the following:

- ➤ Boundaries are explicit

- ➤ Services are autonomous

- ➤ Services share schema and contract, not class

- ➤ Service compatibility is based on policy

Boundaries Are Explicit

When working in a SOA approach, the boundaries a consumer needs to cross to reach the implementation should be defined explicitly. Services run in a process and memory space separated from the clients using them. Up-front thinking is needed to define the boundaries and should be communicated to each possible participant. The boundaries are defined by means of the contract and the address where a service can be reached. This information should be considered important and be easily accessed.

It is impossible to execute the logic in a service without having a contract and address. The logic is allowed to execute only in one way. This is by calling the contract, which is considered as the boundary. Boundaries are explicit, which means the client only needs to be aware of the existence of functions in the service that can only be executed via the contract This tenet also means that all possible exceptions must be described and a method can only stop executing by either giving the needed answer as an explicitly known data structure or as a structure containing the details of the exception. No data enters the service operation and no data leaves the service operation without a clear allowance to do so.

Services Are Autonomous

Services are considered standalone pieces of code that do not rely on the behavior of other services. Services are considered available without the need to explicitly instantiate it. They should be deployed and versioned independently from each other, and installing a new version of a service should not influence the behavior of other service operations. Services should not be coupled to each other as classes are coupled in a compiled executable. Services should instead use a loosely coupled architecture.

Services Share Schema and Contract, Not Class

A schema is the definition of a service operation and describes the signature in a platform-neutral way: the name of the functions, types of parameters, and the type of return value. A contract is considered metadata for the service being a black box with only this well-described interface. Schemas are the definition of the structure of the parameters. This tenet clearly indicates that the class itself (in code or as UML notation) is not shared across services and their clients.

As SOA is aimed at cross-platform interaction between different parts, it is not useful to bring the code for a class to other parties. In a lot of cases that code is meaningless. The inner workings (behavior of the code) of the class are not relevant to the consumer. The application (or other service) that uses a service is only interested in the outcome of the service operation. Clients send messages to part of the schema operations that conform to this contract to obtain this outcome.

Clients should interact with a service and back through an explicitly defined public interface including faults. Each version of a service should have one version of the interface. After an interface is in production it should not change, as changing the interface would be the result of modifications in the behavior of some service operations and should result in a new version of the interface.

Service Compatibility Is Based On Policy

This tenet means that a service decides which conditions process the message. A policy is used to negotiate elements in the communication, such as message format and security requirements. The policy is there to further indicate the semantics of the service and its expectation of the behavior on client side.

ANATOMY OF A SERVICE

A human body and a service both have an anatomy containing different parts related to each other that form a whole. Every part has its own purpose and behavior in the system. Describing this anatomy helps you understand how services work and is an introduction to the technical details of an SOA implementation. See Figure 1-1.

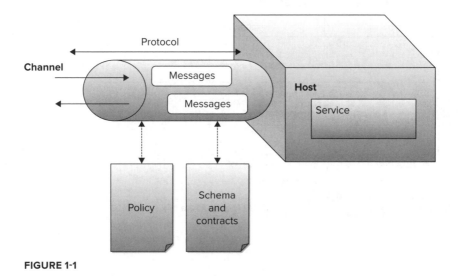

FIGURE 1-1

A service containing methods uses a channel to communicate and to be reachable by service consumers. The service consumers also use a channel, considered to be compatible with the service channel, to actually call the methods and send the needed data to the service. A channel is the combination of the schema, contract, and the policy on one hand and the used protocol at runtime on the other. Messages are sent through this channel in either direction. The channel is bound to a protocol defining in which way and how the service is reachable. A protocol, such as HTTP or MSMQ, is there to transport the data and needs to be supported by the operating system platform on which services are implemented. A channel is a kind of pipe in which messages flow. Messages are put on the channel by clients (or other types of service consumers) and taken out of the channel by the hosting stack of the platform that publishes the services.

A channel is bound to the schema it contracts. The channel is not complete without the definition of the metadata of service operations contained in schemas and contracts.

The channel also knows the policy which a service consumer has to implement.

Service Ecosystem

From a higher point of view a service is living in an ecosystem where a few concepts form part of the SOA paradigm. This ecosystem describes the place of these concepts and how they are related to each other. See Figure 1-2.

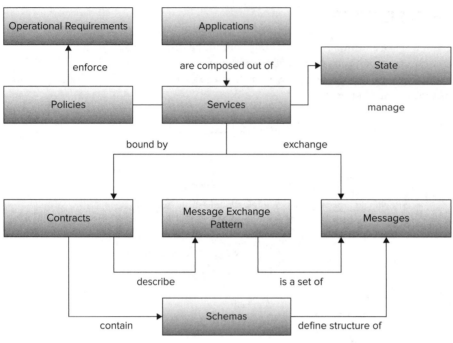

FIGURE 1-2

Applications Are Composed of Services

The heart of the ecosystem is the service itself. Services are the building blocks out of which applications can be composed. Applications can be end-user tools with clear user interface parts or business processes which access the services in a predefined sequence. As the SOA approach allows you to see the services as units of behaviors, you can build applications by picking the ones needed to compose another part of the software solution.

Services Manage State

The responsibility of a service and its operations is often to persist data to a database and read the data again at a later time. A service is actually managing a state. Although services are stateless, meaning they don't remember this data in memory, they are calling to a database to persist the state. Services will not call to a database directly, but in a good architecture they will depend on other layers to communicate to the database.

Services Enforce Policies

A service has the right to define policies concerning the usage of its logic. Policies describe prerequisites about how the service consumer should behave. You can think of a policy being an agreement on a condition that has to be fulfilled before a client is allowed to communicate with the service. Most often this is an agreement on security.

Policies Enforce Operational Requirements

By defining policies, a service can enforce the operational requirements of the calling platform. The policies can be organized in such a way that a certain measure of security must be implemented on the client.

Services Are Bound by Contracts

Services only exist if a contract is present which describes the signatures of its operations. This contract is the agreement between client and service. The contract has to be defined clearly and bound to the service at runtime. The contract is needed to create a proxy class for the client tier used to program against the service as if it is a local class. Without a contract the service cannot be consumed by a client application.

Contracts Describe Message Exchange Patterns

A message exchange pattern is the definition of how and in which sequence messages are sent from one party to another. The patterns influence how the service can be called either synchronously or asynchronously and defines whether answers are expected from the operation or not. Message exchange patterns can be the following:

➤ **Request-response:** Most-used pattern, every call is returned by another message directly.

➤ **One-way:** There is no answer coming from the service and the operation can thus be called asynchronously.

➤ **Duplex:** A service operation can call back to the client during the method call. In this way the operation can ask more information from the client before returning the final answer.

A message exchange pattern is visible on a functional level where developers implement service operations. On a deeper technical level of the protocol, a message exchange pattern is present but mostly invisible. When using a wsHttpBinding for calling an operation, client and service will not only exchange the message with the data. The functional call will be preceded and followed by some other technical messages. We can consider these messages as handshaking messages that are part of the WS-protocol. These messages can negotiate a security context. They are also needed to ensure reliability that the service has received the data and that the service can be sure the client has received the answer as expected. This additional communication is done by the protocol and is not to be implemented by the developer.

Contracts Contain Schemas and Schemas Define Message Structure

A schema is the definition of the structure of the parameters for an operation. It describes these parameters in terms of an XSD file. XSD is the metadata language that defines messages going into a service operation or the result of a service operation. Schemas are used so service operation consumers can format data. It can be interpreted by the service when called so the service can access the data again. This is called serialization and deserialization.

A Message Exchange Pattern Is a Set of Messages

The combination and calling order of messages can be described by a more complex exchange pattern. So a message exchange pattern can define which operation must be called first and which one last, or if a complete workflow of the operation can be defined.

Services Exchange Messages

Exchanging messages is the most important part in a service ecosystem. Exchanging messages means calling an operation and receiving answers from it (or raising exceptions). Exchanging messages is simply a way to allow that operations are called on another machine. A message transports the input parameters from client to service and another message transports the answer back to the caller.

ORCHESTRATING SERVICES IN BUSINESS PROCESSES

As services are building blocks of applications in a service-oriented architecture, the operations in it can also be called by a workflow. This workflow is a definition of the order and dependencies between incoming and outgoing calls. The workflow orchestrates the interaction between consumers and services to fulfill a business process. Workflows know the contracts and schema of the services they are using or implementing.

A workflow is like programming sequences and branches around receiving operations and calling other operations in other services. Instead of programming these sequences and branches in a programming language, the flow is defined declaratively as a meta-language. This meta-language can be interpreted to form the integration between multiple parts of the application at runtime. In this way a workflow describes a very functional and complex message exchange pattern. As the main goal of SOA is building reusable components for an application, the use of workflows is an enabler to define the logic of integration and business processes.

The requirement of a business process forms the base of the definition of the contracts and schemas. Looking at these requirements should be the start of the analyzing process.

Figure 1-3 shows an example of an orchestration.

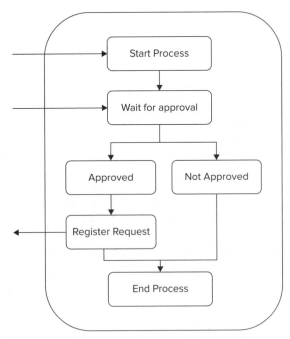

FIGURE 1-3

TECHNOLOGIES BEHIND SOA

To implement an SOA application, you need to have technologies and protocols. As SOA is intended to create distributed and cross-platform applications, these supporting technologies and protocols need to be industry standards. The following sections describe some of the most used standards in the SOA world.

SOAP

Simple Object Access Protocol (SOAP) is an XML specification for exchanging data as structured information in messages. SOAP standardizes how data is exchanged on the wire. As it's based on XML, it is platform agnostic. A SOAP message simply carries the data as a message. A SOAP envelope contains a (optional) header and a (required) body element. The header can contain information needed for the underlying technical infrastructure to support the communication and is not related to the business functionality. The body element contains the functional data as payload. Each parameter for the service operation is present in the body as the serialized representation of the data. This is an example of a SOAP message:

```
<soap:Envelope
    xmlns:soap="http://www.w3.org/2001/12/soap-envelope"
    soap:encodingStyle="http://www.w3.org/2001/12/soap-encoding">

    <soap:Body xmlns:m="http://www.example.org/stock">
    <m:GetStockPrice>
    <m:StockName>XYZ</m:StockName>
    </m:GetStockPrice>
    </soap:Body>

</soap:Envelope>
```

WS-* Protocols

SOAP is only a specification describing how functional data in the body and technical data in headers is formatted. SOAP itself does not always define a meaning to the header. WS-* are protocols that standardize how to implement certain needs and behaviors when working with distributed messages using SOAP messages. These protocols describe how the plumbing needs to exchange messages in a secure, transactional, and reliable way by using the headers in the SOAP message. WS-* is a set of protocols where each protocol has its own purpose.

WCF can implement the WS-* protocols by using a binding called `WsHttpBinding`. This binding makes use of some of the WS-* protocols and adds the needed behaviors, such as transactional message calls, reliability, discovery, and addressing.

WSDL

WSDL is a XML-formatted definition of the contract. It contains all metadata for the interface of the service including function names, parameter names, and their types and the types of return values. The purpose of a WSDL file is to define this contract in a cross-platform way as the types are expressed in XML types. The WSDL file can be used by non-.NET development environments to create classes in their programming language (such as J2EE) to act as proxies for the real centralized implementation class.

See Figure 1-4 as an example of a WSDL file. This file can be shown in a browser when browsing to a dedicated URL on which the WCF service exposes metadata.

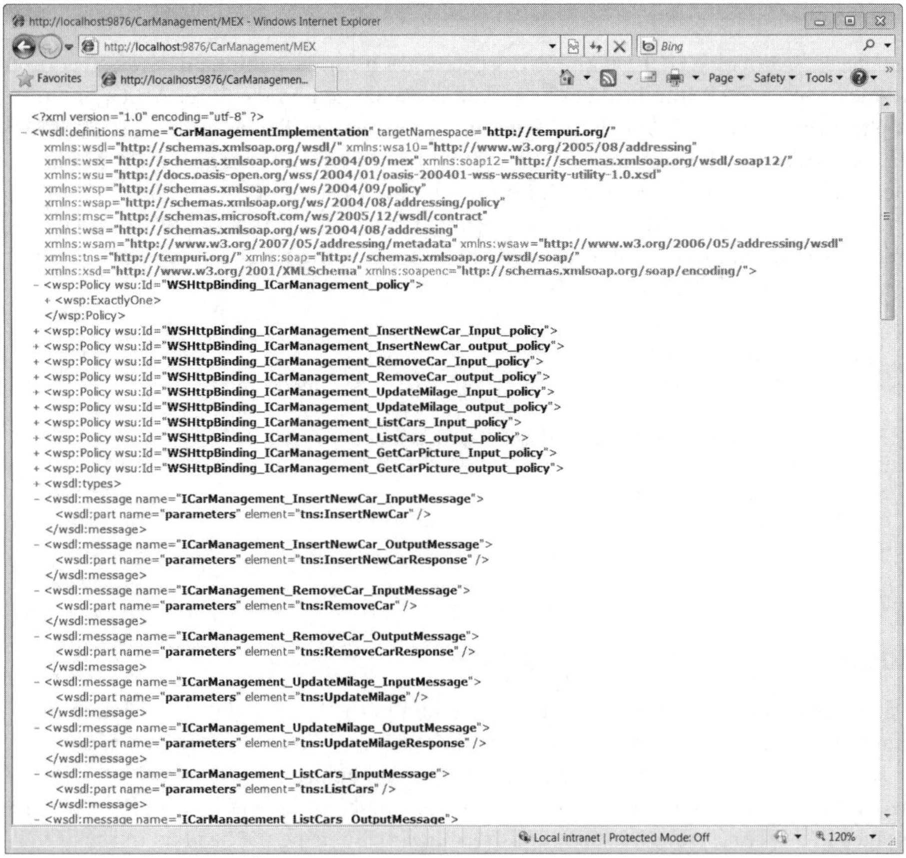

FIGURE 1-4

CONTRACT-FIRST PRINCIPLE

Designing services for an application starts with analyzing the requirements. It's not a good idea to open Visual Studio first and start coding immediately. Analysts should start by working together with the people needing the application and carefully interpreting what they say the requirements are for the services. Meetings with all stakeholders are needed to define what the services should do and what their logic is.

The first thing that should be clearly defined is the contract of a service. Analyzing a service-oriented application is not about drawing screens for the user interface or defining tables and building a relational diagram for them. It's about defining the contract first.

Of course, at the end of a functional analysis there are three basic layers in an application:

➤ UI: Contains the screens, validation logic, and interaction between user controls

➤ Logic: Implements the requirements, business rules, calculations, and reporting

➤ Database: Stores data and referential integrity across tables

In a SOA approach, it's clear that UI and database are not the first layers being analyzed. SOA is focused in the business aspect and deals with separating the logic from the look and feel of screens and how the data is stored. Neither UI nor database is really related to the business requirements. In most cases the business is not interested in how the data is stored or how it's represented to the end user.

You want to make the logic contained in services accessible to multiple user interfaces. The user interface is developed by another team that is only responsible for the UI and has no relation to the business. Remember that services are black boxes; they are used to get results from them.

You want to make the logic independent of the database store. It's up to the DBA administrators to come up with a design for the tables unless the database is already in place.

This leads to the contract first principle. The first thing you should analyze is the contracts. You should have a clear view of what to expect from a service, what methods are part of the service, and what the structure of the parameters for these methods are. The design of this contract is very much influenced by the business and should be driven by it. It's up to the software and business analysts to define a contract.

HOW WCF AND .NET SERVICES IMPLEMENT SOA PATTERNS

Patterns are a description of a reusable solution to a well-known problem in typical situations. The idea of a design pattern is to describe the solution for the problem in an understandable language before it's translated to code. One could say that a design pattern is a blueprint or template for a possible solution. It is used for discussing the problem before programming it in a language. It is agnostic of the development stack or of the used technology.

Patterns

Patterns are languages used by architects or the designers of the needed integrations where people can start discussing and using the patterns in their communication.

Phrases such as "I would suggest using an enricher pattern before the messages are sent to the broker . . ." and "for this functional requirement I don't see the need for a correlation pattern here . . ." are typical in conversations when doing an analysis for service-oriented or integration-based solutions.

These phrases are clear enough for the process designers and architects and are a valid way of communicating before development starts. After designers agree on the design they can draw it in a schema. Design patterns often have a counterpart as a schema with a big diagram describing the whole picture of communication and integration. This schema contains a combination of the patterns and is the ideal base for developers to create code and system engineers to set up the implementation.

Decoupled Contract: Interface vs. Implementation

WCF supports the separation and implementation of interfaces by using interfaces as part of the C# or VB.NET languages. All operations, their types of parameters and type of return values for a service, can be expressed in interfaces. These interfaces can be created in a separate class library project. The data contracts describing the structures of parameters or return values are also defined in classes.

Typically these interfaces and classes are stored in a class library which contains no implementation. The implementation of the services is done in a different class library. It's just a matter of referencing the needed interface library from within the implementation project and implementing the interfaces in the classic way that is supported by .NET languages.

This separation allows sharing the interface with other projects that need them but cannot provide the implementation as with the client applications.

Interfaces and their operation signatures are attributed with metadata attributes so WCF can recognize them as contracts that are part of the service ecosystem. These attributes are placed on top of the code elements and they form an additional layer of metadata which is understandable by the WCF runtime to give the code meaning in terms of contracts and schemas. The metadata for defining these contracts and schemas contained in the attributes is thus separated from the interface, and the implementation only knows the interface. This makes the contract decoupled from the implementation. In the metadata the name of operations and XML structure of the SOAP message can be defined without the implementation having to know these.

Those attributes are `[ServiceContract Attribute]`, `[OperationContractAttribute]`, `[DataContractAttribute]`, and `[DataMemberAttribute]`.

Proxy Pattern

The proxy pattern is used by WCF by allowing building and using a class in the project which consumes the services. This class acts like it is the implementation but it's actually a class that implements the same shared interface as the implementation of the real logic. As the interface together with the extra metadata for the SOAP messages defined in attributes is also available in the client project, this proxy class can mimic the implementation by implementing the interface.

WCF provides the `ClientBase<T>` class for these proxy classes to inherit from. This base class has the needed logic to set up communication with the service and transform the operation calls. The consumers execute against the proxy into SOAP messages and send them to the service using the defined binding.

`ClientBase<T>` is a generic class that needs to know the type of the interface. This class has a protected property, only visible in the classes that inherit from it. This property is the channel and is of the generic type used by the proxy. This means the channel has the same list of methods as the actual implementation of the logic on the server side.

OperationContext Pattern

The goal of the `OperationContext` pattern is to decouple the functional input parameters from technical information the method needs to execute. WCF provides a class called `System .ServiceModel.OperationContext` that is useable during the execution of the implementation methods to obtain the execution and message context for the current method. This class can provide the executing method with information about the call, like a session ID, the incoming message headers in the SOAP envelope, information about the identity of the caller, and how the authorization of the call was executed. The context contains a lot of information that is nonfunctional and therefore should not be part of the parameters of the `DataContract` of the method being called. When working in a duplex communication mode, the `OperationContext` provides the channel to be used to call back to the client during the execution of the call. WCF 3.5 also supports an additional context called `WebOperationContext` that provides a method with more information about the request in terms of Http properties.

Concurrent Contracts

WCF supports concurrent contracts by implementing multiple interfaces simultaneously combined with allowing a service to have multiple endpoints configured. Each endpoint configuration has its own address and is referred to one of the interfaces. This results in the possibility for a single service implementation to implement a set of operations coming from multiple interfaces in which some operations are reserved for one particular interface in combination with operations that are defined in multiple interfaces. The list of operations that is accessible by an interface is defined by the endpoint configuration as this configuration is aware of the interface it's exposing.

Data Confidentiality

Security and data confidentiality is implemented extremely well in WCF. WCF supports cross-platform security by using the WS-* protocols stack for message level security and can additionally use transport security on a higher level in addition to the security applied through these WS-* enhancements. The level of security is defined by the selected binding.

Atomic Service Transactions

WCF supports transactions by implementing the WS-Atomic Transaction (WS-AT) protocol. Most often transactions on the service level lead to transactions on the database level. WCF communicates with the distributed transaction coordinator of the database to set up the transactions. The WS-Atomic Transaction specifications define mechanisms to execute transactions across service boundaries. It allows transactions to span multiple calls from a client so the transaction is distributed beyond the facade of the session. This makes it possible for a client to start the transaction, call different operations on the service, and consider all the operation calls as one transaction. The transaction flows from client to service and the operation in the service participates in (sometimes expressed as "follows") the transaction started by the client.

This means that the service keeps the transaction alive until the client decides the transaction is complete. When this happens, the service signals to the distributed transaction coordinator to commit the transactions.

Distributing transactions also means that when something goes wrong at the service level during one of the calls instantiated by the client, the transaction is considered ended and thus rolled back.

How a service behaves concerning transactions can be defined by the [TransactionFlow] attributes on the operation in the interface and by [OperationBehavior] attributes on the implementation.

Session Facade

The session facade in WCF is built up by the implementation classes. These classes form the first wall of code a client reaches when executing an operation in a service. It's up to these implementation classes to call the business logic in other layers of the application. This could be the business logic, a workflow, or the data access layer.

Exception Shielding

WCF automatically shields away all exceptions occurred in or behind the facade and does not show the details of these exceptions to the calling clients. When exceptions occur at service side, the client is only informed about the fact that something went wrong. By default the detailed information about the error, the inner exception and stack trace, are not visible for the client. This client only sees a very generic error. Receiving this exception causes the channel of the client to come into a faulted state.

This is not only done from a security perspective — you would not want to give information about the stack trace to a potential hacker, for example. But also because sending the details of a .NET exception to a client in a SOA architecture would be useless as the clients are not always .NET clients. As SOA has this cross-platform approach, it's possible that the clients are not running in the .NET environment but possibly in a J2EE or other framework where receiving a .NET exception would be useless and could not be interpreted.

WCF supports a more cross-platform way of carrying information about exceptions in a SOAP fault. Transporting a SOAP fault and serializing/deserializing the content is defined by the SOAP standard and is cross-platform and more SOA-oriented.

Using SOAP faults in WCF is done by defining a data contract like any other DataContract used by the interface. This data contract can have a customized structure containing only the data about the exception and what the service wants to reveal and thinks is useful to its clients and the end user. The operations that will send this custom fault contract need to know this contract by adding the Fault Contract attribute to the operation.

The methods in which the .NET exception takes place need to catch this exception and translate it to this DataContract. It's up to the client to react to this exception.

COMMUNICATION AND INTEGRATION PATTERNS

Communication and integration are the most important aspects of WCF. These are the areas of software development where WCF really shines and where it has great value — what WCF is really built for. Developers can take advantage of a rich set of features in WCF that support them by building distributed applications that communicate data and create integrations between each other.

WCF is an acronym for Windows Communication Foundation, meaning the core WCF is really targeted to communication. Here you have the background of the need for integration, the different ways communication is used, and the patterns of how messages are exchanged for integration are described.

The need for communication and integration comes from the fact that enterprises are typically comprised out of a large number of different applications. Each of these have their own functionality, built in different architectural styles, using different technologies, and implemented on different operating systems. It's not uncommon that enterprises have a broad set of applications, either custom-made or bought as a package running on different platforms and locations with each fulfilling only a small part of the business requirements. Solid integration infrastructure is needed as well as a platform-agnostic way of communicating that provides an efficient, controllable, and maintainable exchange of data between multiple applications.

All communication leading to the exchange of data is based on sending messages. This data is either a set of parameters for a question to obtain information or is information that is the answer to these questions. These messages are formatted and serialized according to an industry-wide standard. This standard is SOAP, which is based on XML. The purpose of formatting messages in the SOAP standard is interoperability. SOAP is understood by many technology stacks used for communication and integration. SOAP and the additional WS standards support not only cross-platform formatting but also additional functionalities such as security, reliability, and transactional behavior.

Communication and integration is the technical part of applications that allow functions in a distributed environment to talk to each other and that know how to exchange the data they need. In almost every environment, lots of smaller applications or services, each executing a single responsibility, form a much bigger application.

In many cases applications are distributed by nature. Services are implemented close to the database, applications are run on desktops, and data has to be moved between multiple branches of a company. In between them, the data has to be enriched, aggregated, or somewhere a decision has to be made about where data is to be delivered. Most often data is sent dynamically.

Integration Styles

Throughout the history of software architecture, a number of integration styles were introduced and each of them was based on the needs and requirements for that time — the availability of technology stacks and the standardization of protocols and existence of the communication infrastructure.

We recognize four styles:

- ➤ Import/export files
- ➤ Shared database

➤ Remote procedure calls

➤ Message Bus

Import/Export Files

At first, when no communication infrastructure was present, the need for integration was low. There were not many applications to integrate and all environments had a closed architecture — the only possible integration was to export data into a file from one application and import the file containing the data into another application. The file could be a delimited or positional flat file.

This was originally a manual process where people could export and move the files on disk or use a FTP connection to a place where the receiving application could reach the file again to import it by a manual action. This process was done later in a more automated way using scripts run by an operating system or custom application that could execute macros in the application and automate a FTP connection.

A lot of these applications still exist in many enterprises keeping this first wave of integration styles alive. It's clear that this integration is a pure peer-to-peer integration and that the process doing the integration is strongly coupled to the application at both ends of the communication channel.

This style is always communicating data in a delayed fashion where imports and exports were scheduled during night. This was okay at those times but nowadays, a faster, real-life integration is needed in our set of applications.

Shared Database

Another style of integration was built on top of a shared database. Instead of exporting data to files, the data was copied to a central database form where it could be picked up by other applications having access to the same database. This was possible as the access to databases was standardized and most databases were open and reachable by middleware (think ODBC) on different platforms. Integration in this style also became more focused on the multiuser aspect of applications where different applications were accessing this shared data simultaneously and data was exchanged nearly immediately instead of by scheduled imports and exports.

This style also resulted in a coupling between applications and a relation structure somewhere in a database. Changing the data structure for one of the integrations could impact the correctness of other integrations. It uses the same structures in the database for their integration needs.

Remote Procedure Calls

Styles evolved and it became clear that applications should be able to talk to each other without the need for import/export procedures and that a shared database was hard to maintain in large integration scenarios. So the remote procedure call style was taking over.

In a RPC (remote procedure call), style applications can send data to other applications by simply calling their methods and crossing memory and physical network boundaries. Some technologies such as CORBA were created for this style of integration. But a problem with these first-generation RPC technologies is that their implementation is somewhat proprietary and not available on every platform.

SOAP later became a solution, not only in the SOA area but also by providing its value in the integration area. But again RPC, even with an open technology, has its drawbacks. The fear of coupling applications too tightly with RPC calls is present. Another drawback is the creation of lots of connections between multiple applications where every new integration results in creation code at the client side and code to receive it on the other side.

Message Bus

The last style is the Service (or Message) Bus. In this style a new infrastructure is introduced as a bus where messages can be sent by an application and picked up again by other applications. This could be done by publish and subscribe patterns. Data is published onto the bus and other applications subscribe to data on the bus. Even when no subscribers are available the bus can take the initiative itself to resend the data later. On the other hand, the bus can also act as a reader to read external data and resend it to the subscribers.

Publishing data and subscribing to data is based on schemas declared by data contracts. Most often an XSD file is used to not only declare the structure of messages but also as the unit of subscription. Subscribing in a Service Bus is done by expressing interest in a certain namespace or the root element name defined in XSD scheme. All data flowing into the bus in a XML message conforms to this schema and is automatically pushed toward the receiver. The advantage of the bus is that new applications interested in receiving data already published into the bus for another integration scenario can simply be plugged into the bus without the need to change the code of the sender and redeploy the client application.

The main reason to use a bus is if the data is already published on the bus for another application, the new application can also profit from this. It could subscribe to the same data. Even when the data that is already being sent into the bus does not perfectly fit the needs, because the receiving application needs less or possibly other data, it is possible to work with this approach. Data can be filtered and or aggregated with other data flowing into the bus to form a new stream of data onto which the subscriber can plug in to also consume this data.

A Service Bus is there to allow other integrations in the future without impact on already existing integrations.

INTEGRATION OF LEGACY APPLICATIONS WITH A NEW ENVIRONMENT

Legacy applications are software written years ago, using technology present at that time. It was not meant to be re-engineered or thrown away when new requirements arrived, because the investment would be too large to migrate them to new technologies.

They tend to have a closed and monolithic approach, sometimes tightly coupled to the dataset or user interface. Most often these types of applications are stable, doing their job perfectly, and are the core of the enterprise.

When new requirements are needed, these applications remain unchanged but need to integrate with the new applications or services built for these requirements.

Integration is needed to exchange data—the legacy application exports data and the new service needs this data to fulfill the business requirement.

Message Exchange Patterns

Message exchange patterns (sometimes called MEPs) are descriptions of common ways to have two parts: communication and message exchange.

Request-Response

The most commonly used pattern. The client requests information from the service by sending a request message and expects a response message from the service. This means the service has to be reachable and the client waits for the answer for a defined timeout. The client has a clear definition of what the structure of the answer will be. In case of an exception occurring while processing the request, a message containing the fault is sent. See Figure 1-5.

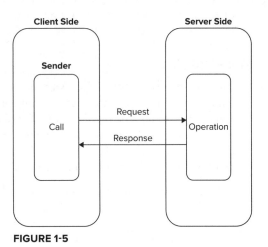

FIGURE 1-5

In most cases the request-response pattern is used to organize communication between applications. Almost every communication has a client requesting data from a service which sends a response.

WCF supports this by simply allowing the developer to define a method in C# or VB.NET where the methods have one or more input parameters and can have a return type. These parameters can be of any type, such as primitive strings and integers or more complex types defined in classes.

The approach of WCF is that these method signatures can be defined in an interface, which is a C# or VB.NET language element. This interface has the signatures of the methods together with attributes to indicate that the method is reachable from a remote client. By having the operating class implement this interface, WCF supports the separation of the metadata indicating it's an operation from the actual implementation. The classes are just implementing the interface, they are not aware that they are called by a remote client. These attributes are [ServiceContract] for the interface and [OperationContract] for the method signatures.

The attributes on the interface indicate that the methods are implementing the request-response pattern. The attributes have additional parameters to further define the details of the request and the response, like the namespace for the contract and the SOAP action and reply action values.

One-Way

Messages are sent from client to server in one direction. The client sends the message but does not expect an answer back. In many scenarios it even forgets about sending it. The server simply processes the message and does not calculate an answer or send acknowledgements back to the client. It's clear that not all communication can be done by this pattern. Whenever an answer is needed directly, it's not useable. See Figure 1-6.

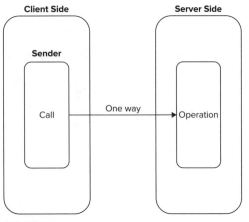

FIGURE 1-6

The biggest value of this pattern is the ability to work asynchronously, allowing the client to continue its work while the receiver processes the message at its own pace. This results in the illusion that communication is very fast as the client is responsive again immediately after sending the request, but it's up to the service to process the request. Processing at the server side can be done in a multithreaded approach so the service can consume multiple messages simultaneously.

Another, perhaps most important, value is the ability to create a guaranteed delivery environment. By using a one-way pattern it's possible to send the message through a queuing system such as MSMQ. A queue at the client side receives the message and tries to send it to the receiver. When the receiver is not available for one reason or another, this mechanism resends the message and delivers it when the other end is back online. The queuing system can also be configured to persist the data when delivery is not possible so the messages survive a reboot.

Having a method executing in the one-way pattern is defined partly at the level of the operation itself by indicating that the return type is void or defining the method as a subroutine instead of a function in VB.NET.

This has to be done in combination with specifying the use of the one-way pattern on the interface by setting the `IsOneWay` parameter to True on the `OperationContract` attributes.

Duplex Messaging

In the duplex pattern, client and server exchange messages without a predefined pattern. The client sends an initial request to the service waiting for a response but allows the service that sends the response to call back to the client to ask for more information. The service can call back to the client dynamically and possibly multiple times before sending the response to the initial request. See Figure 1-7.

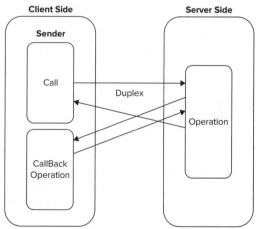

In this pattern the client becomes a service for the code while executing. The code which was considered as the service can now act as a client to call a function during the processing of the call.

A distinct communication mechanism is used when a duplex communication calls back to a client during execution. It also needs the signatures of

FIGURE 1-7

the operation that is called by service to reach the client available in both service and client. First the service needs to use a duplex-enabled way of communicating; there is no way for a service to call back to the client without this.

This is done by selecting one of the duplex bindings supported by WCF and indicating this in the configuration. The signatures of the methods that are implemented in the client need to be defined at service level and also be present at the client to have them implemented.

WCF allows defining a callback contract as a normal interface and indicates at the service interface that it could call one of its methods in the callback interface. This is done by specifying the type of callback interface at the [Service Contract] of the service.

In this way, the definition of the callback contract is part of the WSDL file. The client can implement a class based on this interface. The service knows exactly what methods it can call back to the client as it knows the signatures of the methods available on the client.

Duplex simply means that the service is operating temporarily as a client and needs to have a channel back to reach the client. During the execution of a method the service has access to a context which has a reference to this callback channel. Calling methods on this channel result in calling methods on the client.

Streaming

In the streaming pattern the client initiates a request to get a very large set of data. The service chunks up the data in smaller pieces and sends them to the client one by one. The data is so big that the service has to read this data from a file system or database in chunks. The data chunks are sent to the client in an ordered way as the receiver wants to consume them in that same ordered way. This would be the case in streaming video.

In this pattern there is one request asking for the data followed by a large set of answers which each contain a subset of all the data as a result of the call. It is up to the sender to indicate in the last message that the datastream is finished so the client doesn't expect more data to come. See Figure 1-8.

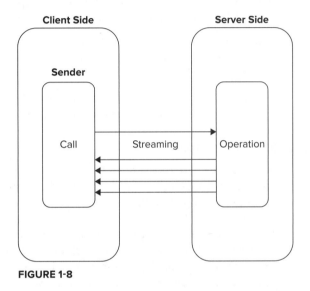

FIGURE 1-8

Pub-Sub

Pub-sub is the pattern where you see applications publishing data on a regular basis and a number of other applications interested in this data and subscribing to this publication. For example, a stock quote system that publishes quotes frequently is received by interested parties.

In the pub-sub pattern the publisher is typically unaware who the subscribers are and what they are doing with the received data. The publisher doesn't even care whether there are subscribers. The publisher just cares about sending data out of its system. The pattern indicates an event-driven approach; the publisher raises an event into the client applications. These client applications act to this event by consuming the received data. This consumption can be different: they can show the information to the end user, they can store it in their persistence environment, or they can decide to send the data to other applications. See Figure 1-9.

In the pub-sub pattern there is always an explicit action, called the subscription, where an application expresses interest in the information from the publisher. Most often a subscriber is not interested in all the information the publisher sends. By subscribing, it can express a condition for the data as a filter. The publisher keeps a list of references to the subscribers together with the filter conditions, and every time it has new information to be sent it iterates through all the interested subscribers, checks interest in the information, and publishes the data.

In many cases the information provider itself does not do this subscription management and broadcasting of the data. Instead the provider sends its data to a generic service which is responsible for the publication of the data. This additional service manages subscriptions and can publish the received data to all subscribers.

WCF 4.0 has no direct support for the pub-sub pattern. The pub-sub pattern can be implemented by using the same construction for the duplex pattern. The implementation of pub-sub could be made by having a subscription service that maintains a list of references to the callback channels of the subscribers in memory.

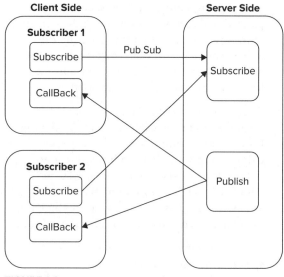

FIGURE 1-9

When the service needs to send data to all subscribers, it can iterate through all these subscribers and call a method to broadcast this data. There is no polling involved in this scenario as the subscribers are acting as a host waiting for methods to be called by services.

.NET services (as part of the Azure AppFabric) has support for the pub-sub pattern without using duplex communication but by using a communication mechanism implemented by the eventRelay bindings.

Clients can register their own address to the .NET Service Bus in the cloud. The AppFabric records where the client is. When data needs to be published to all subscribers, it's only a matter of sending a message to the Service Bus. The Service Bus relays this message to all subscribers as it knows all subscriber addresses.

Implied Order Invocation

When using multiple operations in a contract in some sequential order to fulfill one logical unit of work at the service, it's useful to define the order that operations can be called. By defining an implied order invocation the client is aware of this order, and this results in the fact that some operations cannot be executed before others are executed first.

This could be the case when operations rely on a state that must be created by operations called earlier. Implied order invocation allows describing which operations can be used to start this logical group of calls and which method could violate this logical order when called.

It also allows defining methods that are considered last in the logical order. Calling these terminating methods indicates to the client that there is no use calling the other methods as the logical unit of work is considered finished.

This pattern is not a pure message exchange pattern as the calls to the methods participating in the ordered invocation can have their own implementation of another pattern. It's more a pattern that groups multiple operations into one logical unit of work. See Figure 1-10.

WCF provides the `OperationContract` attribute where you can specify the constraints for invoking operations in order. It allows defining a method that can be used to start the conversation by specifying the `IsInitiating` parameter as false. Specifying the `IsTerminating` as true means that calling this method indicates that the conversation is over.

By default, when the parameters are not specified explicitly, every method has

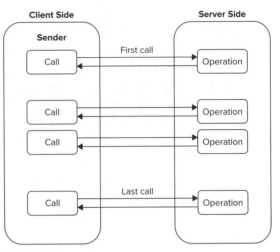

FIGURE 1-10

`IsInitiating` set to true and every method has `IsTerminating` set to `false`. This means every method is allowed to be called first and no method terminates the conversation. It's up to you to decide otherwise and specify which methods cannot be used as the first (`IsInitiating` = `false`) and which methods will close the conversation (`IsTerminating` = `false`).

The important aspect here is that the client also knows this order invocation as it's defined on interface level. So the proxy will not call methods that it's not allowed to call. Either because it's calling a method as the first, which is not initiating, or calling a method after it has called a terminating method.

Another way to declare an order in the invocation of methods in a service is by implementing them as a workflow service. This has a more flexible model that defines the order. A workflow service is a declarative definition of a sequence of operations in the form of a flowchart.

In this definition you can clearly define the order of the methods. You can define an expected number of methods out of the interface that are called in a certain step in the process by placing them inside a listen activity. A listen activity groups operations together and stops the process until one of the methods is called. This call executes the workflow continuously with the rest of the process, meaning the other methods in the same listen activity are no longer available.

This definition of the order is not known by the client. This would be too complex for the proxy and is useless as the workflow can behave very dynamically. It could branch to another set of methods in a listen activity based on input from a previous call. When a client calls a method that is not currently available, the client receives an error message indicating that the requested operation is not found.

In workflow services, operations can be defined as either instantiating a new process or participating in existing and already running processes. Typically, the first operation in the workflow instantiates the process, and the other methods follow.

Messaging Patterns

Messaging patterns can be used in a variety of ways, from enriching content to routing messages to intercepting filters and more. Their versatility makes use of the WCF runtime architecture. The following sections will explore messaging patterns in more detail.

WCF Runtime Architecture

To dive into more messaging patterns, you first have to know how the WCF runtime architecture looks. This runtime has a layered architecture where messages travel from the client application down to a stream transporting the message. This message travels up to the implementation of the service on the other side.

Meanwhile the message is passed by the proxy layer on the client and the dispatcher layer on the service. This multilayered runtime architecture allows different messaging patterns to be implemented. It offers lots of extensibility to hook custom code into places to add logic or to change the behavior when calling operations.

Simply put, the proxy translates calls to methods into WCF messages, sends them through the channel, and the dispatcher picks up the WCF messages from the channel and translates them into calls to the code. See Figure 1-11.

In this architecture you see a proxy that is pushing the message on the channel. When the message is on the channel it is passing other layers such as the protocol layer and the encoder layer before it's actually sent on the wire to the services. At the service side, the message is received by a corresponding channel stack that sends it through the corresponding layers upward. It passes the encoder and protocol layer and is received by the dispatcher. This dispatcher examines the message and figures out which methods to call.

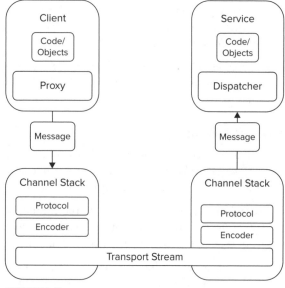

FIGURE 1-11

Content Enricher

The content enricher is a pattern which operates on a functional level. In cases where applications send data which does not contain all information that the receiver is expecting, a content enricher is needed.

The reason for this lack of information can be historical — maybe at the time of writing there was no need to have that information as part of messages as it was always available in the database. But in a distributed environment, not all services have access to the database. Between sender and receiver, another service needs to pick up the message, examine it, and add the needed information to it. Looking up that extra information can be done by querying a database, executing business rules, or simply hard coding it.

Enriching data is something that an implementation of a service operation executes. Enriching the content could potentially mean that the datacontract is changing dynamically. The behavior to enrich data could result in adding an extra property to the datacontract and giving this new property some content and then sending the changed datacontract further to other services.

To do this in a generic approach means WCF needs a way to receive messages for which the datacontract is not defined in the signature of the operation and needs to send the message further in a datacontract that is also not known by the code. Most often content enrichers are just generic functions receiving data in a generic format (XML), changing this format and sending this data further to another service.

WCF supports receiving untyped data by the message class. A function receives one parameter of type message and answers with a message to the call or will not send something back in case of a one-way void method. The message class is a kind of catchall datacontract. In an operation with the message class as inputparameter, every message can be received that is not already mapped to another operation. So creating a generic content enricher is done by creating a service that has one operation with the message parameter.

Of course this code does not have direct typed access to the datacontract as it does not know the details of it. But this code can read the data on the XML level and change the content or add XML nodes where needed.

Message Routing

In many cases the sender of a message does not always know where to send the message. The actual receiver is not known by the client so a routing mechanism determines the real address of the endpoint. The route can perform different kinds of processing during the routing.

This decision can be influenced by the content of the message in combination with a set of business rules. Or the actual endpoint can just be hardcoded. In all cases the idea is to decouple the senders from receivers across the organization in a flexible way.

When the actual endpoint is determined by a value or combination of multiple values in the content of this message, it is called *content-based routing*.

It's often a business requirement that data be sent to one of possible multiple receivers which is interested in this data and can fulfill the request while other receivers cannot.

Since .NET 4.0, WCF has great support for implementing message routing. It supports this by allowing the host of a service to use a class which has no functional behavior but has only the purpose of routing messages to another service somewhere else that needs implementation.

This class can implement interfaces in the System.ServiceMode.Routing namespace to define the message exchange patterns needed. This router service determines what the target service is by the evaluation of the incoming message against a set of message filters.

This routing service is hosted and configured as any other service. This means it has multiple endpoints defining an address: binding and a contract. You can configure this service by adding a service behavior that manages the routing table. This routing table is a list of references to client endpoints in the same configuration together with a list of references to filters. So you configure the exact reason for the routing based on the filter criteria. These filters can work on the WS-addressing values to determine the route, work on endpoint names, or use an XPath expression to evaluate an incoming message.

This routing mechanism also supports protocol bridging by simply specifying the needed bindings in the configuration of the target endpoints referenced by the routing table.

Protocol Bridging

When messages flowing into the router are formatted in a protocol which cannot be understood by possible receivers, it is the router's responsibility to switch to the needed protocol.

This is done by reading the data out of the message in the source protocol and copying the data into a message of the destination protocol. Bridging can be done by reformatting data out of a closed proprietary format to XML, according to a schema. But also on the transport level, bridging can switch from one transport protocol to another.

The router functionality of WCF 4.0 can also act as a bridge between protocols. The use of a certain protocol is defined by the binding configured at an endpoint together with the address to reach the endpoint. To change the protocol and send the message with the request to another endpoint with a different binding, the routing system in WCF can be used. WCF automatically translates the protocol.

Message Filters

Message filters are the key to configuring message routing. They allow expressing conditions in a declarative way to support the routing mechanism that makes decisions about where to route incoming messages. With a message filter you can declare that for some SOAP WS-addressing actions the message must be routed to other services. So it's possible to have a dedicated service for each SOAP action. Not only can message filters be based on SOAP actions but also on other information identified for the request. XPath queries looking into the content of the message or to the SOAP headers are also useful as a message filter.

Backup Endpoint

Routing can also be useful for implementing a backup endpoint. In this case you have a routing table configured with multiple endpoints which are not related to any message filter or used for protocol bridging.

But the routing table defines which would be an alternative endpoint if the first endpoint is not available. This provides an escape route if the targeted service going down the routing mechanism decides to send the message to an alternative route.

Multicast Behavior

With this behavior, the routing mechanism delivers the message to multiple receivers. This can be done by overlapping message filters. The incoming message is compared to all filters and is sent to the endpoint for each matching filter found. It's clear that this multicast behavior is only applicable for the one-way MEP, as routing the question to more than one receiver could result in multiple answers to the client.

Discovery

Discovery can be used when the runtime location of services is dynamically changing as new services join the network and others disappear. Discovery can also be used when the implementation of the hosting of service is not under the control of the client and their network administrators.

When using discovery, clients can look up the needed address themselves by sending a probe for service endpoints on the network. This probe knows what the needed criteria are for evaluation. Finding a match results in the discovery of the service and its network location in the form of an URI. Most often these criteria are the contract. This means the contents of the WSDL for a service is used to look up a service which can fulfill the required contract.

When the address of the endpoint is figured out, the client can talk to this service as it has the correct contract.

Besides this ad-hoc way of working where a polling broadcast is sent across the network to find the correct endpoint, there is a more network-friendly way for services starting up to announce themselves to possible listeners.

WCF implements the SOAP-based WS-Discovery protocol and can make a service discoverable by configuring the behavior for the services. This results in the service being discoverable over UDP on the local subnet. Clients can use the WS-Discovery protocol to find out the actual address of the running service.

Clients can do this by using the `DiscoveryClient` class. This class provides a method that specifies the criteria to find a service on the network. This will most often be the type of interface the client wants to use to talk to the service. After a corresponding service is found, the client has access to the address and can use it to specify the address of the real proxy that is used for the conversation. Clients can narrow the results by specifying a more detailed scope. Services can also announce whether they are active and have joined the network. This signal can be heard by clients that implement the WS-Discovery announcement protocol. To do this the client has to instantiate the `AnnouncementService` which has events to detect when services get online or go down. WCF also provides a discovery proxy to build a central service as a hub between multiple services and multiple clients.

Intercepting Filters

Using the intercepting filters pattern allows you to add logic that executes right after receiving the call, and just before the operation in a service is executed. It could also be immediately after the end of the execution and before the answer is sent back to the client.

The logic intercepts the call and does some preprocessing and/or post-processing. In this processing you have the opportunity to check authentication, decide on creating a session, decode data, start transactions if needed, and provide defaults for missing data sent by clients with older versions of a data contract.

The purpose is to centralize and reuse this processing logic for multiple operation calls in a service and to not have the technical code for this behavior mixed with the functional code of the implementation of the service operation. With the use of intercepting filters, which are executed at server side, neither client nor services are coupled to this technical logic. Neither client nor services are aware of the processing logic being executed.

WCF supports intercepting filters implemented in the `System.ServiceModel.Dispatcher` namespace. This namespace contains classes and interfaces to modify the runtime execution of the WCF application at the dispatcher level. The dispatcher gets the message from the channel stack and calls the methods. This execution can be influenced by custom code.

This code can intercept the call and executes the desired behavior before the implementation if the operation is executed. There are extensibility points to execute parameter inspections, transform messages, set up output caching, authorize, and perform message logging and many other patterns.

Creating an extensibility point is most often a matter of creating a class that implements one or more of the interfaces found in the dispatcher namespace and writes custom code implementing the interfaces.

Context Objects

The context object pattern describes that there is data available with technical details of the call and the service instance during the execution of the call. This means that the implementation cannot only rely on the incoming functional parameters but that it also has access to an object, called the context, where more technical data is stored.

This data is about the call in general or the running instance of the service. By accessing the object context the operation has access to information about the associated channel referring back to the client, possible security information about the user calling the operation, header information in the message, session ID, and so on.

BUSINESS PROCESS PATTERNS

When trying to describe a business process in a written or schematized form, some recurring scenarios are discovered. These typical scenarios can be considered common patterns which are applicable in lots of scenarios and are present in nearly all business processes.

Process Manager

This is the high-level pattern on business processes. It describes the infrastructure and concepts needed to execute the defined steps in business processes, allows applications to participate in the process, exchanges data with the process, and reaches the goal of the process.

It's clear that processes need to be managed. This means there is an environment that runs the processes, allows starting instances of a process, deals with exceptions, stores the state of a process, and can put the process into an idle mode.

Processes are a declaration of a list of steps to be undertaken to fulfill a goal. This goal gathers information, makes decisions on the information, and distributes the information.

The start of a process is triggered by some event in the business. For example: a process has to be started when a new employee starts working at the company. The goal of the process is to fulfill a number of registrations in different applications, assign a new employee to a manager, give the new employee access to intranet applications, and allow the employee to order a car.

A number of actions occur when the employee starts working. In some cases the actions have to occur in a predefined order where it's not possible to continue before the previous step is finished.

The execution of the process is also influenced by the availability of information and is not able to continue before this information is known to the process. Allowing the process to wait for information before continuing is the most important responsibility of the process manager.

In the declaration of the process it is indicated that more information is needed. When the process detects this situation, figures out what information is needed, and from what source it will come, the process manager puts the process in an idle state and persists all information already known by the process.

When reaching this waiting state the process and all the data it is using is released from memory. The process manager persists this to a database and a pointer to the place where the process stopped is remembered. The process manager is then responsible for listening for incoming information. When new information arrives from the needed source, the process manager checks the content of the information and selects the correct instance of the persisted processes. It then loads it into memory again, fills the process with all the data it had before it came to the waiting state, and restarts the process from the point where it was left.

In this way it is like the process was never stopped, only delayed while waiting for a piece of data.

The process manager is thus responsible for starting processes, persisting them when needed, waiting for incoming data, and restarting the processes.

The process manager must also act when a process does not get the needed information in a timeframe defined by the process. This means the process manager must not only look for incoming data, it also must frequently check the database with persisted processes to figure out if the idle situation of an instance of the process hasn't timed out.

Start-Listen-Action Pattern

In its simplest form, every process has three stages. It gets started by the process manager and triggered by an application. After this the process comes in the listen state and the process manager does its work to persist the process, and waits for new information before continuing.

When the data arrives, the process manager reactivates the process and the process takes action to process this new information. The pattern can be present in a more complex form where decisions influence where to listen.

You could say that if there is no start-listen-action pattern to be recognized in your requirements, it's not really a process that needs to be managed by a process manager. See Figure 1-12.

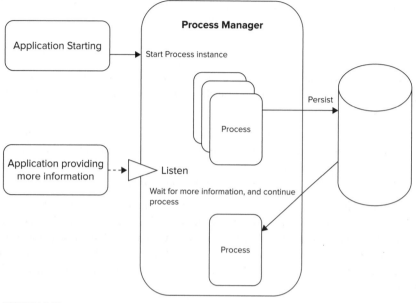

FIGURE 1-12

Patterns in Workflows Declaration

To define the declaration of the process you need a typical combination of activities. This combination can also be seen as patterns.

Sequence

One step (considered an operation) is executed after the previous one. It's the basic and fundamental pattern for organizing processes. It enables a top-down approach where a process starts and continues by doing the next defined step in a sequence.

Parallel Split

In a parallel split the process is split into more than one branch. Each branch runs simultaneously and does its work independently of the other branch. In a parallel split there is no way to know which one of the branches will be completed first. It's possible that one branch has only a small step that executes fast and a second branch that waits for human interactions. The finishing time of the second branch is not predictable.

Synchronization

This pattern is often found together with the parallel split. A parallel split has a wait-for-everybody-to-complete-before-continuing approach. Every branch does its work and the steps in the sequence after the split are only executed when all branches report that they have finished their job.

This parallel looks like the multithreading features found in an operating system but in fact it is the process manager who does the scheduling of the steps in all branches.

Listen Pattern

Also called the exclusive choice. In this pattern a set of branches is declared of which only one is executed during the process. The pattern is based on a mechanism that can decide which one of the branches needs to be executed.

This mechanism is either a delay that times out or an incoming message with the information the process instance was waiting for. In the listen pattern a few conditions are described that can become true while the process is in an idle state. Being in idle state means that the process cannot decide for itself what to do next. It will wait for a signal before continuing.

As the content of the signal is important for this decision, multiple branches are described in the listen pattern. Every branch has this condition as the first element and has a sequence of steps just after this condition. When the signal comes in, all conditions are evaluated. When a match is found for the branch the process continues with the steps defined in that branch. It only executes the step defined in its branch; the other branches for which the condition is not satisfied are discarded and the steps in these branches are never executed.

Listen for Incoming Messages during a Predefined Time

In all situations where the listen pattern is used there will be at least one branch which defines a delay. This indicated process will listen for the defined condition fulfilled by incoming messages for only a specified amount of time. If this timeout is reached before any condition is met, the branch for the delay is executed. The branch will most often execute a backup scenario informing the logging system that the needed trigger, with possible answers for the condition of the other branches, has not been executed.

With this branch, the process can take action and reminds other applications and humans using them to take action. The process can decide to continue in the listen shape and wait again for the input needed to execute one of the other actions.

Convoy Patterns

In a convoy pattern, multiple messages are related to each other and must all be received by the process to achieve a result. This indicates that the process does not have all the information it needs just by receiving one message. In convoys there is always a first message that starts the convoy and the expectation by the process to receive other related messages. The process waits for more messages which are related to the first one and can only continue after all information is received. The combination of all the messages is what the process is looking for. Either it needs multiple messages to work with the set as one big piece of related data or it needs at least a number of messages to make a decision from different sources to continue. The data to fulfill the request is split into pieces which are given to the process one by one.

The reason behind this chunking could be technical, with some kind of memory limit enforcing us to split data into multiple parts. But the reason can also be functional because the input for the process is just an aggregation of data coming from multiple applications which can only send the data they own themselves. Aggregation data from various sources is exactly why business processes are needed.

Here are some examples:

> ➤ A process fulfills an order and receives multiple messages. It contains order lines because the sending application cannot send them with the order because of technical limitations.

> ➤ A process needs a supplier and waits until at least three price quotes are received before deciding on a supplier.

Sequential Convoy

In a sequential convoy, different messages have a predefined order. The process needs multiple messages for a result but can only receive one message at a time. This is the message it is expecting according to the place in the sequence of the previous one. This could be the case if data in the messages is needed to make a decision about what messages to expect next. If the content of the messages is indicating some kind of priority needed for executing, a sequential convoy is needed.

Parallel Convoy

In a parallel convey, messages do not have a strict order. The process can consume messages in any order. But as in the parallel pattern, the process only continues after it has received all messages of the convoy. In a parallel convoy either the number of messages to be expected is known before the messages start coming in or a property of the messages indicates whether it's the last message in the convoy or not.

2

Service Contracts
and Data Contracts

WHAT'S IN THIS CHAPTER?

➤ Explaining contracts

➤ Implementing service contracts

➤ Implementing data contracts

➤ Using different serializers

➤ Implementing message contracts

Contracts in general are very important in our daily lives. Contracts ensure that each party is aware of what his or her efforts will return. If you put your signature at the end of 17 pages of a business document or make a verbal agreement, expectations are given and agreed on. A contract should be well-defined and understandable without leaving any leeway for interpretation.

One thing is certain: in a service-oriented environment where different parties (software components) communicate with each other and use different technologies and platforms, it is indispensable to have a clear definition of the how and what.

WCF (Windows Communication Foundation) uses the concept of contracts to define the service and its operation as a whole, to explain the data which are transferred by wire, and if needed, to directly define the SOAP messages exchanged between the client and the service. WCF uses WSDL and XSD to deliver service metadata.

WCF differentiates between three types of contracts: service, data, and message.

Each of these contracts defines a certain behavior. The one needed depends on your architecture. The most frequently used contract type is the service contract — it can be used in nearly every scenario. The service contract also stands for the C in the ABC of an endpoint. As you may know, a service endpoint is an addressable unit which is typically used by the client to send and receive messages.

Contracts in the context of SOA provide the necessary metadata to communicate with the service — they describe things such as data types, operations, message exchange patterns, and the transport protocol that are used. Contracts are typically delivered in a standardized platform and language-neutral XML format that allow different parties to consume and interpret the definition. In WCF, the service metadata is typically described by a WSDL document (Web Services Description Language). More information is available at http://www.w3.org/TR/wsdl. This standard allows software vendors such as Microsoft, Sun, and IBM to build tools to help developers produce and consume these contracts.

SERVICE CONTRACTS

The *service contract* defines the functionality which is exposed by your service to the outside world. The functionality is expressed in the form of service operations. In a SOA world, you typically exchange a set of SOAP messages, and the schemas of these messages are defined in the service contract. The service contract further defines the message exchange pattern (Request/Reply, One-Way, Duplex) for each service operation.

DATA CONTRACTS

You usually pass one or more arguments to your service operation and expect a return value. The structure of a message argument is explained in the data contract as an XSD schema which is part of the WSDL document. The Data Contract defines the structure and content of the information that is exchanged between the client and the service.

If you use your own objects and complex types as method arguments or return values, you have to inform the runtime how to serialize these types into an XML stream by using the DataContract attribute.

Depending on the granularity of your method arguments, you might use only simple .NET types as method arguments. In this case you do not need to worry about serialization and deserialization because the messaging infrastructure already knows how to deal with those simple .NET types.

MESSAGE CONTRACTS

A *message contract* is an advanced feature which can be used to gain greater control of the SOAP header and/or the SOAP body. The message contract is used to directly interact with the SOAP message (header and body), not just the method body — as is the case if you use a data contract instead of a message contract.

CONTRACTS AND CODE

As a .NET software developer on the service side, it is not your daily job to produce metadata documents in the form of WSDL — you would normally design interfaces and classes, write methods, implement business logic, and then write unit tests to check your logic. To help software developers produce these metadata artifacts from source code without fundamentally changing the programming, WCF offers different tools, attributes, and classes which are explained in more detail on the following pages.

If you use WCF to implement your SOA architecture, you can choose from different approaches — depending on your requirements — to automatically generate those metadata documents from scratch, based on your code. You can use .NET attributes, configuration settings, and directly leverage the API — provided by WCF — to get absolute control of the metadata generation.

But how can you consume those metadata from a client and interact with the service? To complete the story, assume that you have already generated the service specification in the form of a WSDL document. Then assume that the service is up and running. If you want to communicate with the service, you have to create an XML message in the right format, send the messages to the service endpoint, wait for a response message, and finally extract your values from the XML document. Thanks to the standard of WSDL and tools such as svcutil.exe and VS 2010, it is very easy to create source code (a proxy) which mimics the behavior of the service and handles all the communication and serialization details for you.

As mentioned earlier, there are different approaches to instructing the runtime. Knowing which parts of your code should be reflected as metadata in WSDL, without knowing the exact specification of WSDL, is what you need to figure out.

It is helpful to know some basic elements of WSDL to get a good understanding of what is going on under the hood and to interpret the generated metadata document. To get a basic idea of the correlation between elements in the WSDL document and your code, start with a simple example to see which code fragment leads to which element in the WSDL document.

CAR RENTAL SERVICE — IMPLEMENTATION EXAMPLE

So far contracts in general have been explained — automatic metadata generation and the use of proxies. Now it is time to see all these concepts in action.

To give you a short and compact overview of how to create a service contract, a simplified implementation of a fictive car rental service is shown, explaining in further detail about the basis of the code listings. If you choose the contract-first approach, you typically start by defining the WSDL document and not by writing code.

When using the code-first approach, you start with a .NET interface definition and decorate your service contract with the `[ServiceContract]` attribute and your methods with the `[OperationContract]` attribute from the `System.ServiceModel` namespace.

Step 1: Service Contract Definition

The service contract definition as shown in Listing 2-1 should live in its own assembly because there are several advantages if you use a separate Class Library for your interface and your service contract — such as versioning, decoupling the abstract definition from the concrete implementation, and deployment.

LISTING 2-1: Service Contract Definition

```
using System;
using System.ServiceModel;

namespace Wrox.CarRentalService.Contracts
{
  [ServiceContract()]
  public interface ICarRentalService
  {
    [OperationContract]
    double CalculatePrice(DateTime pickupDate, DateTime returnDate,
    string pickupLocation, string vehiclePreference);
  }
}
```

As you can see in Listing 2-1, the example service interface is quite simple and contains just one method called `CalculatePrice` with four arguments and a return type of `double`.

To define a service contract, just apply the `[ServiceContract]` attribute to the interface definition and the `[OperationContract]` attribute to each method you want included as a service operation in the WSDL document. If the interface contains a method without the `[OperationContract]` attribute, the method will not be included in the generated service metadata. This is also called an opt-in model.

It is possible to annotate a class — the concrete service implementation — with the `[ServiceContract]` attribute and its methods with the `[OperationContract]` attribute. However, there are several reasons why this is not recommended. One reason is that you will mix the "outside world" (the service contract) with the "inside world" (your implementation code), and this breaks the rule about having explicit boundaries. You should always decouple the abstract service definition from the concrete implementation, if you want to produce production code.

If you apply the attribute at the interface level, you can additionally create different implementations of the same service contract and expose those different implementations at various service endpoints.

After compiling the source code, obtain an Assembly called `Wrox.CarRentalService.Contracts.dll` which contains the interface/service contract definition.

Step 2: Extract the Service Metadata

To give you a better understanding of how each part of the interface definition correlates with the WSDL document, the WSDL document is generated first.

If the service exposes a Metadata Exchange Endpoint (MEX), you can directly browse to this endpoint and see the generated metadata.

Because you do not have a MEX, you will use svcutil.exe to generate the WSDL file. The ServiceModel Metadata Utility Tool (svcutil.exe) can be found at the Windows SDK installation location and provides you with a number of functionalities:

➤ Code generation from running services or static metadata documents

➤ Metadata export from compiled code

➤ Validation of compiled service code

➤ Download of metadata documents from running services

➤ Generation of serialization code

Use the command `svcutil.exe Wrox.CarRentalService.Contracts.dll` at the Visual Studio command prompt to get the three files shown in Table 2-1.

TABLE 2-1: The WSDL and XSD Files

FILENAME	DESCRIPTION
tempuri.org.wsdl (see Listing 2-2)	The WSDL document with a reference to the XSD files, message definitions, port types, and service operations.
tempuri.org.xsd (see Listing 2-3)	The XSD schema for the method attributes.
schemas.microsoft.com.2003.10.Serialization.xsd (see Listing 2-4)	The standard XSD schema for simple .NET types.

> *Visit the W3C site at* `http://www.w3.org/XML/Schema` *for more information about schemas.*

LISTING 2-2: WSDL

```
<?xml version="1.0" encoding="utf-8"?>
<wsdl:definitions xmlns:soap="http://schemas.xmlsoap.org/wsdl/soap/"
xmlns:soapenc="http://schemas.xmlsoap.org/soap/encoding/"
 xmlns:wsu="http://docs.oasis-open.org/wss/2004/01/
oasis-200401-wss-wssecurity-utility-1.0.xsd"
```

continues

LISTING 2-2 *(continued)*

```
xmlns:xsd="http://www.w3.org/2001/XMLSchema"
xmlns:soap12="http://schemas.xmlsoap.org/wsdl/soap12/"
xmlns:tns="http://tempuri.org/"
xmlns:wsa="http://schemas.xmlsoap.org/ws/2004/08/addressing"
xmlns:wsp="http://schemas.xmlsoap.org/ws/2004/09/policy"
xmlns:wsap="http://schemas.xmlsoap.org/ws/2004/08/addressing/policy"
xmlns:wsaw="http://www.w3.org/2006/05/addressing/wsdl"
xmlns:msc="http://schemas.microsoft.com/ws/2005/12/wsdl/contract"
xmlns:wsa10="http://www.w3.org/2005/08/addressing"
xmlns:wsx="http://schemas.xmlsoap.org/ws/2004/09/mex"
xmlns:wsam="http://www.w3.org/2007/05/addressing/metadata"
targetNamespace="http://tempuri.org/"
xmlns:wsdl="http://schemas.xmlsoap.org/wsdl/">
  <wsdl:types>
    <xsd:schema targetNamespace="http://tempuri.org/Imports">
      <xsd:import namespace="http://tempuri.org/" />
      <xsd:import namespace="http://schemas.microsoft.com/2003/10/
Serialization/" />
    </xsd:schema>
  </wsdl:types>
  <wsdl:message name="ICarRentalService_CalculatePrice_InputMessage">
    <wsdl:part name="parameters" element="tns:CalculatePrice" />
  </wsdl:message>
  <wsdl:message name="ICarRentalService_CalculatePrice_OutputMessage">
    <wsdl:part name="parameters" element="tns:CalculatePriceResponse" />
  </wsdl:message>
  <wsdl:portType name="ICarRentalService">
    <wsdl:operation name="CalculatePrice">
      <wsdl:input wsaw:Action="http://tempuri.org/ICarRentalService/CalculatePrice"
message="tns:ICarRentalService_CalculatePrice_InputMessage" />
      <wsdl:output wsaw:Action="http://tempuri.org/ICarRentalService/
CalculatePriceResponse" message=
"tns:ICarRentalService_CalculatePrice_OutputMessage" />
    </wsdl:operation>
  </wsdl:portType>
  <wsdl:binding name="DefaultBinding_ICarRentalService"
type="tns:ICarRentalService">
    <soap:binding transport="http://schemas.xmlsoap.org/soap/http" />
    <wsdl:operation name="CalculatePrice">
      <soap:operation soapAction="http://tempuri.org/ICarRentalService/
CalculatePrice" style="document" />
      <wsdl:input>
        <soap:body use="literal" />
      </wsdl:input>
      <wsdl:output>
        <soap:body use="literal" />
      </wsdl:output>
    </wsdl:operation>
  </wsdl:binding>
</wsdl:definitions>
```

LISTING 2-3: XSD File

```xml
<?xml version="1.0" encoding="utf-8"?>
<xs:schema xmlns:tns="http://tempuri.org/" elementFormDefault="qualified"
targetNamespace="http://tempuri.org/" xmlns:xs="http://www.w3.org/2001/XMLSchema">
  <xs:element name="CalculatePrice">
    <xs:complexType>
      <xs:sequence>
        <xs:element minOccurs="0" name="pickupDate" type="xs:dateTime" />
        <xs:element minOccurs="0" name="returnDate" type="xs:dateTime" />
        <xs:element minOccurs="0" name="pickupLocation" nillable="true"
type="xs:string" />
        <xs:element minOccurs="0" name="vehiclePreference"
nillable="true" type="xs:string" />
      </xs:sequence>
    </xs:complexType>
  </xs:element>
  <xs:element name="CalculatePriceResponse">
    <xs:complexType>
      <xs:sequence>
        <xs:element minOccurs="0" name="CalculatePriceResult" type="xs:double" />
      </xs:sequence>
    </xs:complexType>
  </xs:element>
</xs:schema>
```

LISTING 2-4: schemas.microsoft.com.2003.10.Serialization

```xml
<?xml version="1.0" encoding="utf-8"?>
<xs:schema xmlns:tns=http://schemas.microsoft.com/2003/10/Serialization/
 attributeFormDefault="qualified" elementFormDefault="qualified"
targetNamespace="http://schemas.microsoft.com/2003/10/Serialization/"
xmlns:xs="http://www.w3.org/2001/XMLSchema">
  <xs:element name="anyType" nillable="true" type="xs:anyType" />
  <xs:element name="anyURI" nillable="true" type="xs:anyURI" />
  <xs:element name="base64Binary" nillable="true"
type="xs:base64Binary" />
  <xs:element name="boolean" nillable="true" type="xs:boolean" />
  <xs:element name="byte" nillable="true" type="xs:byte" />
  <xs:element name="dateTime" nillable="true" type="xs:dateTime" />
  <xs:element name="decimal" nillable="true" type="xs:decimal" />
  <xs:element name="double" nillable="true" type="xs:double" />
  <xs:element name="float" nillable="true" type="xs:float" />
  <xs:element name="int" nillable="true" type="xs:int" />
  <xs:element name="long" nillable="true" type="xs:long" />
  <xs:element name="QName" nillable="true" type="xs:QName" />
  <xs:element name="short" nillable="true" type="xs:short" />
  <xs:element name="string" nillable="true" type="xs:string" />
  <xs:element name="unsignedByte" nillable="true"
type="xs:unsignedByte" />
  <xs:element name="unsignedInt" nillable="true"
```

continues

LISTING 2-4 *(continued)*

```
  type="xs:unsignedInt" />
   <xs:element name="unsignedLong" nillable="true"
type="xs:unsignedLong" />
   <xs:element name="unsignedShort" nillable="true"
type="xs:unsignedShort" />
   <xs:element name="char" nillable="true"
type="tns:char" />
   <xs:simpleType name="char">
     <xs:restriction base="xs:int" />
   </xs:simpleType>
   <xs:element name="duration" nillable="true"
type="tns:duration" />
   <xs:simpleType name="duration">
     <xs:restriction base="xs:duration">
       <xs:pattern value=
"\-?P(\d*D)?(T(\d*H)?(\d*M)?(\d*(\.\d*)?S)?)?" />
       <xs:minInclusive value="-P10675199DT2H48M5.4775808S" />
       <xs:maxInclusive value="P10675199DT2H48M5.4775807S" />
     </xs:restriction>
   </xs:simpleType>
   <xs:element name="guid" nillable="true" type="tns:guid" />
   <xs:simpleType name="guid">
     <xs:restriction base="xs:string">
       <xs:pattern value=
"[\da-fA-F]{8}-[\da-fA-F]{4}-[\da-fA-F]{4}-
[\da-fA-F]{4}-[\da-fA-F]{12}" />
     </xs:restriction>
   </xs:simpleType>
   <xs:attribute name="FactoryType" type="xs:QName" />
   <xs:attribute name="Id" type="xs:ID" />
   <xs:attribute name="Ref" type="xs:IDREF" />
 </xs:schema>
```

As you can see in Listing 2-2 (WSDL) and Listing 2-3 (XSD), different parts of the XSD and WSDL come directly from your source code. To override the default naming behavior and gain further control, you can use the members of the `[ServiceContract]` and the `[OperationContract]` attributes. Table 2-2 describes the mapping between your code and the WSDL document.

TABLE 2-2: Mapping between Source Code and WSDL Elements

WSDL ELEMENT	SOURCE CODE
Message name: ICarRentalService_CalculatePrice	Interface name + method name + input/output
portType name: ICarRentalService	Interface name
Operation name: CalculatePrice	Method name

As you have seen so far, you can generate metadata from code by defining an interface, putting some methods in it, and decorating the interface name with the [ServiceContract] attribute and your methods with the [OperationContract] attribute. The WCF infrastructure uses reflection to build the WSDL document.

Step 3: Service Implementation

To complete the service side, you need one or more concrete implementations of the service interface. As a recommended practice, the concrete service implementation should be placed in a separate Class Library. As in Listing 2-5, there is no need to use WCF-specific elements in the service implementation code.

You may see the use of the [ServiceBehavior] and [OperationBehavior] attributes in the implementation code. Behaviors in general are internal implementation details and therefore are not included in the WSDL file.

LISTING 2-5: Service Implementation

```
using System;
using Wrox.CarRentalService.Contracts;

namespace Wrox.CarRentalService.Implementations.Europe
{
    public class CarRentalService: ICarRentalService
    {
        public double CalculatePrice
                    (
                    DateTime pickupDate,
                    DateTime returnDate,
                    string pickupLocation,
                    string vehiclePreference
                    )
        {
            //call to some internal business logic
            Random r = new Random(DateTime.Now.Millisecond);
            return r.NextDouble()*500;
        }
    }
}
```

Step 4: The Client

The metadata can be used to generate the necessary client code. For this purpose the client would use svcutil.exe or Add Service Reference from within Visual Studio to obtain a proxy which mimics the functionality of the service. You will find more details about this topic in Chapter 5. Listing 2-6 demonstrates the use of the generated proxy within your client app; Listing 2-7 displays the request SOAP message; and Listing 2-8 displays the response message.

LISTING 2-6: Client Code

```
using System;
using Wrox.CarRentalService.ConsoleClient.CarRentalProxy;

namespace Wrox.CarRentalService.ConsoleClient
{
    class Program
    {
        static void Main(string[] args)
        {
            using (CarRentalServiceClient
                carRentalClient = new CarRentalServiceClient())
            {
                double price = carRentalClient.CalculatePrice
                    (
                     DateTime.Now, DateTime.Now.AddDays(5),
                     "Graz", "Pickup"
                    );
                Console.WriteLine("Price {0}",price );
            }
        }
    }
}
```

LISTING 2-7: SOAP Messages

```
<s:Envelope xmlns:s="http://schemas.xmlsoap.org/soap/envelope/">
 <s:Body>
  <CalculatePrice xmlns="http://tempuri.org/">
   <pickupDate>2010-01-09T19:15:25.2392813+01:00</pickupDate>
   <returnDate>2010-01-14T19:15:25.2402578+01:00</returnDate>
   <pickupLocation>Graz</pickupLocation>
   <vehiclePreference>Pickup</vehiclePreference>
  </CalculatePrice>
 </s:Body>
</s:Envelope>
```

LISTING 2-8: SOAP Response Message

```
<s:Envelope xmlns:s="http://schemas.xmlsoap.org/soap/envelope/">
 <s:Body>
  <CalculatePriceResponse xmlns="http://tempuri.org/">
   <CalculatePriceResult>357.7265724808567</CalculatePriceResult>
  </CalculatePriceResponse>
 </s:Body>
</s:Envelope>
```

[ServiceContract] and [OperationContract]

The automatically generated WSDL document sometimes needs further enhancements — you should at least provide a meaningful namespace for the service to prevent name clashes with other services. Sometimes there are some internal coding styles and naming patterns for interfaces, classes, and methods which are not allowed or recommended in a service description, or you just don't want to expose your internal names to the outside world.

To further enhance and gain additional control of the generated WSDL document, Table 2-3 (from MSDN) describes the members of the [ServiceContract] and the [OperationContract] in detail.

TABLE 2-3: [ServiceContract] Members

SETTING	DESCRIPTION
CallbackContract	Gets or sets the type of callback contract when the contract is a duplex.
ConfigurationName	Gets or sets the name used to locate the service in an application configuration file.
HasProtectionLevel	Gets a value that indicates whether the member has a protection level assigned.
Name	Gets or sets the name for the <portType> element in WSDL.
Namespace	Gets or sets the namespace of the <portType> element in WSDL.
ProtectionLevel	Specifies whether the binding for the contract must support the value of the ProtectionLevel property.
SessionMode	Gets or sets whether sessions are allowed, not allowed, or required.

As it applies to the [ServiceContract] attribute, the same goes for the [OperationContract] attribute — sometimes you need more control over the generation of the WSDL document. See Table 2-4.

TABLE 2-4: [OperationContract] Members

SETTING	DESCRIPTION
Action	Specifies the action that uniquely identifies this operation. WCF dispatches request messages to methods based on their action.
AsyncPattern	Indicates that the operation is implemented or can be called asynchronously using a Begin/End method pair.
HasProtectionLevel	Indicates whether the ProtectionLevel property has been explicitly set.

continues

TABLE 2-4 *(continued)*

SETTING	DESCRIPTION
IsOneWay	Indicates that the operation only consists of a single input message. The operation has no associated output message.
IsInitiating	Specifies whether this operation can be the initial operation in a session.
IsTerminating	Specifies whether WCF attempts to terminate the current session after the operation completes.
ProtectionLevel	Specifies the message-level security that an operation requires at runtime.

Listing 2-9 demonstrates the use of some common attributes. Some of the other attributes are described in Chapter 3.

LISTING 2-9: [ServiceContract] and [OperationContract] Attributes

```
using System;
using System.ServiceModel;

namespace Wrox.CarRentalService.Contracts
{
    [ServiceContract(Namespace="http://wrox/CarRentalService/2009/10",
                     Name="RentalService")]
    public interface ICarRentalService
    {
        [OperationContract(Name = "GetPrice")]
        double CalculatePrice(DateTime pickupDate, DateTime returnDate,
        string pickupLocation, string vehiclePreference);

        [OperationContract( Name = "GetPriceOverloaded")]
        double CalculatePrice(string pickupLocation,
        string vehiclePreference);

        [OperationContract(IsOneWay=true,
        ProtectionLevel=System.Net.Security.ProtectionLevel.None )]
        void UpdatePrice(string vehicleId, double newPrice);
    }
}
```

The result of these attributes is reflected in the WSDL fragment shown in Listing 2-10.

LISTING 2-10: WSDL Document

```
<?xml version="1.0" encoding="utf-8"?>
<wsdl:definitions . . ..
xmlns:xsd="http://www.w3.org/2001/XMLSchema" targetNamespace=
```

```
"http://wrox/CarRentalService/2009/10"
xmlns:wsdl="http://schemas.xmlsoap.org/wsdl/">

  <wsdl:message name="RentalService_GetPrice_InputMessage">
    <wsdl:part name="parameters" element="tns:GetPrice" />
  </wsdl:message>
  <wsdl:message name="RentalService_GetPrice_OutputMessage">
    <wsdl:part name="parameters" element="tns:GetPriceResponse" />
  </wsdl:message>
  <wsdl:message name="RentalService_GetPriceOverloaded_InputMessage">
    <wsdl:part name="parameters" element="tns:GetPriceOverloaded" />
  </wsdl:message>
  <wsdl:message name="RentalService_GetPriceOverloaded_OutputMessage">
    <wsdl:part name="parameters" element="tns:GetPriceOverloadedResponse" />
  </wsdl:message>
  <wsdl:message name="RentalService_UpdatePrice_InputMessage">
    <wsdl:part name="parameters" element="tns:UpdatePrice" />
  </wsdl:message>
  <wsdl:portType name="RentalService">
    <wsdl:operation name="GetPrice">
      <wsdl:input wsaw:Action=
"http://wrox/CarRentalService/2009/10/RentalService/GetPrice"
 message="tns:RentalService_GetPrice_InputMessage" />
      <wsdl:output wsaw:Action=
"http://wrox/CarRentalService/2009/10/RentalService/GetPriceResponse"
 message="tns:RentalService_GetPrice_OutputMessage" />
    </wsdl:operation>
    <wsdl:operation name="GetPriceOverloaded">
      <wsdl:input wsaw:Action=
"http://wrox/CarRentalService/2009/10/RentalService/GetPriceOverloaded"
 message="tns:RentalService_GetPriceOverloaded_InputMessage" />
      <wsdl:output wsaw:Action=
"http://wrox/CarRentalService/2009/10/RentalService
/GetPriceOverloadedResponse"
message="tns:RentalService_GetPriceOverloaded_OutputMessage" />
    </wsdl:operation>
    <wsdl:operation name="UpdatePrice">
      <wsdl:input wsaw:Action=
"http://wrox/CarRentalService/2009/10/RentalService/UpdatePrice"
 message="tns:RentalService_UpdatePrice_InputMessage" />
    </wsdl:operation>
  </wsdl:portType>
</wsdl:definitions>
```

DATA CONTRACTS

Previous examples have demonstrated the use of the attributes [OperationContract] and
[ServiceContract]. The [OperationContract] attribute essentially determines which operations
are provided by your service.

The data which is transferred depends on the individual transfer parameters and the return data
type. The specific value of a parameter is typically derived from a .NET object in memory.

This object is converted into a corresponding form and is embedded in the SOAP message. On the other hand, the parameters are extracted from the SOAP message and provided to you as a .NET object. This conversion is performed by special serializer classes.

WCF supports different types of serialization/deserialization, whereby some serializers have been specially developed for WCF, and some have existed in the framework since .NET 1.0/.NET 2.0 and can also be used with WCF.

WCF uses the `DataContractSerializer` class from the namespace `System.Runtime.Serialization` as standard to serialize or deserialize its objects. This serializer has been specially developed for WCF and is particularly fast, effective, and powerful, which makes it the preferred choice. However, should your requirements exceed the capability of the `DataContractSerializer`, you can revert to classical XML serialization.

The `DataContractSerializer` supports various data types, including the following:

➤ Primitive data types

➤ Data types with the `[DataContract]` attribute

➤ Classes which are marked as serializable

➤ Classes which implement the `IXmlSerializable` interface from the namespace `System.Xml.Serialization`

➤ Enumerations, collections, and generic collections

In the previous examples, there was no need for additional serialization measures because primitive data types are already serializable. However, if you have to work with complex data types as method parameters or return values, you have to use the appropriate attributes (`[DataContract]`, `[DataMember]`) to determine how this data is serialized.

These two attributes from the namespace `System.Runtime.Serialization` are a design-time construct which tells the `DataContractSerializer` how to serialize a special type. Because the structure of the data being exchanged also belongs to the contract, of course, the application of the `[DataContract]` and `[DataMember]` attributes affects the prepared WSDL document directly. The definition of the data is incorporated into the contract (WSDL) in a format which is independent of platform and programming languages, namely XSD. Therefore, the client and the server cannot agree on the exchange of .NET data types, but are compatible with regard to the neutral XML schema definition format.

To this effect, look at the simple example in Listing 2-11 which does not include the use of the `[DataContract]` and `[DataMember]` attributes and produces a WSDL document shown in Listing 2-12.

LISTING 2-11: Service Operation with Simple Types

```
using System;
using System.ServiceModel;

namespace Wrox.CarRentalService.Contracts
```

```
    {
        [ServiceContract(
                Namespace = "http://wrox/CarRentalService/2009/10",
                Name = "RentalService")]

        public interface ICarRentalService
        {
            [OperationContract]
            double CheckAvgPricePerDay(string carType);
        }
    }
```

LISTING 2-12: WSDL Document with Simple Types

```
<?xml version="1.0" encoding="utf-8"?>
<xs:schema xmlns:tns="http://wrox/CarRentalService/2009/10" elementFormDefault=
"qualified"
targetNamespace="http://wrox/CarRentalService/2009/10"
 xmlns:xs="http://www.w3.org/2001/XMLSchema">
  <xs:element name="CheckAvgPricePerDay">
    <xs:complexType>
      <xs:sequence>
        <xs:element minOccurs="0" name="carType"
nillable="true" type="xs:string" />
      </xs:sequence>
    </xs:complexType>
  </xs:element>
  <xs:element name="CheckAvgPricePerDayResponse">
    <xs:complexType>
      <xs:sequence>
        <xs:element minOccurs="0"
name="CheckAvgPricePerDayResult"
type="xs:double" />
      </xs:sequence>
    </xs:complexType>
  </xs:element>
</xs:schema>
```

In the example defined in Listing 2-11, neither the [Serializable] attribute nor the [DataContract] attribute have been used with their corresponding [DataMember] attribute. This is possible because the DataContractSerializer class can work with simple .NET data types without the need for any precautionary measures.

However, in most cases you will not use simple data types as the content of your methods in a message-oriented architecture; instead, consideration should be given to the structure of the data being exchanged and make this known in the form of a contract.

In this case you can use the [DataContract] and [DataMember] attributes to tell the DataContractSerializer how and in which form its objects are to be converted.

If you use complex data types in your operations without informing the DataContractSerializer how they are to be handled, all publicly visible members are automatically serialized. This enables you to serialize POCOs (plain old CLR objects) without additional changes in your code. You can exclude individual members with the [IgnoreDataMember] attribute. Listing 2-13 shows a service contract with a method called CalculatePrice, an input parameter of type PriceCalculationRequest. The return type is defined as PriceCalculationResponse.

LISTING 2-13: Service Contract with Complex Types

```
namespace Wrox.CarRentalService.Contracts
{
    [ServiceContract(
            Namespace = "http://wrox/CarRentalService/2009/10",
            Name = "RentalService")]
    public interface ICarRentalService
    {
        [OperationContract]
        PriceCalculationResponse CalculatePrice
        (
            PriceCalculationRequest  request);
        }
    }
}
```

Listings 2-14 and 2-15 demonstrate the use of POCOs, the [IgnoreDataMember] attribute, and the resulting WSDL document.

LISTING 2-14: POCOs and [IgnoreDataMember]

```
using System;
using System.Runtime.Serialization;
using System.Xml.Serialization;

namespace Wrox.CarRentalService.Contracts
{
    public class PriceCalculationRequest
    {
        public DateTime PickupDate { get; set; }
        public DateTime ReturnDate { get; set; }
        public string PickupLocation { get; set; }
        public string ReturnLocation { get; set; }
        private string VehicleType { get; set; }
        [IgnoreDataMember]
        public string Color { get; set; }
    }
}
```

LISTING 2-15: WSDL Document

```
<?xml version="1.0" encoding="utf-8"?>
<xs:schema xmlns:tns="http://schemas.datacontract.org/2004/07/
Wrox.CarRentalService.Contracts"
```

```
elementFormDefault="qualified"
targetNamespace="http://schemas.datacontract.org/2004/07/
Wrox.CarRentalService.Contracts"
xmlns:xs="http://www.w3.org/2001/XMLSchema">
  <xs:complexType name="PriceCalculationRequest">
    <xs:sequence>
      <xs:element minOccurs="0" name="PickupDate" type="xs:dateTime" />
      <xs:element minOccurs="0" name="PickupLocation"
nillable="true" type="xs:string" />
      <xs:element minOccurs="0" name="ReturnDate" type="xs:dateTime" />
      <xs:element minOccurs="0" name="ReturnLocation"
nillable="true" type="xs:string" />
    </xs:sequence>
  </xs:complexType>
  <xs:element name="PriceCalculationRequest"
nillable="true" type="tns:PriceCalculationRequest" />
  <xs:complexType name="PriceCalculationResponse">
    <xs:sequence>
      <xs:element minOccurs="0" name="Flag" type="xs:int" />
      <xs:element minOccurs="0" name="Price" nillable="true" type="xs:string" />
    </xs:sequence>
  </xs:complexType>
  <xs:element name="PriceCalculationResponse"
nillable="true" type="tns:PriceCalculationResponse" />
</xs:schema>
```

However, you will only be able to disclose your business objects including all public properties as standard in very rare cases.

It is important to define contracts explicitly in an SOA scenario and to request control of the names including namespaces of your elements, the order in which the individual attributes occur, and whether or not this is absolutely necessary.

Consequently, the data contract and the service contract together serve to form a formal agreement between service and client and provide a detailed description of the structure of the data which is exchanged.

The `DataContractSerializer` uses the `[DataContract]` and `[DataMember]` attributes to control the exact serialization process. A `[DataContract]` is an opt-in model which means that only properties or member variables which have been explicitly assigned the `[DataMember]` attribute are serialized. The visibility of the properties is of no consequence. Listing 2-16 demonstrates the use of the `[DataContract]` and `[DataMember]` attributes. Listing 2-17 displays the resulting XSD part.

LISTING 2-16: [DataContract] and [DataMember] Attributes

Available for
download on
Wrox.com

```
using System;
using System.Runtime.Serialization;
using System.Xml.Serialization;

namespace Wrox.CarRentalService.Contracts
{
    [DataContract]
```

continues

LISTING 2-16 *(continued)*

```
public class PriceCalculationRequest
{
    [DataMember]
    public DateTime PickupDate { get; set; }
    [DataMember]
    public DateTime ReturnDate { get; set; }
    [DataMember]
    public string PickupLocation { get; set; }
    [DataMember]
    public string ReturnLocation { get; set; }
    public string Color { get; set; }
}
}
```

LISTING 2-17: XSD Part

```
<xs:complexType name="PriceCalculationRequest">
    <xs:sequence>
        <xs:element minOccurs="0" name="PickupDate" type="xs:dateTime" />
        <xs:element minOccurs="0" name="PickupLocation"
nillable="true" type="xs:string" />
        <xs:element minOccurs="0" name="ReturnDate" type="xs:dateTime" />
        <xs:element minOccurs="0" name="ReturnLocation"
nillable="true" type="xs:string" />
    </xs:sequence>
</xs:complexType>
```

The characteristics of the schema, which are automatically generated by WCF, include the following:

➤ Namespaces: `http://schemas.datacontract.org/2004/07/` + CLR and
   `http://schemas.datacontract.org/2004/07/Wrox.CarRentalService.Contracts`

➤ Attributes are arranged in alphabetical order

   ➤ `<xs:element minOccurs="0" name= PickupDate "`

   ➤ `<xs:element minOccurs="0" name="PickupLocation "`

➤ The `minOccurs` attribute is set to a value of 0, which means that this attribute is optional

➤ The primitive CLR data types are automatically shown in the form of XSD data types.
   `DateTime PickupDate` becomes `xs: dateTime`

Data Contract in Detail

As you have seen from the previous examples, your data classes are typically assigned the `[DataContract]` attribute and the individual member variables are assigned the `[DataMember]` attribute.

Listing 2-18 demonstrates additional possibilities when using the [DataContract] and [DataMember] attributes to influence the generated schema.

LISTING 2-18: [DataContract] and [DataMember] Attributes

Available for
download on
Wrox.com

```
[DataContract(
Name="PriceCalculationRequest",                              Namespace=
"http://schemas.datacontract.org/2004/07/
Wrox.CarRentalService.Contracts")
]
public class PriceReq
{
    [DataMember(Name="PickupDate",Order=1, IsRequired=true )]
    private DateTime FromDate { get; set; }
    [DataMember(Name = "ReturnDate", Order = 3)]
    public DateTime ToDate{ get; set; }
    [DataMember( Order = 2)]
    public string PickupLocation { get; set; }
    [DataMember(Order = 4)]
    public string ReturnLocation { get; set; }
    public string CarType { get; set; }
}
```

Even though the original definition of the PriceCalculationRequest class has undergone significant changes, no problems occur when serializing an instance followed by comparison with the schema prepared beforehand. The [DataContract] and [DataMember] attributes create an XML info set which is valid in accordance with the contract (XSD).

To illustrate this, refer to the newly prepared schema in Listing 2-19 which is compatible with the original schema.

LISTING 2-19: Equivalent XSD

Available for
download on
Wrox.com

```
<xs:complexType name="PriceCalculationRequest">
  <xs:sequence>
    <xs:element minOccurs="0" name="PickupDate" type="xs:dateTime" />
    <xs:element minOccurs="0" name="PickupLocation"
        nillable="true" type="xs:string" />
    <xs:element minOccurs="0" name="ReturnDate" type="xs:dateTime" />
    <xs:element minOccurs="0" name="ReturnLocation"
        nillable="true" type="xs:string" />
  </xs:sequence>
</xs:complexType>
```

The following observations are made when using the [DataContract] and [DataMember] attributes from the namespace System.Runtime.Serialization:

➤ The default namespace can be overwritten by the namespace property.

➤ The name property of the [DataContract] attribute serves to define the name of the complex type in XSD.

➤ The access modifier of a member variable is ignored.

➤ `CarType` does not appear as an element opt-in model — only member variables which are explicitly assigned the `[DataMember]` attribute are serialized.

➤ If the property is `IsRequired=true`, the attribute is no longer optional. If this attribute is not located during deserializing, an error occurs.

➤ The order can be determined explicitly with the order property.

➤ The name property for the `[DataMember]` attribute is used to determine the name of the XSD element.

The properties of the `[DataContract]` and `[DataMember]` attributes primarily play an important role during versioning or in interop scenarios. If, for example, you have to keep a default XML schema but do not wish or are unable to make any or only minor changes to your .NET classes, you can attempt to create a compatible data contract with the attributes and properties previously mentioned.

KnownTypes

In object-oriented programming you frequently use a reference to an inherited class instead of the base class. This concept of polymorphism is frequently used, although if done in conjunction with WCF, an error occurs if special precautionary measures are not taken.

The method signature typically only contains the base class and consequently, the definition of the inherited classes is not included in the WSDL document either. This naturally also means that the inherited class for the generated proxy code is unknown and can therefore not be deserialized.

The same problem also occurs, for example, if the parameter which you use is a non-generic collection class as shown in Listing 2-20.

LISTING 2-20: Base Class Response Argument and ArrayList

```
namespace Wrox.CarRentalService.Contracts
{

    [ServiceContract(
        Namespace = "http://wrox/CarRentalService/2009/10",
        Name = "RentalService")]
    [ServiceKnownType(typeof(PriceCalculationResponseDetailed))]
    public interface ICarRentalService
    {
        [OperationContract]
        PriceCalculationResponse        CalculatePrice
        (
            PriceCalculationRequest  request
        );

        [OperationContract]
        System.Collections.ArrayList GetPrices();
    }
```

However, the specific implementation of the method from Listing 2-20 does not use the `PriceCalculationResponse` base class as a return value; it uses an inherited version named `PriceCalculationResponseDetailed`. Listing 2-21 shows the inherited class and the concrete service implementation.

LISTING 2-21: Inherited Class and Service Implementation

```
[DataContract]
public class PriceCalculationResponseDetailed
                    : PriceCalculationResponse
{
  [DataMember]
  public string  Currency { get; set; }
}


public PriceCalculationResponse
       CalculatePrice(PriceCalculationRequest  request)
{
    PriceCalculationResponseDetailed resp = null;
    reps=new PriceCalculationResponseDetailed();
    resp.Price = 120;
    resp.Currency = "euro";
    return resp;
}
```

Now, if the client proxy calls the method `CalculatePrice` the return is not expected and therefore produces the following error:

```
There was an error while trying to serialize parameter http://wrox/
CarRentalService/2009/10:CalculatePriceResult. The InnerException message was
'Type 'Wrox.CarRentalService.Contracts.PriceCalculationResponseDetailed' with
data contract name 'PriceCalculationResponseDetailed:http://schemas.datacontract
.org/2004/07/Wrox.CarRentalService.Contracts' is not expected. Consider using a
DataContractResolver or add any types not known statically to the list of known
types — for example, by using the KnownTypeAttribute attribute or by adding them to
the list of known types passed to DataContractSerializer.'
```

As the error message shows, this problem can be solved with the `KnownType` attribute. The `KnownType` attribute enables the inherited data type to be added to the data contract, thereby facilitating correct serialization and deserialization.

You should use either the `[KnownType]` attribute in your data class or the `[ServiceKnownType]` attribute in the definition of your service contract or operation contract (regardless of whether you wish to use the inherited class or the base class throughout, or whether you only wish to permit this for special service contracts or service operations).

A simple use of the `[KnownType]` attribute exists in enumerating all the derived classes in the data contract for the base class.

Listing 2-22 demonstrates the use of the `[KnownType]` attribute.

LISTING 2-22: KnownType on DataContract

```
[DataContract]
[KnownType(typeof(PriceCalculationResponseDetailed))]
public class PriceCalculationResponse
{
    [DataMember]
    public double  Price { get; set; }
}
```

This attribute tells the `DataContractSerializer` to include the inherited class in the data contract in addition to the base contract. The inheritance hierarchy is also retained in the XSD, as you can see in Listing 2-23.

LISTING 2-23: XSD and Inheritance

```
<xs:complexType name="PriceCalculationResponseDetailed">
  <xs:extension base="tns:PriceCalculationResponse">
   <xs:sequence>
    <xs:element minOccurs="0" name="Currency" type="xs:string" />
   </xs:sequence>
```

If you only expect to encounter an instance of an inherited class in certain methods, or if an inherited version is permitted in all the operations of a service contract, you can use the `[ServiceKnownType]` attribute either at service level (Listing 2-24) or at the operational level, as shown in Listing 2-25. Using the `[ServiceKnownType]` at the operational level means that the inherited class is only accepted for this method. Using the attribute at the service level means that every method accepts the inherited version.

LISTING 2-24: [ServiceKnownType] for One Method

```
[OperationContract]
[ServiceKnownType(typeof(PriceCalculationResponseDetailed))]
PriceCalculationResponse CalculatePrice(PriceCalculationRequest  request);
```

LISTING 2-25: [ServiceKnownType] at the Service Level

```
[OperationContract]
[ServiceKnownType(typeof(PriceCalculationResponseDetailed))]
PriceCalculationResponse CalculatePrice(PriceCalculationRequest  request);
```

Disclosing a more flexible `KnownType` variant involves swapping this information to the configuration file in the `system.runtime.serialization` section, as shown in Listing 2-26.

LISTING 2-26: dataContractSerializer Section in the Config File

```
<system.runtime.serialization>
    <dataContractSerializer>
      <declaredTypes>
        <add type="Wrox.CarRentalService.
            Contracts.PriceCalculationResponse,
            Wrox.CarRentalService.Contracts">
          <knownType type="Wrox.CarRentalService.Contracts.
            PriceCalculationResponseDetailed,
            Wrox.CarRentalService.Contracts"/>
        </add>
      </declaredTypes>
    </dataContractSerializer>
  </system.runtime.serialization>
```

There is a certain degree of inflexibility in telling the previous types (KnownType, ServiceKnownType, config) of WCF which inherited classes are supported. For example, every time you derive a new class, you would have to add an additional [KnownType] attribute to your base contract. Therefore, WCF offers you other possibilities for disclosing KnownTypes. Instead of specifying a fixed set of derived classes, you provide the name of a method which returns a list of derived classes. This can be done both with the [KnownType] and [ServiceType] attributes. Listing 2-27 displays the use of the [KnownType] attribute with a static method called GetTypes.

LISTING 2-27: Dynamic Known Types

```
[DataContract]
[KnownType("GetTypes")]
public class PriceCalculationResponse
{
    static Type[] GetTypes()
    {
      Type[] t = { typeof(PriceCalculationResponseDetailed) };
      return t;
    }
}
```

SERVICE AND DATA CONTRACT VERSIONING

Software development is particularly given to ongoing changes in requirements and, thus, in the offered functionality and structure of the data being exchanged. In principle, any minor change in your operations or data can bring about a change in the WSDL document, leading to a new version of your service. Generally speaking, however, it is neither organizationally nor technically feasible to update your service components continually and to respond to changes in the services offered.

Therefore, you will be shown techniques and processes in this chapter which permit you to maintain the exchange of compatible messages in spite of changes in the service or data contract. These changes are also regarded as changes which do not lead to a break of the contract. While the contracts do not have to be identical so-to-speak, it is imperative that they are compatible. In the case of a service contract, this would mean, for example, that the addition of a new method would not lead to incompatibilities because the client is unfamiliar with this new method anyway. The same applies in data contracts; if a new optional field is added, for example, this field is simply ignored by the DataContractSerializer and filled with a default.

However, a new contract is unavoidable in certain situations — for example, if the name of an operation is changed, or if a mandatory field is added. Changes of this type result in a break of contract, creating the need for a new version. In this case, you are advised to adapt the namespaces to the new version and to host your service at a new endpoint.

Data Contract Versioning

The WCF or the DataContractSerializer is very tolerant of changes in the structure of the data contract.

For example, it is easy to add additional data members or to leave out data members in which the IsRequired attribute is set to false. One benefit to this is that there is no need to worry about these types of minor details; however, in a service-oriented environment it is important to adhere to contracts or, where changes are necessary, to disclose them formally and officially.

Let's assume that a client makes the following changes to version 1 of the service contract/data contract shown in Listing 2-28.

LISTING 2-28: Service and Data Contract Version 1

```
[ServiceContract(
    Namespace = "http://wrox/CarRentalService/2009/10",
    Name = "RentalService")]
public interface ICarRentalService
{
    [OperationContract]
    PriceCalculationResponse CalculatePrice
    (
       PriceCalculationRequest  request, int priority
    );
}


[DataContract]
public class PriceCalculationRequest
{
    [DataMember]
    public DateTime PickupDate { get; set; }
    [DataMember]
    public DateTime ReturnDate { get; set; }
    [DataMember]
    public string PickupLocation { get; set; }
    [DataMember]
    public string ReturnLocation { get; set; }

}
```

The changes to the operation and data contract in Listing 2-29 would lead to compatible contracts.

LISTING 2-29: Service and Data Contract Version 2

```
[ServiceContract(
    Namespace = "http://wrox/CarRentalService/2009/10",
    Name = "RentalService")]
public interface ICarRentalService
{
    [OperationContract]
    PriceCalculationResponse CalculatePrice
    (
        PriceCalculationRequest  request, string someData
    );
}

[DataContract]
public class PriceCalculationRequest
{
    [DataMember]
    public DateTime PickupDate { get; set; }
    [DataMember]
    public DateTime ReturnDate { get; set; }
    [DataMember]
    public string PickupLocation { get; set; }
    [DataMember]
    public string Color { get; set; }
}
```

The following conclusions can be drawn from the previous example:

➤   Method parameters can be deleted or added

➤   Data members can be deleted or added

➤   Data types may be changed provided they remain compatible

➤   Methods can be added

These changes would not lead to any problems of a technical nature. However, you would have to define details of procedures for dealing with missing values, for example. It is possible that a member may no longer be required and can therefore be ignored without any problems.

Round-Trip Versioning

A problem that arises again and again in connection with the versioning of data contracts is the newly added attribute in which deserialization to an old data contract is ignored.

Let's take a closer look at the original example relating to the price inquiry — the client sends a price inquiry to the service and receives a reply object including a flag and a price. The client can confirm the offered price by calling the ConfirmPrice method again, as shown in Listing 2-30. Listing 2-31 displays the service contract and data contract.

LISTING 2-30: ConfirmPrice Service Contract

```
[ServiceContract(
    Namespace = "http://wrox/CarRentalService/2009/10",
    Name = "RentalService")]
public interface ICarRentalService
{
[OperationContract]
PriceCalculationResponse CalculatePrice
    (
        PriceCalculationRequest  request
    );
[OperationContract]
bool ConfirmPrice(PriceCalculationResponse resp);
}
[DataContract]
public class PriceCalculationResponse
{
    [DataMember]
    public int Flag { get; set; }
    [DataMember]
    public string  Price { get; set; }
}
```

LISTING 2-31: ConfirmPrice Client Code

```
using (RentalServiceClient carRentalClient = new RentalServiceClient())
{
    PriceCalculationRequest req = new PriceCalculationRequest();
    req.PickupDate  = System.DateTime.Now.AddDays(5);
    req.ReturnDate  = System.DateTime.Now.AddDays(7);
    req.PickupLocation = "Graz";
    req.ReturnLocation = "Villach";
    PriceCalculationResponse resp;
    resp = carRentalClient.CalculatePrice(req);
    Console.WriteLine("Price {0}", resp.Price);
    Console.WriteLine(carRentalClient.ConfirmPrice(resp));
}
```

During internationalization, add the Currency attribute to the data contract.

Your service can still use the client code because the additional field does not lead to any problems if the IsRequired property does not apply. However, the value of the Currency attribute is lost on the client side because the client is unfamiliar with this newly added attribute and is also unable to deserialize its content.

IExtensibleDataObject

The solution to this round-tripping problem is to implement the IExtensibleDataObject interface and the requisite ExtensionDataObject field. If the DataContractSerializer detects unknown elements in the XML document, they are written to the ExtensionDataObject property bag during deserialization. The content of the `ExtensionDataObject` is retained when further use is made of this object, resulting in no data loss between different versions of data contracts.

If you use the Add Service Reference dialog box, the data classes on the client side automatically implement this interface. If you wish to reciprocate on the server side, you have to implement the interface manually in the data classes — the code in Listing 2-32 is sufficient for this.

LISTING 2-32: IExtensibleDataObject

```
[DataContract]
public class PriceCalculationResponse :IExtensibleDataObject
{
    public ExtensionDataObject ExtensionData { get; set; }

    [DataMember]
    public int Flag { get; set; }
    [DataMember]
    public double   Price { get; set; }
    [DataMember]
    public string Currency { get; set; }
}
```

> *You can also prevent* `ExtensionData` *in general by setting a service behavior in your configuration file with the property* `<dataContractSerializer ignoreExtensionDataObject="true"/>`*. You should take particular care when working with extension data on the server side because it may cause a security gap.*

Best Practices of Service Contract Versioning

If precise compliance between schemas is required, you should assign a new version to your contract every time a change is implemented.

If there is no need for precise compliance between schemas, you should heed the following points:

➤   You can add new methods at any time

➤   You may not delete any existing methods

➤   The parameter data types must remain compatible

Best Practices of Data Contract Versioning

If precise compliance between schemas is required, you should assign a new version to your contract every time a change is implemented.

If there is no need for precise compliance between schemas, you should heed the following points:

➤ Data contracts should not be assigned new versions as a result of inheritance. Create a new independent data class instead.

➤ To facilitate round-tripping, you should implement the IExtensibleDataObject interface at the start.

➤ If you have to change the name of your data class or of some members, compatible data contracts can be created using the DataContract or DataMember attributes.

➤ Do not make subsequent changes to your data types.

➤ Do not change the order in which your data members appear by using the property [DataMember(Order=?)].

➤ Leave the default IsRequired value (false) unchanged.

➤ You can add additional data members at any time but you should remember that this would change the serialization order. This problem is avoided by setting the Order property for new members to the current version's value. Therefore, data members added in version 2 should be assigned Order=2.

➤ Data members should not be deleted.

➤ Subsequent changes should not be made to the IsRequired property.

Listing 2-33 displays some of the recommended practices.

LISTING 2-33: Best Practices of Versioning

```
[DataContract(
    Name="PriceCalculationRequest",
    Namespace="http://schemas.datacontract.org/2004/07/
    Wrox.CarRentalService.Contracts")]
public class PriceReq //Version 1
{
    [DataMember()]
    private DateTime PickupDate { get; set; }
    [DataMember()]
    public DateTime ReturnDate { get; set; }
    [DataMember()]
    public string PickupLocation { get; set; }
    [DataMember()]
    public string ReturnLocation { get; set; }
}

[DataContract(
    Name = "PriceCalculationRequest",
    Namespace = "http://schemas.datacontract.org/2004/07/
    Wrox.CarRentalService.Contracts")]
public class PriceReq //Version 2
```

```
{
    [DataMember(Name = "PickupDate")]
    private DateTime FromDate { get; set; }
    [DataMember(Name = "ReturnDate")]
    public DateTime ToDate { get; set; }
    [DataMember(Order = 2)]
    public string PickupLocation { get; set; }
    [DataMember()]
    public string ReturnLocation { get; set; }
    [DataMember(Order=2)] //from Version 2
    public string CarType { get; set; }
}
```

MESSAGE CONTRACTS

At the start of this chapter, it was explained that SOAP messages are exchanged between the client and the server. However, you have only been able to influence the content of the SOAP body up to now. In most cases, you will be able to manage with data contracts and operation contracts, which is recommended. However, in certain situations you may have to gain total control of the entire SOAP message (header and body). The SOAP header is a suitable method for transferring additional data without extending the data class (for example, a security token).

Message contracts give you complete control over the content of the SOAP header, as well as the structure of the SOAP body. Up to now you have used data contracts as transfer or return parameters — these are now simply replaced by message contracts. If you opt for message contracts, it is important to use message contracts for all the parameters — methods cannot contain a mixture of data contracts and message contracts.

Listing 2-34 shows how the three attributes [MessageContract], [MessageHeader], and [MessageBody] are used. In addition to the price request object, a username is also transferred in the SOAP header.

LISTING 2-34: [MessageContract], [MessageHeader], and [MessageBody]

```
[ServiceContract(
    Namespace = "http://wrox/CarRentalService/2009/10",
    Name = "RentalService")]
public interface ICarRentalService
{
    [OperationContract]
    PriceCalculationResp  CalculatePrice(PriceCalculation  request);
}


[MessageContract]
public class PriceCalculation
{
    [MessageHeader]
```

continues

LISTING 2-34 *(continued)*

```csharp
    public CustomHeader SoapHeader { get; set; }

    [MessageBodyMember]
    public PriceCalculationRequest  PriceRequest { get; set; }
}

[DataContract]
public class CustomHeader
{
    [DataMember]
    public string Username { get; set; }
}

[DataContract]
public class PriceCalculationRequest
{
    [DataMember]
    public DateTime PickupDate { get; set; }
    [DataMember]
    public DateTime ReturnDate { get; set; }
    [DataMember]
    public string PickupLocation { get; set; }
    [DataMember]
    public string ReturnLocation { get; set; }
    }
```

Listing 2-35 illustrates the usage on the client side and Listing 2-36 shows the SOAP message.

LISTING 2-35: Message Contracts — Client Side

```csharp
using (RentalServiceClient carRentalClient = new RentalServiceClient())
{
    PriceCalculation calc = new PriceCalculation();
    PriceCalculationRequest req = new PriceCalculationRequest();
    req.PickupDate = System.DateTime.Now.AddDays(5);
    req.ReturnDate = System.DateTime.Now.AddDays(7);
    req.PickupLocation = "Graz";
    req.ReturnLocation = "Villach";
    calc.PriceRequest = req;

    CustomHeader sHeader = new CustomHeader();
    sHeader.Username = "Johann";
    calc.SoapHeader = sHeader;

    PriceCalculationResp  resp= carRentalClient.CalculatePrice(calc);
}
```

LISTING 2-36: SOAP and Message Headers

```
<s:Envelope xmlns:s="http://schemas.xmlsoap.org/soap/envelope/">
 <s:Header>
  <h:SoapHeader xmlns:h="http://wrox/CarRentalService/2009/10"
    xmlns:i="http://www.w3.org/2001/XMLSchema-instance">
   <Username xmlns="http://schemas.datacontract.org/2004/07/
    Wrox.CarRentalService.Contracts">
    Johann
   </Username>
  </h:SoapHeader>
 </s:Header>
 <s:Body>
  <PriceCalculation xmlns="http://wrox/CarRentalService/2009/10">
   <PriceRequest
    xmlns:a=
"http://schemas.datacontract.org/2004/07/
Wrox.CarRentalService.Contracts"
    xmlns:i="http://www.w3.org/2001/XMLSchema-instance">
    <a:PickupDate>2010-01-15T14:15:08.1683905+01:00</a:PickupDate>
    <a:PickupLocation>Graz</a:PickupLocation>
    <a:ReturnDate>2010-01-17T14:15:08.1693671+01:00</a:ReturnDate>
    <a:ReturnLocation>Villach</a:ReturnLocation>
   </PriceRequest>
  </PriceCalculation>
 </s:Body>
</s:Envelope>
```

You can find other specific examples of how message contracts are used in Chapter 7.

XML Serialization

As already mentioned in the introduction, WCF supports a number of types of serialization. By default, WCF uses the `DataContractSerializer` class to serialize your CLR objects. In the previous examples you have also seen the use of different properties in connection with the `[DataContract]` and `[DataMember]` attributes. To an extent, you can control the structure of the generated XML info set.

The `DataContractSerializer` is optimized for performance, although it offers fewer possibilities as far as influencing the structure of the created document is concerned. If the possibilities offered do not meet your needs, you can switch to the XML Serializer. The XML Serializer also offers you more control in interop scenarios or in communication with old ASP.NET Web Services.

To instruct WCF to use the XML Serializer, you can simply assign your service contract the `[XmlSerializerFormat]` attribute. However, should you only wish to use the XML Serializer for certain operations, you can also apply this attribute to your methods. Note that the XML Serializer also serializes all public properties by default. You can find further information about these classes in the Framework Documentation on MSDN.

Listing 2-37 demonstrates the use of the `[XMLSerializerFormat]` with attributes from the System.XML.Serialization namespace and Listing 2-38 displays the XSD for the `PriceCalculationRequest` type.

LISTING 2-37: XML Serialization

```
[XmlSerializerFormat]
[ServiceContract(
    Namespace = "http://wrox/CarRentalService/2009/10",
    Name = "RentalService")]
public interface ICarRentalService
{
    [OperationContract]
    PriceCalculationResponse CalculatePrice
    (
     PriceCalculationRequest request
    );
}

[XmlRoot("PriceRequest")]
public class PriceCalculationRequest
{
    [XmlAttribute()]
    public  string PickupLocation { get; set; }
    [XmlElement(ElementName="ReturnLoc")]
    public string ReturnLocation { get; set; }
    [XmlIgnore()]
    public DateTime PickupDate { get; set; }
    private  DateTime ReturnDate { get; set; }
}
```

LISTING 2-38: XSD for the PriceCalculationRequest Type

```
<xs:element name="CalculatePrice">
 <xs:complexType>
  <xs:sequence>
<xs:element minOccurs="0" maxOccurs="1"
   name="request"
   type="tns:PriceCalculationRequest" />
</xs:sequence>

</xs:complexType>
</xs:element>
<xs:complexType name="PriceCalculationRequest">
 <xs:sequence>
  <xs:element minOccurs="0" maxOccurs="1" name="ReturnLoc"
    type="xs:string" />
  </xs:sequence>
 <xs:attribute name="PickupLocation" type="xs:string" />
</xs:complexType>
<xs:element name="CalculatePriceResponse">
 <xs:complexType>
  <xs:sequence>
   <xs:element minOccurs="0" maxOccurs="1"
```

```
    name="CalculatePriceResult"
    type="tns:PriceCalculationResponse" />
  </xs:sequence>
 </xs:complexType>
</xs:element>
...
</xs:complexType>
```

3

Bindings

WHAT'S IN THIS CHAPTER?

➤ Understanding bindings

➤ Defining addresses

➤ Applying behaviors

➤ Creating your own bindings

Windows Communication Foundation (WCF) provides a programming framework that abstracts out the complexities of creating services. It does this for nearly every element of the service and bindings is probably one of the most important areas. This allows you as the programmer to concentrate on the problem at hand, and not worry about how to create architecture that allows your system to work. The foundation is there already.

To define a service endpoint (as described in previous chapters), you must implement the ABCs of WCF. This stands for Address, Binding, and Contract — or the Where, How, and What of a service.

➤ The Address is where the service is hosted, either for the service as a reference, or so the client knows where to send the message.

➤ The Binding is the how of the services, and defines how the messages are sent and received.

➤ The Contract is the definition of what the message contains. There are many types of contracts described in depth in Chapter 2.

The ABCs make up an endpoint in WCF. They need to be set for both the client and the service.

Bindings incorporate three main areas:

➤ Transport protocol — The protocol to use. Examples are Http and TCP.

➤ Encoding format — The details of how to encode the message as it goes down the wire, such as plain text, binary, and so on.

➤ Other messaging protocol details — Used for the communication channel. This could be reliable messaging requirements or security requirements such as SOAP message.

A *binding* is actually a group of binding elements; each element is responsible for different things, such as message encoding or security (see later in this chapter for a full list of WCF binding elements). The WCF pre-configured bindings bring groups of binding elements together to address common scenarios that developers need, which abstract out the common scenarios to bring together defined standards. Each channel within the binding is part of the overall communication. This allows for re-use within WCF and allows you to create your own binding using pre-configured elements that already exist. You can use one of the many pre-defined bindings provided for you by the WCF framework, which try to address many different scenarios that are commonly used at the time. If the binding that is provided by the framework doesn't quite address your specific needs, you have a few options.

First you can tweak one of the pre-defined bindings that closely match your needs by setting one of the many binding properties. You can also define your own binding by selecting existing binding elements and creating a group of binding elements.

For the most part, you will be able to use one of the default WCF bindings. This speeds up development time immensely, as you don't have to write code to transport messages over the wire. You are able to define the ABCs and then everything is taken care of for you. Due to having these binding implementations set for you by WCF, you can have multiple endpoints with different bindings. This is a fundamental part of WCF — interoperability. So your same service method could implement several different protocols and transport options. This allows you to quickly expose your service to any kind of client that needs to access it. You could use a .NET-specific binding to communicate with .NET clients to take advantage of the built-in WCF security and performance capabilities. However, you can also expose your service using WS-* standards for Java, PHP, or any compatible clients that implement the specifications. Otherwise you can use a binding that allows web clients to connect to your service with a simplified interface already known as a *REST* (*Representational State Transfer*) interface. This also allows you to quickly swap a binding out, or change a binding to test performance.

> *With respect to SOA, REST provides an alternative way to allow operations on a remote resource. Working with REST is treated in more detail in Chapter 4.*

When choosing the best binding and properties for a solution you can create multiple endpoints with a range of different endpoint and configuration options. This means you can run performance tests for the response time of each binding. The logic/contract and business logic are all the same, only the binding config differs. This means you are literally just changing the transport. Doing this without WCF would mean learning .NET remoting and ASMX web services and all the things in between. Then you'd have to implement each of them and host them all in different ways before testing them. If you want a range of these implemented on your production servers, you would again need it to be deployed differently depending on the technology. It's easy to see the benefits of WCF for all the SOA scenarios.

HOW THE BINDINGS WORK

As previously described, WCF allows sending and receiving messages by using different kinds of transport protocols. To establish how your service communicates with the external world, you can also decide the message encoding (text, binary, or Mtom) or the standards protocols to enable interoperable, secure, and reliable communication. The binding is the key element of the WCF architecture. It allows you to specify how the message is handled before the specific service implementation on the service provider side, or after the client implementation on the consumer side.

A binding is composed of a set of binding elements. This is explained in more depth next in this chapter. Here it is sufficient to know that each binding element corresponds to the transport and to the protocol channels located in something known as the *channel stack*. The channel stack is the sequence of channels that a message passes through to the runtime execution.

The type and order of binding elements are important. They determine the execution of the channels within the service runtime, as shown in Figure 3-1.

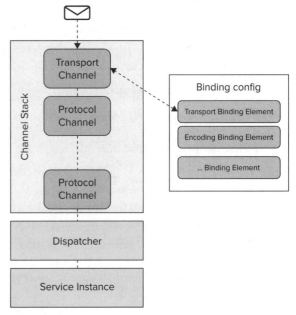

FIGURE 3-1

Note that the transport element and the encoding element have to be the first and second element specified because they enable the correct communication between the channels. In fact, when a message arrives, it is received by a transport channel (e.g., a TCP channel that listens on a predefined port), and is then passed to the encoding channel. Finally it is passed to all other protocol channels defined in the binding via binding elements. This is an important thing to keep in mind when configuring and using a binding.

It is also possible to implement custom channels to achieve an unsupported scenario, but rarely do you need to create, for example, your custom transport in place of Http or TCP protocol. You do need to know that you can do it and that WCF offers you this great level of flexibility.

All these things are addressed in this chapter, but first, a concept should be clarified — what the address and the behaviors are and how they can be used in the WCF architecture.

ADDRESSES

The *address* is the first of the ABCs. Each endpoint must have a unique address; this is the location of the service. It can be any type of address, IP address, server name, URL, etc. You need an address to know where the service is hosted, similar to the URL of a web site. It contains a lot of the necessary information needed to connect to the service within the address itself. An address is composed of the following parts:

➤ Transport scheme — Beginning part of the address that sets the protocol the service uses.

➤ Server location — Actual address or location of the server where the service is hosted. This can be local to your network (`http://localserver/`), or across the Web (`http://www.webserver.com` or `http://216.239.59.104`).

➤ Port — Can be specified if you are not using the default port for that protocol.

➤ Path — The relative location of the resource on the server; if the resource filename is not specified, the server could return the default file.

The format of the address would be this:

```
scheme://SERVERLOCATION[:port]/path/subpath
```

A simple example would be this:

```
http://myserver.com/service
```

From this address you can see that the transport scheme is Http; the server location is myserver.com; and no port was specified, meaning that it would use the default port for Http, which is 80; and the path is /service. Table 3-1 shows a set of examples for each available transport protocol.

TABLE 3-1: WCF Address Examples per Transport Protocol

TRANSPORT PROTOCOL	EXAMPLE ADDRESS
Http	`http://localhost:8001` `http://localhost:8001/Service1`
Http (Secure)	`https://localhost:8001`
TCP Peer network	`net.tcp://localhost:8002/Service1` `net.p2p://localhost/`
IPC (Inter-process communication over named pipes)	`net.pipe://localhost/PipeService1`
MSMQ (Microsoft Message Queue)	`net.msmq://localhost`

Transport Protocols

WCF allows you to communicate with clients over any protocol you wish. Unlike ASMX web services, which were just over Http, you now have a choice depending on your client.

➤ **Http:** This is the chosen protocol for communication over the Web, and allows you to integrate your service with open standards, allowing you to serve clients on many different architectures.

➤ **TCP:** A fast binary format protocol. It allows for high-performance communication in WCF-to-WCF, where it is the best choice in intranet scenarios.

➤ **Named pipes:** This transport allows a fast, reliable communication between the client and the service when run on the same machine. It works only WCF-to-WCF by using a section of shared memory used by the processes.

➤ **MSMQ:** Microsoft Message Queue allows the queuing of messages and it is very useful in disconnected communications between a client and a service. The net.msmq transport is used when a client wants to enqueue a message that a service can then consume later.

➤ **Custom protocol:** WCF allows you to communicate over the wire with all previous protocols. On very rare occasions, you may need to define your own protocol.

BEHAVIORS

By applying behaviors to different parts of your system you are able to influence WCF service in regard to things such as Session Management, Concurrency, Throttling, and Transactions. Some of these things can only be applied at certain levels: Service, Endpoint, Operation, and Contract.

Depending on the level, there are different ways you can set up the behaviors. A lot can be done within configuration or within attributes that are provided. But some will have to be implemented within your code itself, although a lot can be done within the configuration.

Behaviors are applied locally on either the clients or services, so they are not exposed in the WSDL for the service.

Service Behaviors

The [ServiceBehavior] attribute allows you to apply rules and behavior on a service-wide level. At design time, this allows you to control things such as Concurrency, Instancing, Throttling, Transaction, Session Management, and Thread behavior by setting its properties:

➤ `AddressFilterMode:` This allows you to change the Message Filter. The `AddressFilterMode` property has three values: `Any`, `Exact`, and `Prefix`. This setting is used by the dispatcher to identify the correct endpoint responsible to handle incoming messages.

➤ `AutomaticSessionShutdown:` This is a Boolean field that stops the server from closing the session when all messages have been processed. By default this is `true`; by setting it to `false`, you are able to have control of session lifetime.

➤ `ConcurrencyMode:` This sets if the service can run on one thread or on multiple threads. By default it is set to `Single`. Setting to multiple means you must implement thread safety into your service.

➤ `IgnoreExtensionDataObject:` This is a Boolean with a `false` default. If set to `true`, any extra unknown serialization data is not sent with the message.

➤ IncludeExceptionDetailInFaults: You have to set this property to true if you want to get an unhandled exception sent to the client as SOAP fault. This produces a big SOAP message with some internal information (e.g., the stack trace) that a client usually doesn't have to know. Set to true if you are in a development environment, but set to false in a production environment.

➤ InstanceContextMode: This property is used to set the lifetime of the service instance. The allowed values are PerSession, PerCall, and Single. The instance management is treated in more depth in Chapter 4.

➤ MaxItemsInObjectGraph: This sets the maximum allowed items in the serialized/ deserialized object graph. Sometimes you receive an exception if your objects exceed the maximum number of items that can be serialized or deserialized. Increase this property to match your case.

➤ ReleaseServiceInstanceOnTransactionComplete: If this property is set to true, the service object is released when the active transaction is complete.

➤ TransactionAutoCompleteOnSessionClose: Set this property to true if you want to mark as complete the active transaction when the session is closed by the client without an error.

➤ TransactionIsolationLevel: Specify the isolation level enabled on the current object when a transaction is active. The possible values are Serializable, RepeatableRead, ReadCommitted, ReadUncommitted, Snapshot, Chaos, and Unspecified.

➤ TransactionTimeout: Sometimes a transaction can take a long time to complete. You can set a timeout after which the transaction is considered aborted and the rollback process is activated.

➤ UseSynchronizationContext: This property can be used to specify whether the affinity between the user interface thread and the service is required.

➤ ValidateMustUnderstand: This is used to turn off the validation of SOAP Headers that have been marked as MustUnderstand. This is a Boolean field and by default is false.

To use the [ServiceBehavior], as with any other attribute in .NET, you can mark the service class and set the appropriate properties — as seen in Listing 3-1.

LISTING 3-1: Usage of Service Behavior

```
using System;
using Wrox.CarRentalService.Contracts;

namespace Wrox.CarRentalService.Implementations.Europe
{
    [ServiceBehavior(InstanceContextMode = InstanceContextMode.PerCall)]
    public class CarRentalService : ICarRentalService
    {
        // service operations
    }
}
```

In this sample code the [ServiceBehaviorAttribute] is used to establish the service instance lifetime by using the PerCall mode. The ServiceBehaviorAttribute is only a special case of service behavior. Indeed, any ServiceBehavior implements a specific interface called IServiceBehavior with the following methods:

➤ AddBindingParameters: Use this method, called only one time for each endpoint, to inspect the current service description and modify the binding parameters according to service behavior needs.

➤ ApplyDispatchBehavior: This is the most important method of the interface. You could use it to apply the service behavior logic to the runtime. An example is to set a MessageInspector to log the incoming and outgoing messages.

➤ Validate: As the name implies, this method should be used to check the service description and optionally throw an exception if it doesn't meet the service behavior needs.

Besides the ServiceBehaviorAttribute, there are many other behaviors implementing the IServiceBehavior interface configurable by using both the config file and the programmatic approach. One of the most used behaviors is the ServiceMetadataBehavior that allows you to publish the service metadata.

As demonstrated in the Listing 3-2, in the config file, under the <system.serviceModel> <behaviors> section, you can set the service behaviors you would like to use.

LISTING 3-2: Enable Metadata Publishing on the Service in Config

```xml
<?xml version="1.0" encoding="utf-8" ?>
<configuration>
  <system.serviceModel>
    <services>
      <service name="Wrox.CarRentalService.Implementations.Europe.CarRentalService"
behaviorConfiguration="CarRentalServiceBehavior">
        <endpoint address="http://localhost:8000/CarRentalService"
          contract="Wrox.CarRentalService.Contracts.ICarRentalService"
          binding="basicHttpBinding">
        </endpoint>
      </service>
    </services>
    <behaviors>
      <serviceBehaviors>
        <behavior name="CarRentalServiceBehavior">
          <serviceMetadata httpGetEnabled ="true"/>
        </behavior>
      </serviceBehaviors>
    </behaviors>
  </system.serviceModel>
</configuration>
```

This sample config enables the publishing of the metadata information about your service by using the ServiceMetadataBehavior. This allows a client to make a request and get a set of information that describes your service in a standard format based on a WSDL (Web Services Description

Language) standard specification or a WS-Metadata Exchange. Alternatively you could also use the programmatic approach to set the behaviors, as in Listing 3-3.

LISTING 3-3: Enable Metadata Publishing on the Service in Code

```
using Wrox.CarRentalService.Implementations.Europe;
using Wrox.CarRentalService.Contracts;
...

ServiceHost host = new ServiceHost(typeof(CarRentalService));

ServiceMetadataBehavior serviceMetadata =
host.Description.Behaviors.Find<ServiceMetadataBehavior>();
if (serviceMetadata == null)
{
    serviceMetadata = new ServiceMetadataBehavior();
    host.Description.Behaviors.Add(serviceMetadata);
}
serviceMetadata.HttpGetEnabled = true;

BasicHttpBinding binding = new BasicHttpBinding();
host.AddServiceEndpoint(typeof(ICarRentalService),
                        binding,
                        "http://localhost:8080/CarRentalService");
```

This code checks whether the current `ServiceHost` instance already has an instance of the `ServiceMetadataBehavior`. It creates a new one if it does not exist and then sets to `true` the `HttpGetEnabled` property, as in the configuration file. Only one instance of the same `ServiceBehavior` type can exist at the same time for each `ServiceDescription`.

> The ServiceHost is treated in depth in Chapter 14. For now just know that it is used to host and manage the service instance in a .NET application, such as a Windows Service, a WindowsForms, or a Console application.

Operation Behaviors

Using the `OperationBehavior` attribute you are able to control class methods, which allow you to be more specific with certain areas of your service. The things you are able to control at this level are Transactional, Caller Identity, and Object recycling.

➤ `AutoDisposeParameters`: This property enables the auto dispose of input, output, and reference parameters. The default value is `true`.

➤ `TransactionAutoComplete`: When the transaction is enabled, this property sets the transaction as completed if no errors occur in the current method. Otherwise the transaction is aborted. When this property is set to `false`, you must manually set the transaction as completed or as aborted.

➤ `TransactionScopeRequired`: This property is used to set if a transaction is required for the current method.

➤ `Impersonation`: Sometimes you have the need to execute operations with the caller's identity. Set this property to Required or Allowed, the default value, to meet your requirements.

➤ `ReleaseInstanceMode`: This property allows overriding the value of `InstanceContextMode` recycle settings for the service object. The possible values are `None`, `BeforeCall`, `AfterCall`, and `BeforeAndAfterCall`.

The `OperationBehaviorAttribute` allows managing settings that are strictly related with the service operations. You can simply apply the attribute on the operation you want to manage and then set the appropriate properties to obtain the desired behavior, based on the specific needs. See Listing 3-4.

LISTING 3-4: Define the OperationBehavior on Service Implementation

```
using System;
using Wrox.CarRentalService.Contracts;

namespace Wrox.CarRentalService.Implementations.Europe
{
    public class CarRentalService : ICarRentalService
    {
        [OperationBehavior(
            AutoDisposeParameters = true,
            Impersonation = ImpersonationOption.NotAllowed,
            ReleaseInstanceMode = ReleaseInstanceMode.None,
            TransactionAutoComplete = true,
            TransactionScopeRequired = false)]
        double CalculatePrice(DateTime pickupDate, DateTime returnDate,
    string pickupLocation, string vehiclePreference)
        {
            // method code here
        }
    }
}
```

In this sample code, all the properties of the `OperationBehaviorAttribute` are set with the default values.

Endpoint Behaviors

Although the service behavior is only usable on the service side, the endpoint behaviors could be used both in services and client side. Some things, such as client credential usage or serializer settings, can be managed by applying the specific behavior to the endpoint. WCF provides a predefined set of behaviors, each of which implements the `IEndpointBehavior` interface:

➤ `AddBindingParameters`: Use this method, called only one time for each endpoint, to inspect the current service description and modify the binding parameters according to endpoint behavior needs.

➤ `ApplyDispatchBehavior`: This is the most important method of the interface. You could use it to apply the endpoint behavior logic at the service side.

➤ ApplyClientBehavior: On the client side you can use this method to apply the endpoint behavior logic at runtime.

➤ Validate: As the name implies, this method should be used to check the service description and optionally throw an exception if it doesn't meet the endpoint behavior needs.

You are able to set the various endpoint behaviors by using the config file, the programmatic approach, or a combination. Unlike ServiceBehaviorAttribute, an Endpoint Behavior can be used on both the client and the service. Another big difference, on the service side, is that the endpoint behavior settings are valid only at endpoint level, while the service behavior settings are valid at service level. By the way, some special implementation may allow only client usage, as in the ClientCredential behavior.

By using the config file, you can specify and configure the endpoint behaviors. For example, on the client side, if you want to indicate the credentials that a client must use when calling the relative endpoint, you can use the ClientCredential behavior. See Listing 3-5.

LISTING 3-5: Set the ClientCredentials on the Config File

```xml
<?xml version="1.0" encoding="utf-8" ?>
<configuration>
  <system.serviceModel>
    <services>
      <service
        name="Wrox.CarRentalService.Implementations.Europe.CarRentalService"
        behaviorConfiguration="CarRentalServiceBehavior">
        <endpoint address="http://localhost:8000/CarRentalService"
          contract="Wrox.CarRentalService.Contracts.ICarRentalService"
          binding="basicHttpBinding"
          behaviorConfiguration="carRentalEndpointBehavior">
        </endpoint>
      </service>
    </services>
    <behaviors>
      <serviceBehaviors>
        <behavior name="CarRentalServiceBehavior">
          <serviceMetadata httpGetEnabled ="true"/>
        </behavior>
      </serviceBehaviors>
      <endpointBehaviors>
        <behavior name="carRentalEndpointBehavior">
          <clientCredentials>
            <clientCertificate findValue="CN=client_cert"
                               storeLocation="CurrentUser"
                               storeName="My"
                               x509FindType="FindBySubjectDistinguishedName"/>
          </clientCredentials>
        </behavior>
      </endpointBehaviors>
    </behaviors>
  </system.serviceModel>
</configuration>
```

If the config file is not the right solution, it is also possible to set the behavior programmatically on the client side. See Listing 3-6.

LISTING 3-6: Set the ClientCredentials on the Client in Code

```
CarRentalServiceClient client = new CarRentalServiceClient();

try
{
    client.ClientCredentials.ClientCertificate.SetCertificate(
        StoreLocation.CurrentUser,
        StoreName.My,
        X509FindType.FindBySubjectDistinguishedName,
        "CN=client_cert");

    // other code

    client.Close();
}
catch (Exception ex)
{
    client.Abort();
    throw;
}
```

The code is different if you want to set an endpoint behavior on the server side (see Listing 3-7). As seen for service behavior, if you don't use the config file, the ServiceHost class helps us.

LISTING 3-7: Set the ServiceCredentials on the Service in Code

```
using Wrox.CarRentalService.Implementations.Europe;
...

ServiceHost host = new ServiceHost(typeof(CarRentalService));

try
{
    BasicHttpBinding binding = new BasicHttpBinding();
    ServiceEndpoint serviceEndpoint =
        host.AddServiceEndpoint(typeof(ICarRentalService),
        binding,
        "http://localhost:8080/CarRentalService");

    ServiceCredentials credentials = new ServiceCredentials();
    credentials.ServiceCertificate.SetCertificate(
        StoreLocation.CurrentUser,
        StoreName.My,
        X509FindType.FindBySubjectDistinguishedName,
        "CN=service_cert");

    host.Open();

    // other code here ...

    host.Close();
```

continues

```
}
catch (Exception)
{
    host.Abort();
}
```

The `ClientCredentials` behavior is not usable on the service side. In this sample code you see how to set the service certificate by using the `ServiceCredentials` behavior. Security settings and the other WCF security topics are addressed Chapters 7, 8, and 9.

Contract Behaviors

The `IContractBehavior` interface can be implemented to extend or modify any aspect of your contracts. This is applied throughout the use of your contract. This interface has four methods which you can implement to modify contracts. You cannot apply contract behaviors in configuration so you must do it in code or by attributes. The four methods are shown here:

➤ `AddBindingParameters`: This method allows you to add custom parameters useful to execute the behavior. This method is called once for each endpoint.

➤ `ApplyClientBehavior`: Use this method to apply the behavior logic on the client side.

➤ `ApplyDispatchBehavior`: Implement this method by applying the behavior logic on the service client.

➤ `Validate`: This is useful if you want to validate the runtime context for behavior execution.

As for the `IEndpointBehavior`, the `IContractBehavior` can be applied both on client and service side to the contract interface. But otherwise, an `IContractBehavior` implementation cannot be added at runtime with the configuration file. It can be added only at design time by using attributes or programmatically.

There is only one predefined `IContractBehavior` implementation: the `DeliveryRequirementsAttribute`. This behavior acts as a validator versus a feature that is loaded at runtime from a configuration file. See Listing 3-8.

LISTING 3-8: Usage of a Contract Behavior

```
using System;

namespace Wrox.CarRentalService.Contracts
{
    [DeliveryRequirements(
    QueuedDeliveryRequirements = QueuedDeliveryRequirementsMode.NotAllowed,
    RequireOrderedDelivery = true)]
    public class ICarRentalService
    {
        // service operations
    }
}
```

The `DeliveryRequirements`, in this example, indicates that this contract does not allow the queued contracts but requires the message ordered delivery. You can also set the behavior programmatically (see Listing 3-9).

LISTING 3-9: Usage of a Contract Behavior Programmatically on the Client Side

```
DeliveryRequirementsAttribute deliveryRequirements =
    new DeliveryRequirementsAttribute();
deliveryRequirements.RequireOrderedDelivery = true;
deliveryRequirements.QueuedDeliveryRequirements =
    QueuedDeliveryRequirementsMode.NotAllowed;

CarRentalServiceClient client = new CarRentalServiceClient();
client.Endpoint.Contract.Behaviors.Add(deliveryRequirements);
```

On the server side, instead, you can do it by using the `ServiceHost`, as shown in Listing 3-10.

LISTING 3-10: Usage of a Contract Behavior Programmatically on the Server Side

```
using Wrox.CarRentalService.Implementations.Europe;
...

ServiceHost host = new ServiceHost(typeof(CarRentalService));

BasicHttpBinding binding = new BasicHttpBinding();
ServiceEndpoint serviceEndpoint =
host.AddServiceEndpoint(typeof(ICarRentalService),
                    binding,
                    "http://localhost:8080/CarRentalService");

DeliveryRequirementsAttribute deliveryRequirements = new
DeliveryRequirementsAttribute();
deliveryRequirements.RequireOrderedDelivery = true;
deliveryRequirements.QueuedDeliveryRequirements =
QueuedDeliveryRequirementsMode.NotAllowed;
serviceEndpoint.Contract.Behaviors.Add(deliveryRequirements);

host.Open();
```

THE BINDINGS

WCF provides a bunch of different bindings which will hopefully allow you to develop your service without having to go through much code. Patterns and commands used over and over by other developers have been brought together, which allows you to get the "standard" services into production fast. If you have different needs, you can still develop a custom binding with minimal fuss, but you need to know what is out there to see if there is already a binding that will fit your needs.

Bindings that are prefixed with "net" mean they were designed to take advantage of .NET and perform many performance-enhancing operations. Bindings that are prefixed with "ws" are to be used with all systems and conform to set web standards. A brief discussion of the currently available standard bindings is available in Table 3-2.

TABLE 3-2: Standard Bindings Found in the System.ServiceModel Namespace

BINDING NAME	DESCRIPTION
`basicHttpBinding`	This uses WS-I Basic Profile 1.1 (`http://www.ws-i.org/Profiles/ BasicProfile-1.1-2004-08-24.html`) which is the profile for old ASMX web services. It allows you to create and consume ASMX-style services within WCF. It uses Http for transport and encodes the message in UTF-8 text by default.
`webHttpBinding`	This allows you to expose your services as Http requests, as used for REST-based services to output XML or JSON.
`wsHttpBinding`	This uses advanced WS-* based profiles to create web services. This is for many profiles such as WS-Security, WS-Transactions, WS-BusinessActivity, etc.
`wsDualHttpBinding`	This uses the same profiles as the wsHttpBinding but for duplex contracts. This means that services and clients can both send and receive messages.
`wsFederationHttpBinding`	To be used for advanced WS-* based web services using federated identity.
`netTcpBinding`	Use this binding to communicate over TCP across two machines within your network. This requires both the service and the client to use WCF. Features include transactions and security optimized for WCF.
`netNamedPipeBinding`	This is optimized for on-machine communication.
`netPeerTcpBinding`	This binding still communicates over TCP but it uses a peer-to-peer (P2P) network. Each participant (node) acts as a client and a server to the other nodes in the network. This relies on name resolution systems to resolve each other's network locations from names. The Peer Name Resolution Protocol (PNRP) is used and specified within the binding. P2P is used heavily in file sharing such as torrent, which has been made famous during the last few years.
`netMsmqBinding`	Binding for asynchronous communication using MSMQ (Microsoft Message Queue).
`msmqIntegrationBinding`	This binding allows WCF developers to communicate with existing systems that communicate via MSMQ.

BasicHttpBinding and WSHttpBinding

In a scenario with a lot of heterogeneous clients that should have access to your service, the use of interoperable protocols is a prerequisite that must be respected. WCF provides the BasicHttpBinding and the WSHttpBinding as two kinds of bindings that use Http (HyperText Transfer Protocol) as transport protocol. These are the most interoperable bindings that are useable.

The BasicHttpBinding provides a high level of interoperability between WCF and the other framework for building services such as ASP.NET ASMX. In terms of standards, it is the implementation of the WS-I Basic Profile 1.1 specification. It supports SOAP 1.1 as a messaging protocol. The security is based on the underlying transport protocol (Http) for authentication and encryption, or on WS-Security 1.0 for message security. Because the usage of BasicHttpBinding is useful only for backward interoperability with ASP.NET ASMX, because the ASMX ASP.NET doesn't support WS-Security, and the entire payload is sent in plain text, there aren't many reasons to use it.

Though it offers a great level of interoperability, there are many scenarios where it is unusable. The WSHttpBinding, as the name suggests, allows you to use various WS-* specifications such as WS-Security 1.1, WS-Reliable Messaging (for reliable and ordered message delivery), WS-Atomic Transaction, WS-Trust, and so on. This allows you to create a great and robust service infrastructure.

Obviously, using all these specifications could generate a lot of message exchanges between the client and the services. Definitively, the support of standards make WSHttpBinding more secure and reliable than BasicHttpBinding. Finally, if compatibility is not required, WSHttpBinding is the choice.

NetTcpBinding

NetTcpBinding allows using the TCP protocol with the message binary encoding. By default, all the binding settings are turned off. If you want to use the security, you have to set it. If you want to use the reliable and ordered delivery with WS-ReliableMessaging or if you want to make atomic your communication, you have to enable it.

NetTcpBinding is a faster and more reliable protocol, compared with the Http protocol bindings. However, it is only usable when communication is WCF-to-WCF. This scenario represents the best applicable solution.

NetMsmqBinding

BasicHttpBinding, WSHttpBinding, and NetTcpBinding are solutions for connected scenarios. Sometimes you want or have the need to decouple the service provider and consumer. This usually happens if the service processes the message at a different time than the client. The client, in turn, doesn't know the exact endpoint of the services that consume and process the message.

NetMsmqBinding allows using a MSMQ to enqueue and dequeue messages. A typical scenario uses a service to receive messages from clients, enqueue the messages, then dequeue the message and process it at the backend. This allows decoupling the client and service, while the queue is the duty free zone where messages are exchanged.

In the .NET Framework you can find another binding that uses MSMQ as a message transport protocol: the `MsmqIntegrationBinding`. This binding differs from the `NetMsmqBinding` because it allows communication with the existing applications that use the `System.Messaging` or COM API. You cannot use `NetMsmqBinding` to read messages written with `MsmqIntegrationBinding` or vice versa because of their totally different message formatting.

Context-Enabled Bindings

WCF provides a special set of context management–enabled bindings for a range of different standard bindings. Context-enabled bindings allow you to send extra parameters to the service to exchange context by using the HttpCookies or the SOAP Header. These bindings are inherited from their main binding, and are utilized in the same way as that binding.

The following context bindings are provided for you by WCF:

➤   `BasicHttpContextBinding`

➤   `NetTcpContextBinding`

➤   `WSHttpContextBinding`

These bindings allow the implementation of durable services. A WCF durable service is a service in which the state is maintained during the different calls. The following SOAP message demonstrates the usage of a SOAP Header to transfer the context between client and services. See Listing 3-11.

Available for download on Wrox.com

LISTING 3-11: SOAP Message Sent When the Binding Has Context Exchange Enabled

```xml
<s:Envelope xmlns:s="http://www.w3.org/2003/05/soap-envelope"
    xmlns:a="http://www.w3.org/2005/08/addressing">
    <s:Header>
        <a:Action s:mustUnderstand="1">
            http://tempuri.org/IService1/GetData
        </a:Action>
        <a:MessageID>
            urn:uuid:32186d9f-573f-4252-989f-ad94a469271b
        </a:MessageID>
        <a:ReplyTo>
            <a:Address>
                http://www.w3.org/2005/08/addressing/anonymous
            </a:Address>
        </a:ReplyTo>
        <Context xmlns="http://schemas.microsoft.com/ws/2006/05/context">
            <Property name="instanceId">
                1507fdf6-a27b-40f2-b339-f331baa937f1
            </Property>
        </Context>
        <a:To s:mustUnderstand="1">http://fabio-nb:10101/IService</a:To>
    </s:Header>
    <s:Body>
```

```
        <GetData xmlns="http://tempuri.org/">
            <value>1</value>
        </GetData>
    </s:Body>
</s:Envelope>
```

The Context SOAP Header has a child element named `Context` that maintains the service instance ID in an element *property*. This is used on server side to retrieve the instance and resume the persisted durable service.

So Many Bindings to Choose From

All these built-in bindings are built on standards that work for specific scenarios, but will also work if you choose the wrong or less-efficient one. So how do you choose which one is right for your situation?

The most obvious decision is if you need to interact with non-WCF applications. If your service is to communicate with WCF clients, then you can use one of the bindings prefixed with "net." Remember you can define several endpoints for the same service which would use different bindings. This allows you to take advantage of performance optimizations for WCF clients, but still provide support for ASMX services and WS-* standards. These provide further security and other features which many clients take advantage of.

For example, if you want to establish a WCF-to-WCF communication, choosing a `NetTcpBinding` with a binary encoding makes the communication four or five time faster than a `BasicHttpBinding` with text encoding.

These WCF-provided bindings should cover most cases that you need: however, if you need to change or create an entirely new binding, WCF allows you do this very simply. This will be discussed later in this chapter.

CONFIGURING BINDINGS

You can define your binding along with your endpoint either in configuration or in code. It is generally accepted to set your endpoints in configuration, as you won't usually know where the address of your service will be hosted while you're in development. Even if you do have a good idea where it will be, by defining it in configuration you are able to change the location at a later date without having to re-build the code and deploy. Your service may be in place for many years and its location may be moved as network infrastructure changes within your company or organization. This allows administrators to make this change without you by editing the XML. Other developers can also easily make this change without digging through your code.

Your configuration resides inside your App.config (or Web.config) file. You can edit this directly (as in the examples provided) or you can use the WCF Configuration Editor (see Figure 3-2) by right-clicking your App.config/Web.config file and selecting Edit WCF Configuration. This is a great tool. For these examples, however, the XML that is produced is shown. The tool speaks for itself and knowing the code will help you in both learning the code and doing difficult configuration without the editor at a later date.

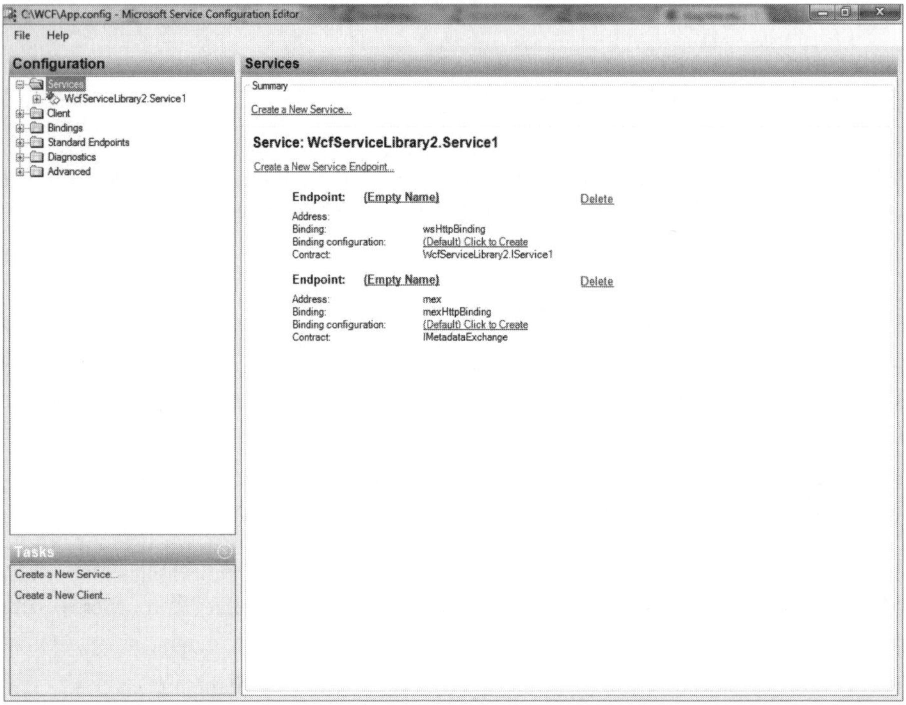

FIGURE 3-2

In the config file there is a special configuration section called `system.serviceModel`. In this section you can define all the settings for your service or client implementation: the endpoints, the binding, the behaviors, the diagnostics, and so on. Listing 3-12 shows you how to create an endpoint in the configuration file by using the `wsHttpBinding` with the contract `IMyService` service contract.

LISTING 3-12: Configuring a Binding Declaratively

Available for download on Wrox.com

```
<?xml version="1.0" encoding="utf-8" ?>
<configuration>
  <system.serviceModel>
    <services>
      <service name="HelloWorldService" >
        <endpoint
          address="http://localhost:8080/HelloWorldService"
          binding="wsHttpBinding"
          contract="IMyService" />
      </service>
    </services>
    <bindings>
      <wsHttpBinding>
      </wsHttpBinding>
     </bindings>
  </system.serviceModel>
</configuration>
```

As shown in Listing 3-13, you can obtain the exact same result by configuring the service with the programmatic approach.

LISTING 3-13: Configuring a Binding Programmatically

```
ServiceHost host = new ServiceHost(typeof(HelloWorldService));

wsHttpBinding binding = new wsHttpBinding();

host.AddServiceEndpoint(typeof(HelloWorldService),
                        binding,
                        "http://localhost:8731/HelloWorldService");
```

Base Addresses

You don't have to explicitly set your address in each endpoint. You can set a base address in your configuration, and then use a relative address inside each of your endpoints. This allows you to have multiple endpoints which all use the same base address, meaning that if you change the URL of the service location, you can do it in one place instead of having to do it in multiple places for each endpoint. This might not sound like a big issue when you have only one or two endpoints, but if you have a whole library of endpoints it quickly becomes a chore. This also leaves you less prone to spelling mistakes of each address and allows for more reuse.

Listing 3-14 appends the relative address set inside the endpoint with the base address. So essentially it is the same as the previous configuration.

LISTING 3-14: Configuring Base Address in Config

```
<?xml version="1.0" encoding="utf-8" ?>
<configuration>
  <system.serviceModel>
    <services>
      <service name="HelloWorldService" >
        <endpoint
          address="HelloWorldService"
          binding="wsHttpBinding"
          contract="IMyService" />
<host>
    <baseAddresses>
        <add baseAddress="http://localhost:8080/" />
    </baseAddresses>
</host>
      </service>
    </services>
    <bindings>
      <wsHttpBinding>
      </wsHttpBinding>
    </bindings>
  </system.serviceModel>
</configuration>
```

You can have multiple base addresses for each service, but only one for each protocol. WCF will then automatically map the correct address based on the binding configuration of the endpoint.

Listing 3-15 defines two endpoints, one which has no address using the `basicHttpBinding`. This means it will be mapped to the base address path for the base address defined with Http. And the second, which has TCP as the address using the `netTcpBinding`, has the full address as `net.tcp://localhost:9090/tcp`.

LISTING 3-15: Multiple Base Addresses

```xml
<?xml version="1.0" encoding="utf-8" ?>
<configuration>
  <system.serviceModel>
    <services>
      <service name="HelloWorldService" >

        <endpoint
          address=""
          binding="basicHttpBinding"
          contract="IMyService" />
        <endpoint
          address="tcp"
          binding="netTcpBinding"
          contract="IMyService" />
<host>
    <baseAddresses>
        <add baseAddress="http://localhost:8080/" />
        <add baseAddress="net.tcp://localhost:9090/" />
    </baseAddresses>
</host>
      </service>
    </services>
  </system.serviceModel>
</configuration>
```

Default Configurations

A new group of features to WCF 4.0 tries to simplify configurations by defining default configurations for several aspects of WCF. As a whole this allows for much smaller (or nonexistent) configuration files. The WCF configuration schema is very large and difficult to configure features. Mistakes also happen and services are deployed with missing configuration information. (This is especially useful for development purposes.) Although it may not be apparent with very simple services, when you have large-scale enterprise services with many endpoints and many different configuration settings for each, you can see where editing these settings becomes a difficult prospect for developers and administrators alike. (This is especially true for administrators who won't necessarily know the implications of changing these configuration files, but are responsible for them on production servers.)

The following changes are new to WCF 4.0 and will generate runtime exceptions if using these configurations in pre-4.0. However, when you upgrade your WCF 3/3.5 app to WCF 4.0, it still works with the WCF 3.x configuration. But you are able to re-factor your configuration files to take advantage of this increased simplicity if you wish.

Automatic Endpoints

If you do not configure any `<service>` attributes inside your configuration file (or if no configuration file is present), and no service endpoint is programmatically added to the host, then endpoints will automatically be added to your service. One will be configured for each service and each contract, and the endpoint address will be appended to the base address.

When you host your service in IIS, the list of base addresses is automatically retrieved from the hosting settings. If the web site allows the usage of both Http and Https protocols, you'll find two addresses. With the usage of Windows Activation Services (WAS) on IIS, you can use protocols other than Http. Also in this case, if the web site is configured to support a NET.TCP protocol, you'll find your service exposed with the relative endpoint.

The different hosting options are discussed in Chapter 14.

Default Bindings

Default bindings allow you to create a service that automatically sets the correct binding by working it out from the protocol schema that you specified in the address of your service (or the base address). This is done by using protocol mapping.

WCF has pre-defined protocol mapping, which maps protocol schema to a WCF binding. The defaults are shown in Table 3-3.

TABLE 3-3: Default WCF Protocol Mapping

SCHEMA	WCF BINDING
Http	`basicHttpBinding`
net.tcp	`netTcpBinding`
net.msmq	`netMsmqBinding`
net.pipe	`netNamedPipeBinding`

You can override the default mappings provided to you by WCF 4.0 by inserting the following into your configuration file of your service and changing the defaults. This makes the changes to your applications specifically. Alternatively, if you know that you want to do this machine-wide, you can do the same in your machine.config. See Listing 3-16.

> *There will be a performance hit when services with bindings set in configuration need to run the protocol mapping in your machine.config. Do this in each configuration or add a new configuration further up which each of your service configuration files can use.*

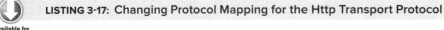

LISTING 3-16: Default Protocol Mapping Provided by WCF 4.0

```
<system.serviceModel>
    <protocolMapping>
        <add scheme="http" binding="basicHttpBinding"/>
        <add scheme="net.tcp" binding="netTcpBinding"/>
        <add scheme="net.pipe" binding="netNamedPipeBinding"/>
        <add scheme="net.msmq" binding="netMsmqBinding"/>
    </protocolMapping>
</system.serviceModel>
```

You can change any of these settings, or add your own. As shown in Listing 3-17, if you know that all your services will use the webHttpBinding, you can change the default protocol mapping for Http (basicHttpBinding by default) to wsHttpBinding.

LISTING 3-17: Changing Protocol Mapping for the Http Transport Protocol

```
<system.serviceModel>
  <protocolMapping>
    <add scheme="http" binding="wsHttpBinding"/>
  </protocolMapping>
</system.serviceModel>
```

Listing 3-18 creates a mapping between Https and webHttpBinding.

LISTING 3-18: Changing Protocol Mapping for the Https Protocol

```
<system.serviceModel>
  <protocolMapping>
    <add scheme="https" binding="wsHttpBinding"/>
  </protocolMapping>
</system.serviceModel>
```

Default Behaviors

Default behaviors allow you to not have to explicitly set the behaviors you want to apply using the behaviorConfiguration attribute in your configuration file.

Listing 3-19 shows the differences made to configuration files.

LISTING 3-19: Configuration without Default Behavior

```
<?xml version="1.0" encoding="utf-8" ?>
<configuration>
  <system.serviceModel>
    <services>
      <service name="MyService"
               behaviorConfiguration="MyServiceBehavior">
```

```
        <endpoint address="http://localhost/MyService/"
                  binding="wsHttpBinding"
                  contract="IMyService" />
      </service>
    </services>
    <behaviors>
      <serviceBehaviors>
        <behavior name="MyServiceBehavior">
          <serviceMetadata httpGetEnabled="True" />
        </behavior>
      </serviceBehaviors>
    </behaviors>
  </system.serviceModel>
</configuration>
```

Note the explicit declaration of the behavior name. Listing 3-20, instead, shows how to write a default behavior without specifying the name.

LISTING 3-20: Configuration with Default Behavior

```
<?xml version="1.0" encoding="utf-8" ?>
<configuration>
  <system.serviceModel>
    <behaviors>
    <behaviors>
      <serviceBehaviors>
        <behavior>
          <serviceMetadata httpGetEnabled ="true"/>
        </behavior>
      </serviceBehaviors>
    </behaviors>
  </system.serviceModel>
</configuration>
```

Standard Endpoints

Standard endpoints allow for a pre-defined set of endpoints and WCF provides some of these for you. Some of these endpoints have things that will be the same for all services — MEX, for example, will have the same contract and binding. You can also define your own standard endpoints.

Following are the standard endpoints:

➤ mexEndpoint

➤ webHttpEndpoint

➤ webScriptEndpoint

➤ workflowControlEndpoint

➤ announcementEndpoint

➤ discoveryEndpoint

➤ udpAnnouncementEndpoint

➤ udpDiscoveryEndpoint

To use these standard endpoints, you can use the `kind` attribute within a normal endpoint, as shown in Listing 3-21.

LISTING 3-21: Standard Endpoint

```xml
<?xml version="1.0" encoding="utf-8" ?>
<configuration>
  <system.serviceModel>
    <services>
      <service name="MyService1">
        <endpoint kind="mexEndpoint">
      </service>
    </services>
  </system.serviceModel>
<configuration>
```

Setting Multiple Bindings

You will often have clients connecting to your service from many different types of systems and applications, i.e., WCF, ASMX, and JSON. You can specify multiple endpoints with different bindings allowing different clients to connect to your service using whichever transport they support.

Listing 3-22 adds two endpoints with different bindings: `wsHttpBinding` and `basicHttpBinding`.

LISTING 3-22: Configuring Multiple Bindings Declaratively

```xml
<?xml version="1.0" encoding="utf-8" ?>
<configuration>
  <system.serviceModel>
    <services>
      <service name="HelloWorldService" >
        <endpoint
          address="http://localhost:8080/HelloWorldService"
          binding="wsHttpBinding"
          contract="IMyService" />
        <endpoint
          address="http://localhost:8080/HelloWorldService/basic"
          binding="basicHttpBinding"
          contract="IMyService" />
      </service>
    </services>
    <bindings>
      <wsHttpBinding>
      </wsHttpBinding>
    </bindings>
  </system.serviceModel>
</configuration>
```

Notice the two differences in declaring these endpoints: the first is obviously the binding, which is exactly as it should be. Also, the addresses are different. Remember that addresses must be unique. You have to create a new address for the `basicHttpBinding` to use. If you add a `netTcpBinding`, it would have a unique address, as the protocol scheme at the beginning would no longer be `http://` and would be replaced by `net.tcp://`. Also, if you are using a different contract, your endpoint can have the same address and also the same binding. If the address is not unique, and the contracts are the same, then an exception will be thrown.

MODIFYING BINDINGS

Even though WCF has a large range of bindings provided for you, which hopefully will meet your needs most of the time, there will be times when you need to define your own for scenarios that weren't provided for you. You can do this by either tweaking the provided bindings using the properties that the bindings expose, or by creating your own custom binding. If you can use the provided bindings with some small changes to the properties, then this is the simplest and most ideal. However, WCF provides a very easy way to create your own bindings using the built-in binding elements which are the building blocks for each provided binding.

Bindings Properties

The WCF-provided bindings all have default properties which you are able to modify to suit your own scenarios. Each binding has similar properties but differ from binding to binding.

For this example, the `basicHttpBinding` is used, which is the binding you would use to communicate with ASMX web services. Table 3-4 shows the `basicHttpBinding` properties, a brief description, and the default value for each of them.

TABLE 3-4: basicHttpBinding Properties

PROPERTY NAME	DESCRIPTION	DEFAULT VALUE
AllowCookies	Sets if the client accepts cookies.	False
BypassProxyOnLocal	Set to `true` to bypass the proxy server for local addresses.	False
CloseTimeout	Value of time that a connection will wait upon closing before it times out.	One minute
HostNameComparisonMode	Whether the hostname is used to match to the service.	"StrongWildCard" (ignores the hostname)
MaxBufferPoolSize	Sets the maximum memory to be used by the message buffers.	524,288 bytes
MaxBufferSize	Sets the maximum size for each buffer to receive a message.	65,536 bytes

continues

TABLE 3-4 *(continued)*

PROPERTY NAME	DESCRIPTION	DEFAULT VALUE
MaxReceivedMessageSize	Sets the maximum message size that can be received for this binding.	65,536 bytes
MessageEncoding	Sets the type of encoding used.	Text
Name	Sets the name of the binding.	null
Namespace	Sets the XML namespace.	http://tempura.org/
OpenTimeout	Sets the maximum time that the opening of the binding has before timing out.	One minute
ProxyAddress	Sets the address for the proxy.	Null
ReceiveTimeout	Sets the maximum time that the message receive operation has before timing out	00:10:00
SendTimeout	Sets the maximum time that the message send operation has before timing out	00:01:00
TextEncoding	Sets the text encoding used for the messages	UTF8
TransferMode	Sets the message transfer mode (buffered or streamed)	Buffered
UseDefaultWebProxy	Sets if the system proxy should be used	true

You modify the MessageEncoding property from its default Text to Mtom. Mtom (*Message Transmission Optimization Mechanism*) allows for smaller messages when sending large amounts of data by sending SOAP messages as raw bytes. You should see a big performance difference in changing this.

To change this property, first create a new config section inside your basicHttpBinding section. This includes a name to reference, and then set the property (or multiple properties) that you want to change. You can then reference that in your endpoint configuration by the name created (in the following example, the name is Encode). You do this by using the bindingConfiguration property in the endpoint configuration. You can then re-use this configuration for other endpoints in your configuration, or maybe more importantly, choose to not use this configuration for other endpoints. This gives you complete flexibility with the configuration, but minimizes duplicating the configuration of properties by allowing this re-use. Listing 3-23 shows how you can change the default property values in app.config.

LISTING 3-23: Modifying Default Property Values in App.config

```
<system.serviceModel>
    <services>
      <service name="MyService1">
        <endpoint address="http://localhost:8080/MyService1"
                  contract="Service1"
                  binding="basicHttpBinding"
                  bindingConfiguration="Encode">
        </endpoint>
      </service>
    </services>
    <bindings>
      <basicHttpBinding>
        <binding name="Encode" messageEncoding="Mtom"></binding>
      </basicHttpBinding>
    </bindings>
  </system.serviceModel>
```

The same can be done programmatically when you create the new `basicHttpBinding` object. As shown in Listing 3-24, you can then change the properties of that object just as any other object's property. This also gives you the beauty of Visual Studio's Intellisense so you can see all the options for the binding you are configuring.

LISTING 3-24: Modifying Default Property Values Programmatically

```
ServiceHost host = new ServiceHost(typeof(MyService1.Service1));

BasicHttpBinding binding = new BasicHttpBinding();
binding.MessageEncoding = "Mtom";

host.AddServiceEndpoint(typeof(MyService1.IService1),
                        binding,
                        "http://localhost:8080/MyService1");
```

When editing the App.config, you need to explicitly set the `bindingConfiguration` to use, but within the code you just modified the actual instance of the `BasicHttpBinding` class that you created.

Creating Custom Bindings

There are times when you must create your own binding; a couple of examples would be custom security and additional transport protocols. This can be done within your configuration or in code.

To create your own custom binding, build up a collection of binding elements. You need to be familiar with the binding elements that are defined within WCF. This allows you to define the specifics of your custom binding.

Binding Elements

Binding elements inherit from `System.ServiceModel.Channels.BindingElement`. When adding your binding elements you need to keep them in the correct order. Table 3-5 shows the binding elements provided to you in the order that they must be added to your binding collection.

TABLE 3-5: Protocol Elements

PROTOCOL BINDING ELEMENTS	CLASS NAME
Transaction Flow	`TransactionFlowBindingElement`
Reliable Messaging	`ReliableSessionBindingElement`
Security	`SecurityBindingElement`
Duplex Communication Element	
Composite Duplex	`CompositeDuplexBindingElement`
Message Encoding Elements	
Message Encoding	**Class Name**
Text	`TextMessageEncodingBindingElement`
Mtom	`MtomMessageEncodingBindingElement`
Binary	`BinaryMessageEncodingBindingElement`
Transport Security Elements	
Security	**Class Name**
Windows	`WindowsStreamSecurityBindingElement`
SSL	`SslStreamSecurityBindingElement`
Transport Elements	
Protocol	**Class Name**
Http	`HttpTransportBindingElement`
Https	`HttpsTransportBindingElement`
TCP	`TcpTransportBindingElement`
Named pipes	`NamedPipeTransportBindingElement`
MSMQ	`MsmqTransportBindingElement`
MSMQ	`MsmqIntegrationBindingElement`
P2P	`PeerTransportBindingElement`

To create your custom binding, you need to choose which binding elements you want to include and then add them to the custom binding in the correct order as previously listed. As shown in Listing 3-25, a custom binding needs to have a transport binding element and a message encoding element (although if you don't specify message encoding, WCF will automatically add Text for Http and binary for all other transports).

LISTING 3-25: Custom Binding Using Http as Transport and Binary Encoding

```
<customBinding>
  <binding name="binHttp">
     <binaryMessageEncoder />
     <httpTransport />
  </binding>
</customBinding>
```

As explained at the start of this chapter, the order of the binding elements is much more important. Starting from the bottom, the first binding element must define the transport. The second binding element must define the encoding to use. The order of the other binding elements, however, is not as important as the first two.

If you don't want to use the configuration file, you can also create your custom binding programmatically, as shown in Listing 3-26.

LISTING 3-26: Configuring a Custom Binding Programmatically

```
using Wrox.CarRentalService.Implementations.Europe;
...

CustomBinding binding = new CustomBinding();
binding.Elements.Add(new BinaryMessageEncodingBindingElement());
binding.Elements.Add(new HttpTransportBindingElement());

ServiceHost host = new ServiceHost(typeof(CarRentalService));

ServiceEndpoint serviceEndpoint =
host.AddServiceEndpoint(typeof(ICarRentalService),
                  binding,
                  "http://localhost:8080/CarRentalService");

host.Open();
```

In this code, you can simply add the binding elements to the elements collection of custom binding. This determines how the custom binding works.

A Reusable Custom Binding

Sometimes you may need to create a custom binding and reuse it in various solutions. Because each binding inherits from the base abstract class `System.ServiceModel.Channels.Binding`, you can simply create your own binding class and implement the `CreateBindingElements` to achieve this requirement. Listing 3-27 shows how you can extend the `Binding` base class to create and reuse your own implementation.

LISTING 3-27: Creating a Custom Reusable Binding

```
public class NetTcpTextBinding : Binding
{
    private TcpTransportBindingElement transport;
    private TextMessageEncodingBindingElement encoding;

    public NetTcpTextBinding()
        : base()
    {
        this.Initialize();
    }

    public override BindingElementCollection CreateBindingElements()
    {
        BindingElementCollection elements = new BindingElementCollection();
        elements.Add(this.encoding);
        elements.Add(this.transport);
        return elements;
    }

    public override string Scheme
    {
        get { return this.transport.Scheme; }
    }

    private void Initialize()
    {
        this.transport = new TcpTransportBindingElement();
        this.encoding = new TextMessageEncodingBindingElement();
    }
}
```

In the sample NetTcpTextBinding shown in Listing 3-28, a custom binding is set that encodes messages using text encoding protocol on a TCP transport. It is a very simple implementation that demonstrates how you can customize WCF to achieve every need.

As with every other binding, you can use it with ServiceHost or ChannelFactory to configure the service endpoint.

LISTING 3-28: Using the NetTcpTextBinding

```
NetTcpTextBinding binding = new NetTcpTextBinding();

ServiceHost host = new ServiceHost(typeof(Service1));
host.AddServiceEndpoint(typeof(IService1),
                        binding,
                        "net.tcp://localhost:10101/IService");

host.Open();
```

One step over allows developers to use the custom binding via configuration file. As shown in Listing 3-29, you must extend the BindingCollectionElement abstract base class and then implement the required methods.

LISTING 3-29: Implement the NetTcpTextBindingCollectionElement

```
using System.Configuration;
...

public class NetTcpTextBindingCollectionElement : BindingCollectionElement
{
    public override Type BindingType
    {
        get { return typeof(NetTcpTextBinding); }
    }

    public override ReadOnlyCollection<IBindingConfigurationElement>
    ConfiguredBindings
    {
        get
        {
            return new ReadOnlyCollection<IBindingConfigurationElement>(
                    new List<IBindingConfigurationElement>());
        }
    }

    public override bool ContainsKey(string name)
    {
        throw new NotImplementedException();
    }

    protected override Binding GetDefault()
    {
        return new NetTcpTextBinding();
    }

    protected override bool TryAdd(
        string name, Binding binding, Configuration config)
    {
        throw new NotImplementedException();
    }
}
```

The property that you must implement is BindingType. It allows defining the binding type target of the current configuration. The other important property is the ConfiguredBindings that retrieves all the binding configuration elements.

The code shown in Listing 3-29 is a really simple implementation that could be extended, for example, with the definition of custom binding elements. You should implement the IBindingConfigurationElement interface to permit a great level of customization at runtime.

Now, if you want to use the NetTcpTextBinding in the configuration file, you have to configure the NetTcpTextBindingCollectionElement by using the binding extensions (see Listing 3-30). Indeed, if you want to use your custom binding implementation, you have to define it.

LISTING 3-30: Using the NetTcpTextBinding in the Configuration File

```
<system.serviceModel>
  <services>
    <service name="WcfServiceLibrary2.Service1">
      <endpoint address="net.tcp://localhost:10101/IService"
                binding="netTcpTextBinding"
                contract="WcfServiceLibrary2.IService1">

      </endpoint>
    </service>
  </services>
  <extensions>
    <bindingExtensions>
      <add name="netTcpTextBinding"
           type="ConsoleApplication1.NetTcpTextBindingCollectionElement,
           ConsoleApplication1,
           Version=1.0.0.0, Culture=neutral, PublicKeyToken=null" />
    </bindingExtensions>
  </extensions>
</system.serviceModel>
```

The value of the name attribute defined in the binding extensions section corresponds to the name usable in the service element. Finally, you can use the binding in the endpoint element of the service section.

DUPLEX DURABLE SERVICES

Earlier in this chapter, context bindings were discussed. Introduced in .NET Framework 3.5, context bindings enable the exchange of a property called instance id that is used to identify persisted services. That feature allows a service to remember its status by using a durable and reliable storage that handles unexpected scenarios such as host or service restart. This is the important difference between durable services versus session, available since .NET Framework 3.0.

It is most common to have a scenario when processes can hold on for a long time. Windows workflow provides support for long-running scenarios by persisting its state in a database such as SQL Server. Durable service allows you to store the current state of services in the same manner as you can persist a running workflow. Though the context bindings could be used without a workflow, they are designed with the previous scenario in mind.

With the .NET Framework 4.0, the WSHttpContextBinding and the NetTcpContextBinding have a new property called ClientCallbackAddress. This property accepts a URI that represents the client address usable to receive the callback message from the invoked service. As shown in Figure 3-3, if the first workflow calls the second workflow, and the second workflow takes a long time to complete its work, the first workflow is persisted. Now, the ClientCallbackAddress with the context binding allows waking up the first workflow.

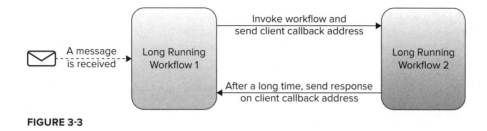

FIGURE 3-3

How the durable duplex binding works differs from the already known duplex binding because it works on context property and storage rather than channel level.

Configuring the Bindings for Duplex Durable Services

Not all context bindings support the duplex durable correlation services. In effect, the `BasicHttpContextBinding` doesn't support the `ClientCallbackAddress` property — it instead supports both in the `WSHttpContextBinding` and `NetTcpContextBinding`.

To enable the correlation, you have to set `ClientCallbackAddress` in your context binding configuration, as shown in Listing 3-31.

LISTING 3-31: Configure Binding to Enable Duplex Durable Correlation

```
<system.serviceModel>
  <services>
    <service name="WorkflowService1">
      <endpoint address=""
                binding="wsHttpContextBinding"
                contract="IWorkflowService"
                bindingConfiguration="contextCorrelationBinding">
      </endpoint>
      <endpoint address=""
                binding="wsHttpContextBinding"
                contract="IWorkflowServiceCallback"
                bindingConfiguration="contextCorrelationBinding">
      </endpoint>
    </service>
  </services>
  <bindings>
    <wsHttpContextBinding>
      <binding name="contextCorrelationBinding"
clientCallbackAddress="http://localhost/DurableDuplex/
WorkflowService1.xamlx">
      </binding>
    </wsHttpContextBinding>
  </bindings>
</system.serviceModel>
```

In the previous configuration section, two endpoints were defined: one for the service and the other for the callback calls. Both endpoints use the `WSHttpContextBinding` and the value of the `clientCallbackAddress` property in the relative section named `contextCorrelationBinding`. This is the only setting you need to create the correlation.

It is also possible to create your custom binding and define the context binding element, as shown in Listing 3-32.

LISTING 3-32: Create Custom Binding with Context Correlation Enabled

```
<bindings>
    <customBinding>
        <binding name="netMsmqContextBinding">
            <context clientCallbackAddress="net.msmq://localhost/private/
WorkflowService1.xamlx"/>
            <msmqTransport />
        </binding>
    </customBinding>
</bindings>
```

The context bindings and the correlation system is an implementation of the Microsoft Context Exchange Protocol (`http://msdn.microsoft.com/en-us/library/bb924468.aspx`).

POLLINGDUPLEXHTTPBINDING: HTTP POLLING

The changing needs of users have led to the creation of web sites being increasingly interactive. In this context, Silverlight offers a powerful development platform to create rich, interactive applications. Silverlight runtime runs as a client in the user's browser process. As with any clients, it needs to access data remotely, often exposed as service. The more convenient and obvious platform to develop this service is WCF.

The most common scenario enables a request-reply message exchange pattern where the Silverlight client sends a request and receives a reply from the service. But sometimes, the service needs to inform or notify the client when something happens on the other side. The service needs to push data to the client. `PollingDuplexHttpBinding`, available since Silverlight v3 in the System. ServiceModel.PollingDuplex.dll, is designed to accomplish this communication protocol.

`PollingDuplexHttpBinding` is the implementation of the WS-MakeConnection v1.1 OASIS Specification (`http://docs.oasis-open.org/ws-rx/wsmc/v1.1/wsmc.html`). In practice, when a session is established, the client sends the request to the service and the service replies with an Http response only when it needs to push data to the client — meaning only when there are data for the client. This is done with a mechanism already known as *long polling*. If there aren't data for the client, the service holds on to the latest Http request until there are available data or a timeout is reached. If the client wants to get more information after receiving one, it re-sends a new Http request. The communication goes on until an active Http request is alive.

On client side you have to reference the client version of the `PollingDuplexHttpBinding` from the System.ServiceModel.PollingDuplex.dll in the Silverlight v3 SDK Libraries path. Then configure the binding as shown in Listing 3-33.

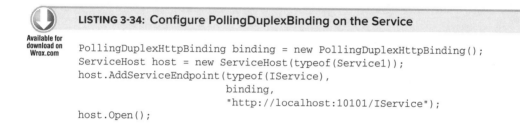

LISTING 3-33: Configure PollingDuplexBinding in the Client Environment

```
PollingDuplexHttpBinding binding = new PollingDuplexHttpBinding()
{
    InactivityTimeout = TimeSpan.FromMinutes(10),
    ReceiveTimeout = TimeSpan.FromMinutes(30),
    SendTimeout = TimeSpan.FromSeconds(30)
};
ChannelFactory<IService1> factory =
    new ChannelFactory<IService1>(binding, "http://localhost:10101/IService");
```

Also, on the service side, you can simply use the `PollingDuplexHttpBinding` to enable the communication, as shown in Listing 3-34.

LISTING 3-34: Configure PollingDuplexBinding on the Service

```
PollingDuplexHttpBinding binding = new PollingDuplexHttpBinding();
ServiceHost host = new ServiceHost(typeof(Service1));
host.AddServiceEndpoint(typeof(IService),
                        binding,
                        "http://localhost:10101/IService");
host.Open();
```

`PollingDuplexHttpBinding` is able to manage the communication problem and doesn't require further configurations settings to work well. As you can see, the Http long polling is different from the traditional polling system, where typically a client sends messages to inquire the service state at predefined time intervals. This produces a lot of traffic and sometimes causes network congestion. To limit this problem, many browsers, such as Internet Explorer 8, allow a max of six connections to a specific host.

You have to pay attention to this usage limit, although the long polling technique may be a big advantage. It may easily exceed the browser connection limit if the usage in the Silverlight client is too massive.

NetTcpBinding in Silverlight 4

With Silverlight 4 you are able to handle a duplex connection between a Silverlight client and a WCF Service by also using a net.tcp transport protocol.

Compared with the `PollingDuplexHttpBinding`, the net.tcp in Silverlight 4 dramatically affects the performance, and it should be the preferred solution only when you are in an intranet environment. Indeed, the net.tcp protocol is subject to some restrictions. You can use only ports 4502–4534, and in intranet environments you can control the firewall settings to meet the requirements. Finally, the transport security settings (SSL) with the net.tcp transport protocol in Silverlight are not supported. If you don't need to use transport security, then this limit is not as important.

The net.tcp protocol in Silverlight is a great improvement and a good alternative to the Http protocol, although it has a limited usage due to the above-mentioned constraints.

> *At the time of this writing, Silverlight 4 is in Release Candidate and what is discussed in this section may change in the final version.*

4

Clients

WHAT'S IN THIS CHAPTER?

➤ Implementing WCF clients

➤ Implementing and using RESTful services

➤ AJAX-enabling your service

➤ Using WCF from Silverlight

Some of the other chapters have focused primarily on implementation on the server side. The main tasks involved in developing WCF services include the design of service and data contracts, the selection of a suitable InstanceContextMode and ConcurrencyMode, and last but not least, the use of a suitable binding.

In this chapter, a closer look at the client side is taken. You have probably already come across some examples where .NET has been used on the client side and communication takes place between the client application and service using a generated proxy. The proxy can be created with Add Service Reference or svcutil.exe (SLsvcutil.exe for Silverlight applications) and a reference to a WSDL file or an MEX endpoint. However, if you have absolute control of the server and client code, you can also dispense with the generated proxy and communicate directly with the service using a reference to the service assembly and make use of the ChannelFactory class.

In a service-oriented world in which components are operated on a very diverse range of platforms and with very different technologies, your services may be consumed by other technologies — such as ASP.NET AJAX, Java, PHP, and Silverlight.

Depending on the expected clients, it may also make sense, under certain circumstances, not to use the entire set of features offered by WCF. For example, an AJAX client can handle JSON-encoded messages much better than extensive SOAP messages. Other clients, in turn, may support very few WS* protocols, if indeed any at all. In these scenarios it makes sense to agree on the lowest common denominator (Basic Profile 1.1). Last but not least,

REST represents an architectural alternative to the heavyweight SOA world with SOAP, as well as to extensive WS* protocols — some of which are difficult to implement. REST concentrates on addressable resources and their different characteristics; it uses an intuitive and uniform API to read and manipulate data.

Each of these aspects is described in more detail in the following sections.

BASIC PROFILE 1.1

With Basic Profile 1.1, the parties involved must abide by certain rules to ensure that communication between different worlds work correctly.

Numerous institutions are working on the standardization of protocols, formats, and definitions. In web services applications, Basic Profile 1.1 is the lowest common denominator when it comes to the exchange of messages, the provision of metadata, the description of services, and of security-related definitions. Basic Profile 1.1 was published by the web services Interoperability Organization (WS-I), under the URL `http://www.ws-i.org/Profiles/BasicProfile-1.1.html`. The standards described and recommended include the likes of SOAP 1.1, WSDL 1.1, UDDI 2.0, XML 1.0, and several more.

You only need to use the binding `basicHttpBinding` to make your WCF service compatible with Basic Profile 1.1.

> *WCF 4.0 also adds support for Basic Profile 1.2.*

However, should your service wish to employ and use advanced technologies such as transactions, reliability, and special security mechanisms, you should use the appropriate WS* protocol. You will also run the risk, however, that your service may only be used by very specific clients.

.NET CLIENTS

When it comes to implementing service clients for WCF in .NET, there are various techniques you can use. You can use the provided WSDL document to generate a proxy and use the proxy for communication with the service. Or your .NET client may share the same data contract assembly as the service. Next you will explore some of these options in more detail.

Sharing WSDL-Contracts

Should you wish to use a service offered by a particular service provider in a service-oriented world, you are not normally supplied with any DLLs or other binaries. Instead, the WDSL document, which is provided by the service provider, is all the client and server have in common. This document contains all the requisite details, such as service operations, structure of the data being exchanged, as well as any policies such as security and reliability about how the service deals with extended functionalities.

This variant makes sense and is recommended in a loosely coupled system. The client does not require any knowledge of the internal implementation, but relies solely on the WDSL document supplied. Because the client does not share any code with the service, it does not necessarily have to be a .NET client either. It might, for example, also be a PHP or Java application.

If you use a .NET application as a client, you generally don't program directly contrary to the service offered; you rely on the functionalities of a generated proxy. The proxy takes on such tasks as sending SOAP messages to the service, receiving the response, and making it available as an object. In addition to the service operations provided, the WCF proxy also features additional functions such as opening and closing, or other properties such as the endpoint or the inner channel to read out the session ID or endpoint-specific information.

The proxy is normally generated by using Add Service Reference, as shown in Figure 4-1, or the svcutil.exe tool. If you are in Visual Studio, it is definitely simpler and more convenient to proceed via the Add Service Reference menu. If when you create the proxy, however, you require options other than those offered by the Add Service Reference dialog box shown in Figure 4-2, or you wish to export service metadata from an assembly, you can also use svcutil.exe directly.

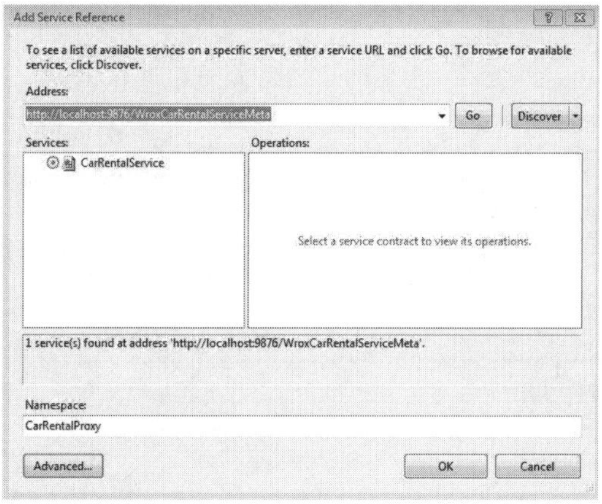

FIGURE 4-1

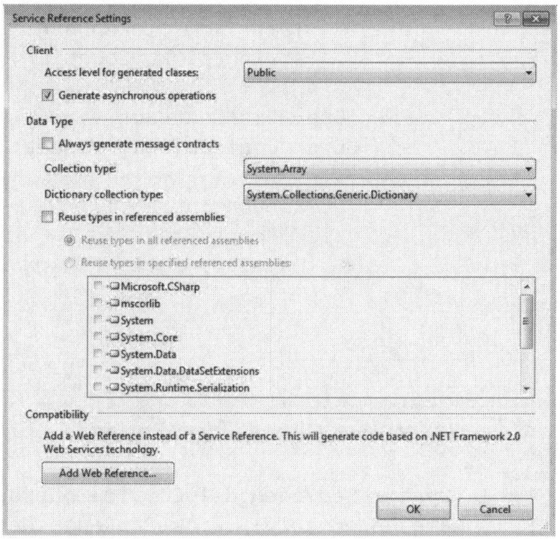

FIGURE 4-2

If you add a service reference, you will essentially receive two files:

➤ The code file, which is used for communication with the service, including the service proxy, data classes, and interfaces.

➤ A configuration file, in which the client endpoint is defined.

The code which is generated by svcutil.exe extends the base class `System.ServiceModel` `.ClientBase<T>` and implements the service interface and, thus, the service operations which are provided. The service data classes are also replicated on the client side and are assigned the attributes `[DataContract]` and `[DataMember]`. In principle, the `ClientBase<T>` class is nothing other than a wrapper for the `ChannelFactory<T>` class and is a quick and easy way of communicating with the service.

For example, the service code in Listing 4-1 would lead to the following client artifacts displayed in Listings 4-2 through 4-4.

LISTING 4-1: Service Contract

```
using System;
using System.ServiceModel;

namespace Wrox.CarRentalService.Contracts
{
    [ServiceContract(
     Namespace = "http://wrox/CarRentalService/2009/10",
     Name = "RentalService")]
    public interface ICarRentalService
    {
        [OperationContract()]
        PriceCalculationResponse CalculatePrice
            (DateTime pickupDate, DateTime returnDate,
             string pickupLocation, string returnLocation);

        [OperationContract]
        Guid  Confirm(Guid requestID);

        [OperationContract()]
        void  ReportCrash
            (DateTime date, String location, Guid  confirmationID);
    }
}
```

LISTING 4-2: Client-Side - Service Contract Interface

```
[System.ServiceModel.ServiceContractAttribute(
Namespace="http://wrox/CarRentalService/2009/10",
ConfigurationName="CarRentalProxy.RentalService")]
public interface RentalService {

[System.ServiceModel.OperationContractAttribute(
Action="http://wrox/CarRentalService/2009/10/RentalService/CalculatePrice",
ReplyAction="http://wrox/CarRentalService/2009/10/RentalService/
CalculatePriceResponse")]
Wrox.CarRentalService.ConsoleClient.CarRentalProxy.PriceCalculationResponse
        CalculatePrice(
              System.DateTime pickupDate, System.DateTime returnDate,
              string pickupLocation, string returnLocation);

[System.ServiceModel.OperationContractAttribute(AsyncPattern=true,
Action="http://wrox/CarRentalService/2009/10/RentalService/CalculatePrice",
```

```
ReplyAction="http://wrox/CarRentalService/2009/10/RentalService/
CalculatePriceResponse")]
System.IAsyncResult BeginCalculatePrice
                    (System.DateTime pickupDate, System.DateTime returnDate,
                     string pickupLocation, string returnLocation,
                     System.AsyncCallback callback, object asyncState);


Wrox.CarRentalService.ConsoleClient.CarRentalProxy.PriceCalculationResponse
                EndCalculatePrice(System.IAsyncResult result);
```

LISTING 4-3: Client-Side - ClientBase<T>

```
public partial class RentalServiceClient :
        System.ServiceModel.ClientBase
            <Wrox.CarRentalService.ConsoleClient.CarRentalProxy.RentalService>,
            Wrox.CarRentalService.ConsoleClient.CarRentalProxy.RentalService
{
```

LISTING 4-4: Client-Side Configuration File

```
<configuration>
    <system.serviceModel>
        <client>
            <endpoint address="http://localhost:9876/WroxCarRentalService"
                binding="basicHttpBinding"
                contract="CarRentalProxy.RentalService" />
        </client>
    </system.serviceModel>
</configuration>
```

When you use the proxy as shown in Listing 4-5, you must remember to close it if you no longer require it. Or you may also use the proxy within a using statement to guarantee that the Dispose method is called up automatically at the end and valuable resources are released.

LISTING 4-5: Using the Client Proxy

```
namespace Wrox.CarRentalService.ConsoleClient
{
    class Program
    {
        static void Main(string[] args)
        {

            using (CarRentalProxy.RentalServiceClient
                rentalServiceClient = new
                CarRentalProxy.RentalServiceClient())
            {

                CarRentalProxy.PriceCalculationResponse resp = null;
```

continues

LISTING 4-5 *(continued)*

```
            resp = rentalServiceClient.CalculatePrice
                (DateTime.Now, DateTime.Now.AddDays(5),
                 "Graz", "Vinna");
            Console.WriteLine("Price to Vienna {0}",
                                    resp.Price);
        }
        Console.WriteLine("Proxy closed");
    }
  }
}
```

Sharing WSDL-Contracts and DataContract-DLLs

If you are responsible both for the server and for the client implementation and have complete control of the code which is created, it may make sense under certain circumstances to prevent new data classes from being created every time the service reference is added, which would cause it to be duplicated and therefore require multiple maintenance. Shared data contracts can also be used to prevent your code from looking different on the server side and on the client side. For example, List<string> on the server side would become a string array on the client side. Some aspects could be controlled by the Add Service Reference - Advanced dialog box as well.

In these cases you can assign the parameter /r to svcutil.exe as an instruction to use data classes from a referenced DLL and not to create any new data classes. Another advantage of shared data classes is that you can use data classes of any complexity provided they can be serialized.

The service class is still supplied to your client code in the form of a proxy which is inherited by System.ServiceModel.ClientBase<T>, and which the service interface implements. However, the service data classes are no longer simulated on the client side. They are loaded directly from the shared assembly.

Sharing Interfaces and DataContract-DLLs

The narrowest form of binding between the client and server generally involves dispensing with a WSDL document and making direct reference instead to the ServiceContract or DataContract assemblies. Of course, this is only possible and worthwhile in a very closely coupled system in which you have absolute control of the client and server code. The ChannelFactory class is used for communication with the service, not the proxy which is created, as shown in Listing 4-6. ChannelFactory objects are used primarily in middle-tier scenarios, where the aim is to increase performance where there is no need to instantiate a new proxy for every client every time. The ChannelFactory object, however, is simply used to open a separate channel for each client. Furthermore, in environments in which frequent changes are made to the service contract (most notably at the start of a project), it may make perfectly good sense and be helpful not to create a new proxy code every time, but to use the server assembly directly.

LISTING 4-6: ChannelFactory<T>

```csharp
using System;
using System.Collections.Generic;
using System.Linq;
using System.Text;
using System.ServiceModel;
using Wrox.CarRentalService.Contracts;

namespace Wrox.CarRentalService.ConsoleClient
{
    class Program
    {
        static void Main(string[] args)
        {
            ChannelFactory<ICarRentalService> factory = null;
            try
            {
                BasicHttpBinding binding = new BasicHttpBinding();
                EndpointAddress address = new
                  EndpointAddress("http://localhost:9876
                                          /WroxCarRentalService");

                factory = new
                  ChannelFactory<ICarRentalService>(binding, address);

                ICarRentalService channel = factory.CreateChannel();

                PriceCalculationResponse resp =
                    channel.CalculatePrice
                        (DateTime.Now, DateTime.Now.AddDays(5),
                         "Graz", "Wien");
                Console.WriteLine("Price to Wien {0}", resp.Price);

                factory.Close();
            }
            catch (CommunicationException)
            {
                if (factory != null)
                {
                    factory.Abort();
                }
            }
            catch (TimeoutException)
            {
                if (factory != null)
                {
                    factory.Abort();
                }
            }
            catch (Exception ex)
            {
                if (factory != null)
```

continues

LISTING 4-6 *(continued)*

```
            {
                factory.Abort();
            }
            Console.WriteLine(ex.ToString());
        }

        Console.WriteLine("Proxy closed");
    }
  }
}
```

In the sample displayed in Figure 4-3, the client makes direct reference to the service assembly and to the `DataContract` assembly.

However, there is no need for a reference to specific implementation of the service class because communication between the client and the server still takes place via the standard WCF route.

REST

REST stands for Representational State Transfer and was looked at in the dissertation by Roy Thomas Fielding.

Some of the most important aspects of the REST environment are uniquely addressable resources, their different characteristics

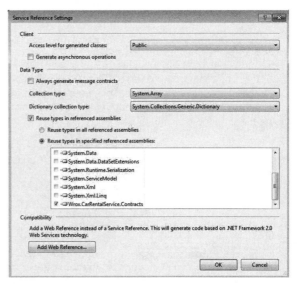

FIGURE 4-3

and formats, a uniform and easy-to-follow programming interface, and the facilitation of a highly scalable environment.

Implemented today, REST mainly entails the use of technologies which are already well established in practice on the Web and which have been used to outline the advantages of REST. HTTP or HTTPS, for example, may be used as the transfer protocol. URLs including query strings are used to address resources, and the representation formats supported range from HTML and XML to JSON and ATOM, as well as to sound and video files. The simple and intuitive programming interface previously mentioned is achieved by using HTTP verbs and status codes.

If, for example, you point your browser at the URL `http://p2p.wrox.com/content/blogs`, status code 200 is returned and your browser displays the returned HTML in the form of a web site. In keeping with normal web practices, the following page also contains links to other resources and topics:

```
http://p2p.wrox.com/content/blogs/danm/announcing-virtualdnug
```

In the URL above you can also see how intuitively these URLs are structured. Or use the following URL to receive an RSS feed:

```
http://www.wrox.com/WileyCDA/feed/RSS_WROX_ALLNEW.xml
```

In contrast to SOA with SOAP, REST is not concerned with the definition of messages and the design of methods; central components are resources and actions which can affect those resources. The actions which affect resources are mainly CRUD (Create, Read, Update, and Delete) methods. What should be done with a resource is determined by means of an HTTP verb, and the success of the action is ascertained by querying the HTTP status code.

In the following example, a GET at `http://localhost:1234/CarPool` shows all the cars in the fleet in the form of an XML document. Status code 200 indicates success.

```
URL: http://localhost:1234/CarPool
Verb: GET
Status-Code: 200
Response-Body:
<Cars xmlns="http://schemas.datacontract.org/2004/07/Wrox"
xmlsn:i="http://www.w3.org/2001/XMLSchema-
instance"><Car><Make>Dodge</Make><Name>Dakota</Name><Seats>8</Seats><Type>Pickup

Truck</Type></Car><Car><Make>Audi</Make><Name>TT</Name><Seats>2</Seats><Type>Sport
Car</Type></Car><Car><Make>Seat</Make><Name>Leon</Name><Seats>5</Seats><Type>Sport
Car</Type></Car></Cars>
```

In the following example, a GET at `http://localhost:1234/CarPool/TT` shows the Audi TT in the form of an XML document. Status code 200 indicates success. Status code 404, for example, would mean not found.

```
http://localhost:1234/CarPool/TT
Verb: GET
Status-Code: 200
Response-Body:
<Car xmlns="http://schemas.datacontract.org/2004/07/Wrox"
xmlsn:i="http://www.w3.org/2001/XMLSchema-
instance"><Make>Audi</Make><Name>TT</Name><Seats>2</Seats><Type>Sport
Car</Type></Car>
```

In the following example, a GET at `http://localhost:1234/CarPool/TT?format=json` shows the Audi TT in the form of a JSON document. Status code 200 indicates success. Status code 404, for example, would mean not found.

```
URL: http://localhost:1234/CarPool/TT?format=json
Verb: GET
Status-Code: 200 (OK)
Response-Body:
{"Make":"Audi","Name":"TT","Seats":2,"Type":"Sport Car"}
```

In the following example, a PUT at `http://localhost:1234/CarPool/Leon` with the requisite XML data in the request body would mean that the car is to be added to the car pool. Status code

201 means created. As a result of the POST action, the added object is normally returned, along with any further details or links to other objects.

```
URL: http://localhost:1234/CarPool/Leon
Verb: PUT
Request-Body:
<Car xmlns="http://schemas.datacontract.org/2004/07/Wrox"
 xmlns:i="http://www.w3.org/2001/XMLSchema-instance">
<Make>Seat</Make><Name>Leon</Name><Seats>4</Seats><Type>Sport
Car</Type></Car>
Status-Code: 201 (Created)
Response-Body:
<Car xmlns="http://schemas.datacontract.org/2004/07/Wrox"
xmlsn:i="http://www.w3.org/2001/XMLSchema-
instance"><Make>Seat</Make><Name>Leon</Name><Seats>4</Seats><Type>Sport
Car</Type></Car>
```

Apart from GET and PUT, which have already been seen, the verbs most commonly used also include DELETE and POST.

GET is used exclusively to retrieve data and, therefore, the result can also be buffered without any concerns. It also offers a major advantage over SOAP messages in which the actual call cannot be identified straight away as a reading call. Therefore, they are also difficult to buffer.

DELETE is used for deleting resources. It should be called up as often as you wish without any concerns about side effects. When http://localhost:1234/CarPool/Leon is called up for the first time, for example, the Leon is deleted. The next time the same URL is called up, the resource is no longer available and can, therefore, not be deleted either.

PUT is used to add or change a resource if you can define the URL yourself. For example, a PUT at http://localhost:1234/CarPool/Leon along with corresponding details in the request body means that this resource is added anew with the URL used. If you assign a PUT to this URL with other values in the request body, it would lead to an update in the resource.

POST is an exception in certain regards. First of all, POST is frequently misused as DELETE and PUT, because the use of DELETE and PUT is either not permitted or technically impossible from the browser's perspective. Secondly, POST is used to add new resources to a container without having control of the URL created. Thus, for example, a POST to http://localhost:1234/CarPool with corresponding details in the body would mean that a new car is being added to the carpool. However, in this case the POST call would have to return the URL of the newly created resource.

In any event, the REST is stateless. Therefore, whenever a call is made, all the requisite values are either transferred in the address of the resource or as additional parameters. This behavior also means that REST applications are generally much easier to scale because there is no need to be concerned about which server to send the query to in a load-balanced environment.

REST and WCF

WCF not only provides a platform for SOAP messages, it is also a means of offering RESTful services.

The essential components that allow you to create a REST application can be found in `System.ServiceModel.Web.dll`. The most important elements of a REST application include the `[WebGet]` and `[WebInvoke]` attributes and the new binding `webHttpBinding` in connection with the `webHttp` endpoint behavior.

> If you use `[WebGet]` or `[WebInvoke]`, the `[OperationContract]` attribute is optional.

Should you wish to create a RESTful solution from your SOAP-based solution, theoretically you would simply have to change the binding to `webHttpBinding` and configure the endpoint with the `webHttp` behavior.

This binding has the following effect: If you send a SOAP message to an endpoint in a classical SOA environment, the content of the message will normally be checked first. The correct operation will be called up depending on the content of the message.

In REST, however, the method which is called up is dependent on the URL and on the verb used. This altered dispatch behavior is made possible by the binding `webHttpBinding` and the `webHttp` endpoint behavior. Furthermore, the `WebHttpBehavior` class or the endpoint behavior also enables you to choose from two different serialization formats:

➤ POX (Plain old XML) uses XML alone without the SOAP overhead.

➤ JSON (JavaScript Object Notation) is a very compact and efficient format, primarily in connection with JavaScript.

The service contract shown in Listing 4-7 in connection with the changed configuration displayed in Listing 4-8 would, for example, prompt you to make a POST at `http://localhost:1234/HelloWorld`, resulting in a receipt of an XML document with "Hello World".

LISTING 4-7: Service Contract

```
[ServiceContract()]
    public interface ICarRentalService
    {
        [OperationContract]
        string HelloWorld();
```

LISTING 4-8: Configuration File with webHttpBinding and webHttp Behavior

```
<configuration>
  <system.serviceModel>
      <services>
      <service name="Wrox.CarRentalService">
        <endpoint
```

continues

LISTING 4-8 *(continued)*

```
            address="http://localhost:1234/"
            contract="Wrox.ICarRentalService"
            binding="webHttpBinding"
            behaviorConfiguration="web"/>
      </service>
    </services>
    <behaviors>
      <endpointBehaviors>
        <behavior name="web">
          <webHttp/>
        </behavior>
      </endpointBehaviors>
    </behaviors>
  </system.serviceModel>
</configuration>
```

Instead of the configuration entries in the config file, you can also use the new `WebServiceHost` class. The `WebServiceHost` class inherits from `ServiceHost` and automatically assigns the correct binding and behavior to your endpoint. Consequently, you no longer need to be concerned about the content of your configuration file and you can host your service without a config file. Alternatively, if you are hosting your service in IIS, you can use the `WebServiceHostFactory` class. For example:

```
<% @ServiceHost Factory= "System.ServiceModel.Web.WebServiceHostFactory"
```

The configuration file could remain blank with the server code shown in Listing 4-9.

LISTING 4-9: WebServiceHost

```
namespace Wrox.ConsoleHost
{
    class Program
    {
        static void Main(string[] args)
        {
            WebServiceHost webHost = null;
            try
            {
                webHost = new WebServiceHost(
                        typeof(Wrox.CarRentalService),
                        new Uri("http://localhost:1234")
                        );
                webHost.Open();
                Console.ReadLine();
            }
            catch (Exception ex)
            {
                if (webHost != null)
```

```
                webHost.Abort();
            Console.WriteLine(ex.ToString());
            }
        }
    }
}
```

However, the disadvantage of this standard `webHttpBinding` behavior in conjunction with `enableWeb` is that, firstly, `POST` is used as a standard verb and, secondly, the URL used is simply the name of the method. However, this does not reflect the idea behind REST. In contrast to SOA, it is not the messages which are of prime importance; instead it is the resources, the URLs, and the verbs used.

You can obtain complete control of the URL being used by using the two attributes `[WebGet]` and `[WebInvoke]` in combination with your `OperationContract` attribute (the `OperationContract` attribute is obsolete).

Use `[WebGet]` whenever you require read-access to the resource, i.e., when you wish to use the HTTP verb `GET`.

Use `[WebInvoke]` for all other scenarios (`POST`, `PUT`, `DELETE`).

`[WebGet]` and `[WebInvoke]` also give you the opportunity to use a URI template with constant and variable parts. Furthermore, these two attributes also allow you to determine the serialization format (XML or JSON).

> *The `automaticFormatSelectionEnabled` attribute uses the Accept Header of the incoming message to automatically choose between JSON or XML.*

Listing 4-10 shows examples of how `[WebGet]` and `[WebInvoke]` are used (assumption of the base address `http://localhost:1234`).

LISTING 4-10: REST Implementation

```
namespace Wrox
{
    public class Car
    {
        public string Name { get; set; }
        public string Make { get; set; }
        public string Type { get; set; }
        public int Seats { get; set; }
    }

    [System.Runtime.Serialization.CollectionDataContract(Name="Cars")]
    public class CarPool: List<Car>
    {
        private CarPool()
```

continues

LISTING 4-8 *(continued)*

```csharp
        {
            this.Add(new Car() { Name = "Dakota",
                Make = "Dodge", Type = "Pickup Truck", Seats = 8 });
            this.Add(new Car() { Name = "TT",
                Make = "Audi", Type = "Sport Car", Seats = 2 });
        }
        private static CarPool AllCars = null;

        public static CarPool GetCarPark()
        {
            if (AllCars ==null)
                AllCars = new CarPool();

            return AllCars;
        }

    }

[ServiceContract()]
public interface ICarRentalService
{
    [OperationContract]
    string HelloWorld();

    [OperationContract]
    [WebGet(UriTemplate = "/CarPool")]
    CarPool GetAllCars();

    [OperationContract]
    [WebGet(UriTemplate = "/CarPool/{carName}")]
    Car GetCar(string carName);

    [OperationContract]
    [WebGet(UriTemplate="/CarPool/{carName}?format=xml",
    ResponseFormat = WebMessageFormat.Xml)]
    Car GetCarXML(string carName);

    [OperationContract]
    [WebGet(UriTemplate = "/CarPool/{carName}?format=json",
    ResponseFormat = WebMessageFormat.Json)]
    Car GetCarJSON(string carName);

    [OperationContract]
    [WebInvoke(UriTemplate = "CarPool/{carName}", Method = "PUT")]
    Car AddCar(string carName, Car car);

    [OperationContract]
    [WebInvoke(UriTemplate = "/CarPool/{carName}",
    Method = "DELETE")]
    void DeleteCar(string carName);

}
```

```
[ServiceBehavior(InstanceContextMode=InstanceContextMode.Single)]
public class CarRentalService: ICarRentalService
{
    public string HelloWorld()
    {
        WebOperationContext.Current.OutgoingResponse.StatusCode =
            System.Net.HttpStatusCode.OK ;
        return "Hello World";
    }
    public CarPool GetAllCars()
    {
        return CarPool.GetCarPark();
    }

    public Car  GetCar(string carName)
    {
        return CarPool.GetCarPark().Find(e => e.Name == carName);
    }
    public Car GetCarXML(string carName)
    {
        return GetCar(carName);
    }
    public Car GetCarJSON(string carName)
    {
        return GetCar(carName);
    }
    public void DeleteCar(string carName)
    {
        Car found = CarPool.GetCarPark().Find
            (e => e.Name == carName);
        if (found == null)
            WebOperationContext.Current.OutgoingResponse
                .SetStatusAsNotFound();
        else
            CarPool.GetCarPark().Remove(found);

    }

    public Car AddCar(string carName, Car car)
    {
        WebOperationContext.Current.OutgoingResponse
            .SetStatusAsCreated
          (
            new Uri("http://localhost:1234/CarPool/" + car.Name)
          );
        CarPool.GetCarPark().Add(car);
        return car;
    }

}
}
```

In the following example, the HTTP GET URL is fixed text and does not contain a variable element.

```
[OperationContract]
[WebGet(UriTemplate = "/CarPool")]
CarPool GetAllCars();
```

This is how the operation GetAllCards can be invoked (Sending a HTTP GET to the address below).

```
GET http://loalhost:1234/CarPool
[OperationContract]
[WebGet(UriTemplate = "/CarPool/{carName}")]
Car GetCar(string carName);
```

When the following line is invoked, Leon is passed as the variable {carName} to the operation GetCar (Sending an HTTP GET to the address below):

```
GET http://localhost:1234/CarPool/Leon
```

The following example is similar to the previous example. {carName} is written to the variable carName. Furthermore, a fixed query string is also stated, and the response format is set to JSON.

```
[OperationContract]
[WebGet(UriTemplate = "/CarPool/{carName}?format=json", ResponseFormat =
WebMessageFormat.Json)]
Car GetCarJSON(string carName);
```

As shown in the following example, in contrast to WebGet, the verb can be specified in WebInvoke. The variable carName is taken from the URL and the content of the car object is taken from the request body.

```
[OperationContract]
[WebInvoke(UriTemplate = "CarPool/{carName}", Method = "PUT")]
Car AddCar(string carName, Car car);
```

You previously saw how the new webHttpBinding is used together with webHttp and [WebGet] or [WebInvoke] to assist in creating a RESTful application. The addressable resources are defined with the aid of URI templates, and you can use the RequestFormat or ResponseFormat properties to determine whether to use XML or JSON as the format. The intuitive API is made possible by using HTTP verbs.

Use HTTP status codes and HTTP headers to determine whether an operation was successful or whether, for example, a resource has limited accessibility and can be retrieved only with a username and password. Access to these HTTP-specific elements is obtained via the WebOperationContext.

If a call was successful, for example, the status code returned would be 200, whereas 403 would be returned if a resource was not found. To help you to work with these status codes, you can either use the enum System.Net.HttpStatusCode or auxiliary methods from the OutgoingWebResponseContext class.

The following line would return a status code 200 from the service.

```
WebOperationContext.Current.OutgoingResponse.StatusCode =
System.Net.HttpStatusCode.OK ;
```

On the contrary, the following line would return a status code 403 (Resource not found):

```
WebOperationContext.Current.OutgoingResponse.SetStatusAsNotFound();
```

Working with REST Clients

In contrast to WCF with SOAP, the REST variant does not provide any means of creating a WSDL document. Therefore, the quick and easy variant Add Service Reference is not available.

However, this isn't altogether disadvantageous; it also brings with it certain advantages. As the use of the REST API is limited to a few verbs and avoids the exchange of complicated SOAP messages, a separate proxy is relatively easy to create with a suitable stack which supports HTTP, verbs, and status codes.

For example, you could use System.Net.WebRequest and System.Net.WebResponse for this purpose or leverage the WebChannelFactory class from the System.ServiceModel.Web.dll. In this case you also have absolute control over communication between the server and client and do not have to worry about any hidden activities and functionalities in the proxy you create.

In contrast to SOAP, REST is also interoperable to a higher degree because it is theoretically sufficient if the client has a command of HTTP and XML or JSON. Therefore, there is no need for an extensive SOAP stack with the support of all the WS* protocols to communicate with the REST service.

Using the REST Starter Kit

Because support for REST has only been available since .NET Framework 3.5 and there is still a lack of support in some areas (error handling, hosting, client, caching), you can also revert to using the REST Starter Kit. The REST Starter Kit is available as a download in CodePlex and offers a wide range of classes and extension methods for programming with REST on the server side and for REST calls on the client side.

The server-side functionality which can be found in the Microsoft.ServiceModel.Web.dll assembly includes, for example, simplified working with status codes, intuitive error handling with throw, ASP.NET-based caching support, and a separate service host which saves you having to create a documentation page manually. The generated help page is created similar to WSDL on the basis of your service code and can be adapted further by using [WebHelp].

HttpClient is surely the most important class on the client side. This class simplifies how REST operations are called up and supports GET, PUT, DELETE, and POST. The entire client functionality is located in the Microsoft.Http.dll assembly and in Microsoft.Http.Extensions.dll.

Listing 4-11 illustrates how the HttpClient class is used to send a GET request for a readout of all available cars. Furthermore, the use of the PUT method is also demonstrated in this example.

LISTING 4-11: REST Client - HttpClient

```
namespace Wrox.RestClient
{
    class Program
    {
        static void Main(string[] args)
        {
            using (HttpClient restClient = new HttpClient())
            {
                HttpResponseMessage resp =
                restClient.Get("http://localhost:1234/CarPool");
                    resp.EnsureStatusIsSuccessful();
                Console.WriteLine(resp.Headers.ToString());

                var result = resp.Content.ReadAsString();

                Console.WriteLine(result);

                string newCar = "<Car
                xmlns=\"http://schemas.datacontract.org/2004/07/Wrox\">
                <Make>Seat</Make><Name>Leon</Name>
                <Seats>5</Seats><Type>Sport Car</Type></Car>";

                restClient.Put("http://localhost:1234/CarPool/Leon",
                    "application/xml",
                    HttpContent.Create(newCar));
                Console.WriteLine(resp.StatusCode);

            }
        }
    }
}
```

Therefore, the REST Starter Kit provides you with an extensive collection of classes and methods which is worth taking a look at. However, the starter kit not only contains the assemblies, it also contains the entire code from which you can also get a wide range of ideas for implementing your REST application.

> *In addition to the REST Starter Kit, WCF 4.0 introduces additional features to ease programming with REST, like a new Visual Studio Template, support for ASP.Net caching, automatic generated help pages, WebFaultException, JSONP, conditional GET, and ETag support.*

AJAX AND WCF

AJAX is a popular programming model used in conjunction with web sites to avoid reloading entire pages just to change specific parts of the page. The aim is to provide a sophisticated, interactive page without having to put up with disruptive delays during rendering. This means that the gulf between simple web sites and interactive desktop applications is becoming ever smaller.

The AJAX concept is based on the fact that the browser or the code on the client side sends an asynchronous call to the server to obtain further information and changes the contents of the page with the data returned.

AJAX previously stood for *Asynchronous JavaScript and XML* because JavaScript was mainly used as a programming language, and XML documents were exchanged between the browser and the server. However, this has become significantly less common in recent times; nowadays, in principle, an AJAX application involves an asynchronous call from the client side which is processed further with the aid of the data received.

That said, JavaScript is still in very common usage and, therefore, JSON is much better suited as a data exchange format than XML. JSON is somewhat narrower than XML and can be deserialized more quickly by most script languages, such as JavaScript or PHP. You can call up a REST service, for example, when using JavaScript with XMLHttpRequest. The returned XML document would then have to be deconstructed bit by bit with suitable classes and methods and processed further.

However, if you use WCF and ASP.NET as a technology, you can shorten the lengthy route via an XMLHTTPRequest and issue a direct instruction to your WCF service to download JavaScript code. It can then be used as a proxy for communication with the service. This is very similar to the popular and convenient use of automatically generated proxies on the basis of a WSDL file for your .NET applications.

To enable the JavaScript proxy code to be generated, simply replace the webHttp behavior with the enableWebScript behavior. As shown in Listing 4-12, you can obtain the source code of the automatically generated JavaScript code via the endpoint with the addition of /js.

LISTING 4-12: AJAX Proxy

```
Type.registerNamespace('wrox.CarRentalService._2009._10');
wrox.CarRentalService._2009._10.RentalService=function() {
wrox.CarRentalService._2009._10.RentalService.initializeBase(this);
this._timeout = 0;
this._userContext = null;
this._succeeded = null;
this._failed = null;
}
wrox.CarRentalService._2009._10.RentalService.prototype={
_get_path:function() {
 var p = this.get_path();
 if (p) return p;
 else return
wrox.CarRentalService._2009._10.RentalService._staticInstance.get_path();},
GetAllCars:function(succeededCallback, failedCallback, userContext) {
return this._invoke(this._get_path(), 'GetAllCars',false,{},succeededCallback,
failedCallback,userContext); },
AddCar:function(car,succeededCallback, failedCallback, userContext) {
return this._invoke(this._get_path(), 'AddCar',false,{car:car},succeededCallback,
failedCallback,userContext); }}
...
```

However, instead of making a change in the configuration file, you can also use a special class again which automatically configures the endpoint with the correct binding and behavior, namely `WebScriptServiceHost`.

But if you wish to provide your WCF service with the aid of a generated JavaScript proxy, you should be aware that the only verbs permissible are GET and POST, and that the use of URI templates is not supported.

To access the generated proxy from your ASPX side, you normally use a `ScriptManager` control and add the endpoint address of the service as a `ServiceReference`, as shown in Listing 4-13.

LISTING 4-13: ScriptManager

```
<asp:ScriptManager ID="ScriptManager1" runat="server">
        <Services>
                <asp:ServiceReference Path="http://hansAt7:1234" />
        </Services>
</asp:ScriptManager>
```

As a result, when you download the page the JavaScript proxy code is downloaded from the server first and can then be used for communication.

Listings 4-14, 4-15, and 4-16 illustrate both the code required for this on the server side and the content of the ASPX page. Note that the proxy is accessible via the class `wrox.CarRentalService._` `2009._10.RentalService` which is derived by `namespace + servicename`.

LISTING 4-14: REST Service Contract

```
namespace Wrox.RestClient
{
  [ServiceContract(
     Namespace = "http://wrox/CarRentalService/2009/10",
     Name = "RentalService")]
     public interface ICarRentalService
     {
         [OperationContract]
         CarPark  GetAllCars();

         [OperationContract]
         [WebInvoke(Method = "POST",
           RequestFormat = WebMessageFormat.Xml,
           ResponseFormat = WebMessageFormat.Xml)]
         Car AddCar(Car car);

     }
```

LISTING 4-15: AJAX-Enabled Configuration File

```
<services>
      <service name="Wrox.CarRentalService" >
        <endpoint
            address="http://hansat7:1234/"
            contract="Wrox.ICarRentalService"
            binding="webHttpBinding"
            behaviorConfiguration="webScript"/>
      </service>
  </services>
  <behaviors>
    <endpointBehaviors>
      <behavior name="webScript">
        <enableWebScript/>
      </behavior>
    </endpointBehaviors>
  </behaviors>
```

LISTING 4-16: Default.aspx

```
<%@ Page Title="Home Page" Language="C#" MasterPageFile="~/Site.master"
AutoEventWireup="true"
    CodeBehind="Default.aspx.cs" Inherits="WebAjaxClient._Default" %>
<asp:Content ID="HeaderContent" runat="server"
ContentPlaceHolderID="HeadContent">
</asp:Content>
<asp:Content ID="BodyContent" runat="server"
ContentPlaceHolderID="MainContent">
    <asp:ScriptManager ID="ScriptManager1" runat="server">
        <Services>
            <asp:ServiceReference Path="http://hansAt7:1234" />
        </Services>
    </asp:ScriptManager>
    <script>
        function ajaxTest() {
            var myProxy =
            new wrox.CarRentalService._2009._10.RentalService();

            var myCar = new Wrox.Car();
            myCar.Make = "Mercedes";
            myCar.Name = "SLK";
            myProxy.AddCar(myCar, onSuccessAdd, onFailAdd, myProxy);
            myProxy.GetAllCars(onSuccessGetAll, onFailGetAll, myProxy);

        }
        function onSuccessAdd(result) {
            $get("divAddCar").innerText = result;
        }
```

continues

LISTING 4-16 *(continued)*

```
        function onFailAdd(result) {
            alert(divAddCar);
        }

        function onSuccessGetAll(result) {
            var allCars = "";

            for (var i = 0; i < result.length; i++) {
                allCars += " " + result[i].Name + " " + result[i].Make;
            }

            $get("divAllCars").innerText += allCars;
        }
        function onFailGetAll(result) {
            alert(result);
        }

    </script>
    <h2>
        Test for the CarRentalService REST API
    </h2>
    <p>
        WCF Service
        <input type="button" value="Test" onclick="ajaxTest()" />
    </p>
    Add Cars
    <div id="divAddCar">
    </div>
    <p>
        All Cars
        <div id="divAllCars">
        </div>
    </p>
</asp:Content>
```

The result is shown in Figure 4-4.

TEST FOR THE CARRENTALSERVICE REST API

WCF Service Test

Add Cars
<Car xmlns="http://schemas.datacontract.org/2004/07/Wrox" xmlns:i="http://www.w3.org/2001/XMLSchema-instance"><Make>Mercedes</Make><Name>SLK</Name><Seats>0</Seats><Type i:nil="true"/></Car>

All Cars

Dakota TT

FIGURE 4-4

WCF 4.0 AND SILVERLIGHT

What is true for classic .NET clients and for AJAX clients also works for Silverlight. There is an easy way to use an existing WCF service by just using Add Service Reference to generate a proxy and program against the proxy. If you already have a Silverlight-Webcontainer, you can use the new Visual Studio item template called Silverlight-enabled WCF service to add a .svc file and the associated code-behind file to your project (see Figure 4-5). Note that issues such as security and threading are not discussed here.

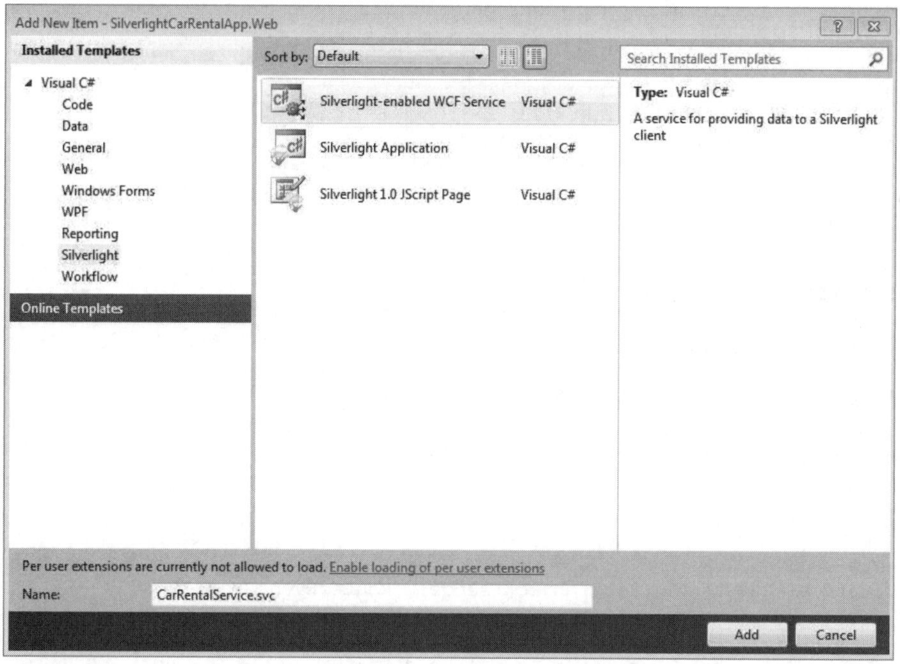

FIGURE 4-5

Listing 4-17 shows the content of the CarRentalService.svc.cs which contains a test method called `HelloWorld`.

LISTING 4-17: HelloWorld for Silverlight

Available for download on Wrox.com

```
namespace SilverlightCarRentalApp.Web
{
[ServiceContract(Namespace = "http://WCFBook/SilverlightSamples")]
    [AspNetCompatibilityRequirements(
    RequirementsMode = AspNetCompatibilityRequirementsMode.Allowed)]
    public class CarRentalService
    {
        [OperationContract]
        public string  HelloWorld()
        {
            return "Hello Silverlight";
        }
    }
}
```

To create a proxy for your Silverlight-App, just add a service reference to your project. Listing 4-18 shows the markup and Listing 4-19 demonstrates the use of the generated proxy within your Silverlight-App. Note that the proxy offers only async-calls to prevent deadlocks in your main thread.

LISTING 4-18: MainPage.xaml

```xml
<StackPanel>
    <Button Content="Button" Height="23"
    Name="button1" Width="75" Click="button1_Click" />
    <TextBox Height="23" Name="textBox1" Width="120" />
</StackPanel>
```

LISTING 4-19: Silverlight WCF Proxy

```csharp
namespace SilverlightCarRentalApp
{
    public partial class MainPage : UserControl
    {
        public MainPage()
        {
            InitializeComponent();
        }

        private void button1_Click(object sender, RoutedEventArgs e)
        {
            CarRentalProxy.CarRentalServiceClient myClient =
            new CarRentalProxy.CarRentalServiceClient();
            myClient.HelloWorldCompleted += new
              EventHandler<CarRentalProxy.HelloWorldCompletedEventArgs>
              (myClient_HelloWorldCompleted);
            myClient.HelloWorldAsync();
        }

        void myClient_HelloWorldCompleted(object sender,
                CarRentalProxy.HelloWorldCompletedEventArgs e)
        {
            textBox1.Text = e.Result;
        }
    }
}
```

5
Instancing

Your proxy on the client side (typically derived from ClientBase<T>) communicates with objects on the server side via the so-called channel stack. The service host accommodates these objects on the server side. As you will have learned in previous chapters, SOAP messages are exchanged between the proxy and the object on the server side. The InstanceContextMode determines whether the client proxy now communicates with one and the same instance of the server object during a session (PerSession), or whether a new instance is created every time the server object is used (PerCall) and is then deleted again as soon as the method call is ended, or whether, last but not least, only one single server instance is created (Single), irrespective of the number of clients.

There is an assumption in classical object-oriented applications that an instance of a class is created and used for work or communication for a certain length of time. If certain properties are set for the object beforehand, they remain in place while there is a valid reference to the object, and the methods which are called up can work with the values which are set beforehand. If the Dispose method is called and the object reference is set to null, important resources are released, and the object can be deleted from the garbage collector during the next cycle. This is a similar type of instance management possible with WCF through PerSession mode.

However, the situation is rather different in distributed development — references do not point to local objects, they point to remote objects on a server or, in another application domain. Therefore, a different approach to classical, *local* programming is taken to create scalable environments which are as efficient as possible in terms of utilizing resources. The server objects are generally instantiated for the short duration of a method call and are released again immediately afterward. Values which are used for processing the method are either transferred again each time the method is called, or they are loaded from a persistent storage, such as a database. Consequently, it does not matter on which server the objects are created in a load-balanced environment; scaling with thousands of clients does not present a problem either (in this scenario, the database may become a bottleneck). Deleted object references must not be explicitly released either — if a client application crashes, objects are not orphaned because they are destroyed immediately after each call. This type of instance management is achieved by `PerCall` mode in WCF.

> *It is also occasionally advantageous to have only one instance of a server object, irrespective of the number of clients. This is achieved in Single mode. However, you should only choose this variant if you really only have to work with a single central resource.*

INSTANCECONTEXTMODE

When instantiating the server object, WCF distinguishes between three different variants: `PerCall`, `PerSession`, and `Single`.

Your choice of instantiation is only visible on the server side and is not reflected in the WSDL document. Because the client doesn't know whether it will receive the same instance whenever the method is called, and remembers all previously set values, or if the instance is newly created each time, you should take particular care in the design of your operations.

As already mentioned, the instantiation behavior is an implementation detail which only concerns the server; it is controlled by the `InstanceContextMode` property of the `ServiceBehavior` attribute. You will hereby assign this attribute to your implementation, not your service contract.

You can see an example of how this attribute is used in Listing 5-1.

LISTING 5-1: [ServiceBehavior]

```
[ServiceBehavior(
    InstanceContextMode = InstanceContextMode.PerCall)
]
public class CarRentalService: ICarRentalService, IDisposable
{
```

The individual `InstanceContextModes` are now explained in detail using various examples and their advantages, disadvantages, and possible uses are described.

PerCall

The proxy on the client side forwards method calls to the server. Every time a method is called, a new instance of the server object is created (default constructor is called) and as soon as the method is processed, this new instance is released again. If the service object implements the IDisposable interface, the Dispose method is called automatically after the result is sent to the proxy.

> *However, the connection between the proxy and the server is only closed when you call your proxy's* Close *method.*

The object is released again after every call, which makes this variant extremely scalable. However, bear in mind that the content of your instance variables is lost after every call, and that you have to transfer it every time, or buffer the values and reload the required data every time you call the method. In addition to the advantage of scalability, there is also no need to worry about threading problems because each call is assigned a separate instance.

Listing 5-2 illustrates two ways in which a client can supply the required data to the server object.

LISTING 5-2: PerCall state management

Available for
download on
Wrox.com

```
double price = 0;
Guid confirmationID;
CarRentalProxy.RentalServiceClient carRentalClient = new
CarRentalProxy.
RentalServiceClient();

Console.WriteLine("Version 1");
price= carRentalClient.CalculatePriceV1(DateTime.Now,
DateTime.Now.AddDays(5),
"Graz", "Wien");
Console.WriteLine("Price to Wien {0}", price);
confirmationID = carRentalClient.ConfirmV1(DateTime.Now,
DateTime.Now.AddDays(5),
"Graz", "Wien", price);
Console.WriteLine("ConfirmationID {0}",confirmationID );

Console.WriteLine("Version 2");
CarRentalProxy.PriceCalculationResponse resp =
carRentalClient.CalculatePriceV2(
DateTime.Now, DateTime.Now.AddDays(5), "Graz", "Wien");
Console.WriteLine("Price to Wien {0}", resp.Price );
confirmationID = carRentalClient.ConfirmV2(resp.RequestID );
Console.WriteLine("ConfirmationID {0}", confirmationID);

carRentalClient.ReportCrash(DateTime.Now,"Hartberg",confirmationID);

carRentalClient.Close();
```

As you can see in Listing 5-2, the CalculatePrice method is called first with parameters such as PickupDate and ReturnDate.

In variant 1, only the calculated price is returned. Should you then wish to call up the `Confirm` method, all the parameters, including the value returned beforehand, must be transferred again.

In variant 2, a `requestID` is returned along with the calculated price. This request ID can be used, for example, to perform a Confirm action immediately. In variant 2 it is important for the `Confirm` method to reload the original values using the transferred `RequestID`; these values are generally reloaded from a database.

The `ReportCrash` method works in the same way as variant 2. In this case, a unique `confirmationID` is also transferred to the method.

Listing 5-3 demonstrates the service implementation for the `PerCall` scenario.

LISTING 5-3: Service Implementation

```csharp
using System;
using Wrox.CarRentalService.Contracts;
using System.ServiceModel;

namespace Wrox.CarRentalService.Implementations.Europe
{
    [ServiceBehavior(InstanceContextMode= InstanceContextMode.PerCall )]
    public class CarRentalService: ICarRentalService, IDisposable
    {

        public CarRentalService()
        {
            Console.WriteLine("CarRentalService Constructor");
        }

        public double CalculatePriceV1(DateTime pickupDate,
            DateTime returnDate,
            string pickupLocation, string returnLocation)
        {
            double price = 0;
            if (returnLocation.Equals("Wien"))
                price=120;
            else
                price =100;

            return price ;
        }

        public Guid ConfirmV1(DateTime pickupDate, DateTime returnDate,
            string pickupLocation, string returnLocation, double price)
        {
            Guid confirmationNumber = Guid.NewGuid();
            //save confirmation to database
            return confirmationNumber;
        }

        public PriceCalculationResponse CalculatePriceV2(
            DateTime pickupDate, DateTime returnDate,
```

```
                    string pickupLocation, string returnLocation)
        {
            PriceCalculationResponse resp = null;
            resp = new PriceCalculationResponse();
            Guid requestId = Guid.NewGuid();
            resp.RequestID = requestId;

            if (returnLocation.Equals("Wien"))
                resp.Price =120;
            else
                resp.Price = 100;
            //Save request to database
            return resp  ;
        }

        public Guid  ConfirmV2(Guid requestID)
        {
            //load request from Database
            Guid confirmationNumber = Guid.NewGuid();
           //save confirmation to database
            return confirmationNumber;
        }

        public void ReportCrash(DateTime date,
                    String location, Guid confirmationID)
        {
            //load values from database
            Console.WriteLine(@"
             Crash reported Date {0} Location {1}
             Confirmation ID {2}",
             date,location,confirmationID );
        }
        public void Dispose()
        {
            Console.WriteLine("CarRentalService disposed...");
        }
    }
}
```

Singleton

As the name suggests, there is only one single instance in this variant, irrespective of how many client proxies there are. The object is only instantiated once, and its service life is linked to the ServiceHost.

The primary problem posed by this variant is scalability. The standard threading behavior in WCF is ConcurrencyMode.Single, which means that at any given time the service object can be blocked by a single thread for its exclusive use for the duration of the method call. The object is only released when the entire method has been processed. All other method calls are filed in a queue.

> To ease this problem somewhat, you can change the default ConcurrencyMode manually to ConcurrencyMode.Multiple, although you are then also responsible for synchronizing the threads.

The code in Listing 5-4 illustrates the use of the `InstanceContextMode.Single`. The default `ConcurrencyMode` has also been repeated here explicitly for better legibility.

LISTING 5-4: InstanceContextMode.Single

```
namespace Wrox.CarRentalService.Implementations.Europe
{
    [ServiceBehavior(InstanceContextMode = InstanceContextMode.Single,
        ConcurrencyMode = ConcurrencyMode.Single    )]
    public class CarRentalServiceAT : ICarRentalService, IDisposable
    {
        public int Count { get; set; }
        public CarRentalServiceAT()
        {
            Console.WriteLine("CarRentalService Constructor ");
        }

        public double CalculatePrice(
          DateTime pickupDate, DateTime returnDate,
          string pickupLocation, string returnLocation)
        {

            Count++;
            double returnValue = 0;
            if (returnLocation.Equals("Graz"))
                returnValue = 100;
            else
                returnValue = 150;
            Console.WriteLine("total number of price calculations {0}",
            Count);

            return returnValue;
        }

        public void Dispose()
        {
            Console.WriteLine("CarRentalService disposed ");
        }
    }
}
```

Listing 5-5 shows that the `ServiceHost` class has an overloaded variant to which a ready-made `Singleton` object can be transferred. The `Singleton` object can also be reached via the `SingletonInstance` property of the `ServiceHost`.

LISTING 5-5: ServiceHost and Singleton

```
using System.ServiceModel;
...

CarRentalServiceAT myService = new CarRentalServiceAT();
```

```
myService.Count = 20;

ServiceHost carRentalHost = null;
carRentalHost = new ServiceHost(myService);

carRentalHost.Open();
CarRentalServiceAT singleton = null;
carRentalHost.SingletonInstance as CarRentalServiceAT;
singleton.Count = 0;
```

PerSession

PerSession means that each client proxy communicates with its own single instance on the server side. The object on the server side remains in place as long as the client does not call the proxy's Close method, or the session timeout (default 10 minutes) has already been reached.

After the connection has been explicitly ended by calling the Close method or the PerSession server object has been deleted by the timeout, the proxy can no longer be used. When you attempt to call up a method, you get a CommunicationException.

The advantage of PerSession instantiation is that values which have been set are retained on the server side without any additional measures. However, the disadvantage with this is scalability because every active connection naturally also takes up memory space on the server, regardless of whether the client currently requires it. If the client crashes or the Close method is not called, the values are also held in memory until the end of the session. The code in Listing 5-6 demonstrates the use of InstanceContextMode.PerSession.

LISTING 5-6: InstanceContextMode.PerSession

```
using System;
using Wrox.CarRentalService.Contracts;
using System.Diagnostics;
using System.ServiceModel;

namespace Wrox.CarRentalService.Implementations.Europe
{
    [ServiceBehavior(InstanceContextMode=  InstanceContextMode.PerSession)]
    public class CarRentalService: ICarRentalService, IDisposable
    {
        private DateTime pickupDate, returnDate;
        private String pickupLocation, returnLocation;
        private  string  confirmationNumber;
        public CarRentalService()
        {
            Console.WriteLine("CarRentalService Constructor");
        }
        public void SetValues(DateTime pickupDate, DateTime returnDate,
            string pickupLocation, string returnLocation)
        {
            this.pickupDate = pickupDate;
            this.returnDate = returnDate;
```

continues

LISTING 5-6 *(continued)*

```
            this.pickupLocation = pickupLocation;
            this.returnLocation = returnLocation;
        }

        public double CalculatePrice()
        {
            double price = 0;
            if (returnLocation.Equals("Wien"))
                price=120;
            else
                price =100;

            return price ;
        }

        public string  Confirm()
        {
            confirmationNumber = OperationContext.Current.SessionId ;

            return confirmationNumber;
        }

        public void Dispose()
        {

            Console.WriteLine("CarRentalService disposed...");
        }
    }
}
```

As shown in Listing 5-7, when the first call is made, the values are set and the private instance variables can be used in subsequent calls without transferring twice from the client to the server. The confirmation ID corresponds to the `SessionId`.

LISTING 5-7: PerSession Client

```
using System;
using System.Collections.Generic;
using System.Linq;
using System.Text;

namespace Wrox.CarRentalService.ConsoleClient
{
    class Program
    {
        static void Main(string[] args)
        {

            double price = 0;
            CarRentalProxy.RentalServiceClient carRentalClient = null;
            carRentalClient = CarRentalProxy.RentalServiceClient();
```

```
carRentalClient.SetValues(
                    DateTime.Now, DateTime.Now.AddDays(5),
                    "Graz", "Wien");
price = carRentalClient.CalculatePrice();
Console.WriteLine("Price to Wien {0}", price);

carRentalClient.SetValues(
                    DateTime.Now, DateTime.Now.AddDays(5),
                    "Graz", "Villach");
price = carRentalClient.CalculatePrice();
Console.WriteLine("Price to Villach {0}", price);

string confirmNumber = carRentalClient.Confirm();
Console.WriteLine("Reservation ID {0}", confirmNumber);
carRentalClient.Close();
try
{
    //order is already confirmed and the proxy is closed
    carRentalClient.SetValues(DateTime.Now,
    DateTime.Now.AddDays(5), "Graz", "Salzburg");
    price = carRentalClient.CalculatePrice();
    Console.WriteLine("Price to Salzburg {0}", price);
}
catch (Exception ex)
{
    Console.WriteLine(ex.Message );
}
        }
    }
}
```

PerSession requires you to use a protocol which supports session. For example, you can use the netTcpBinding with the connection-oriented transfer protocol TCP which allows the server to allocate the incoming message to the correct server object. The basicHttpBinding, for example, is unsuitable because the transfer protocol HTTP is connectionless and cannot allocate the incoming message to a dedicated server instance.

However, there are some bindings which use the transfer protocol HTTP and provide additional support in terms of security or reliability. In this case, WCF uses the ID from the security or reliability protocol to establish a unique connection between the proxy and the server object.

Listing 5-8 illustrates the use of wsHttpBinding, which supports both security and reliability. If you only activate security now, for example, WCF uses the security identifier for client-server mapping and for the SessionId, as shown in Figure 5-1.

Available for download on Wrox.com

LISTING 5-8: wsHttpBinding

```
<bindings>
 <wsHttpBinding>
  <binding name="wsReliable" >
   <reliableSession enabled="false"/>
   <security mode="Message"/>
```

continues

LISTING 5-8 *(continued)*

```
    </binding>
   </wsHttpBinding>
  </bindings>
  <service
  behaviorConfiguration="MetaDataBehavior" name="Wrox.CarRentalService.
  Implementations.Europe.CarRentalService">
  <endpoint
      address=""
      binding="wsHttpBinding" bindingConfiguration="wsReliable"
      contract="Wrox.CarRentalService.Contracts.ICarRentalService"
  />
  </service>
```

FIGURE 5-1

> Given the fact that the combination `InstanceContextMode.PerSession` *and*
> *binding* `basicHttpBinding` *does not lead to a runtime error and does not*
> *produce the required behavior — because the server instance behaves as it does in*
> `PerCall` *mode — it is imperative to request or decline a protocol which supports*
> *sessions explicitly. This is done with the* `SessionMode` *property in the service*
> *contract, as shown in Listing 5-9.*

LISTING 5-9: SessionMode.Required to Enforce a Suitable Binding

```
[ServiceContract(
      Namespace = "http://wrox/CarRentalService/2009/10",
      SessionMode = SessionMode.Required ,
      Name = "RentalService")]
public interface ICarRentalService. . .
```

Should you attempt to load this service with the binding `basicHttpBinding`, the following runtime
error occurs when the service definition is read by the service host:

```
Unhandled Exception: System.InvalidOperationException: Contract requires Session,
```

but Binding 'BasicHttpBinding' doesn't support it or isn't configured properly to support it.

On the other hand, the combination of SessionMode.NotAllowed and netTcpBinding leads to the following error message:

```
Unhandled Exception: System.InvalidOperationException: Contract does not
allow Session, but Binding 'NetTcpBinding' does not support
Datagram or is not configured properly to support it.
```

Regardless of the previous configurations, the Reliability property should be kept activated at all times in a PerSession scenario.

SERVICE LIFE

As you have already seen, you can release the server instance explicitly by calling the Close method or wait for the default timeout. However, in connection with sessions it is also often important to call up the methods in a certain order. For example, the SetValues method must be called first, and only then can the price be calculated. Furthermore, when you call up the Confirm method, the contract has been concluded between the customer and the car rental company, and the server object can then be deleted.

Use the properties IsInitiating and IsTerminating to determine the order in which methods have to be called. IsInitiating means that this method can start a session or is involved in an existing session. IsTerminating means that the session is ended if this method is called up; where necessary, the Dispose method for the server object is called, and the proxy is unusable. Setting these properties also affects the generated WSDL document, as shown in Listing 5-10, which means that it can also be seen and used by the client.

LISTING 5-10: IsInitiating and IsTerminating and the Produced WSDL Document

```
<wsdl:operation
    msc:isInitiating="false"
    msc:isTerminating="false"
    name="CalculatePrice"
>
```

If, for example, you define an operation contract as shown in Listing 5-11, the method cannot be called first. However, should the client attempt to call up this method, the following error message is generated:

```
Unhandled Exception: System.InvalidOperationException:
The operation 'CalculatePrice' cannot be the first operation
to be called because IsInitiating is false.
```

LISTING 5-11: IsInitiating and IsTerminating

```
[OperationContract(IsInitiating = false , IsTerminating = false)]
double CalculatePrice();
```

Consequently, the final service contract for the car hire example is shown in Listing 5-12.

LISTING 5-12: Car Hire Service Contract

```
[ServiceContract(
    Namespace = "http://wrox/CarRentalService/2009/10",
    SessionMode = SessionMode.Required ,
    Name = "RentalService")]
public interface ICarRentalService
{
    [OperationContract(IsInitiating=true, IsTerminating =false)]
    void SetValues(DateTime pickupDate, DateTime returnDate,
        string pickupLocation, string returnLocation);

    [OperationContract(IsInitiating = false , IsTerminating = false)]
    double CalculatePrice();

    [OperationContract(IsInitiating = false , IsTerminating = true )]
    string  Confirm();
}
```

A further advanced possibility for influencing the service life of the service instance is to use the `OperationBehavior` attribute together with the `ReleaseInstanceMode` property. In principle, every server instance is surrounded by a context which maintains the actual connection with the client proxy. In certain scenarios it may be advantageous to maintain the context (container for the instance), re-create the instance contained in it before a method is called up, or delete it after a method is called. The `ReleaseInstanceMode` property is actually only used in connection with PerSession scenarios if the user wishes to retain the session but not the instance.

In Listing 5-13, the `SetValues` method has been assigned the `ReleaseInstanceMode.BeforeCall`. As a result of this, the existing instance is deleted and recreated again before every time this method is called.

LISTING 5-13: ReleaseInstanceMode.BeforeCall

```
[OperationBehavior(ReleaseInstanceMode=ReleaseInstanceMode.BeforeCall)]
public void SetValues(DateTime pickupDate, DateTime returnDate,
            string pickupLocation, string returnLocation)
```

In addition, a further method has been incorporated into the service contract, as shown in Listing 5-14, with the name `Reset` and has been assigned the `ReleaseInstanceMode.AfterCall`. The instance is now deleted every time the client calls the `Reset` method.

LISTING 5-14: ReleaseInstanceMode.AfterCall

```
[OperationBehavior(ReleaseInstanceMode=ReleaseInstanceMode.AfterCall )]
public void Reset()
```

Other options would be `ReleaseInstanceMode.BeforeCall` (default) and `ReleaseInstanceMode.BeforeAndAfterCall`.

In principle, this instance management option should only be applied in special exceptions — if you require explicit control over the lifetime of a server instance for reasons of performance or scalability.

SessionId

The `SessionId`, displayed in the form of a GUID, is exchanged between the client and the server and uniquely signifies a connection between the client (proxy) and the server (context). It originates either from the transfer protocol session (TCP) or from a logical session id if you are using `wsHttpBinding`, for example. The `SessionId` is primarily used for logging and protocol purposes and can be applied irrespective of whether you are in `PerCall`, `PerSession`, or `Single` mode.

Therefore, the `SessionID` is always accessible whenever you are using a protocol or a binding which supports session. For example, you can use the TCP protocol, which is connection-oriented anyway, or you can use `wsHttpBinding`, which uses the connectionless HTTP transfer protocol but carries a logical session ID above it.

The uppermost session ID is used if, for example, you have activated `wsHttpBinding` to be secure and reliable. In this scenario the exchanged security identifier is used as a session ID. The connection between the session ID and the security identifier can also be seen in Figure 5-2.

FIGURE 5-2

In any event it is important to activate either reliable sessions or security with the binding being used.

Therefore, the session ID can always be accessed sensibly whenever reliability and/or security are involved. In addition to these restrictions, it is also important for communication to happen beforehand between the proxy and the server for the exchange of the ID. This can be done by opening the proxy manually, which is recommended, or at least by calling one method. If you access the `SessionId` prior to communication or use a protocol which does not support any sessions, you will either receive an incorrect `SessionId` or an error message.

You can access the `SessionId` on the client side via the proxy's `InnerChannel` property. This `SessionId` is provided to you on the server side by the operation context's `Current` attribute.

> *Also bear in mind that if you have activated* `SessionMode.NotAllowed` *on the server side, you can access the* `SessionId`, *even though it remains blank.*

The following conclusion can be drawn from the code in Listing 5-15 and the console output display in Listing 5-16.

LISTING 5-15: Client Side SessionId

```
namespace Wrox.CarRentalService.ConsoleClient
{
    class Program
    {
        static void Main(string[] args)
        {

            CarRentalProxy.RentalServiceClient carRentalClient = null;
            carRentalClient = new CarRentalProxy.RentalServiceClient();

            double price =0;

            try
            {
                Console.WriteLine(
                    carRentalClient.InnerChannel.SessionId);
            }
            catch (Exception ex)
            {
                Console.WriteLine(ex.Message ); ;
            }

            carRentalClient.Open();
            price = carRentalClient.CalculatePrice(
                DateTime.Now, DateTime.Now.AddDays(5), "Graz", "Wien");
            Console.WriteLine("Price {0}", price);
            Console.WriteLine(carRentalClient.InnerChannel.SessionId);

            carRentalClient.Close();
            try
            {
                Console.WriteLine(
                    carRentalClient.InnerChannel.SessionId);
            }
            catch (Exception ex)
            {

                Console.WriteLine(ex.Message); ;
            }

            carRentalClient = new CarRentalProxy.RentalServiceClient();

            price = carRentalClient.CalculatePrice(
                DateTime.Now,DateTime.Now.AddDays(5),"Graz","Villach");
            Console.WriteLine("Price {0}",price );

            Console.WriteLine(carRentalClient.InnerChannel.SessionId);

            price = carRentalClient.CalculatePrice(
                DateTime.Now,DateTime.Now.AddDays(5),"Graz", "Villach");
            Console.WriteLine("Price {0}", price);

            Console.WriteLine(carRentalClient.InnerChannel.SessionId);
```

```
                    Console.WriteLine("try it again ... demo for Single");
                    Console.ReadLine();
                    price = carRentalClient.CalculatePrice(
                        DateTime.Now,DateTime.Now.AddDays(5),"Graz","Villach");
                    Console.WriteLine("Price {0}", price);

                    Console.WriteLine(carRentalClient.InnerChannel.SessionId);
                }
            }
        }
```

LISTING 5-16: Client Output

```
The session channel must be opened before the session ID can be accessed.
Price 120
urn:uuid:9dd6c7de-d89a-4200-9be4-59f9e5dfc0bc
urn:uuid:9dd6c7de-d89a-4200-9be4-59f9e5dfc0bc
Price 120
urn:uuid:c3606853-13a0-4fc0-aa4e-f859a2d0891a
Price 120
urn:uuid:c3606853-13a0-4fc0-aa4e-f859a2d0891a
try it again ... demo for Single

Price 120
urn:uuid:c3606853-13a0-4fc0-aa4e-f859a2d0891a
```

The SessionId can be accessed via the InnerChannel proxy property. To access the SessionId, the connection must be opened between the proxy and the server; this can either be done explicitly via Open or by calling up at least one method. After the proxy has been closed, the old SessionId can be accessed. When the proxy is opened again, a new SessionId is negotiated.

The following conclusion can be drawn from the server code in Listing 5-17 with a configuration shown in Listing 5-18 and the output shown in Listing 5-19.

LISTING 5-17: Server Side SessionId

```
[ServiceBehavior(InstanceContextMode = InstanceContextMode.Single )]
    public class CarRentalService: ICarRentalService, IDisposable
    {
        public CarRentalService()
        {
            Console.WriteLine("CarRentalService Constructor" );
        }

        public double CalculatePrice(
            DateTime pickupDate, DateTime returnDate,
            string pickupLocation, string returnLocation)
        {

            OperationContext ctx = OperationContext.Current;
            Console.WriteLine("CalculatePrice \t{0} ", ctx.SessionId);
            if (returnLocation.Equals("Villach"))
```

continues

LISTING 5-17 *(continued)*

```
                    return 50;
                else
                    return 120;
            }
            public void Dispose()
            {
                OperationContext ctx = OperationContext.Current;
                Console.WriteLine("Disposed \t{0}", ctx.SessionId);

            }
        }
    }
```

LISTING 5-18: Config File

```xml
<system.serviceModel>
  <bindings>
    <wsHttpBinding >
      <binding name="mywsBinding">
        <reliableSession enabled="false"/>
        <security mode="Message"/>
      </binding>
    </wsHttpBinding>
  </bindings>
  <services>
    <service behaviorConfiguration="MetaDataBehavior"
        name="Wrox.CarRentalService.Implementations.
        Europe.CarRentalService">
    <endpoint address=""
          binding="wsHttpBinding"
          bindingConfiguration="mywsBinding"
          contract="Wrox.CarRentalService.Contracts.ICarRentalService"
    />

    </service>
  </services>
</system.serviceModel>
```

LISTING 5-19: Server Output

```
The car rental service is up and running...
CalculatePrice   urn:uuid:9dd6c7de-d89a-4200-9be4-59f9e5dfc0bc
CalculatePrice   urn:uuid:c3606853-13a0-4fc0-aa4e-f859a2d0891a
CalculatePrice   urn:uuid:c3606853-13a0-4fc0-aa4e-f859a2d0891a
CalculatePrice   urn:uuid:c3606853-13a0-4fc0-aa4e-f859a2d0891a
```

The SessionId can be accessed via the OperationContext.Current.SessionId property. The decisive factor for a common SessionId is not the InstanceContextMode, but the binding used. The SessionId can also be accessed in the Dispose method, although this only makes sense in PerCall or PerSession mode.

PERFORMANCE

The performance of your WCF services hinges on a wide range of factors. In addition to general topics such as CPU, RAM, and network performance, WCF-specific considerations such as InstanceContextMode, ConcurrencyMode, DataContract design or the binding used also play an important role.

The InstanceContextMode is used to control the instantiation behavior of your service object — possible variants are PerCall, PerSession, or Singleton.

The binding determines which transfer protocol and which encoding is used. In addition, a wide range of WS* protocols can be used via the binding.

ConcurrencyMode describes whether multiple threads are permitted to access one and the same object at the same time. ConcurrencyMode is controlled via the [ServiceBehavior] attribute, and its default setting is ConcurrencyMode.Single. Further options are ConcurrencyMode.Multiple and ConcurrencyMode.Reentrant. ConcurrencyMode.Single means that a server object can only be accessed by a single thread. Therefore, this setting will not lead to any synchronization problems because other requests are automatically placed in a queue, and the object may only be accessed when the first thread has released the object. ConcurrencyMode.Multiple means that any number of threads may access one and the same object. If necessary, you must take care of thread synchronization manually with classic .NET tools such as Monitor or Mutex.

> ConcurrencyMode.Reentrant *is ultimately important for callback scenarios and is not described here in more detail.*

In principle, however, the ConcurrencyMode you use only plays a role if you use a multithreaded client which accesses a PerSession object or if you use a Singleton. In the case of PerCall scenarios, a new object is created for every method call in any event, avoiding the threading problem from the outset.

The use of the [ServiceBehavior] attribute is shown in Listing 5-20.

Available for download on Wrox.com

LISTING 5-20: [ServiceBehavior]

```
[ServiceBehavior(InstanceContextMode=InstanceContextMode.PerCall,
    ConcurrencyMode=ConcurrencyMode.Single)]
public class CarRentalService: ICarRentalService, IDisposable
{
```

Throttling

WCF offers another possibility for increasing performance and for avoiding server overloads, thereby preventing DoS attacks, for example. You can control the following limits by using the

`<serviceThrottling>` element in the `ServiceBehavior` section of your configuration file, as shown in Listing 5-21 or, of course, by programming the following:

➤ `maxConcurrentCalls`: Maximum number of service operations which can be processed at the same time. If this number is exceeded, other method calls are placed in a queue and processed gradually.

➤ `maxConcurrentSessions`: Maximum number of simultaneous transfer or application sessions.

➤ `maxConcurrentInstances`: Maximum number of instances.

LISTING 5-21: serviceThrottling Behavior

```
<serviceBehaviors>
        <behavior name="throttlingBehavior">
          <serviceThrottling
              maxConcurrentCalls ="5"
              maxConcurrentSessions="2"
              maxConcurrentInstances="3" />
        </behavior>
      </serviceBehaviors>
```

To read out the throttling values you can use the code shown in Listing 5-22.

LISTING 5-22: Read Throttling Values

```
namespace Wrox.CarRentalService.ConsoleHost
{
    class Program
    {
        static void Main(string[] args)
        {
            System.ServiceModel.ServiceHost carRentalHost = null;
            carRentalHost = new ServiceHost(
                typeof(Wrox.CarRentalService.Implementations.
                    Europe.CarRentalService));
            carRentalHost.Open();
            ChannelDispatcher dispatcher =
                carRentalHost.ChannelDispatchers[0]
                as ChannelDispatcher;
            Console.WriteLine("Max concurrent calls {0}",
                dispatcher.ServiceThrottle.MaxConcurrentCalls);
            Console.WriteLine("Max concurrent instances {0}",
                dispatcher.ServiceThrottle.MaxConcurrentInstances);
            Console.WriteLine("Max concurrent sessions {0}",
                dispatcher.ServiceThrottle.MaxConcurrentSessions);
            Console.WriteLine(@"The car rental service is up
                and running...");
            Console.ReadLine();
        }
    }
}
```

By using this `ServiceBehavior`, you have control over how many instances or sessions can exist concurrently, or how many calls are permitted at the same time. The defaults used can be adapted depending on your environment to achieve improved overall performance. However, the throttling values which are most suitable depend on a variety of parameters. You should ask the following questions: How much memory capacity does a session take? How many concurrent clients are expected? Are there multithreaded clients? Which `InstanceContextMode` is used? Which binding is used?

In all tuning scenarios it is important to have a baseline and, after making changes to your configuration, to compare this baseline with the new values to ascertain whether these changes have actually had a positive impact, or whether the overall load on your server has come down at all. WCF offers a variety of performance counters for monitoring the performance or for creating a baseline. Performance counters must be activated by configuration or by programming before they can be read.

An example of activating via configuration file is shown in Listing 5-23.

LISTING 5-23: Activate Performance Counters

```
<system.serviceModel>
 . . .
   <diagnostics performanceCounters="All"/>
 . . .
</system.serviceModel>
```

After you have activated the performance counters and started your service host, you can monitor the current performance values with the Windows Performance Monitor; WCF offers performance indicators for the service as a whole — for endpoints and for operations.

To show what effect the individual components (`serviceThrottling`, `InstanceContextMode`, `ConcurrencyMode`) have, you start with a simple `PerCall` service with `basicHttpBinding` and take a step-by-step look at configuration variants.

The starting point is the existing `CalculatePrice` operation in the `CarRentalService`. To make the effects of throttling more readily visible, greatly reduced throttling settings are shown in Listing 5-24.

LISTING 5-24: Service Throttling

```
<serviceThrottling
 maxConcurrentCalls ="5"
 maxConcurrentInstances="10"
 maxConcurrentSessions="15"
 />
```

The service implementation is shown in Listing 5-25.

LISTING 5-25: Service Implementation

```
namespace Wrox.CarRentalService.Implementations.Europe
{
    [ServiceBehavior(InstanceContextMode=InstanceContextMode.PerCall,
        ConcurrencyMode=ConcurrencyMode.Reentrant)]
    public class CarRentalService: ICarRentalService, IDisposable
    {
        public double CalculatePrice(
                DateTime pickupDate, DateTime returnDate,
                string pickupLocation, string vehiclePreference)
        {
            System.Threading.Thread.Sleep(5000);
            return double.Parse(pickupLocation);
        }
        public double GetDummyNumber()
        {
            return 10;
        }

        public CarRentalService()
        {
            Console.WriteLine("CarRentalService Constructor");
        }

        public void Dispose()
        {
            Console.WriteLine("CarRentalService disposing...");
            System.Threading.Thread.Sleep(2000);
            Console.WriteLine("CarRentalService disposing...");
        }
    }
}
```

The client code shown in Listing 5-26 creates a single proxy outside the loop via the
basicHttpBinding and then calls up the CalculatePrice method asynchronously 40 times.

LISTING 5-26: Client Code

```
namespace Wrox.CarRentalService.ConsoleClient
{
    class Program
    {
        static void Main(string[] args)
        {
            CarRentalProxy.RentalServiceClient carRentalClient = new
CarRentalProxy.RentalServiceClient("NetTcpBinding_RentalService");

            for (int i = 0; i < 40; i++)
            {
                carRentalClient.BeginCalculatePrice
                    (DateTime.Now, DateTime.Now.AddDays(5),
                    i.ToString(),
```

```
                    "Graz",
                    priceCalcFinished,
                    carRentalClient);
            }

            Console.ReadLine();

        }
        public static void priceCalcFinished(IAsyncResult asyncResult)
        {
            Console.WriteLine("priceCalcFinished");
            try
            {
                RentalServiceClient carRentalClient =
                    asyncResult.AsyncState as RentalServiceClient;
                double price = carRentalClient.EndCalculatePrice(asyncResult);
                Console.WriteLine("Price {0}", price);
            }
            catch (Exception ex)
            {
                Console.WriteLine(ex.Message); ;
            }
        }
    }
}
```

After the start of this example, you can see how the price calculations are conducted in blocks of five because a maximum of five calls is permitted at any one time. The remaining calls are buffered and are processed bit by bit. Setting the maxConcurrentInstances attribute to 5 would also lead to the same result. Changing the maxConcurrentSessions attribute makes absolutely no difference in this scenario because neither a connection-oriented transfer protocol nor a WS binding with security or reliability are used. Were the processing of the individual calls to take too long, the client would receive a timeout exception; the default for this is after one minute. The timespan between the method being called and the timeout exception can be changed on the client side by using the sendTimeout attribute in your binding.

If the binding is changed to netTCPBinding, using the maxConcurrentSessions attribute would still not work, even though TCP supports connections at a transfer protocol level. This is because only one proxy has been created on the client side. As a result, the maxConcurrentSessions attribute has no effect.

However, if you move the instantiation of the proxy into the loop, each proxy instance establishes a separate connection with the server side.

Listing 5-27 shows the changed client code.

LISTING 5-27: Change Client Code

```
for (int i = 0; i < 40; i++)
{
   CarRentalProxy.RentalServiceClient carRentalClient = new CarRentalProxy.
RentalServiceClient("NetTcpBinding_RentalService");
```

continues

LISTING 5-27 *(continued)*

```
carRentalClient.BeginCalculatePrice
  (
  DateTime.Now, DateTime.Now.AddDays(5),
  i.ToString(),
  "Graz",
  priceCalcFinished,
  carRentalClient);
}
```

Based on the configuration in Listing 5-28, there may only ever be five instances active. If the values for the other two attributes maxConcurrentCalls or maxConcurrentInstances are lower, they would be referred to as limits, of course.

LISTING 5-28: Changed serviceThrottling

```
<serviceThrottling
maxConcurrentCalls ="100"
maxConcurrentInstances="100"
maxConcurrentSessions="5" />
```

In this scenario it is also extremely important for the proxy to be closed in the callback method as shown in Listing 5-29; otherwise, the session would be maintained and would only be closed after the 10-minute default.

LISTING 5-29: Close Proxy in the Callback Method

```
public static void priceCalcFinished(IAsyncResult asyncResult)
    {
        Console.WriteLine("priceCalcFinished");
        try
        {
            RentalServiceClient carRentalClient =
                asyncResult.AsyncState as RentalServiceClient;
            double price =
                carRentalClient.EndCalculatePrice(asyncResult);
            Console.WriteLine("Price {0}", price);
            carRentalClient.Close();
        }
        catch (Exception ex)
        {
            Console.WriteLine(ex.Message); ;
        }
    }
```

As a final example, here is the use of ConcurrencyMode.Multiple in conjunction with InstanceContextMode.PerSession and a multithreaded client. For this purpose, the server code was adapted in such a way that an instance variable is incremented in the CalculatePrice method as shown in Listing 5-30.

LISTING 5-30: ConcurrencyMode.Multiple with PerSession

```
namespace Wrox.CarRentalService.Implementations.Europe
{
  [ServiceBehavior(InstanceContextMode=InstanceContextMode.PerSession ,
      ConcurrencyMode=ConcurrencyMode.Multiple  )]
    public class CarRentalService: ICarRentalService, IDisposable
    {
        private object myLock = new object();
        private int Counter;
        public double CalculatePrice(
          DateTime pickupDate, DateTime returnDate,
          string pickupLocation, string vehiclePreference)
        {
            lock (myLock)
            {
                int tempValue = Counter;
                tempValue++;
                System.Threading.Thread.Sleep(2000);
                Counter = tempValue;
                Console.WriteLine("Counter {0}", Counter);
            }
            return double.Parse(pickupLocation);
        }

        public CarRentalService()
        {
            Console.WriteLine("CarRentalService Constructor");
        }

        public void Dispose()
        {
            Console.WriteLine("CarRentalService disposing...");
            System.Threading.Thread.Sleep(2000);
            Console.WriteLine("CarRentalService disposing...");
        }
    }
}
```

If the CalculatePrice method is now called up by a multithread client, as shown in Listing 5-31, a logical error occurs in the calculation.

LISTING 5-31: Multithreaded Client

```
namespace Wrox.CarRentalService.ConsoleClient
{
    class Program
    {
        static void Main(string[] args)
        {
            CarRentalProxy.RentalServiceClient carRentalClient = new
CarRentalProxy.RentalServiceClient("NetTcpBinding_RentalService");
```

continues

LISTING 5-31 *(continued)*

```
                for (int i = 0; i < 40; i++)
                {
                    carRentalClient.BeginCalculatePrice(DateTime.Now,
          DateTime.Now.AddDays(5),
                        i.ToString(),
                        "Graz",
                        priceCalcFinished,
                        carRentalClient );
                }

                Console.ReadLine();

            }
            public static void priceCalcFinished(IAsyncResult asyncResult)
            {
                Console.WriteLine("priceCalcFinished");
                try
                {
                    RentalServiceClient carRentalClient =
                     asyncResult.AsyncState  as RentalServiceClient;
                    double price =
                    carRentalClient.EndCalculatePrice(asyncResult);
                    Console.WriteLine("Price {0}", price);

                }
                catch (Exception ex)
                {
                    Console.WriteLine(ex.Message ); ;
                }
            }
        }
    }
```

This problem is solved either by resetting the `ConcurrencyMode` to `Single` or by using manual synchronization in the `CalculatePrice` method.

Best Practices

As you have seen from the previous examples, the overall performance and load limits of your WCF environment are affected by many different factors, such as the `InstanceContextMode`, `ConcurrencyMode`, and throttling behavior. However, you should always initially keep to the defaults or the recommended best practices with regard to tuning. For example, it is advisable to use the `DataContractSerializer` and to favor a `PerCall` architecture with `ConcurrencyMode.Single`. You should only start to adapt the default settings if you notice that these defaults or best practices lead to problems. When tuning, it is always important to have reliable numerical material on hand, confirming whether or not your changes have been successful. As mentioned previously, WCF offers a series of performance counters for general monitoring.

Load Balancing

The typical scale-out scenario involves adding more servers to your environment, if necessary, and using them to take on some of the workload of the other servers. However, load balancing is only possible if the client calls can be passed on to any server for processing. That is generally possible without any problems in a `PerCall` scenario without a session-oriented protocol. The SOAP message is sent to any server, where a new object is created for this call. Where necessary, requisite data is loaded from another data source (e.g., an SQL Server). After the work is done, the object is deleted on the server side again. In the case of `InstanceMode.PerSession`, `InstanceMode.Single`, or a connection-oriented protocol, load balancing with standard WCF technologies is not possible. In `PerSession` mode in particular, WCF is unable to swap session variables to a central state or database server, unlike a classic ASP.NET session state.

6
Workflow Services

WHAT'S IN THIS CHAPTER?

➤ Getting started with workflow services

➤ Implementing message correlation

➤ Configuring workflow services

➤ Hosting workflow services

Workflows are presented in software development as an effective tool for solving problems or accomplishing business goals. By splitting them into smaller and more manageable pieces, they can be coordinated into a single process.

Workflows also bring reusability and maintainability — two core quality principles in software engineering. They are promoted by workflows because they have smaller pieces that can be reused across several processes and are easier to maintain. These pieces or reusable assets receive the name of activities, and usually describe the work performed by the people or software involved in the process.

When designing workflows within an enterprise application using a bottom-up approach, they are first designed as a set of primitive activities to control the execution flow, communicate with the outside world, or execute actions to change the workflow's internal state. These workflows can later be converted to activities and used as a compositional unit for creating other workflows that coordinate work at a higher level. In this way, the design process can be applied recursively to a number of abstraction levels that you might find necessary.

The same design paradigm can be applied in the service-oriented world. A service can be implemented through a combination of primitive activities in a workflow, or a service can be the result of a workflow that orchestrates other services to accomplish a business goal.

For instance, a service for submitting a new order in a supply management application might require the coordination of other services to verify or update the stock level of the ordered product. All the work needed to coordinate these service calls can be modeled through a simple workflow.

However, implementing a service as a workflow is not as simple as it sounds. There are challenges that need to be addressed, and without the help of the right technology, they would be almost impossible to achieve:

➤ A long-running process that interacts with people might take hours or days to complete. For instance, a service that implements a document approval workflow. For this kind of service, a mechanism is needed to save the workflow state across different service calls. You can't keep the state in memory forever, as it is volatile storage and a performance bottleneck when the number of running workflows gets high.

➤ Multiple messages that represent business events might come in or go out from a given service instance. A mechanism to correlate all these messages into the same service instance is required to resume the workflow execution in the correct step and with the correct state.

Workflow Foundation (WF) is the technology that helps you in this area. Fortunately with the introduction of new activities to build workflow-enabled or workflow services, it has been closely integrated with WCF in the .NET Framework 3.5. WCF in that sense provides the necessary infrastructure to communicate the workflows with the external world through incoming and outgoing messages.

Throughout this chapter, you will see this relationship has been improved in version 4.0 with the introduction of new features such as content correlation, declarative services, and the new runtime model and activity library.

ANATOMY OF A WORKFLOW SERVICE

A *workflow service* created with WF maintains state, gets input messages from and sends output messages to the outside world, and executes code that performs the service's work. This is the same as an ordinary stateful service, which preserves a shared state between different operations during its lifetime.

Figure 6-1 shows the anatomy of a simple workflow service. Every workflow service has an outermost activity, the workflow itself, which contains all other activities. This outer activity can take different shapes, and basically determines the way the execution flow goes through different inner activities. WF 4.0 ships with two built-in activities for modeling workflows: a sequence activity that flows from one activity to the next until the last activity is executed, and a flowchart activity that resembles the concepts that many analysts and application designers go through when creating solutions or designing business processes.

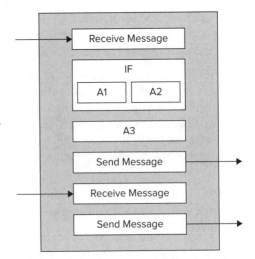

FIGURE 6-1: Anatomy of a workflow service

In this example, the workflow execution begins with a Receive Activity that receives an input message from the external world using a WCF endpoint. This is followed by a branch activity that evaluates a condition before executing one of the activities (named A1 and A2 in Figure 6-1) defined on each branch. The branch activity is followed by the execution of another custom activity (A3), and a message is finally sent to the world beyond this service by the Send Message Activity (which might represent a call to another service). Another Receive Message Activity appears which gets more input, and is followed by a final Send Message Activity that sends out the final service result.

As you can see, every activity in this example represents a piece of a typical service, with the main difference being that many of the built-in language elements found in a traditional program have been replaced by activity classes provided by the WF activity library.

You should also understand that the WF runtime does not know anything about the internal implementation of the activities it is executing, or the way it behaves.

It can only run one activity after another, until the last activity is reached. It can also persist the workflow state at certain points.

Now, you might wonder why you should go with a workflow service when the same service can be implemented manually with code? The answer is, to address some of the benefits that WF can give in this area:

➤ The automatic support for long-running workflows that the WF infrastructure provides is the most evident benefit. The execution of a long-running workflow can be suspended or resumed on multiple points, so the internal state of the execution and activities must be preserved. WF automatically takes cares of saving the workflow state through the use of configurable providers. Therefore, you do not need to worry about these details.

➤ The implementation of a complex service that orchestrates several other services with a certain degree of parallelism gets simplified with the use of a workflow. All the aspects related to message correlation are automatically handled by the WF infrastructure. The same implementation made purely on code would require a lot of plumbing code and some knowledge about concurrent programming. This is necessary to be efficient when coordinating all the service calls and correlating all the responses in the same way WF would do it.

➤ A service might need to execute some kind of compensation logic or be suspended when an unexpected situation or exception occurs during its execution. For instance, a service that depends on other services to perform an action might not be able to complete its execution when any of these are not available, which might lead to some data inconsistencies. If you use a workflow to implement this service, the workflow itself can be suspended and restarted later when the dependent services are available.

➤ The declarative model and visual designer that WF provides becomes handy at the moment of building simple services without worrying about implementation details of the WCF ABC (Address, Binding, and Contract). You can focus on a declarative model that simply creates variables that are handled in the workflow, and activities that initialize these variables and change their values, sending them to the outside world.

DECLARATIVE SERVICES

One of the main problems of implementing workflow services in the .NET Framework 3.5 is that the integration between these technologies leaves something to be desired. You basically have to define all the WCF artifacts using the WCF programming and configuration model, and the workflow using a different model, resulting in a set of multiple artifacts that need to be deployed and managed separately.

However, with the .NET Framework 4.0, you can define all the WCF artifacts, such as contracts and operations, using *XAML* (eXtensible Application Markup Language) together with the workflow definition in the same language, resulting in a single artifact — a XAML-based service.

In other words, you essentially create a model of the service defining what the service should do, rather than writing code to specify how to do it — the traditional way to do things in .NET.

Listing 6-1 shows the XAML representation of a workflow service with a simple operation, `GetData`, that receives an input argument in the variable "data," and returns a string (`data.ToString()`). As you can see, all the activities have been represented as objects with properties using the XAML notation.

LISTING 6-1: XAML Representation

```xml
<WorkflowService ConfigurationName="Service1" Name="Service1" ....>

    <p:Sequence DisplayName="Sequential Service">
      <p:Sequence.Variables>
        <p:Variable x:TypeArguments="CorrelationHandle" Name="handle" />
        <p:Variable x:TypeArguments="x:Int32" Name="data" />
      </p:Sequence.Variables>

      <Receive x:Name="__ReferenceID0" DisplayName="ReceiveRequest"
        OperationName="GetData" ServiceContractName="contract:IService" >
        <Receive.CorrelationInitializers>
          <RequestReplyCorrelationInitializer CorrelationHandle="[handle]" />
        </Receive.CorrelationInitializers>
        <ReceiveMessageContent>
          <p:OutArgument x:TypeArguments="x:Int32">[data]</p:OutArgument>
        </ReceiveMessageContent>
      </Receive>

      <SendReply Request="{x:Reference Name=__ReferenceID0}"
        DisplayName="SendResponse" >
        <SendMessageContent>
          <p:InArgument x:TypeArguments="x:String">[data.ToString()]</p:InArgument>
        </SendMessageContent>
      </SendReply>

    </p:Sequence>

</WorkflowService>
```

In addition, the contract and operations for this service are automatically inferred from the Receive Activity definition.

A great advantage of having a fully declarative service is that you can store the complete definition in a service repository and take full control of the workflow's instances from a hosting environment such as Windows AppFabric.

You can still develop a complete workflow service in WF 4.0 using an imperative .NET programming language such as C# or VB.NET.

WF 4.0 provides a new way to create a complete workflow definition using code without using a designer and the .NET component model. Because this kind of model requires that you define every activity and its properties using code, it might cause maintainability issues when the number of activities increases or the workflow implementation gets complex — you lose the visual definition that you have in the designer.

If you go with this approach, you need to create activities that represent the workflow model, such as Sequence or FlowChart; create messaging activities to interact with the outside workflow, such as Receive or Send Activities; and create other activities to implement the service itself. The contract and operations from the service are still derived from the Receive Activities — there isn't a formal contract definition as in WCF.

```
private static WorkflowServiceImplementation CreateWorkflow()
{
    var result = new Sequence();
    var receivedInput = new Variable<string>();
    result.Variables.Add(receivedInput);

    var handle = new Variable<CorrelationHandle>();
    result.Variables.Add(handle);

    var receive = new Receive()
    {
        OperationName = "HelloWorld",
        ServiceContractName = "HelloWorldService",
        Content =
            ReceiveContent.Create(new OutArgument<string>
            (receivedInput)),
        CorrelatesWith = new InArgument<CorrelationHandle>(handle),
        CanCreateInstance = true
    };

    result.Activities.Add(receive);

    var write = new WriteLine()
    {
        Text = new InArgument<string>(env =>
            string.Format("Hello World!!! '{0}'.",
```

```
                    receivedInput.Get(env)))
        };
        result.Activities.Add(write);

        var reply = new SendReply()
        {
          Request = receive,
          Content = SendContent.Create(new InArgument<string>(env =>
            string.Format("Hello World!!! '{0}'.",
            receivedInput.Get(env))))
        };
        result.Activities.Add(reply);
        var service = new WorkflowServiceImplementation
        {
          Name = "HelloWorldService",
          Body = result
        };
    return service;
}
```

In this example, we receive a message as defined by the Receive Activity Content *property. It is a string assigned to the variable* receivedInput. *The content of the* receivedInput *variable is printed and returned through the* Content *property of the SendReply Activity.*

SEND AND RECEIVE ACTIVITIES

The .NET Framework 3.5 introduced two new activities, Send and Receive, to simplify the integration between WCF and WF. Using these activities, you can essentially enable WCF endpoints on your WF workflows to make it accessible from the external world. On the other hand, you can employ WF as the implementation technology for your WCF services. A workflow that uses these activities is usually known as a workflow service and that terminology is used throughout this chapter.

WF in the .NET Framework 4.0 still ships with these activities for sending and receiving one-way messages through WCF, but it also includes two new activities, SendAndReceiveReply and ReceiveAndSendReply, that represent a higher-level abstraction for request/response operations.

Next, we discuss these four activities in detail and how they can be used.

Receive Activity

The Receive Activity defines an entry point in a workflow that starts receiving messages from the outside world. This entry point takes the form of a WCF endpoint associated to a specific contract and operation. This activity has been improved in the .NET Framework 4.0 with the introduction of significant changes to simplify the service contract and operation definition, as well as other related aspects, such as message correlation.

Some of the properties that you will find in this activity are discussed in Table 6-1.

TABLE 6-1: Receive Activity Properties

PROPERTY	DESCRIPTION
DisplayName	The friendly name that identifies the activity within the workflow. This name is used to reference the activity from other activities, or relate this activity to a SendActivity, which sends the result of the operation execution to the outside world.
ServiceContractName	The name of the WCF contract that is associated with the activity. The name chosen for this contract matters because it represents the service contract that the clients will use to consume the service.
OperationName	The name of the WCF operation that is associated with the activity. This operation is added to the contract specified in the ServiceContractName property. The name of the operation is as important as the name of the contract for the same reasons previously discussed — it is one of the visible parts of the service.
Content	The input parameters or arguments that the operation expects to receive. This content is usually mapped to a workflow variable, so it can be used by other activities.
Action	The SOAP Action that will be used to route the messages to the WCF operation. This value is usually sent by the client in the To address header.
CanCreateInstance	This property specifies whether the activity can create a new instance of the workflow when a new message is received through the associated WCF endpoint. Every workflow service definition must have one Receive Activity that can create instances (CanCreateInstance = true), and that activity must be the first activity in the workflow.
KnownTypes	A collection of .NET types representing existing data contracts or primitive types that needs to be associated to the operation definition as known types. A *known type* is a type that should be included for consideration during the serialization/deserialization process of the send/received messages.
ProtectionLevel	The protection level requirement applied to the operation definition. As discussed in the security chapter, the only possible values for this property are None, Sign, and SignAndEncrypt.

continues

TABLE 6-1 *(continued)*

PROPERTY	DESCRIPTION
SerializerOption	The message serializer associated to the operation. The possible values for this property are `DataContractSerializer` and `XmlSerializer`. These serialization engines were discussed earlier in this chapter.
CorrelatesOn/ CorrelatesWith and CorrelationInitializers	These are properties for resolving and associating a correlation handler for the operation. Message correlation is discussed later in this chapter.

A single Receive Activity in a workflow service represents a one-way operation in the service contract unless you define a new SendReply Activity. It is tied to the Receive Activity to send a reply message with the results of the operation execution.

A SendReply Activity is not an activity that you can simply drag and drop from the toolbox to the workflow instance in the designer. It can only be created from an existing Receive Activity by selecting the option `Create SendReply` in the Receive Activity's context menu.

Figure 6-2 shows a SendReply Activity in action. It has been associated with a Receive Activity `ApplyForJobReceive` that represents an operation `ApplyForJob` and assigns the request message payload to the `JobApp` input variable. As you can see in the figure, the `SendReplyToReceive` Activity has been tied to the Receive Activity through the `Request` property, and the response message payload is a simple string value. In a real service implementation, you are also free to associate a variable to the `Content` property with a value computed during the workflow execution.

FIGURE 6-2: SendReply Activity in action

The equivalent WCF contract for the Receive Activity in Figure 6-2 should be the following:

```
[ServiceContract]
public interface IHRService
{
  [OperationContract]
  string ApplyForJob(JobApp application);
}
```

The content property also supports multiple parameters in case you do not want to assign the received message into a single variable. This is something that can be selected in the `Content` property window when using the workflow designer. Figure 6-3 illustrates a `Receive` operation with the input mapped to multiple arguments.

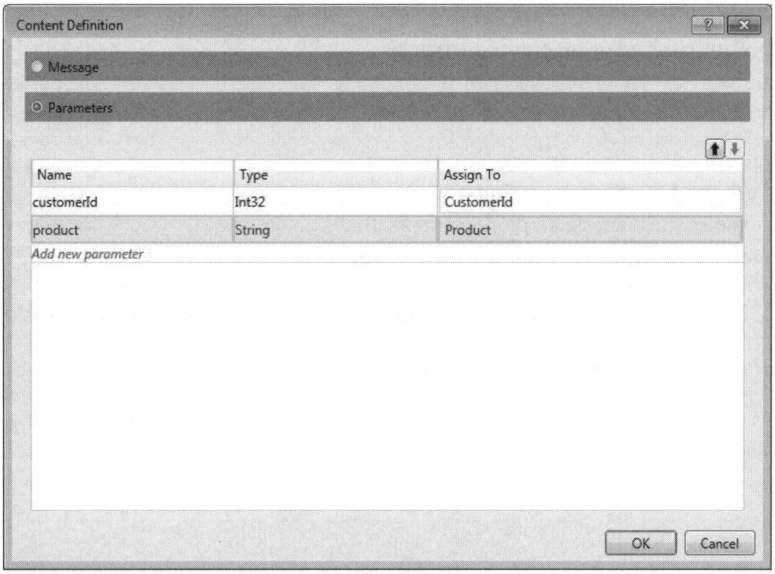

FIGURE 6-3: Receive operation with multiple arguments

> In case you are not familiar with the workflow model in WF 4.0, a variable
> represents a new way to pass values around in the workflow instance. As with
> any programming language, a variable is also associated to a scope, which
> basically determines where the variable can be read from and/or written to
> during its lifetime, or how long it stays in memory. Therefore, the sum of all
> variables in scope in a specific point of time determines the whole workflow state
> at that moment. This is a significant improvement in the way the workflows are
> persisted and loaded into memory from the persistence provider. The WF
> runtime engine can now perform some optimizations and only the variables in
> scope need to be considered for that purpose. In the past, the only way to share
> state between activities within a workflow was to define global variables with
> dependency properties in the workflow itself.

Send Activity

The Send Activity represents the flip side of the Receive Activity. The Receive Activity defines a
WCF entry point for receiving messages, and the Send Activity allows workflows to send messages
to the outside world to execute external WCF services, or send response messages with results of an
operation execution to a service consumer when it is tied to a `ReceiveReply` Activity.

In the same way a single Receive Activity represents a one-way operation in the service contract
by default, the Send Activity does not expect a response message unless it is associated with a
ReceiveReply Activity.

The ReceiveReply Activity is another activity that cannot be directly referenced in an activity toolbox and must be created from an existing Send Activity. You do so by selecting the option `Create ReceiveReply` in the Send Activity's context menu.

Figure 6-4 shows a ReceiveReply Activity in action. It has been associated with the Send Activity `Send` that represents an operation `SubmitOrder` and that gets the request message payload from the Order variable. As you can see in the figure, the `ReceiveReplyForSend` Activity has been tied to the Send Activity through the `Request` property, and the response message payload is returned in the `Result` variable.

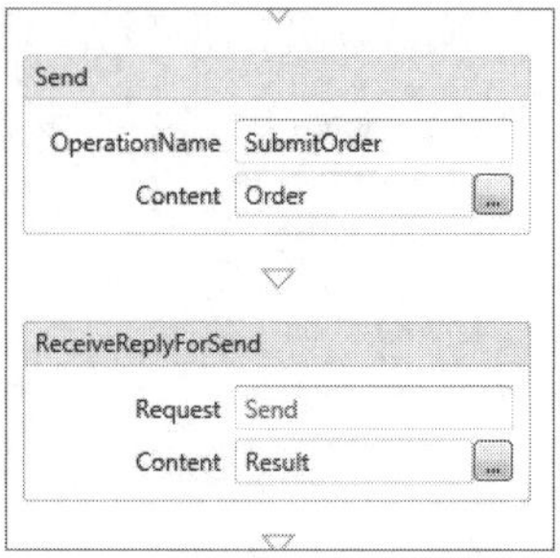

FIGURE 6-4: ReceiveReply Activity in action

Some of the properties that you find in the Send Activity are discussed in Table 6-2.

TABLE 6-2: Send Activity Properties

PROPERTY	DESCRIPTION
Endpoint	The definition of the endpoint that will be used to consume the service. This property is made of two parts, the endpoint address and the WCF binding. The endpoint address is a URI representing the address where the service is listening. The WCF binding is one of the built-in bindings used to set up the channel communication.
EndpointConfigurationName	The friendly name of an endpoint in the WCF configuration section. This property provides the flexibility of specifying all the endpoint settings such as address, binding, and behaviors in the file configuration section. You can either set the Endpoint or EndpointConfigurationName properties but not both.
EndpointAddress	A service endpoint address that overrides the address already defined in the `Endpoint` property or the WCF configuration section — if the `EndpointConfigurationName` property is used.
DisplayName	The friendly name that identifies the activity within the workflow. This name is also used to reference the activity from other activities, or relate this activity to a `ReceiveReply` to receive a service response.
ServiceContractName	The name of the WCF contract that is associated with the activity. The name chosen for this contract matters because it represents the service contract that the WF will use to consume the service. The contract name is made up of two parts, a namespace and the contract name, per se (e.g., `http://wcfbook/}myServiceContract`).

PROPERTY	DESCRIPTION
OperationName	The name of the WCF operation that is associated with the activity. The name of the operation is as important as the name of the contract for the same reasons discussed earlier — it is used to consume the service.
Content	A workflow variable that is mapped to the request message for executing the service's operation.
Action	The SOAP Action that is included in the To address header of the request message for executing the service's operation.
KnownTypes	A collection of .NET types representing existing data contracts or primitive types that needs to be associated with the operation definition as known types. A known type is a type that should be included for consideration during the serialization/deserialization process of the send/received messages.
ProtectionLevel	The protection level requirement that is applied to the operation definition. As was discussed in the security chapter, the only possible values for this property are None, Sign, and SignAndEncrypt.
SerializerOption	The message serializer associated with the operation. The possible values for this property are DataContractSerializer and XmlSerializer. Serialization engines were discussed earlier in this chapter.
CorrelatesWith and CorrelationInitializers	Properties for resolving and associating a correlation handler for the operation. Message correlation is discussed in detail later in this chapter.

The Assign Activity is useful for initializing a variable associated to the Content property of the Send Activity.

The Assign Activity is a new activity introduced in WF 4.0 to assign or initialize the value of a workflow variable. It is made up of two parts — a variable definition, which is assigned to the To property, and an expression to initialize that variable in the Value property.

The expressions for initializing the variable can be simple, such as a scalar value, or something more complex that involves functions or other variables already defined in the workflow. The complex expressions must be defined using VB, so you need to be familiar with that language to create them correctly.

For the example shown in Figure 6-4, the Send Activity uses an Order variable to execute the SubmitOrder operation. As that variable needs to be initialized before executing the operation, the Assign Activity can be used.

The following expression can be assigned to the `Order` variable:

```
Order  = New Order()
With {.ProductName = "foo", .Quantity = 10}
```

As you can see, the VB object initializer syntax has been used to create a new instance of the `Order` class, which represents a data contract in this example.

> *Is C# supported for creating expressions? The answer is no, and the main reason is timing. The VB team provides an in-memory parser for creating expressions within the WF 4.0 RTM timeframe.*

One of the limitations that you will find in the current version is a lack of support for specifying security client credentials through the Send Activity when the target service needs to authenticate the calling application/user. For most scenarios, you can do this through the WCF configuration section using bindings and behaviors. Windows, Certificates, and Issued token credentials can be configured that way, but unfortunately, username token credentials cannot. If that is the case, you will not able to consume the external service unless you create a custom extension or behavior to specify those credentials at runtime.

The Easy Way to Execute External Services

Another interesting feature in WF 4.0 that simplifies the development of workflow services significantly is the automatic generation of typed activities for consuming existing service references in the project. Whenever you add a new service reference in the workflow project, a set of new activities for consuming the service (one per operation) are automatically added to the Visual Studio toolbox. You can simply drag and drop one of those activities within a workflow and fill out all the required properties, such as input/output arguments, to execute service without worrying about the other details already discussed in the Send Activity. The benefits that you get for free by using this generated activity are evident:

➤ Typed properties for the input, and output parameters that the service operation associated to the activity is expecting and returning.

➤ All the details about the contracts exposed by the service are automatically inferred and included in the generated activities.

As recommended, you should always consider this alternative the easiest way to consume external services unless you need more granular control over the details of the WCF client contract or the endpoint settings.

The WCF contract and the XAML representation of activity generated for consuming the `Notify` operation in the contract are shown next:

```
[ServiceContract]
public interface IProductNotification
{
```

```
    [OperationContract]
    bool Notify(string product, int quantity);
}

<psa:Notify NotifyResult="[NotifyResult]" product="[PurchaseOrder.Product]"
quantity="[PurchaseOrder.Quantity]" />
```

SendAndReceiveReply and ReceiveAndSendReply Activities

SendAndReceiveReply and ReceiveAndSendReply were introduced to simplify the definition of request/response operations.

These are equivalent to using a combination of Send/ReceiveReply and Receive/SendReply Activities respectively, with a slight difference, as they are wrapped with a Sequence Activity. That sequence activity, in addition to being an organizational unit, also defines a variable scope that you can optionally use for new variable definitions.

IMPLEMENTING YOUR FIRST WORKFLOW SERVICE

You have seen some introductory theories behind workflow services and the messaging activities that can be used in this kind of service to receive messages or invoke external services. It is now time to jump into a more concrete example to see a workflow service in action.

This example represents the implementation of a service for entering purchase orders into a system. For practical purposes, this service will also invoke an external service for every received order.

Let's start creating a C# class library for including the definition of the contract and implementation of the external service invoked within the workflow service. The implementation is simple enough: it receives the product that was ordered, the quantity associated to the order, and returns a Boolean value specifying the success of the operation. See Listing 6-2.

LISTING 6-2: Contract and Implementation of the Notification Service

```
[ServiceContract]
public interface IProductNotification
{
  [OperationContract]
  bool Notify(string product, int quantity);
}

public class ProductNotification : IProductNotification
{
  public bool Notify(string product, int quantity)
  {
    return true;
  }
}
```

Now that you have the external service implementation, you can focus on the implementation of the first workflow service.

Visual Studio 2010 provides a template WCF Workflow Service Application under the Workflow category, which you can use to create workflow services from scratch. When that template is selected and executed, a new web project is generated with a sample workflow service definition that includes a pair of Receive/Send Activities. Start the implementation of your workflow service by removing those activities.

This service will initially receive a purchase order as it is defined in the `PurchaseOrder` data contract (see Listing 6-3) through a new Receive Activity that you need to create in the workflow. This activity basically represents the initial entry point for the service.

LISTING 6-3: Purchase Order Data Contract

```
[DataContract]
public class PurchaseOrder
{
   [DataMember]
   public string Customer { get; set; }

   [DataMember]
   public string Product { get; set; }

   [DataMember]
   public int Quantity { get; set; }

   [DataMember]
   public decimal UnitPrice { get; set; }
}
```

You should set the Receive Activity properties with the values specified in Table 6-3.

TABLE 6-3: SubmitPOReceive Activity Properties

PROPERTY	VALUE
DisplayName	SubmitPOReceive
OperationName	SubmitPO
ServiceContractName	{http://wcfbook/}IPurchaseOrder
CanCreateInstance	True
Content (Message Data)	PurchaseOrder

Leave the rest of the properties with the default values. The designer will complain that the `PurchaseOrder` variable is not defined, and that is exactly what you do next.

The variables can be defined for a workflow instance in the Variables tab, which usually appears at the bottom margin of the designer. A variable definition is made of three parts: a name, a type, and a scope. The variables, as in any language, are referenced by name, and the type is any valid CLR type shipped as part of the framework or a type created for you. In this case, you define a variable called `PurchaseOrder` whose type is `PurchaseOrder` (a data contract defined in another project) and is scoped to the current workflow service (Sequential workflow service). As you can see, you have a single data contract parameter to receive all the information, so `Message Data` is just fine for that purpose. In case you want to support multiple arguments in the operation signature, you need to use parameters and assign them to the corresponding variables or use VB expressions to do more complex assignments.

The workflow is now ready to start receiving messages containing the purchase order information through the operation `SubmitPO`. As you haven't defined a SendReply Activity, this operation momentarily behaves as one-way.

The next step is to invoke the `ProductNotification` service for every receive order. The easy way to include that service call in the existing workflow is to use the automatic generated activity. The only thing to do is add a service reference for `ProductNotification` as illustrated in Figure 6-5.

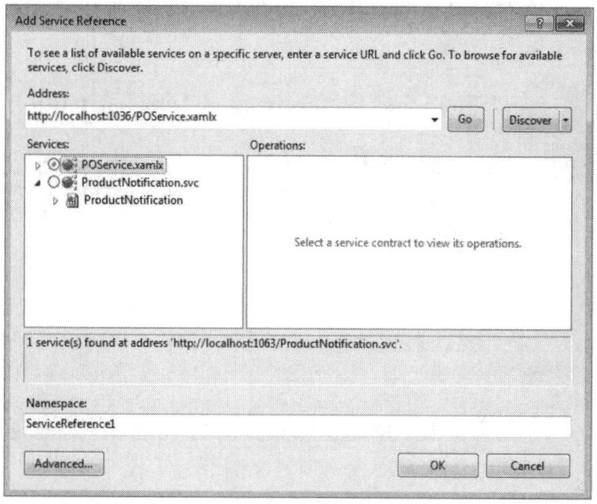

FIGURE 6-5: Service Reference added

When the reference is added to the project, you should be able to see a new activity called Notify with a public interface that resembles the Notify operation in the `IProductNotify` contract. It has two public properties for setting the product and quantity respectively, and a third property for getting access to the operation return value.

You can drag and drop that activity after the Receive Activity and fill out the properties with the values in Table 6-4.

TABLE 6-4: Notify Properties

PROPERTY	VALUE
NotifyResult	NotifyResult
Product	PurchaseOrder.Product
Quantity	PurchaseOrder.Quantity

`NotifyResult` is a new Boolean variable that needs to be defined to receive the result of the operation. The `Product` and `Quantity` input arguments are initialized from the existing variable `PurchaseOrder` by using expressions.

Last but not least, you need to create a new SendReply Activity from the `SubmitPOReceive` Receive Activity to send the results back to the client. The only thing needed is to set up this activity in the `Content` property to use `Message data` and `True` as value, so it will basically return a value indicating the operation was executed successfully.

At this point, the workflow service is ready to use, and any client can access the service WSDL by browsing the POService.xamlx file directly in the corresponding web host (IIS virtual directory or Visual Studio web server). This means that the service behaves as any other WCF service from the point of view of a client application, and a tool such as svcutil can be used to generate the proxy classes to consume it. (See Listing 6-4.)

LISTING 6-4: Code Required for Consuming the Workflow Service

```
PurchaseOrderClient client = new PurchaseOrderClient();
bool? result = client.SubmitPO(new ServiceReference.PurchaseOrder
{
  Customer = "John BarFoo",
  Product = "myproduct",
  Quantity = 10,
  UnitPrice = 1
});

Console.WriteLine(result.GetValueOrDefault());
```

CONFIGURING A WORKFLOW SERVICE

As with any traditional WCF service, you can separate the configuration of a workflow service from the service implementation by defining it either in an app.config for self-hosted services or a web .config for IIS-hosted services. The connection between the workflow service implementation and the corresponding service configuration in the configuration file is specified in the `ConfigurationName` attribute — which maps to the config's service element's name attribute. With this link in place, a workflow service is configured in exactly the same fashion as a traditional WCF service using the service model configuration section. The following text shows how the `ConfigurationName` "MyService" is mapped to the corresponding service configuration section:

```
<WorkflowService mc:Ignorable="sap" ConfigurationName="MyService"
Name="MyService"..>
</WorkflowService>

<system.serviceModel>
    <services>
      <service name="MyService" behaviorConfiguration="myService" >
        <endpoint binding="basicHttpBinding"
                  bindingConfiguration="myService"
                  contract="IService"></endpoint>
      </service>
    </services>
    <bindings>
```

```
        <basicHttpBinding>
          <binding name="myService">
            <security mode="None"></security>
          </binding>
        </basicHttpBinding>
      </bindings>
      <behaviors>
        <serviceBehaviors>
          <behavior name="myService">
            <serviceMetadata httpGetEnabled="true"/>
          </behavior>
        </serviceBehaviors>
      </behaviors>
    </system.serviceModel>
```

The contract name that you need to configure for the service endpoint must match one of the contract names specified in the workflow Receive Activities. For this example, one of the Receive Activities in the workflow has the value `{[namespace]}IService` for the `ServiceContractName` property.

You can still use the new configuration improvements in a workflow service. In fact, the Visual Studio template for workflow services automatically includes a configuration file that only overrides a few default WCF configuration settings to enable the service metadata endpoint and disable the `includeExceptionDetailsInFault` setting:

```
<system.serviceModel>
    <behaviors>
      <serviceBehaviors>
        <behavior>
          <!-- To avoid disclosing metadata information,
set the value below to false and remove the metadata endpoint
above before deployment -->
          <serviceMetadata httpGetEnabled="true"/>
          <!-- To receive exception details in faults for debugging purposes,
set the value below to true.  Set to false before deployment to avoid
disclosing exception information -->
          <serviceDebug includeExceptionDetailInFaults="false"/>
        </behavior>
      </serviceBehaviors>
    </behaviors>
</system.serviceModel>
```

WF Runtime Settings

In addition to the bindings and service settings that you need to configure to expose the service, WF 4.0 provides a set of built-in behaviors to initialize or override some of the WF runtime settings. The most important details about each one of these behaviors is addressed in this section.

WorkflowIdle Service Behavior

This behavior, as its name suggests, gives you control over when idle workflow instances are persisted and unloaded from memory. It contains two properties, `TimeToPersist` and

`TimeToUnload`, that accept a period of time representing the timeout for performing the operations with the same name, persist, and unload the instances. The following example shows how to configure the runtime to persist the idle workflow instances every 10 seconds, and unload them from memory after one minute:

```
<workflowIdle timeToPersist="00:00:10" timeToUnload="00:01:00"/>
```

SqlWorkflowInstanceStore Service Behavior

WF 4.0 comes with a persistence provider out of the box called `SqlWorkflowInstanceStore`, which derives from the abstract class `System.Runtime.Persistence.InstanceStore`, and implements all the abstract methods to save the workflow data in either SQL Server 2005 or 2008. By using this behavior, you can change some of the default settings for this provider like the connection string or whether the instance should be removed from the database after its completion, to name others.

The following example illustrates how the connection string can be configured for this persistence provider.

```
<behaviors>
  <serviceBehaviors>
    <behavior name="ServiceBehavior">
      <sqlWorkflowInstanceStore
        connectionString="Data Source=.\SQLExpress;Initial
        Catalog=WorkflowInstanceStore;Integrated Security=True">
      </sqlWorkflowInstanceStore>
    </behavior>
  </serviceBehaviors>
</behaviors>
```

The SQL scripts for creating the database schema and some store procedures required by this instance provider are available in the .NET framework installation folder (e.g., C:\Windows\Microsoft.NET\Framework\v4.0.21006\SQL\en). The two scripts you need are SqlWorkflowInstanceStoreSchema.sql and SqlWorkflowInstanceStoreLogic.sql.

WorkflowUnhandledException Service Behavior

This behavior enables you to change the action taken by the runtime when an unhandled exception occurs within a running instance. By default, the runtime will leave the instance in the `Abandon` state. Some other possible values for this action are `Cancel`, `Terminate` or `AbandonAndSuspend`.

While the service host will abort the workflow service instance in memory in all cases, only an instance with state `Abandon` or `AbandonAndSuspended` can be resumed later. In addition, when a workflow is `cancelled`, all the cancellation handlers associated to the instance are invoked so it can be terminated in a graceful manner.

WorkflowRuntime Service Behavior

The WorkflowRuntime service behavior allows changing some specific settings in workflow runtime that is used for hosting the workflow services. This behavior also represents a way to additional services into the runtime that the workflow instances can use. Some of the attributes you can find in this behavior are summarized in Table 6-5.

TABLE 6-5: WorkflowRuntime Settings

SETTING	DESCRIPTION
CachedInstanceExpiration	An optional setting that specifies the maximum period of time a workflow instance can stay in memory in idle state before it is forcefully unloaded or aborted.
EnablePerformanceCounters	Another optional setting that specifies whether performance counters are enabled. As happen with performance counters, they provide useful information on various workflow-related statistics, but they cause a performance penalty when the workflow runtime engine starts, and when workflow instances are running.
ValidateOnCreate	A Boolean setting that specifies whether validation of workflow definition will occur when the `WorkflowServiceHost` is opened. It is enabled by default, so the workflow validation is executed every time `WorkflowServiceHost.Open` is called. In case a validation is found, a `WorkflowValidationFailedException` error is thrown.

The following configuration fragment illustrates how some of the settings can be changed for this behavior.

```
<behaviors>
  <serviceBehaviors>
    <behavior name="ServiceBehavior">
      <workflowRuntime name="WorkflowServiceHostRuntime"
                  validateOnCreate="true"
                  enablePerformanceCounters="true">
        <services>
        </services>
      </workflowRuntime>
    </behavior>
  </serviceBehaviors>
</behaviors>
```

IMPLEMENTING MESSAGE CORRELATION

As discussed earlier in this chapter, long-running processes represent a common scenario for workflow services. In this kind of process, an execution is usually made up of multiple execution sequences which may last many days or even weeks. They might involve clients that connect to the service, perform work, transition the workflow to a new state, and then disconnect for an indeterminate amount of time before connecting again for workflow execution. This kind of execution generates questions that need to be addressed when a message leaves a workflow instance, and then another message returns later in the same flow. How does that message know which returning workflow instance to come back to? What if there are thousands of these workflow instances running at a single point in time? For this, WF has correlation, which means that you can specify a set of attributes for a given message that the runtime will use to route the message to the appropriate running workflow instance.

A correlation attribute in this context might be as simple as a unique identifier. It might be more complex, such as a composite key made up of business concepts — a customer identifier or a purchase order number.

The correlation story in WF 3.5 was solved by involving the client applications. Basically, when the first operation that created your workflow instance succeeded, a header or a cookie was attached to the outgoing message containing a workflow instance identifier (consider this the workflow instance primary key). It was the client's responsibility to keep this identifier around and attach it to the messages for executing successive operations in the same workflow instance. As you can see, this got a bit tricky, as the client needed to know some of the implementation details of the services. If the client did not know that an identifier must be obtained from the reply message and used again for the next call, nothing worked.

This is not a big deal if you were developing both the client and the service, but if the client was developed by a third party, it certainly becomes more complex.

Ideally you want the message in the second service operation to have a key value with which you can get the workflow instance back (a correlation attribute). Fortunately, the WF team has included a way to route messages to a workflow instance in a feature called *content-based correlation*.

In this section, the correlation techniques are addressed — the old technique based on the use of a unique identifier or context-based correlation, and the new one based on the use of keys in the message content itself.

Correlation in Action

The correlation mechanisms are based on the use of a few new properties, `CorrelatesOn`, `CorrelatesWith`, and `CorrelationInitializers`, which were previously discussed in the Receive and Send Activities.

The correlation mechanisms work by defining one or more correlation handlers, represented in the workflow as simple variables of the type `CorrelationHandler` — which can be associated to a messaging activity and are initialized according to the strategy specified in the `CorrelationInitializer` function. The WF runtime uses these correlation handlers to determine to which workflow instance the incoming messages should be routed.

The correlation initializer function determines the protocol that the runtime uses for initializing the correlation handlers. Some possible values for this function are `Context correlation initializer`, for context-based routing; `Request-Reply correlation initializer`, for correlating a pair of request and response messages within the same channel; or `Query correlation initializer`, for content-based routing. For example, `Query correlation initializer` also requires an expression that when applied to messages can determine the initial value for the correlation handler.

The other two properties, `CorrelatesOn` and `CorrelatesWith`, are only useful for content-based routing and are discussed in detail in the next sections.

Context-Based Correlation

This context correlation mechanism uses a message protocol for passing the routing information between the client and the workflow service. This information minimally contains a unique identifier also known as instance ID, which is initially generated when a workflow instance is created and sent back to the client on the first message exchange. It is the responsibility of the client application to include this information in all subsequent requests to the same workflow service instance. There are some complex scenarios where a workflow might expect the same message in multiple Receive Activities simultaneously. For those scenarios, the instance identifier is simply not enough, as something else is needed to route the messages to the correct Receive Activity within the workflow — a conversation identifier. Both the `instanceID` and the `conversationID` identifiers can be included as part of the context information.

The implementation of this context exchange protocol in WCF can use either `HttpCookie` or `SOAPHeader` to propagate the context between the service and the client. This protocol is internally implemented through a custom channel that communicates the context to and from the application layer using a `ContextMessageProperty` property.

The value of this property is either serialized as a SOAP header or as a cookie in the Http header before the messages are transmitted over the wire. WCF also ships with a specific binding element `ContextBindingElement` where the purpose is to inject the channel into the WCF channel layer. This binding element exposes a public property `ContextExchangeMechanism` that only accepts two values — `HttpCookie` or `SOAPHeader` — for choosing the serialization mechanism.

An application doesn't usually use binding elements directly, as they are often wrapped in high-level bindings. This is also the case for this content binding element, as WCF provides a set of specific bindings known as context bindings, which hide the underlying details about the context exchange mechanism from the applications.

Table 6-6 shows a list of available context bindings.

TABLE 6-6: Context Bindings

BINDING	DESCRIPTION
`BasicHttpContextBinding`	A variation of `BasicHttpBinding` which supports the context exchange protocol using cookies over http.
`WsHttpContextBinding`	A variation of the `WsHttpContextBinding` that supports the context exchange protocol using either SOAP headers or cookies over http.
`NetTcpContextBinding`	A variation of the `NetTcpContextBinding` that supports the context exchange protocol using SOAP headers over Tcp.

In Table 6-6, you might wonder why `NetMsmqBinding` is missing. `NetMsmqBinding` provides one-way reliable/durable messaging capabilities to a workflow service. However, `ContextBindingElement` requires a channel with an `IReplyChannel` interface and `NetMsmqBinding` actually implements an `IInputChannel` or an `IOutputChannel`. Which one actually depends on whether you are the client or the service. If you think about the way the context exchange mechanism works in workflow services, this restriction makes sense. The `ReceiveActivity` that creates the workflow instance is called without a context, and the context identifier that represents the workflow instance is returned as part of the response messages. Therefore, this protocol leaves out all the one-way messaging implementations, and thereby leaves out `NetMmsqBinding`.

Let's examine how a workflow service with context-based correlation works in action with a concrete example.

Step 1: Implementing the Workflow Service

The workflow service used in this example is made of two Receive Activities — the first activity receives a purchase order, and the second one confirms that order.

The first Receive Activity, which represents the entry point in the service, initially receives a purchase order as it is defined in the data contract `Purchase Order` (see Listing 6-5).

LISTING 6-5: Purchase Order Data Contract

```
[DataContract]
public class PurchaseOrder
{
  [DataMember]
  public string Customer { get; set; }

  [DataMember]
  public string Product { get; set; }

  [DataMember]
  public int Quantity { get; set; }

  [DataMember]
  public decimal UnitPrice { get; set; }
}
```

Set the Receive Activity properties with the values specified in Table 6-7.

TABLE 6-7: SubmitPOReceive Activity Properties

PROPERTY	VALUE
DisplayName	SubmitPOReceive
OperationName	SubmitPO
ServiceContractName	{http://wcfbook/}IService
CanCreateInstance	True
Content (Message Data)	PurchaseOrder

Leave the rest of the properties with the default values, and define a new variable PurchaseOrder to receive the request message payload.

Your workflow is now ready to start receiving messages containing the purchase order information through the operation SubmitPO. Because you haven't yet defined a SendReply Activity, this operation momentarily behaves as a one-way.

The next thing you can do is use an Assign Activity to automatically create a new purchase order identifier (something that you keep in the workflow state as a variable). So, you can define a new variable PONumber of type String, and use the following expression in the Assign Activity to initialize PONumber = 1. (You can later change this routine to dynamically assign new numbers.)

After you have the purchase order number, you can create a SendReply Activity from the SubmitPOReceive Receive Activity to send the content of the PONumber variable back to the client. To accomplish that, you need to set up the Content property to use Message data and PONumber as value, so it will return the generated purchase order number.

As you use context-based routing, the context initializer for the Receive Activity should be set to Context correlation initializer. You can associate this function to the correlation handler __handle1, which is created by default with the Visual Studio template.

You have created a service with a single operation for generating purchase orders in the system. You can now move forward with the next operation for confirming the purchase order. A new pair of Receive and SendReply Activities is required to implement this operation.

You should initialize this new Receive Activity with the values discussed in Table 6-8.

TABLE 6-8: ConfirmPOReceive Activity Properties

PROPERTY	VALUE
DisplayName	ConfirmPOReceive
OperationName	ConfirmPO
ServiceContractName	{http://wcfbook/}IService
CanCreateInstance	False

This activity does not receive any payload, as you do not need anything extra to confirm the purchase order. You already have the information as part of the workflow state. You also might notice that the CanCreateInstance property is set to false, to reuse an existing workflow instance.

The SendReply Activity for this operation sends a response back to the client providing information about the result of the purchase order confirmation. The following expression assigned to the Content property is enough for that purpose: "The purchase order" + PONumber.ToString() + "was confirmed."

Step 2: Configuring the Workflow Service

The next step is to configure the service workflow you created to use one of the available context bindings. For the sake of simplicity, use a `BasicHttpContextBinding` example. As we discussed in the "Configuring a Workflow Service" section, the name of the workflow service is what matters for referencing it in the configuration.

Assuming that you named Service to your workflow service, code Listing 6-6 shows the resulting configuration with the context binding.

LISTING 6-6: Service Configuration with Context Binding

```
<services>
  <service name="Service">
    <endpoint binding="basicHttpContextBinding"
        bindingConfiguration="myService"
        contract="IService"></endpoint>
  </service>
</services>
<bindings>
  <basicHttpContextBinding>
    <binding name="myService" contextManagementEnabled="true"></binding>
  </basicHttpContextBinding>
</bindings>
```

The `contextManagementEnabled` setting specifies that your workflow will use the context exchange protocol to receive the instance and conversation identifiers for correlating messages.

Step 3: Implementing the Client Application

One of the major drawbacks of using the context exchange protocol is that the client needs to be aware of internal details about the service implementation. WCF provides a specific interface named `System.ServiceModel.Channels.IContextManager` with the corresponding concrete implementation `System.ServiceModel.Channels.ContextManager`, which automatically handles most of the details for you at channel level. This class can only be used when one of the context bindings has been configured, and it represents the main entry point for setting the context information — a scenario with a simple string representing the workflow instance identifier.

Code Listing 6-7 shows the general pattern a client application can use to get the initial instance identifier, and passes that identifier in subsequent calls to the service.

LISTING 6-7: Purchase Order Data Contract

```
static void Main(string[] args)
{
    string instanceId;

    string poNumber = SubmitPO(out instanceId);

    Console.WriteLine("The PO Number is {0}", poNumber);
```

```
    string message = ConfirmPO(instanceId);

    Console.WriteLine(message);
  }

  private static string SubmitPO(out string instanceId)
  {
    PurchaseOrder po = new PurchaseOrder
    {
      Customer = "Foo Bar",
      Product = "Product",
      Quantity = 10,
      UnitPrice = 5
    };

    ServiceClient client = new ServiceClient();

    string poNumber = client.SubmitPO(po);

    IContextManager contextManager =
      client.InnerChannel.GetProperty<IContextManager>();
    IDictionary<string, string> context = contextManager.GetContext();

    instanceId = context["instanceId"];

    return poNumber;
  }

  private static string ConfirmPO(string instanceId)
  {
    ServiceClient client = new ServiceClient();

    Dictionary<string, string> context = new Dictionary<string, string>();

    context.Add("instanceId", instanceId);

    IContextManager contextManager =
      client.InnerChannel.GetProperty<IContextManager>();

    contextManager.SetContext(context);

    return client.ConfirmPO();
  }
```

In the first method SubmitPO, a new purchase order is submitted to the service using an operation with the same name, and the instance identifier is retrieved from the channel thanks to the help of the context manager. The second method ConfirmPO receives the instance identifier as input argument, and invokes the service operation for confirming the order by passing that identifier through the context manager. Note that the purchase order identifier was not passed at all to the service because the order itself is stored as part of the workflow state. The service does not need to perform additional lookups in the ConfirmPO operation to retrieve the purchase order from storage — such as you would with a traditional service.

Step 4: Configuring the Client Application

The client needs to be configured with the same binding settings that were set on the service side.

For this example, your binding configuration is shown in code Listing 6-8.

LISTING 6-8: Client Configuration with Context Binding

```
<client>
  <endpoint address="http://localhost:1219/Service.xamlx"
    binding="basicHttpContextBinding"
    bindingConfiguration="myService" contract="ServiceReference.IService"
    name="BasicHttpContextBinding_IService" />
</client>
<bindings>
  <basicHttpContextBinding>
    <binding name="myService" contextManagementEnabled="true" />
  </basicHttpContextBinding>
</bindings>
```

Content-Based Correlation

Content-based correlation is a new mechanism introduced in WF 4.0 for routing messages to an existing workflow instance based on evidence presented in the messages itself — such as an order number or customer identifier, rather than contextual information as the one used by the context bindings. As you can imagine, the advantages of using this new routing technique are quite evident and simplify the workflow development and configuration:

➤ The internal details of the service implementation are not revealed to the external consumer or client applications because the dependency with the context exchange protocol is totally removed.

➤ As the context bindings are not required and the routing information travels with the message itself, this technique is suitable for more scenarios than traditional context-based routing. For instance, scenarios that require the use of reliable/durable messaging capabilities can be used with this routing technique.

This correlation mechanism requires the use of a *Query correlation initializer function*, which is associated with any available messaging activities. It is used for initializing a correlation handler with an XPath expression that is applied over the incoming or outgoing messages.

When a correlation handler is initialized, you can associate it to another Receive Activity thanks to the use of the `CorrelatesWith` and `CorrelatesOn` properties. The `CorrelatesWith` property accepts the correlation handler variable, and the `CorrelatesOn` property allows the specification of a new XPath expression to get one or more values from the incoming message associated with the activity.

The WF runtime knows how to route the messages to the proper instance by matching the value from the XPath expression set in the `CorrelatesOn` property with the value already associated with the correlation handler (which was previously initialized in another Receive Activity with the `CorrelationInitializers` property).

The same example seen previously is discussed with context correlation, but is now using content-based correlation.

Step 1: Implementing the Workflow Service

As the previous example discussed, you use the same Receive Activities — the first activity for receiving a purchase order, and the second one for confirming it.

The first Receive Activity, which represents the entry point in the service, initially receives a purchase order as it is defined in the data contract Purchase Order (see Listing 6-9).

Available for download on Wrox.com

LISTING 6-9: Purchase Order Data Contract

```
[DataContract]
public class PurchaseOrder
{
    [DataMember]
    public string Customer { get; set; }

    [DataMember]
    public string Product { get; set; }

    [DataMember]
    public int Quantity { get; set; }

    [DataMember]
    public decimal UnitPrice { get; set; }
}
```

The first Receive Activity must be initialized with the properties specified in Table 6-9.

TABLE 6-9: SubmitPOReceive Activity Properties

PROPERTY	VALUE
DisplayName	SubmitPOReceive
OperationName	SubmitPO
ServiceContractName	{http://wcfbook/}IService
CanCreateInstance	True
Content (Message Data)	PurchaseOrder

Leave the rest of the properties with the default values, and define a new variable `PurchaseOrder` to receive the request message payload.

The next thing you can do is use an Assign Activity to automatically create a new purchase order identifier (something that is in the workflow state as a variable). So, you can define a new variable

PurchaseOrderId of type String, and use the following expression in the Assign Activity to initialize it: PurchaseOrderId = System.Guid.NewGuid().ToString(). That expression initializes the PurchaseOrderId with an autogenerated Guid identifier to make sure it is unique.

Your workflow is now ready to receive messages containing the purchase order information through the operation SubmitPO. As you haven't yet defined a SendReply Activity, this operation momentarily behaves as a one-way.

After you have the purchase order number, you can create a SendReply Activity from the SubmitPOReceive Receive Activity to send the content of the PurchaseOrderId variable back to the client. To accomplish this, you need to set up the Content property to use Message data and PurchaseOrderId as value, so it will return the generated purchase order number.

At this point, you also need to define the CorrelationInitializers property for this SendReply Activity to use an existing correlation handle variable (you can use __handle1, which is a variable created out of the box by the Visual Studio template), a Query correlation initializer function and the PurchaseOrderId variable that you assigned to the activity content. (The designer will automatically set the XPath expression for you, which looks like this: sm:body()/xgSc: SubmitPOResponse/xgSc:PONumber.) The purchase order identifier is used to correlate subsequent messages that the client sends to the workflow service.

So far you have created a service with a single operation for generating purchase orders in the system. You can now move forward with the next operation to confirm the purchase order. A new pair of Receive and SendReply Activities is required to implement this operation.

Initialize the new Receive Activity with the values discussed in Table 6-10.

TABLE 6-10: ConfirmPOReceive Activity Properties

PROPERTY	VALUE
DisplayName	ConfirmPOReceive
OperationName	ConfirmPO
ServiceContractName	{http://wcfbook/}IService
CanCreateInstance	False
Content(Parameters)	A new parameter PurchaseOrderId of type String. Map this parameter to the existing variable with the same name.

As this activity cannot create instances, you need to define the CorrelatesWith and CorrelatesOn properties so the WF runtime can use them to route the messages to the correct workflow instance.

CorrelatesWith should be initialized with the correlation handler variable that was already specified in the SubmitPO Receive Activity (for example, __handle1). The other property, CorrelatesOn, can be initialized with the parameter PurchaseOrderId (again, the designer will infer the XPath expression automatically).

The SendReply Activity for this operation sends a response back to the client providing information about the result of the purchase order confirmation. The following expression assigned to the Content property is enough for that purpose: `"The purchase order " + PurchaseOrderId .ToString() + " was confirmed."`

Step 2: Configuring the Workflow Service

The main difference with the context-based routing example is that it does not require any specific binding configuration for this one, so you can use the default WCF configuration settings that the Visual Studio template automatically generates for you.

Step 3: Implementing the Client Application

The advantage of using content-based routing is that all the service implementation details are totally hidden from the client application — as should happen with any regular service according to the four service tenets of service orientation. Therefore, you can use the traditional WCF proxy classes for consuming the service, and no extra code or configuration is required for specifying the routing information.

Code Listing 6-10 shows a basic implementation of a client application that consumes your workflow service.

LISTING 6-10: Purchase Order Data Contract

```
static void Main(string[] args)
{
  string purchaseOrderId = SubmitPO();

  Console.WriteLine("The PO Number {0} was submitted", purchaseOrderId);

  string message = ConfirmPO(purchaseOrderId);

  Console.WriteLine(message);

}

private static string SubmitPO()
{
  PurchaseOrder po = new PurchaseOrder
  {
    Customer = "Foo Bar",
    Product = "Product",
    Quantity = 10,
    UnitPrice = 5
  };

  ServiceClient client = new ServiceClient();

  SubmitPOResponse response = client.SubmitPO(po);

  return response.PurchaseOrderId;
}
```

continues

LISTING 6-10 *(continued)*

```
private static string ConfirmPO(string purchaseOrderId)
{
  ServiceClient client = new ServiceClient();

  return client.ConfirmPO(new ConfirmPO { PurchaseOrderId = purchaseOrderId });
}
```

In the first method SubmitPO, a new purchase order is submitted to the service using an operation with the same name, and the purchase order identifier is obtained from the response. The second method ConfirmPO receives the purchase order identifier as an input argument, and invokes the service operation for confirming the order by passing that identifier into the request message. As you can see, all the complexities associated with the context management protocol have been completely removed from the client application, which is a great thing.

> *Message correlation is not the only kind of correlation you will find in WF. As you might guess, WF also needs to support correlation for sharing a WCF channel between Send and Receive activities. And although this type of correlation is explicitly handled by the designer, you must be aware of its existence to use in code workflows. When you create a SendReply activity from an existing Receive activity, or do the same with the ReceiveReply and Send activities, the designer automatically sets a link between the activities through a* Request-Reply Correlation Initializer *function.*

HOSTING THE WORKFLOW SERVICES

The hosting experience for workflow services has also been improved in WF 4.0 with the addition of a native ability to host, support, and maintain .xamlx files (the extension used by workflow services, which is equivalent to .svc for regular services) in IIS and the application server extensions known as Windows AppFabric.

A .xamlx file basically contains all the workflow implementation and configuration in terms of XAML. The experience of hosting a .xamlx is nearly identical to hosting a .svc, as the virtual directory only needs to contain this file, the service configuration in the web.config file, and a bin directory with all the assemblies that the service depends on.

As happens with any application that uses the ServiceHost class for hosting regular WCFs services in a standalone process outside of IIS, there is an equivalent class for doing the same with workflow services — the WorkflowServiceHost class. This class derives from the System. ServiceModel.ServiceHostBase and is responsible for extending the WCF runtime model with all the extensions that the workflow services depend on.

The WorkflowServiceHost provides three overloaded constructors for providing the definition of the workflow service that is hosted:

```
public WorkflowServiceHost(WorkflowService serviceDefinition,
params Uri[] baseAddresses);

public WorkflowServiceHost(Activity activity, params Uri[] baseAddresses);

public WorkflowServiceHost(object serviceObject, params Uri[] baseAddresses);
```

The first constructor receives an instance of a `System.ServiceModel.Activities.WorkflowService` class, which represents the workflow definition itself. Using this new class, you can create, configure, and gain access to all the properties of a workflow service. The other two constructors create and initialize a new `WorkflowService` instance using either a `System.Activities.Activity` (which represents the root activity in the service), or an object (which can be either a `WorkflowService` or Activity instance).

After you have the workflow definition, you can configure the WCF runtime just as you would with any other service using either code or configuration. This allows you to add endpoints or behaviors to the runtime or modify the service description. For example, for adding new service endpoints, you can use either the `WorkflowService.Endpoints` collection as it is shown in the following code or the `AddServiceEndpoint` method directly on the `WorkflowServiceHost` instance — the traditional way to do it with regular WCF services:

```
var service = new WorkflowService();
service.Name = "HelloWorldService";
service.Body = CreateWorkflow();

var endpoint = new Endpoint
{
  AddressUri = new Uri("HelloWorld", UriKind.Relative),
  Binding = new BasicHttpBinding(),
  Name = "HelloWorldService",
  ServiceContractName = "HelloWorldService",
};

service.Endpoints.Add(endpoint);
```

The `WorkflowServiceHost` class also provides a property `DurableInstancingOptions` for configuring the persistence provider that is used by the workflow runtime. Using this property you can change the default `InstanceStore` by the one that persists the workflow instances in a SQL server database (`SqlWorkflowInstanceStore`). This can be accomplished with a few lines of code as is shown here:

```
var host = new WorkflowServiceHost(workflow, baseAddress);
 var connStr =
@"Data Source=.;Initial Catalog=WorkflowInstanceStore;Integrated Security=True";
var instanceStore = new SqlWorkflowInstanceStore(connStr);
host.DurableInstancingOptions.InstanceStore = instanceStore;
```

7

Understanding WCF Security

WHAT'S IN THIS CHAPTER?

➤ Understanding the service security principles

➤ Getting started with WCF security

Security is a critical piece of any programming technology or framework for implementing service-oriented applications.

As you will see throughout this chapter, WCF has been built from the ground up for providing the necessary security infrastructure at the message and service level. In that sense, WCF provides a versatile extensibility model for security that allows developers to customize a large variety of runtime capabilities. The flexibility of incorporating extensions in the security subsystems has made it possible for WCF to support many of the existing security schemas and scenarios used to secure services. Many of the features that WCF provides in this area are covered, as well as some common deployment scenarios you might need while developing service-oriented applications with this technology. You also explore many of the core concepts involved in web service security. By having a previous understanding of these concepts, your learning curve for understanding and taking advantage of the available security features in WCF is more direct.

THE EVOLUTION OF SECURITY IN WEB SERVICES

Security has always been a strong requirement for web services in the enterprise. There is no doubt that security and interoperability are two key contributors in the adoption and success of web services for developing distributed applications in the enterprise.

When the first generation of web services was released in the late nineties, SOAP did not provide a secure message from tampering, nor was there a way to encrypt the messages to provide confidentiality. All the security details were delegated to the transport layer, which was Http at that time. In that way, many of the existing Http/Https security capabilities were leveraged for authenticating clients and securing messages. For example, sending SOAP messages through Https would guarantee confidentiality.

However, relying on the transport layer for proving these security capabilities tied the initial web service implementations to the transport layer, resulting in a big impediment in making SOAP totally independent of the platform.

As the enterprise started demanding more features for the web services, a new generation was born under the umbrella of what was called the WS-* specifications.

WS-*, also known as *web services specifications*, represents a set of protocols and specifications created in combination with big leaders in the industry such as Microsoft, IBM, VeriSign, and SUN among others. It leverages the existing messaging web services capabilities using extensions to the initial SOAP specification.

Back to security, one of most relevant specifications released as part of the WS-* specifications was WS-Security.

Initially released on April 19, 2004, this specification included a new model for securing web services at message level, extending the existing SOAP specification with security capabilities for client authentication and message protection.

A time after the first WS-* specifications were announced, Microsoft released the first version of web services enhancements (WSE), a lightweight framework specially designed for extending the web service stack in the .NET platform with custom implementations of the WS-* protocols. This framework evolved gradually, adding three major versions as more features were required. It was discontinued in 2006 with the announcement of WCF. The last version, WSE 3.0, included implementations of well-known protocols such as WS-Security, WS-Addressing, WS-SecureConversation, MTOM, and WS-ReliableMessaging. If you compare WSE and WCF, it is clear that WSE was the opportunity for Microsoft to get involved in the WS-* world, and all the experience and lessons learned were used to design and develop many of the available features in WCF and Windows Identity Foundation (WIF).

Today, as the business evolves, aspects such as user authentication and authorization are slowly moving toward federated identity management solutions. Federated identity management makes the vision of treating the user identity as a service possible, where authentication and authorization functions are web services available to any application in the enterprise. This also represents a big step toward moving away from the user identity silos that were created in the past to more decentralized authentication and authorization schemas. Microsoft is pushing hard in this direction, and recently announced the Geneva platform as part of the strategy to implement identity management solutions in the .NET platform.

MAIN PRINCIPLES IN WEB SERVICE SECURITY

When you read literature about security for web services, you typically find a consistent set of fundamental principles that apply in any distributed messaging system. You use some of these principles throughout this chapter, so it is a good idea to refresh them before getting specific WCF details.

Authentication

Client *authentication* is the process of uniquely identifying the party that acts as a source of messages to your applications or services. For the purpose of this chapter, "message sender" or "service client" is used for this party.

> *The message sender is not necessarily an end user; it can also be an application or a service.*

The authentication process generally addresses two questions: "Who are you?" and "How do you prove that?"

For the first question, the sender must provide some evidence to prove its identity, which can take the form of intangible credentials such as a pair of usernames and passwords, a Kerberos ticket, a token with cryptographic information, or something more tangible such as an X509 certificate. On the other hand, the service must have a mechanism in place to verify that the presented evidence is legitimate, and whether it can trust or not in that evidence according to the results of the verification. The sender is successfully authenticated only when the verification drops good results.

Client authentication is not the only scenario for authentication. There are some cases where the sender also needs to verify the service identity. This type of authentication is commonly known as Service authentication, and represents a proven practice to prevent phishing attacks.

Phishing in this context represents a common security threat where someone, the attacker, makes available a fake service with the same signature as the original one to capture sensitive or private data about the user.

Mutual authentication is when both the client and the service authenticate each other before any operation is made.

Let's say that a store offering products online provides a service for third-party applications. They can buy products directly without referring users to the website. That service receives sensitive user information such as credit cards and bank account numbers. As a third-party integrator, you should authenticate the server before trusting sensitive information about the user. And as a developer working on the service, you should authenticate the user to associate the purchase information with his profile. As you can see, this is a typical scenario for requiring mutual authentication.

Authorization

Authorization is the process that determines what system resources and operations can be accessed by the authenticated user. It generally addresses the things you are allowed to do.

Authorization decisions are mostly based on evidence presented in the identity of the authenticated user such as user claims, or some other evidence provided by the consumer application.

Continuing the example discussed in authentication, the website might decide to grant different permissions to the users consuming the service based on a specific key or attribute provided by the third-party application.

Message Integrity

Message integrity guarantees that the data in the message is protected from deliberate or accidental modifications. In other words, it ensures that the service receiving the data has not been tampered with or modified in transit.

Integrity for data in transit is generally based on cryptographic techniques such as digital signatures, hashing, and message authentication codes. Integrity is extremely useful to prevent Man-In-The-Middle attacks, where someone intentionally starts sniffing the packets in the network or modifies some of them before the message reaches the service.

Message Confidentiality

Message confidentiality is the process of making sure that the data in the messages remains private and confidential, and that it cannot be read by unauthorized parties. As with message integrity, confidentiality is also based on cryptographic techniques such as data encryption. Different algorithms can be used to encrypt the data, but the most secure are the ones that are based on asymmetric keys such as RSA.

Man-In-The-Middle or Eavesdropping attacks can also be avoided thanks to data encryption.

TRANSPORT SECURITY AND MESSAGE SECURITY

As we already discussed in the section "The Evolution of Security in Web Services," two security models have been traditionally used to secure the communication between client applications as well as web services, transport security, and message security.

Both security models provide some of the aspects or security principles that were mentioned in the last section, in different ways. Security in this context is very important, and it is mainly concerned with providing authentication and guaranteeing the integrity and confidentiality of the service messages as they move across the network.

Knowing the differences between the models will help you choose one model over another according to many of the requirements you have for implementing the right security schema for your services.

Transport Security

Transport security is about leveraging the security capabilities that the different transports provide to secure an end-to-end communication between the message sender or client application and the final service. Because the original SOAP specification lacked any kind of security schema, transport security was best complement for securing communications.

In transport security, all the available authentication mechanisms are tied to the transport implementation. Therefore, this represents a big impediment for creating new kinds of credentials or extending existing ones.

The same thing happens for handling message protection; each transport provides a limited number of built-in options. The most common option for protecting the messages is based on a combination of *TLS (Transport Layer Security)* and *SSL (Security Socket Layer)*, which are used to encrypt and sign the content sent over the wire. A common limitation of SSL/TLS is that they only provide point-to-point security between two endpoints, the client and the server. If a message needs to be sent through different intermediaries, they have to forward the message over a new SSL connection. In addition, after the messages leave the transport, they are no longer secure.

A big advantage of transport security over message security is that the involved parties do not need to understand WS-Security at all, which sometimes represents a big impediment to achieve protocol interoperability between different platforms or web services stacks. This impediment is inherent to two main factors:

➤   The complexity of the WS-Security specification.

➤   The differences in the final implementations on behalf of the web services vendors.

Message Security

When using message security, all the security metadata such as digital signatures, encrypted elements, user credentials, and cryptographic keys are self-contained within the SOAP message. This security model is based on the WS-Security specification, which mainly describes how to sign or encrypt parts of the SOAP envelope using different algorithms or even different keys.

As an XML implementation, WS-Security represents a very flexible solution for supporting different kinds of credentials or creating new ones. The credentials and keys are represented in this specification as security tokens, a generic XML construct that encapsulates specific information about them. In addition, different security tokens have already derived from existing security technologies such as Kerberos, X509 certificates, and usernames and passwords, and are made available in satellite specifications named *token profiles*.

A main difference with transport security is that the messages can be forwarded to other services or intermediary systems without breaking the security — security is always present, no matter whether the messages leave the transport or not. See Figure 7-1.

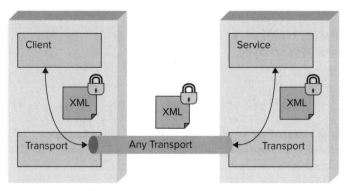

FIGURE 7-1: Message security

Let's discuss how WS-Security works with an example. The message sender modifies part of the message by substituting the message body with encrypted data, and signing other headers. The description of all the transformations that took place is included as part of a special SOAP header called "security." When the service or message receiver gets the message, it can analyze this special security header to discover that the body was encrypted, some headers were signed, and which cryptographic keys and algorithms were used to perform those operations. If it owns the keys, it can decrypt the body and verify that the signatures are valid:

```
<s:Envelope xmlns:s="http://www.w3.org/2003/05/soap-envelope"
xmlsn:a="http://www.w3.org/2005/08/addressing"
xmlsn:u="http://docs.oasis-open.org/wss/2004/01/
oasis-200401-wss-wssecurity-utility-1.0.xsd">
  <s:Header>
    <a:Action s:mustUnderstand="1" u:Id="_2">
       http://tempuri.org/IHelloWorld/Hello
    </a:Action>
    <a:MessageID u:Id="_3">
      urn:uuid:4dabcfb1-6939-402d-919b-8e8486206e1f
    </a:MessageID>
    <o:Security s:mustUnderstand="1" xmlns:o="http://docs.oasis-open.org/
      wss/2004/01/oasis-200401-wss-wssecurity-secext-1.0.xsd">
      <u:Timestamp u:Id="uuid-ea4659dc-85e5-4054-9b0c-c674f0128e7f-11">
        <u:Created>2009-07-27T20:03:36.830Z</u:Created>
        <u:Expires>2009-07-27T20:08:36.830Z</u:Expires>
      </u:Timestamp>
      <!-- Removed for simplicity -->
    </o:Security>
  </s:Header>
  <s:Body u:Id="_0">
    <e:EncryptedData Id="_1" Type="http://www.w3.org/2001/04/xmlenc#Content"
      xmlns:e="http://www.w3.org/2001/04/xmlenc#">
      <e:EncryptionMethod Algorithm="http://www.w3.org/2001/04/xmlenc#aes256-cbc">
      </e:EncryptionMethod>
      <KeyInfo xmlns="http://www.w3.org/2000/09/xmldsig#">
        <o:SecurityTokenReference xmlns:o="http://docs.oasis-open.org/wss/2004/01/
          oasis-200401-wss-wssecurity-secext-1.0.xsd">
          <o:Reference ValueType="http://schemas.xmlsoap.org/ws/2005/02/sc/dk"
            URI="#uuid-ea4659dc-85e5-4054-9b0c-c674f0128e7f-10"></o:Reference>
        </o:SecurityTokenReference>
      </KeyInfo>
      <e:CipherData>
        <e:CipherValue>.....</e:CipherValue>
      </e:CipherData>
    </e:EncryptedData>
  </s:Body>
</s:Envelope>
```

The previous example illustrates how WS-Security is applied to a SOAP message. As you can see, the body has been replaced by an encrypted section that contains references to other security tokens contained within the security headers. Those are the references that the message receiver must resolve to get access to the cryptographic keys.

WCF SECURITY OVERVIEW

At this point you have seen enough of the theory behind security in web services. Now you get your hands dirty with the implementation details of WCF. In the following sections, you see how to use many of the available security settings in WCF, and some common deployment scenarios where the security principles already discussed can be put into practice.

For message protection, WCF supports the two traditional security models, transport security and message security, or a hybrid model of the two (transport security and message credentials). In addition, a great variety of authentication and authorization schemas are supported out of the box to meet the requirements of the most common scenarios. If those schemas do not satisfy your needs, you can easily customize them, as extensibility is one of the strong points of WCF in this area.

Configuring Security in WCF

The binding and behaviors in WCF represent the main entry point for the configuration subsystem and the policies that affect the services at runtime. This rich and configurable environment enables you to create security policies and enforce them at runtime in your services. Choosing the right security schema and policies for your services should only be a matter of determining the initial requirements in terms of message protection, authentication, and authorization.

The bindings, in addition to specifying the communication protocol and encoding for the services, will also allow you to configure the message protection settings and the authentication schema. On the other hand, the behaviors allow you to specify other kinds of security settings such as client and service credentials, credential validators, authorization policies, and managers, to name a few.

The binding selection also influences the available configuration options for the service security policy. For instance, the `BasicHttp` binding only supports legacy web service protocols, and therefore only transport security can be configured with this binding.

All the configuration settings in the bindings and behaviors can be set either as programming against the configuration object model or through a .NET configuration section.

To avoid bad practices when configuring security, the WCF team restricts the number of security settings that can be used in the configuration section. Username and password credentials represent a good example of this. It would not be a good idea to hardcode some passwords in a configuration file, and for that reason, they are only available in the configuration object model.

To simplify the configuration process even more, all the bindings come with a pre-defined configuration schema that satisfies the most common scenarios. In that way, as long as you do not tweak specific settings, WCF tries to use the default security schema.

Table 7-1 summarizes the default security schema for the most common bindings.

TABLE 7-1: Default Security Settings

BINDING	SETTINGS
WsHttpBinding	Message Security with Windows Authentication (NTLM or Kerberos)
BasicHttpBinding	No Security
WsFederationHttpBinding	Message Security with Federated Authentication (Issue Tokens)
NetTcpBinding	Transport Security with Windows Authentication (NTLM or Kerberos)
NetNamedPipeBinding	Transport Security with Windows Authentication (NTLM or Kerberos)
NetMsmqBinding	Transport Security with Windows Authentication (NTLM or Kerberos)

Consider the following service configuration that supports WsHttpBinding:

```
<wsHttpBinding>
  <binding name="UsernameBinding">
    <security mode="Message">
      <message clientCredentialType="UserName"/>
    </security>
  </binding>
</wsHttpBinding>
```

In this example, the service has been configured with message security and the username security token profile. The rest of the security settings for the binding take the default values.

Now we dive into more details about the different security configuration aspects in WCF.

Security Mode

The security mode setting determines two fundamental security aspects for any service: the security model for message protection and the supported client authentication schema.

Each security mode has its own mechanism for passing the authentication credentials to the service, and therefore some authentication options might not be available according to the selected security model.

For example, federated authentication is supported only with message authentication. If you need to support that security schema, message security is the only option you have.

This setting is available in the configuration model through the Mode property in the security element.

The following examples show how to configure the security mode for a WsHttpBinding using the WCF configuration section, and the equivalent version using the code model:

```
<wsHttpBinding>
  <binding name="helloWorld">
    <security mode="TransportWithMessageCredential"></security>
```

```
        </binding>
    </wsHttpBinding>

    WSHttpBinding binding = new WSHttpBinding();
    binding.Security.Mode = SecurityMode.TransportWithMessageCredential;
```

The possible options for this setting are listed in Table 7-2.

TABLE 7-2: Security Modes

MODE	DESCRIPTION
None	The service is available for anyone, and the messages are not protected as they go through the transport. When this mode is used, the service is vulnerable to any kind of attack.
Transport	Uses the transport security model for authenticating clients and protecting the messages. This mode provides the advantages and disadvantages discussed in transport security.
Message	Uses the message security model for authenticating clients and protecting the messages. This mode provides the advantages and disadvantages discussed in message security.
Both	Uses the transport security and message security models at the same time for authenticating the service consumers and protecting the messages. This mode is only supported by the MSMQ bindings and requires the same credentials at both levels.
TransportWithMessageCredentials	The message protection is provided by transport, and the credentials for authenticating the service consumers travel as part of the message. This mode provides the flexibility of using any of the credentials or token types supported in message authentication while the service authentication and message protection is performed at transport level.
TransportCredentialOnly	Uses transport security for authenticating clients. The service is not authenticated, and the messages, including the client credentials, go as plain text through the transport. This security mode can be useful for scenarios where the kind of information transmitted between the client and the service is not sensitive, although the credentials also get exposed to anyone.

Protection Level

By default, WCF encrypts and signs all the messages on wire to provide data confidentiality and integrity. In some circumstances, if the message you are sending through the transport does not contain any sensitive information, you might want to turn off encryption and sign the message to preserve the integrity of the data — without concern about confidentially. For those scenarios, WCF provides the flexibility of changing the default protection level when Message Security mode is used.

The protection level can be configured either at service level in the contract definition or at operation level for a more granular control. When the protection level is defined at both levels, the protection level in operation overrides the existing definition on the service level.

Message contracts also support a way to override the protection level for the operation. The [ProtectionLevel] attribute can be specified in the message contract itself or any specific message header or body.

The supported values for the ProtectionLevel setting are None, Sign, and EncryptAndSign.

None disables the message protection. Sign only provides message integrity against any possible change in the original message, and the last one, EncryptAndSign, provides message confidentiality and integrity.

The protection level is only configurable through attributes in the service definition, and it is not available in the binding configuration settings. The following examples illustrate how this setting can change different levels (an operation or a message contract) in the service definition:

```
[MessageContract(ProtectionLevel = ProtectionLevel.None)]
public class HelloWorldRequestMessage
{
    [MessageHeader]
    public string SampleHeader { get; set; }

    [MessageBodyMember()]
    public string Message { get; set; }
}

[MessageContract]
public class HelloWorldResponseMessage
{
    public string ResponseMessage { get; set; }
}

[ServiceContract(ProtectionLevel = ProtectionLevel.EncryptAndSign)]
public interface IHelloWorld
{
    [OperationContract(ProtectionLevel = ProtectionLevel.Sign)]
    HelloWorldResponseMessage Hello(HelloWorldRequestMessage request);
}
```

The final result, shown in the previous example, is that the request message will not be protected, and the response message will use the protection level defined for the operation, which is sign only.

Algorithm Suite

The `algorithmSuite` setting is something specific to message security and determines the set of algorithms that will be used for message integrity and confidentiality. For practical purposes, you should understand that this setting basically affects the way in which WCF generates the final keys for digitally signing and encrypting the messages. The algorithm suite typically represents a pair of algorithms, an asymmetric algorithm for deriving a symmetric key, and a symmetric algorithm for encrypting and signing the messages.

Performing cryptographic operations such as digitally signing or encrypting information with asymmetric keys is very expensive in terms of computer resources such as CPU or memory. For that reason, WCF first generates and derives a symmetric key by using the asymmetric algorithm, and then uses that symmetric key to effectively perform the cryptographic operations.

> *The default value for this setting is* `Basic256`, *which represents a combination of* `RSA-OAEP` *as the asymmetric algorithm and* `AES256` *as the symmetric one.*

The client and the service must agree on the selected algorithm suite to interoperate well. This is a very important aspect because some platforms or web services stacks only support specific algorithm suites. As long as interoperability is not a concern for you, you should consider leaving the default value for this setting:

```
<netTcpBinding>
  <binding name="helloWorld">
    <security mode="Message">
      <message algorithmSuite="Basic256"/>
    </security>
  </binding>
</netTcpBinding>
```

The previous configuration segment shows how that setting can be changed in a `NetTcpBinding` configured with message security.

Client Credential Type

The client credential type is a very important setting that determines the authentication schema used by your service. It represents the type of credentials expected for authenticating the client or consumer application.

Something that you should know first is that the supported options for this setting will vary according to the selected security mode and transport. Although the available options for message security in the most common bindings are pretty much the same — `None`, `Windows`, `Username`, `Certificate`, and `IssueToken` — the options for transport security are limited by the supported authentication schemas in the transport layer itself.

Tables 7-3 and 7-4 illustrate the available options for message security and transport security with a brief description about each one.

TABLE 7-3: Message Security

CREDENTIAL TYPE	DESCRIPTION
None	The clients are not authenticated by the service. It is equivalent to anonymous authentication.
Windows	The clients are authenticated by the service with traditional Windows authentication through Kerberos or NTLM.
Username	The clients are authenticated by the service with a pair of usernames and passwords.
Certificate	The clients are authenticated by the service using information provided in a X509 certificate.
IssueToken	The clients are authenticated by the service with a token issued by a third party. This is common for federated authentication scenarios.

TABLE 7-4: Transport Security

CREDENTIAL TYPE	DESCRIPTION
None	Equivalent to None in message security.
Windows	Equivalent to Windows in message security.
Certificate	Equivalent to Certificate in message security.
Basic	The clients are authenticated with Http Basic Authentication. This option is specific to Http.
Digest	The clients are authenticated with Http Digest Authentication. This option is specific to Http.
NTLM	The clients are authenticated with Http Windows Integrated Authentication. This option is specific to Http transport.

There are some exceptions to the previous table for the NetMsqmBinding and the NetNamedPipeBinding.

The first binding replaces the clientCredentialType setting with an equivalent one, msmqAuthenticationMode, which supports WindowsDomain for Windows authentication and Certificate for authentication based on certificates.

The NetNamedPipeBinding only supports transport security with Windows authentication.

This setting is available in the configuration model through two elements, `Message` and `Transport`. WCF picks one of these at runtime according to the configured security mode:

```
<wsHttpBinding>
  <binding name="helloWorld">
    <security mode="Transport">
      <transport clientCredentialType="Windows"/>
      <message clientCredentialType="Windows"/>
    </security>
  </binding>
</wsHttpBinding>
```

In this example, WCF uses the client credential type definition in the transport element because the security mode has been set to `Transport`. The message element can still exist in the configuration, but it is ignored by WCF.

Configuring this setting by code can be done in the same way seen with the configuration section:

```
WSHttpBinding binding = new WSHttpBinding();
binding.Security.Mode = SecurityMode.Transport;
binding.Security.Transport.ClientCredentialType = HttpClientCredentialType.Windows;
binding.Security.Message.ClientCredentialType = MessageCredentialType.Windows;
```

Service Credentials Authentication and Negotiation

Services in WCF must provide credentials to clients to support mutual authentication and message protection. In other words, the client uses the service credentials for authenticating it before sending a message, and also provides message protection aspects such as data confidentiality and integrity.

In most cases the credentials are automatically negotiated between the client and the service. The SSL handshake in transport security is a good example of this. This handshake allows the server to authenticate itself to the client by proving an X509 public key, and then allows the client and the server to cooperate in the creation of symmetric keys used for message protection during the secure session that follows.

For some message security authentication schemas, WCF gives the flexibility to change this behavior with a specific setting `negotiateServiceCredentials`. By default, WCF automatically negotiates the credentials at message level using protocols such as `TLSNego` when the client credentials are set to `None`, `Username`, or `Certificate`, or `SPNego` only when they are set to `Windows`. This mechanism to negotiate the credentials is something specific to WCF, so you should disable it to interoperate well with other service stacks or platforms. That can be accomplished as shown next:

```
<wsHttpBinding>
  <binding name="helloWorld">
    <security mode="Message">
      <message clientCredentialType="Certificate"
               negotiateServiceCredential="false" />
    </security>
  </binding>
</wsHttpBinding>
```

When this setting is disabled, in case of certificate credentials, the service certificate must be provided to all the clients prior to establishing a communication with the service, and the clients should refer to the service certificate in their configuration:

```
<clientCredentials>
  <serviceCertificate>
    <defaultCertificate findValue="WCFService"
        storeLocation="LocalMachine" storeName="My"
        x509FindType="FindBySubjectName"/>
  </serviceCertificate>
</clientCredentials>
```

The service authentication is performed by WCF at the moment of establishing the communication by comparing the provided credentials with the configured identity element in the service endpoint. If that element is not configured, WCF will try to assume default values prior to making the comparison. For example, in case you are using certificate credentials, WCF will check whether the subject name in the certificate matches the Internet name of the server.

In most cases, you have to define the service endpoint identity explicitly. That can be done by adding an identity element to the endpoint configuration:

```
<endpoint name="sampleProxy"
    address="http://localhost:8000/helloWorld/"
    bindingConfiguration="sampleBinding"
    behaviorConfiguration="sampleBehavior"
    binding="wsHttpBinding"
    contract="WCFBook.Samples.IHelloWorld">
    <identity>
      <dns value="WCFService"/>
    </identity>
</endpoint>
```

The equivalent version using the object model would be the following:

```
ServiceEndpoint ep = myServiceHost.AddServiceEndpoint(
typeof(WCFBook.Samples.IHelloWorld),
new WSHttpBinding(),
String.Empty);

EndpointAddress myEndpointAdd = new EndpointAddress(
new Uri("http://localhost:8000/helloWorld"),
EndpointIdentity.CreateDnsIdentity("WCFService"));

ep.Address = myEndpointAdd;
```

In the previous example, the service should provide a certificate with a subject name equal to WCFService to be successfully authenticated by WCF.

WCF supports five types of identities for a service. Their uses depend on the scenario you want to implement and the security requirements that the services demand. All the possible values for the identity types are discussed in Table 7-5.

TABLE 7-5: Identity Types

IDENTITY TYPE	DESCRIPTION
Domain Name System (DNS)	This type of identity is valid for X509 certificates or Windows accounts. The value specified in this element must match the Windows account name or the certificate subject name. In case of certificates, as long as the subject name does not change, the identity check is still valid.
Certificate	This type specifies an X509 certificate encoded as Base64. As you need to encode the entire certificate, which includes unique information such as the certificate thumbprint, this identity type represents a more precise alternative to the DNS identity. A downside is that you need to hardcode the complete certificate representation in the WCF configuration.
Certificate Reference	Pretty similar to the previous option. The main difference is that this identity type enables you to specify a certificate name and the location in the certificate store rather than hard coding the credential representation. It requires a previous deployment of the certificate in the Windows certificate store.
RSA	This identity type specifies a certificate RSA key. This option enables you to specifically restrict authentication to a single certificate based on a certificate key. As the certificate option, the key representation must be specified in Base64 encoding.
User Principal Name (UPN)	This identity type is specific to Windows authentication and specifies the UPN that the service is running under. This option is used by default when the service process is not running under of one the system accounts. In other words, it ensures that the service is running under a specific Windows account, which can be either the current logged-on user or any user account.
Service Principal Name (SPN)	This identity type is also specific to Windows authentication and specifies the SPN associated with the account that is running the service process. This option is used by default when the service process is running under the system accounts `LocalService`, `LocalSystem`, or `NetworkService`. WCF can automatically negotiate the value for this identity when the service is configured with Windows authentication and the `negotiateServiceCredential` for message security is set to true.

Secure Sessions

Secure sessions represent the last aspect that we discuss here before jumping into more concrete examples in the next chapter.

Secure sessions or *secure conversations* provide a way to improve the service response time when a client application needs to interchange more than one message with the service.

When this feature is enabled, the credential negotiation and authentication happen once during the first message interchange between the client and the service. Otherwise, these two steps are performed for every service call.

You should not confuse this type of session with typical Http-based sessions. WCF secure sessions are initiated by the clients and are there to support some kind of shared context between the client and the service.

This feature represents a specific implementation of the `WS-SecureConversation` and `WS-Trust` specifications in WCF, and therefore demands the use of message security.

In the way secure conversation works under the hood, the client first sends a special message `RequestSecurityToken` (with SOAP action `http://schemas.xmlsoap.org/ws/2005/02/trust/RST/Issue`) to the service for a session token. This message is part of the `WS-Trust` specification and contains a reference to the client credentials that will be used to create the session token:

```
<s:Envelope xmlns:s="..." xmlns:a="...">
  <s:Header>
    <a:Action s:mustUnderstand="1">
      http://schemas.xmlsoap.org/ws/2005/02/trust/RST/Issue
    </a:Action>
    <a:MessageID>urn:uuid:d55bd2a7-bae8-4751-a010-07e95fd82ee2</a:MessageID>
    <a:ReplyTo>
      <a:Address>http://www.w3.org/2005/08/addressing/anonymous</a:Address>
    </a:ReplyTo>
    <a:To s:mustUnderstand="1">http://localhost/HelloWorld</a:To>
  </s:Header>
  <s:Body>
    <t:RequestSecurityToken Context="uuid-f422503c-7974-42ab-9b8a-c330727290e9-1"
                        xmlns:t="http://schemas.xmlsoap.org/ws/2005/02/trust">
    <t:TokenType>http://schemas.xmlsoap.org/ws/2005/02/sc/sct</t:TokenType>
    <t:RequestType>
      http://schemas.xmlsoap.org/ws/2005/02/trust/Issue
    </t:RequestType>
    <t:KeySize>256</t:KeySize>
    <t:BinaryExchange
      ValueType="http://schemas.xmlsoap.org/ws/2005/02/trust/spnego"
      EncodingType="http://docs.oasis-open.org/wss/2004/01/
        oasis-200401-wss-soap-message-security-1.0#Base64Binary">
    </t:BinaryExchange>
    </t:RequestSecurityToken>
  </s:Body>
</s:Envelope>
```

After the service receives the message and authenticates the client credentials, it creates a new session token called *Secure Context Token (SCT)* which references the client credentials and a symmetric key to perform cryptographic operations such as encrypt or sign messages (message confidentiality and integrity).

The service sends the session token back to the client using a `RequestSecurityTokenResponse` message (with SOAP action `http://schemas.xmlsoap.org/ws/2005/02/trust/RSTR/Issue`), and keeps track of the original credentials using different strategies such as encrypted Http cookies or in-memory caches:

```
<s:Envelope xmlns:s="..." xmlns:a="...">
  <s:Header>
    <a:Action s:mustUnderstand="1">
      http://schemas.xmlsoap.org/ws/2005/02/trust/RSTR/Issue
    </a:action>
    <a:RelatesTo>urn:uuid:d55bd2a7-bae8-4751-a010-07e95fd82ee2</a:RelatesTo>
  </s:Header>
  <s:Body>
  <t:RequestSecurityTokenResponse
      Context="uuid-f422503c-7974-42ab-9b8a-c330727290e9-1"
      xmlns:t="http://schemas.xmlsoap.org/ws/2005/02/trust"
      xmlns:u="http://docs.oasis-open.org/wss/2004/01/
        oasis-200401-wss-wssecurity-utility-1.0.xsd">
    <t:BinaryExchange
      ValueType="http://schemas.xmlsoap.org/ws/2005/02/trust/spnego"
      EncodingType="http://docs.oasis-open.org/wss/2004/01/
        oasis-200401-wss-soap-message-security-1.0#Base64Binary">
    </t:BinaryExchange>
  </t:RequestSecurityTokenResponse>
  </s:Body>
</s:Envelope>
```

In that way, the client can later protect messages with the symmetric key included in the session token or use the session token itself as a client credential.

The most important benefits of using a SCT to protect communication between the client and service are as follows:

1. The service response time is three or four times faster than the same execution with other credentials as the client is authenticated only the first time and the symmetric session key is used to protect communication.

2. It is valid for a short time but it can be automatically renewed as it is used. As a consequence, the client application does not need to keep the original credentials. This is an important aspect when the original credentials contain sensitive information such as a username or password.

From the perspective of the client application, secure conversation is something completely transparent that WCF keeps at channel level. For that reason, the session token is reused as long as the client application uses the same instance of the client channel.

When the client channel is closed in a normal fashion, a message is sent to the service to shut down the session and release all the associated resources. If the channel closes abruptly, the session will eventually be shut down on the service side after a fixed period of inactivity.

This feature is enabled by default for all the bindings that support message security (WS-Security). The custom binding also offers the possibility of enabling Secure Conversation by setting the value `SecureConversation` to the `authenticationMode` attribute. In addition, you can configure a binding that will be initially used to negotiate the session token by means of the element `secureConversationBootstrap`.

The following configuration shows how secure conversation can be enabled for a `wsHttpBinding`, and the equivalent version with a custom binding:

```
<bindings>
  <wsHttpBinding>
    <binding name="ServiceBinding">
      <security mode="Message">
        <message clientCredentialType="Certificate"
           establishSecurityContext="true"/>
      </security>
    </binding>
  </wsHttpBinding>

  <customBinding>
    <binding name="ServiceBinding">

      <security authenticationMode="SecureConversation"
           requireSecurityContextCancellation ="false">
        <secureConversationBootstrap authenticationMode="MutualCertificate">
        </secureConversationBootstrap>
      </security>
      <httpTransport/>
    </binding>
  </customBinding>
</bindings>
```

The attribute `requireSecurityContextCancellation` in the previous configuration specifies whether the client application must send a shutdown message to the service after closing the client channel. When this attribute is set to false, WCF uses an encrypted cookie to keep the state of the session token instead of keeping it in memory on the service side. As the cookies travel in every message to the service, they are ideal for web farm scenarios where intermediary servers or load balancers are used, and there is no guarantee that all the messages are handled by the same server.

You cannot reuse the client channel for sending more than one message to the same service because the benefits of using secure conversation get lost. The extra overhead associated with the initial handshake will affect your service performance, and you should consider disabling this feature when that happens.

8

WCF Security in Action

WHAT'S IN THIS CHAPTER?

➤ Understanding authentication in WCF

➤ Getting started with claim-based security

➤ Authorizing service consumers in WCF

In the previous chapter we discussed fundamental aspects needed to choose the right security schema for your WCF services.

In this chapter, the focus is on applying those concepts in real scenarios, using examples that will guide you step by step. We also discuss alternatives that WCF provides for authenticating and authorizing clients when the client credentials reach the service, giving emphasis to the claims-based security model.

FIRST STEPS IN AUTHENTICATION

The right choice for your services authentication schema is typically based on several factors, such as the location of clients on the intranet or Internet, facility to deploy credentials in the clients, or the number of potential clients that will consume the services.

As previously discussed, authentication in the context of WCF typically refers to mutual authentication.

Mutual authentication is a bidirectional process where the clients and services authenticate each other. This kind of authentication is extremely important for services exposed on the Internet. An attacker might be able to spoof one of the services and intercept the client calls to get access to sensitive data.

The service credentials depend on the client authentication schema and the security mode you choose. Usually, if you use client authentication schemas such as username or certificate authentication with message security, a service certificate is needed for both service authentication and message protection. If you use Windows authentication, the Windows credentials of the service process can be used for service authentication and message protection.

Because the number of possible authentication schemas that a service should handle is the result of any possible combination between client credential types and security modes, WCF introduced a new way to represent the client identity through a uniform authentication model based on claims. In that way, the services get decoupled from the implementation details of every supported authentication mechanism, and only rely on claims to know more about the client's identities.

Claims-Based Identity Model

A *claim* in terms of WCF describes a piece of information about the identity of a subject (the service client) in a specific context, or an individual right or action applicable to a particular resource.

A claim is made of four main parts:

> ➤ The type of claim

> ➤ Information or content specific to the claim

> ➤ Information about the issuer of the claim

> ➤ Whether the claim describes the identity or capability of the subject.

The information about the issuer also plays a role in this model because the service can trust or not in the information provided by the claim based on the claim issuer.

Here's an example in the real world: when you present a driver's license in a winery to prove that you are of legal age to buy alcohol, you are giving evidence about your identity to a third party in the form of claims. Every claim in the license matches with a specific piece of information about you or the license itself, such as the legal name, birthday, or expiration date.

In that example, the person selling you the wine would probably only be interested in the claim that represents your age, which can be inferred from your birthday. That person would also verify that the license is valid, and was issued by a trusted party (authentication). The situation would be different if you present a card issued by a non-trusted source, such as a fake card. The seller would surely reject it.

In WCF, every credential type or security token successfully authenticated is mapped to a set of claims and passed to the service through the security context associated with the operation being executed.

These claims not only contain information about the client identity, but information that the service can use to take authorization decisions in the execution of the operation.

In WCF, a claim is represented by a class known as `System.IdentityModel.Claims.Claim`, which is part of the `System.IdentityModel` assembly. Most of the classes for handling different authentication aspects in WCF are located in that assembly:

```
[DataContract(Namespace = "http://schemas.xmlsoap.org/ws/2005/05/identity")]
public class Claim
{
  [DataMember(Name = "ClaimType")]
```

```
    public string ClaimType { get; set; }

    [DataMember(Name = "Resource")]
    public object Resource { get; set; }

    [DataMember(Name = "Right")]
    public string Right { get; set; }
}
```

As you might notice, this class is also decorated with the `DataContract`/`DataMember` attributes, so it can be transmitted over the wire to cross service boundaries.

The `ClaimType` property is a unique string identifier typically associated with a pre-defined URI that represents the kind of information contained within the claim. For example, the type `http://schemas.xmlsoap.org/ws/2005/05/identity/claims/name` would represent the claim that contains the username.

WCF already provides a set of predefined claim types in the `System.IdentityModel.Claims.ClaimTypes` class, but you are still free to use any schema to represent a type. The idea is that you can reuse most of them, and create new ones as you need them for representing types specific to the service business domain.

Some of the predefined claim types that you can find in that class are enumerated in Table 8-1.

TABLE 8-1: Claim Types

TYPE	VALUE
Name	http://schemas.xmlsoap.org/ws/2005/05/identity/claims/name
Surname	http://schemas.xmlsoap.org/ws/2005/05/identity/claims/surname
E-mail	http://schemas.xmlsoap.org/ws/2005/05/identity/claims/emailaddress
Country	http://schemas.xmlsoap.org/ws/2005/05/identity/claims/country

The `Resource` property references the actual claim value. As this property is an object, you can associate any kind of information to claim, from simple values such as strings to more complex object graphs. If you are planning to serialize the claims, make sure that the values assigned to them can be serialized as well.

The last but not least property, `Right`, specifies whether the claim represents identity information about the authenticated subject such as the name, or some additional information for taking authorization decisions such as user e-mail, phone number, and so on. These two possible values for the `Right` property are available as properties in the `System.IdentityModel.Rights` class. (See Table 8-2.)

TABLE 8-2: Right Types

TYPE	VALUE	PURPOSE
Identity	http://schemas.xmlsoap.org/ws/2005/05/identity/right/identity	A claim with this right uniquely identifies the subject it describes.
PossessProperty	http://schemas.xmlsoap.org/ws/2005/05/identity/right/possessproperty	A claim with this right provides additional information about the subject.

As happens with the claim types, the value for this property is also a simple string, so again you are open to providing your own schema for claim rights.

WCF by default generates a new set of claims for every authenticated security token or client credential. Clients usually send one security token per message, which receives the name of the primary token and can be any of the available credential types in WCF or a custom one. However, the client is not limited to send just one token: in some circumstances it might send more than one. These additional security tokens receive the name of supporting tokens, and typically provide additional information about the client.

A set of claims in WCF is represented by the abstract class `System.IdentityModel.Claims.ClaimSet`, which holds the list of claims as well as a reference to the issuer of those claims:

```
[DataContract(Namespace = "http://schemas.xmlsoap.org/ws/2005/05/identity")]
public abstract class ClaimSet : IEnumerable<Claim>
{
    public abstract IEnumerable<Claim>
        FindClaims(string claimType, string right);
    public abstract IEnumerator<Claim> GetEnumerator();
    public abstract int Count { get; }
    public abstract ClaimSet Issuer { get; }
    public abstract Claim this[int index] { get; }
}
```

Three specific implementations of this class are shipped as part of WCF. A generic one, `System.IdentityModel.Claims.DefaultClaimSet`, is for storing any kind of claim used to add or send additional claims to the service. The other two are for converting X509 certificates and Windows tokens to claims. These are `System.IdentityModel.Claims.X509CertificateClaimSet` and `System.IdentityModel.Claims.WindowsClaimSet` respectively.

As you can see, a basic implementation of this class involves different methods to enumerate or find existing claims in the claim set, or provide additional information about the issue of the claims.

All the claim sets generated by WCF can be accessed at runtime in the operation through the `System.ServiceModel.ServiceSecurityContext` class, which is available in the current `OperationContext`:

```
ServiceSecurityContext securityContext
= OperationContext.Current.ServiceSecurityContext;
```

The security context is available for any authorization code involved in the execution of the operation, and we discuss it more in detail later on in the section about authorization. For now, let's focus only on how to use this class to query some of the claims generated by WCF after the authentication:

```
ServiceSecurityContext securityContext =
OperationContext.Current.ServiceSecurityContext;

IEnumerable<Claim> claims = securityContext.
AuthorizationContext.ClaimSets[0].FindClaims
                (ClaimTypes.Name, Rights.Identity);
foreach (Claim claim in claims)
{
  string name = claim.Resource as string;
  Console.WriteLine("Your name is {0}", name);
}
```

Authentication in Action

You have seen so far how WCF authenticates clients, and transforms the information provided in the security tokens into claims that can be consumed by the service. It is now time to walk through more concrete examples and end-to-end scenarios using some of the authentication schemas that WCF provides out of the box. Some of the schemas in this section are username authentication over message and/or transport security, Windows authentication over message security, Mutual X509 authentication over message security, and finally an authentication scenario that combines username and certificate authentication over message security using the supporting tokens feature.

Username Authentication Over Message Security

Username authentication often receives the name *direct authentication*, as the client provides authentication credentials in the form of a username and password during the request to the service, and the service can validate or authenticate the credentials itself against an identity store without going to a third party or authentication broker. (See Figure 8-1.)

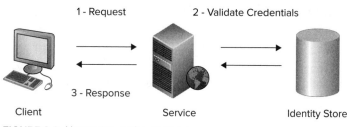

FIGURE 8-1: Username authentication

The main characteristics of username authentication are summarized in the following list:

➤ The credentials presented to the service by the client are based on a combination of username and password. This means that the client and the service must exchange the passwords securely before the first interaction using an out-of-band mechanism.

➤ The service can validate the client credentials (username and password) against an identity store. Different strategies can be used to implement the identity store, ranging from a simple solution such as a file to more complex ones using the Windows user account, a database, or a LDAP directory.

➤ The service is relatively simple, and does not require support for capabilities such as single sign-on (SSO). Without single sign-on, the client might be forced to authenticate prior to every service call or cache the user's credentials within the application.

➤ The client and the service trust each other to manage the credentials securely. If one of the parties manages the credentials in an insecure manner, there is no guarantee that the mishandled credentials will prove the identity of the client.

In the WCF implementation of username authentication over message security, the client passes the credentials to the service as part of a secure message exchange. The messages in this case are protected using an X509 certificate provided by the service. This certificate also works as a mechanism for the client to authenticate the service as part of the mutual authentication process.

The service credentials (the X509 certificate) can be transmitted to the client during the first message exchange or using an out-of-band mechanism according to the value of the negotiateServiceCredential setting.

The mechanism for authenticating the user credentials against an identity store is implemented through the abstract class System.IdentityModel.Selectors.UsernamePasswordValidator in the System.IdentityModel.Selectors assembly:

```
public abstract class UserNamePasswordValidator
{
  public abstract void Validate(string userName, string password);
}
```

The signature of the only method available in this class is quite evident. The username and password received as part of the client credentials is passed by WCF to this class for validation. In case the credentials cannot be validated, it is the responsibility of this class to throw an exception.

WCF ships with two internal implementations of this class, System.IdentityModel.Selectors .MembershipProviderValidator for validating the credentials against an existing ASP.NET Membership provider, and System.IdentityModel.Selectors.NoneUsernamePasswordValidator for not validating anything. These two implementations can be accessed through public members in the base UsernamePasswordValidator class:

```
public abstract class UserNamePasswordValidator
{
  public static UserNamePasswordValidator
```

```
CreateMembershipProviderValidator(MembershipProvider provider);

    public static UserNamePasswordValidator None { get; }
}
```

The static method `CreateMembershipProviderValidator` returns an instance of the `MembershipProviderValidator` that wraps the `MembershipProvider` passed as an argument. The static property `None` returns an instance of the `NonUsernamePasswordValidator` class.

The following code snippet shows a simple implementation of this class that validates the username and password against hardcoded strings:

```
public class MyUserNamePasswordValidator : UserNamePasswordValidator
{
  public override void Validate(string userName, string password)
  {
    if (userName != "joe" || password != "bar")
      throw new
  SecurityTokenValidationException("The user could not be authenticated");

  }
}
```

If the username is different from "Joe," or the password is not "bar," it throws an exception so WCF will assume the client could not be authenticated.

However, the default behavior for authenticating username and password credentials in WCF is to validate them against the Windows account store. Unless you do not override this setting through a specific element `<usernameAuthentication>` under the service behavior `<serviceCredentials>` to use a `UsernamePasswordValidator`, WCF will always use the Windows account store:

```
    <bindings>
      <wsHttpBinding>
        <binding name="HelloWorld">
          <security mode="Message">
            <message clientCredentialType="UserName"
                     negotiateServiceCredential="true"/>
          </security>
        </binding>
      </wsHttpBinding>
    </bindings>
    <behaviors>
      <serviceBehaviors>
        <behavior name="HelloWorld">
          <serviceCredentials>
            <userNameAuthentication userNamePasswordValidationMode=
  "Windows|MembershipProvider|Custom"/>
          </serviceCredentials>
        </behavior>
      </serviceBehaviors>
    </behaviors>
```

The setting `usernamePasswordValidationMode` in the `<usernameAuthentication>` element allows changing the mode that WCF uses to authenticate the username credentials. Windows is the default value, but also supports `MembershipProvider` for using a ASP.NET membership provider (internally uses the already discussed `MembershipProviderValidator`) or `Custom` to specify a custom implementation of `UsernamePasswordValidator` in case you want to provide something not supported by the other options. (The `MyUsernamePasswordValidation` implementation is an example of a custom implementation.)

Based on the value you chose for this setting, you need to provide additional values for other related settings.

In validation mode, `Windows` supports three optional settings:

1. `CacheLogonTokens`: Specifies whether the Windows tokens are cached and reused for the same username/password pair. Authenticating and creating a Windows logon token can be an expensive operation, so WCF caches the logon tokens returned by Win32's `LogonUser` function when this setting is turned on.

2. `CachedLogonTokenLifetime`: Specifies the maximum length of time that the Windows tokens are cached when the `CacheLogonToken` setting is on.

3. `MaxCachedLogonTokens`: Specifies the maximum number of Windows tokens to cache when the `CacheLogonToken` setting is on.

```
<serviceCredentials>
        <userNameAuthentication userNamePasswordValidationMode="Windows"
                                cacheLogonTokens="true"
                                cachedLogonTokenLifetime="00:01:00"
                                maxCachedLogonTokens="10"/>
</serviceCredentials>
```

The validation mode `MembershipProvider` requires an additional setting `membershipProviderName` to provide the name of an already configured ASP.NET membership provider. (That name should exist in the configured membership providers.)

```
<behavior name="HelloWorld">
    <serviceCredentials>
        <userNameAuthentication userNamePasswordValidationMode=
            "MembershipProvider"
            membershipProviderName="MyProvider"/>
    </serviceCredentials>
  </behavior>
 </serviceBehaviors>
<system.web>
   <membership>
     <providers>
       <add name="MyProvider" type="..."/>
     </providers>
   </membership>
</system.web>
```

Finally, the validation mode `Custom` requires the setting `customUsernamePasswordValidatorType` to specify the .NET type of the custom implementation:

```
<behavior name="HelloWorld">
  <serviceCredentials>
    <userNameAuthentication userNamePasswordValidationMode="Custom"
  customUserNamePasswordValidatorType=
"MyCustomUsernamePasswordValidator, MyAssembly"/>
    </serviceCredentials>
</behavior>
```

The X509 certificate used to protect the communication must be configured by using the
`<serviceCertificate>` element within the `<serviceCredentials>` behavior as shown in this
configuration fragment:

```
<behavior name="HelloWorld">
  <serviceCredentials>
    <serviceCertificate findValue="CN=WCFServer" storeLocation="LocalMachine"
  storeName="My" x509FindType="FindBySubjectDistinguishedName"/>
    <userNameAuthentication userNamePasswordValidationMode="Windows"/>
  </serviceCredentials>
</behavior>
```

When you reference a X509 certificate either in the configuration section or the object model, you
often need to specify different settings that WCF will use to resolve the certificate location in the
Windows certificate store. These settings are summarized in Table 8-3.

TABLE 8-3: Certificate Resolution Settings

SETTING	DESCRIPTION
StoreLocation	Specifies the location of the certificate store. Possible values for this setting are `LocalMachine`, for the store assigned to the local machine or `CurrentUser`, for the store used by the current user.
StoreName	Specifies the name of the certificate store. The most common values for this setting are `My`, for personal certificates, or `TrustedPeople`, for certificates associated directly with trusted people or resources.
X509FindType	Specifies the way WCF finds the certificate using the `FindValue` setting. The most common values for this setting are `FindBySubjectName`, to find certificates by the `SubjectName` attribute in the certificate, or `FindBySubjectDistinguishedName`, to perform a more specific search using the `SubjectDistinguishedName` attribute.
FindValue	Specifies the value that WCF uses to search the certificate.

Now that you have a basic understanding of the different settings required to run an end-to-end
scenario with a username authentication schema, let's walk through a complete example for
a service that returns the claims of the authenticated user.

Step 1: Create the Service Implementation

Your service implementation is quite simple: it basically returns the claims passed by WCF in the security context as a list of strings. (See Listing 8-1.)

LISTING 8-1: Service Implementation

```
namespace WCFBook.Samples
{
  [ServiceContract()]
  public interface IEchoClaims
  {
    [OperationContract]
    List<string> Echo();
  }
}
public class EchoClaims : IEchoClaims
{
  public List<string> Echo()
  {
    List<string> claims = new List<string>();

    foreach (ClaimSet set in
          OperationContext.Current
            .ServiceSecurityContext
            .AuthorizationContext
            .ClaimSets)
    {
      foreach (Claim claim in set)
      {
        claims.Add(string.Format("{0} - {1} - {2}",
                claim.ClaimType,
                claim.Resource.ToString(),
                claim.Right));
      }
    }

    return claims;
  }

}
```

The service is hosted in a console application using the http transport (see Listing 8-2).

LISTING 8-2: Service Host

```
class Program
{
  static void Main(string[] args)
  {
    ServiceHost host = new ServiceHost(typeof(EchoClaims),
                new Uri("http://localhost:8000"));
```

```
      try
      {
        host.Open();

        Console.WriteLine("Service running....");
        Console.WriteLine("Press a key to quit");
        Console.ReadKey();
      }
      finally
      {
        host.Close();
      }
    }
  }
```

Step 2: Configure the Service with WsHttpBinding, Username Authentication, and Message Security

In this step you need to configure the service host to expose the `EchoService` service using a `WsHttpBinding` (as the service uses Http) with username authentication over message security.

1. Add the service description with the corresponding endpoint to the `system.ServiceModel` configuration section:

```
<system.serviceModel>
  <services>
    <service name="WCFBook.Samples.EchoClaims"
             behaviorConfiguration="echoClaimsBehavior">
    <endpoint address="EchoClaims"
              contract="WCFBook.Samples.IEchoClaims"
              binding="wsHttpBinding"
              bindingConfiguration="echoClaimsBinding"></endpoint>

    </service>
  </services>
```

2. Configure the `WsHttpBinding` to use message security with username authentication:

```
<bindings>
  <wsHttpBinding>
    <binding name="echoClaimsBinding">
      <security mode="Message">
        <message clientCredentialType="UserName"
                 negotiateServiceCredential="true"/>
      </security>
    </binding>
  </wsHttpBinding>
</bindings>
```

The service credentials will automatically be negotiated, so the client application does not need to install it using an out-of-band mechanism.

3. Configure the `serviceBehavior` with the service certificate and the username authentication mode:

```
<behaviors>
  <serviceBehaviors>
    <behavior name="echoClaimsBehavior">
      <serviceCredentials>
        <serviceCertificate
          findValue="CN=WCFServer"
          storeLocation="LocalMachine"
          storeName="My"
          x509FindType="FindBySubjectDistinguishedName"/>
        <userNameAuthentication
          userNamePasswordValidationMode="Windows"/>
      </serviceCredentials>
      <serviceMetadata httpGetEnabled="true"/>
    </behavior>
  </serviceBehaviors>
</behaviors>
```

For the purpose of the first sample, you configure the service to authenticate the users against the Windows account store (a valid Windows account and password must be provided by the client application).

The X509 certificate `CN=WCFServer` is a test certificate created for this sample using the `makecert.exe` tool. A script `SetupCerts.bat` has been included with the samples to automatically create and register the X509 certificates in the Windows certificate store. Make sure to run this script before playing with the samples.

Step 3: Implement the Client Application

The client application is a basic console application that collects the username and password from the standard input, and calls the service to obtain the user claims (see Listing 8-3).

LISTING 8-3: Service Implementation

```
static void Main(string[] args)
{
    Console.WriteLine("Enter a valid username");
    string username = Console.ReadLine();

    Console.WriteLine("Enter the password");
    string password = Console.ReadLine();

    EchoClaimsReference.EchoClaimsClient client = new
    Client.EchoClaimsReference.EchoClaimsClient();
    client.ClientCredentials.UserName.UserName = username;
    client.ClientCredentials.UserName.Password = password;

    try
```

```
        {
            string[] claims = client.Echo();

            foreach (string claim in claims)
            {
                Console.WriteLine(claim);
            }
        }
        catch (TimeoutException exception)
        {
            Console.WriteLine("Got {0}", exception.GetType());
            client.Abort();
        }
        catch (CommunicationException exception)
        {
            Console.WriteLine("Got {0}", exception.GetType());
            client.Abort();
        }
    }
```

`ClientCredentials` is a property of the type `System.ServiceModel.ClientCredentials` exposed by `System.ServiceModel.ClientBase<T>`, a class that any WCF channel inherits from.

That class contains different properties that the client application can use to set the right credentials to consume the service. In this example, the username credentials are used.

Step 4: Configure the Client with WsHttpBinding, Message Security, and Username Authentication

The last step is to configure the client application to use the same security settings as you configure on the service side. That is, a client endpoint that uses `WsHttpBinding` with message authentication over message security.

1. Add the client endpoint to the `system.ServiceModel` configuration section:

```
<client>
        <endpoint address="http://localhost:8000/EchoClaims"
                  binding="wsHttpBinding"
                  bindingConfiguration="echoClaimsBinding"
                  contract="EchoClaimsReference.IEchoClaims"
                  name="WSHttpBinding_IEchoClaims"
                  behaviorConfiguration="echoClaimsBehavior">
            <identity>
              <dns value="WCFServer"/>
            </identity>
        </endpoint>
    </client>
```

The endpoint identity must match the certificate configured on the service side; otherwise WCF will throw an exception at the moment of authenticating the service.

2. Configure the `WsHttpBinding` to use message security with username authentication:

```
<bindings>
  <wsHttpBinding>
    <binding name="echoClaimsBinding">
      <security mode="Message">
        <message
          clientCredentialType="UserName"
          negotiateServiceCredential="true"/>
        </security>
      </binding>
    </wsHttpBinding>
</bindings>
```

3. As you use test certificates, you need to skip the X509 certificate validations performed by WCF at the moment of authenticating the service credentials. This step is optional if you are using X509 certificates obtained from a trusted certificate authority:

```
<behaviors>
  <endpointBehaviors>
    <behavior name="echoClaimsBehavior">
      <clientCredentials>
        <serviceCertificate>
          <authentication
            certificateValidationMode="None"
            revocationMode="NoCheck"/>
          </serviceCertificate>
        </clientCredentials>
      </behavior>
    </endpointBehaviors>
</behaviors>
```

Variant 1: Using a Custom Membership Provider as the Identity Store

Instead of validating the user credentials with the Windows account store, this variant describes how to configure the service to a custom membership provider as the identity store.

For the purpose of this example, you implement a basic ASP.NET membership provider. For more complex scenarios, you can reuse some of the built-in providers such as `SqlMembershipProvider` for validating credentials against a SQL database.

Step 1: Implement a Custom ASP.NET Membership Provider

Any membership provider must derive from the base class `System.Web.MembershipProvider` and implement different methods to authenticate and manage the users in an application. In the case of WCF, only the method `ValidateUser` is used to validate the user credentials, and the rest of the implementation can be omitted:

```
public class MyMembershipProvider : MembershipProvider
{

    public override bool ValidateUser(string username, string password)
```

```
    {
        if (username != "joe" ||
            password != "bar")
        {
            return false;
        }

        return true;
    }
}
```

This implementation is quite simple as it only validates the credentials when the username is equal to "Joe" and the password is equal to "bar." It returns false for any other credential and therefore WCF sends an exception back to the client.

Step 2: Configure the Service to Use the Custom Membership Provider

Two additional steps are required to configure the membership provider for the service. The custom membership implementation must be registered as a valid provider under the system.web configuration section:

```xml
<system.web>
  <membership>
    <providers>
      <add name="MyMembershipProvider" type="Common.MyMembershipProvider, Common"/>
    </providers>
  </membership>
</system.web>
```

The service must reference this membership provider in the <usernameAuthentication> element:

```xml
<serviceBehaviors>
  <behavior name="echoClaimsBehavior">
    <serviceCredentials>
      <serviceCertificate
        findValue="CN=WCFServer"
        storeLocation="LocalMachine"
        storeName="My"
        x509FindType="FindBySubjectDistinguishedName"/>
      <userNameAuthentication
        userNamePasswordValidationMode="MembershipProvider"
        membershipProviderName="MyMembershipProvider"/>
    </serviceCredentials>
    <serviceMetadata httpGetEnabled="true"/>
  </behavior>
</serviceBehaviors>
```

Variant 2: Using a Custom UserNamePasswordValidator Implementation

The last variant involves the implementation of a custom UsernamePasswordValidator class for validating the user credentials against a custom identity store.

Step 1: Implement a Custom UserNamePasswordValidator

As you already saw, a custom username validator must derive from the base class UserNamePasswordValidator and provide the implementation for the method Validate as is shown in Listing 8-4.

LISTING 8-4: Custom UserNamePasswordValidator Implementation

```
public class MyUserNamePasswordValidator : UserNamePasswordValidator
{
    public override void Validate(string userName, string password)
    {
        if (userName != "joe" || password != "bar")
            throw new SecurityTokenValidationException("The user could not
            be authenticated");

    }
}
```

The implementation of the custom validator used here is the same one used for the MembershipProvider, except it validates the credentials when the username is equal to "joe" and the password is equal to "bar". It throws an exception for any other credential.

Step 2: Configure the Service to Use the Custom UserNamePasswordValidator

The configuration for the custom validator in the <system.ServiceModel> section is quite straightforward. The service configuration must reference this implementation type in the <usernameAuthentication> element, and the userNamePasswordValidationMode must be set to "Custom":

```
<serviceBehaviors>
  <behavior name="echoClaimsBehavior">
    <serviceCredentials>
      <serviceCertificate
        findValue="CN=WCFServer"
        storeLocation="LocalMachine"
        storeName="My"
        x509FindType="FindBySubjectDistinguishedName"/>
      <userNameAuthentication
        userNamePasswordValidationMode="Custom"
            customUserNamePasswordValidatorType=
              "Common.MyCustomUsernamePasswordValidator, Common"/>
    </serviceCredentials>
    <serviceMetadata httpGetEnabled="true"/>
  </behavior>
```

Username Authentication Over Transport Security

Username authentication over transport security is another classic example of direct authentication. The client provides credentials in the form of a username and password during the request to the service using any built-in transport authentication mechanism, such as basic authentication. The service can then validate or authenticate the credentials against an identity store without using a third party or authentication broker. In addition, all the messages and credentials exchanged between the client and service are protected with security mechanisms provided by the transport, such as SSL/TLS.

In case of SSL, the service credentials (the X509 certificate) are always transmitted to the client during the SSL handshake when the connection is established, and before any message is sent by the client to service.

The first WCF version did not include a way to validate the user credentials against a custom identity store — the credentials were always validated against the Windows account store. Version 3.5 introduced improvements in this aspect, allowing the configuration of the custom `userNamePasswordValidator` to change this default behavior when the services are not hosted in IIS.

Plugging a custom extension to validate the credentials against a custom identity store for IIS-hosted services can be accomplished by means of an extension at IIS level — such as a custom ASP.NET module or a WCF custom channel that emulates Basic Authentication. These alternatives are not addressed in detail in this book.

The next example is based on a service hosted in IIS that uses SSL for transport security and Basic Authentication to authenticate the clients. The client and service implementations are the same as for message authentication.

Step 1: Configure a Virtual Directory in IIS for SSL

Go to the Internet Information Services (IIS) Manager and configure a server certificate under the Bindings configuration of the default web site, as shown in Figure 8-2. (You can use the certificate created by the script included with the samples, WCFServer.)

Then configure the default web site to require SSL under the SSL settings properties. (See Figure 8-3.)

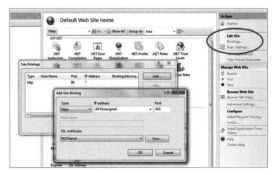

FIGURE 8-2: Virtual directory configuration   **FIGURE 8-3:** SSL Settings

Step 2: Create a Virtual Directory in IIS Configured with Basic Authentication

After SSL is configured for the default web site, you are ready to create a virtual directory to host the services. The virtual directory must also be configured for Basic Authentication as it will be the authentication mechanism that you use for authenticating the clients in the service. (See Figure 8-4.)

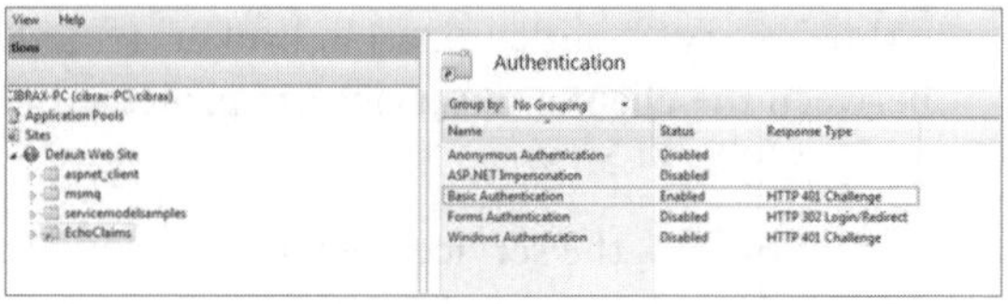

FIGURE 8-4: Basic Authentication settings

That can be accomplished in the authentication options of the virtual directory properties. (You also need to disable anonymous authentication for the virtual directory, which is the default option when a new virtual directory is created.)

Step 3: Configure the Service with WsHttpBinding, Basic Authentication, and Transport Security

In this step you configure the service host to expose the `EchoService` service using a `wsHttpBinding` (as the service uses Http) with basic authentication over transport security.

1. Add the service description with the corresponding endpoint to the `system.ServiceModel` configuration section:

```
<system.serviceModel>
  <services>
    <service name="WCFBook.Samples.EchoClaims"
             behaviorConfiguration="echoClaimsBehavior">
    <endpoint address="EchoClaims"
              contract="WCFBook.Samples.IEchoClaims"
              binding="wsHttpBinding"
              bindingConfiguration="echoClaimsBinding"></endpoint>

    </service>
  </services>
```

2. Configure the `WsHttpBinding` to use transport security with Basic Authentication:

```
<bindings>
  <wsHttpBinding>
    <binding name="echoClaimsBinding">
      <security mode="Transport">
        <transport clientCredentialType="Basic"/>
      </security>
    </binding>
  </wsHttpBinding>
</bindings>
```

Step 4: Configure the Client with WsHttpBinding, Transport Security, and Basic Authentication

The last step is to configure the client application to use the same security settings as you configured on the service side. That is, a client endpoint that uses `WsHttpBinding` with basic authentication over transport security.

1. Add the client endpoint to the `system.ServiceModel` configuration section:

```
<client>
        <endpoint address="http://localhost:8000/EchoClaims"
                  binding="wsHttpBinding"
                  bindingConfiguration="echoClaimsBinding"
                  contract="EchoClaimsReference.IEchoClaims"
                  name="WSHttpBinding_IEchoClaims"
                  behaviorConfiguration="echoClaimsBehavior">
            <identity>
              <dns value="WCFServer"/>
            </identity>
        </endpoint>
    </client>
```

The endpoint identity must match the certificate configured on the service side; otherwise WCF throws an exception at the moment of authenticating the service.

2. Configure the `WsHttpBinding` to use transport security with Basic Authentication:

```
<bindings>
  <wsHttpBinding>
    <binding name="echoClaimsBinding">
      <security mode="Transport">
        <transport clientCredentialType="Basic"/>
      </security>
    </binding>
  </wsHttpBinding>
</bindings>
```

3. As you use test certificates, skip the X509 certificate validations performed by WCF at the moment of authenticating the service credentials. This step is optional if you are using X509 certificates obtained from a trusted certificate authority:

```
<behaviors>
  <endpointBehaviors>
    <behavior name="echoClaimsBehavior">
      <clientCredentials>
        <serviceCertificate>
          <authentication
            certificateValidationMode="None"
            revocationMode="NoCheck"/>
        </serviceCertificate>
      </clientCredentials>
    </behavior>
  </endpointBehaviors>
</behaviors>
```

Mutual X509 Certificate Authentication Over Message Security

Mutual X509 certificate authentication is typical of what is called brokered authentication, as the service trusts the client based on credentials issued by a third party — the authentication broker.

In this scenario, the client provides authentication credentials in the form of X509 certificates issued by a certificate authority (CA) in a public key infrastructure (PKI). The client application attaches the public key of the client's X509 certificate to the request message (or a reference to that certificate), and digitally signs the message with the client's private key. When the service receives the message, it verifies that the message signature is valid using the attached public key, and optionally performs additional validations to ensure that the X509 certificate provided by the client has not expired and was issued by a CA it trusts. The client is authenticated when all these validations pass successfully. (See Figure 8-5.)

FIGURE 8-5: Mutual certificate authentication

The main characteristics of X509 mutual authentication are summarized in the following list:

➤ The credentials presented to the service by the client are based on X509 certificates. This means that a PKI infrastructure is required to issue certificates for any service client.

➤ The trust relationship between clients and services is established by means of an intermediary, the certificate issuer authority.

As it happens with any authentication mechanism based on message security, the client passes the credentials to the service as part of a secure message exchange. The messages in this case are protected using an X509 certificate provided by the service. This certificate also works as a mechanism for the client to authenticate the service as part of the mutual authentication process. The service credentials (the X509 certificate) can be transmitted to the client during the first message exchange or by using an out-of-band mechanism according to the value of the `negotiateServiceCredential` setting.

The strategy for authenticating X509 certificates is implemented in WCF through the abstract class `System.IdentityModel.Selectors.X509CertificateValidator` in the `System.IdentityModel.Selectors` assembly:

```
public abstract class X509CertificateValidator
{
   public abstract void Validate(X509Certificate2 certificate);
}
```

The X509 certificate received as part of the client credentials are passed by WCF to this class for validation. In case the credentials cannot be validated, it is the responsibility of this class to throw an exception.

WCF ships with four internal implementations of this class:

➤ `System.IdentityModel.Selectors.PeerValidator` validates the incoming certificates against the certificates installed in the Trusted People certificate folder.

➤ `System.IdentityModel.Selectors.ChainTrustValidator` validates that the incoming certificates were used by a CA with a certificate installed in the CA Trusted certificate folder.

➤ `System.IdentityModel.Selectors.PerOrChainTrustValidator` is a combination of the first two validators.

➤ `System.IdentityModel.Selectors.NoneX509CertificateValidator` doesn't validate anything. These four implementations can be accessed through public properties in the base `X509CertificateValidator` class.

```
public abstract class X509CertificateValidator
{
  public static X509CertificateValidator ChainTrust { get; }
  public static X509CertificateValidator None { get; }
  public static X509CertificateValidator PeerOrChainTrust { get; }
  public static X509CertificateValidator PeerTrust { get; }
}
```

The following code shows a simple implementation of this class that validates the certificate subject name against hardcoded strings:

```
public class MyX509CertificateValidator : X509CertificateValidator
{
    public override void Validate(X509Certificate2 certificate)
    {
        if (certificate.Subject != "CN=WCFClient")
        {
            throw new SecurityTokenValidationException(
                "The X509 client certificate can not be authenticated");

        }
    }
}
```

If the certificate subject name is different from CN=WCFClient, it throws an exception so WCF assumes the client could not be authenticated.

The settings for changing the X509 client credentials validation mode WCF are available through the configuration element `<clientCertificate/authentication>` under the service behavior `<serviceCredentials>`:

```
<behaviors>
  <serviceBehaviors>
    <behavior name="echoClaimsBehavior">
      <serviceCredentials>
        <clientCertificate>
```

```
                <authentication certificateValidationMode=
  "None|PerTrust|ChainTrust|PerOrChainTrust|Custom"
                             revocationMode="NoCheck|Online|Offline"
                                   />
          </clientCertificate>
        </serviceCredentials>
      </behavior>
    </serviceBehaviors>
  </behaviors>
```

The setting certificateValidatorMode in the <authentication> element allows changing the mode that WCF uses to authenticate the certificate credentials. None, PerTrust, ChainTrust, or PerChainTrust maps with the internal implementations of the validators that were already discussed. The value Custom allows configuring a custom implementation of X509CertificateValidator in case you want to provide something not supported by the other options. (The MyX509CertificatePasswordValidation implementation is an example of a custom implementation.)

Based on the value you chose for this setting, you will need to provide additional values for other related settings.

The validation modes PerTrust, ChainTrust, and PerChainTrust support two optional settings:

1. TrustedStoreLocation: Specifies the location of a trusted certificate folder. The only two possible values for this setting are CurrentUser, for the store used by the current user or LocalMachine, for the store assigned to the machine.

2. RevocationMode: Specifies how the validators will check that the certificates are not revoked. This validation is performed by checking that the certificate is not in the certificate revocation list. The possible values for settings are Online, for checking against the online certificate revocation list, Offline, for using a cached revocation list, or NoCheck, for turning off this validation:

```
    <serviceCredentials>
      <clientCertificate>
        <authentication certificateValidationMode="PerTrust"
                        trustedStoreLocation="LocalMachine|CurrentUser"
                        revocationMode="NoCheck|Online|Offline"/>
      </clientCertificate>
    </serviceCredentials>
```

And finally, the validation mode Custom requires the setting customCertificateValidatorType to specify the .NET type of the custom validator implementation:

```
<serviceBehaviors>
      <behavior name="echoClaimsBehavior">
        <serviceCredentials>
          <clientCertificate>
            <authentication certificateValidationMode="Custom"
                            customCertificateValidatorType=
  "WCFBook.Samples.MyX509CertificateValidator, MyAssembly"
                                 />
          </clientCertificate>
```

```
          </serviceCredentials>
        </behavior>
      </serviceBehaviors>
```

The X509 certificate used to protect the communication must be configured by using the
`<serviceCertificate>` element within the `<serviceCredentials>` behavior as is shown in this
configuration fragment:

```
<serviceBehaviors>
  <behavior name="echoClaimsBehavior">
    <serviceCredentials>
      <serviceCertificate
              findValue="CN=WCFServer"
              storeLocation="LocalMachine"
              storeName="My"
              x509FindType="FindBySubjectDistinguishedName"/>
      <clientCertificate>
        <authentication certificateValidationMode="None"/>
      </clientCertificate>
    </serviceCredentials>
    <serviceMetadata httpGetEnabled="true"/>
  </behavior>
</serviceBehaviors>
```

The instructions for referencing a certificate in this section are the same as seen in the username
authentication scenario.

If you decide to buy certificates from a well-known certificate authority such as Verisign, Thawte,
or Comodo, make sure that the certificates contain the following attributes:

```
KeyUsage:
Digital Signature, Non-Repudiation, Key Encipherment, Data Encipherment (f0)
Enhanced Key Usage: Client Authentication (1.3.6.1.5.5.7.3.2)
```

Most SSL certificates meet these requirements, so it might be a good idea to stick to a SSL in case
you are not sure.

It is time now to walk through a complete example for a service that authenticates the certificates
using a custom validator, and returns the claims of the authenticated certificate.

Step 1: Create the Service Implementation

The service implementation for this sample is quite simple: it basically returns the claims passed
by WCF in the security context as a list of strings. (See Listing 8-5.)

LISTING 8-5: Service Implementation

```
namespace WCFBook.Samples
{
  [ServiceContract()]
  public interface IEchoClaims
```

continues

LISTING 8-5 *(continued)*

```
  {
    [OperationContract]
    List<string> Echo();
  }
}
public class EchoClaims : IEchoClaims
{
  public List<string> Echo()
  {
    List<string> claims = new List<string>();

    foreach (ClaimSet set in
          OperationContext.Current
            .ServiceSecurityContext
            .AuthorizationContext
            .ClaimSets)
    {
      foreach (Claim claim in set)
      {
        claims.Add(string.Format("{0} - {1} - {2}",
                claim.ClaimType,
                claim.Resource.ToString(),
                claim.Right));
      }
    }

    return claims;
  }

}
```

The service is hosted in a console application using the http transport (see Listing 8-6).

LISTING 8-6: Service Host Implementation

```
class Program
{
  static void Main(string[] args)
  {
    ServiceHost host = new ServiceHost(typeof(EchoClaims),
                new Uri("http://localhost:8000"));
    try
    {
      host.Open();

      Console.WriteLine("Service running....");
      Console.WriteLine("Press a key to quit");
      Console.ReadKey();
    }
```

```
    finally
    {
      host.Close();
    }
  }
}
```

Step 2: Configure the Service with WsHttpBinding, Certificate Authentication, and Message Security

In this step you need to configure the service host to expose the EchoService service using a wsHttpBinding (as the service uses http) with certificate authentication over message security.

1. Add the service description with the corresponding endpoint to the system.ServiceModel configuration section:

```
<system.serviceModel>
  <services>
    <service name="WCFBook.Samples.EchoClaims"
             behaviorConfiguration="echoClaimsBehavior">
    <endpoint address="EchoClaims"
              contract="WCFBook.Samples.IEchoClaims"
              binding="wsHttpBinding"
              bindingConfiguration="echoClaimsBinding"></endpoint>

    </service>
  </services>
```

2. Configure the wsHttpBinding to use message security with certificate authentication:

```
<bindings>
  <wsHttpBinding>
    <binding name="echoClaimsBinding">
      <security mode="Message">
        <message clientCredentialType="Certificate"
                 negotiateServiceCredential="true"/>
      </security>
    </binding>
  </wsHttpBinding>
</bindings>
```

The service credentials are automatically negotiated, so the client application does not need to install it using an out-of-band mechanism.

3. Configure the serviceBehavior with the service certificate and the certificate authentication mode:

```
<behavior name="echoClaimsBehavior">
  <serviceCredentials>
    <serviceCertificate
             findValue="CN=WCFServer"
             storeLocation="LocalMachine"
             storeName="My"
             x509FindType="FindBySubjectDistinguishedName"/>
```

```
              <clientCertificate>
                    <authentication certificateValidationMode="Custom"
                                    customCertificateValidatorType=
        "WCFBook.Samples.MyX509CertificateValidator, Common"
                                    />

              </clientCertificate>
          </serviceCredentials>
          <serviceMetadata httpGetEnabled="true"/>
      </behavior>
```

The service authenticates the client certificates using a custom validator implementation provided in the type WCFBook.Samples.MyX509CertificateValidator.

The X509 certificate CN=WCFServer is a test certificate created for this sample using the makecert.exe tool. A script SetupCerts.bat has been included with the samples to automatically create and register the X509 certificates in the Windows certificate store. Make sure to run this script before playing with the samples.

Step 3: Implement the Custom X509CertificateValidator

As already seen, a custom certificate validator must derive from the base class X509CertificateValidator and provide the implementation for the method Validate as shown in Listing 8-7.

LISTING 8-7: Custom X509CertificateValidator Implementation

```
public override void Validate(X509Certificate2 certificate)
    {
        if (certificate.Subject != "CN=WCFClient")
        {
            throw new SecurityTokenValidationException(
                "The X509 client certificate can not be authenticated");

        }
    }
```

The implementation of the custom validator only checks the certificate subject name. It throws an exception for any certificate that does not match the subject name CN=WCFClient.

Step 4: Implement the Client Application

The client application is a basic console application that calls the service to obtain the user claims. The client credentials in this case are specified through the configuration file (see Listing 8-8).

LISTING 8-8: Client Application Implementation

```
static void Main(string[] args)
    {
        EchoClaimsReference.EchoClaimsClient client = new
```

```
Client.EchoClaimsReference.EchoClaimsClient();

try
{
    string[] claims = client.Echo();

    foreach (string claim in claims)
    {
        Console.WriteLine(claim);
    }
}
catch (TimeoutException exception)
{
    Console.WriteLine("Got {0}", exception.GetType());
    client.Abort();
}
catch (CommunicationException exception)
{
    Console.WriteLine("Got {0}", exception.GetType());
    client.Abort();
}
}
```

In case you decide to initialize the client credentials through code, the `ClientCredentials` property of the channel contains a method `SetCertificate` that becomes handy for this purpose:

```
client.ClientCredentials.ClientCertificate.SetCertificate(
    StoreLocation.LocalMachine,
    StoreName.My,
    X509FindType.FindBySubjectDistinguishedName,
    "CN=WCFClient");
```

Step 5: Configure the Client with WsHttpBinding, Message Security, and Certificate Authentication

The last step is to configure the client application to use the same security settings configured on the service side. That is, a client endpoint that uses `wsHttpBinding` with certificate authentication over message security.

1. Add the client endpoint to the `system.ServiceModel` configuration section:

```
<client>
        <endpoint address="http://localhost:8000/EchoClaims"
                  binding="wsHttpBinding"
                  bindingConfiguration="echoClaimsBinding"
                  contract="EchoClaimsReference.IEchoClaims"
                  name="WSHttpBinding_IEchoClaims"
                  behaviorConfiguration="echoClaimsBehavior">
          <identity>
            <dns value="WCFServer"/>
          </identity>
        </endpoint>
    </client>
```

The endpoint identity must match the certificate configured on the service side; otherwise WCF will throw an exception at the moment of authenticating the service.

2. Configure `WsHttpBinding` to use message security with certificate authentication:

```
<bindings>
  <wsHttpBinding>
    <binding name="echoClaimsBinding">
      <security mode="Message">
        <message
          clientCredentialType="Certificate"
          negotiateServiceCredential="true"/>
      </security>
    </binding>
  </wsHttpBinding>
</bindings>
```

3. As you use test certificates, you need to skip the X509 certificate validations performed by WCF at the moment of authenticating the service credentials. This step is optional if you are using X509 certificates obtained from a trusted certificate authority:

```
<behaviors>
  <endpointBehaviors>
    <behavior name="echoClaimsBehavior">
      <clientCredentials>
        <serviceCertificate>
          <authentication
            certificateValidationMode="None"
            revocationMode="NoCheck"/>
        </serviceCertificate>
      </clientCredentials>
    </behavior>
  </endpointBehaviors>
</behaviors>
```

Kerberos Authentication Over Message Security

Kerberos authentication is another example of brokered authentication, where the service trusts the client based on certain credentials (a Kerberos ticket) issued by a third party.

In this scenario, the client provides authentication credentials in the form of a Kerberos ticket issued by a Kerberos Key Distribution Center (KDC).

Describing how Kerberos works in detail is beyond the scope of this book. However, it is important to understand that the client must be first authenticated against the broker, the KDC, and have access to a Kerberos ticket before it can request access to a service.

When Kerberos authentication is used, the client application requests a service ticket from a KDC for communicating with a specific service. The KDC creates a new session key and service ticket on behalf of the client's request. The ticket is encrypted with a key that is only known by the service (the service's master key). After the client receives the ticket and the session key, it uses both to create a Kerberos security token that will be included as the client credentials in the request message to the service. The session key is not included in the token, it is only included in the service ticket, which is what the service uses to validate the token.

The client protects the request message (signs and optionally encrypts the message) for the service using the session key, and includes the Kerberos token as client credentials. The service receives the request message, uses its master key to decrypt the service ticket found in the security token, and retrieves the session key. The session key is used to verify the message signature and optionally decrypts the message. Optionally, the service returns a response to the client. To provide mutual authentication in this scenario, the response should contain information that is encrypted with the session key to prove to the client that the service knows the session key.

The main characteristics of Kerberos authentication are summarized in the following list:

➤ Kerberos provides SSO capabilities, which allow a client to authenticate only once per logon session.

➤ As Kerberos is closely integrated with the Windows operating system, this enables the operating system to provide additional capabilities, such as impersonation and delegation.

➤ Kerberos supports mutual authentication without needing X509 certificates. The service only needs to send a response that contains data encrypted with the shared session key to prove its identity to the client.

➤ The client and the service must both be in the same Active Directory forest to use Kerberos, which is typically only valid for intranet scenarios.

➤ Kerberos requires that the KDC be available at all times. If the KDC fails, the clients will not be able to establish a trust relationship with the services.

The negotiateServiceCredential setting works slightly differently in Kerberos compared to the rest of authentication schemas that use X509 certificates as service credentials. When this setting is set to false, the account running the service process must be associated with a Kerberos service principal name (SPN). To accomplish this, the service should run under the network service account or local system account. Alternatively, a SPN should be associated to the account using the SetSpn.exe tool. In either case, the client must specify the correct SPN in the endpoint identity as in the next sample:

```
<client>
    <endpoint address="http://localhost:8000/EchoClaims"
                binding="wsHttpBinding"
                bindingConfiguration="echoClaimsBinding"
                contract="EchoClaimsReference.IEchoClaims"
                name="WSHttpBinding_IEchoClaims"
                behaviorConfiguration="echoClaimsBehavior">
        <identity>
          <servicePrincipalName value="HOST/MyMachine"/>
        </identity>
    </endpoint>
</client>
```

Kerberos authentication does not provide any kind of high-level class to validate the received credentials you have with Username and Certificate. The validation can be done, but at a much deeper level in the WCF stack with a custom `SecurityTokenAuthenticator` — this kind of extensibility point is not discussed in this chapter.

Let's walk through a complete example for a service that authenticates clients using Kerberos, and returns after the claims are extracted from the WCF security context.

Step 1: Create the Service Implementation

The service implementation for this sample is quite simple: it basically returns the claims passed by WCF in the security context as a list of strings. (See Listing 8-9.)

LISTING 8-9: Service Implementation

```
namespace WCFBook.Samples
{
  [ServiceContract()]
  public interface IEchoClaims
  {
    [OperationContract]
    List<string> Echo();
  }
}
public class EchoClaims : IEchoClaims
{
  public List<string> Echo()
  {
    List<string> claims = new List<string>();

    foreach (ClaimSet set in
          OperationContext.Current
            .ServiceSecurityContext
            .AuthorizationContext
            .ClaimSets)
    {
      foreach (Claim claim in set)
      {
        claims.Add(string.Format("{0} - {1} - {2}",
              claim.ClaimType,
              claim.Resource.ToString(),
              claim.Right));
      }
    }

    return claims;
  }

}
```

The service is hosted in a console application using the http transport. (See Listing 8-10.)

LISTING 8-10: Service Host Implementation

```
class Program
{
  static void Main(string[] args)
  {
    ServiceHost host = new ServiceHost(typeof(EchoClaims),
                       new Uri("http://localhost:8000"));
    try
    {
      host.Open();

      Console.WriteLine("Service running....");
      Console.WriteLine("Press a key to quit");
      Console.ReadKey();
    }
    finally
    {
      host.Close();
    }
  }
}
```

Step 2: Configure the Service with WsHttpBinding, Windows Authentication, and Message Security

In this step you need to configure the service host to expose the `EchoService` service using a `wsHttpBinding` (as the service uses Http) with Windows authentication over message security.

1. Add the service description with the corresponding endpoint to the `system.ServiceModel` configuration section:

```
<system.serviceModel>
  <services>
    <service name="WCFBook.Samples.EchoClaims"
             behaviorConfiguration="echoClaimsBehavior">
    <endpoint address="EchoClaims"
              contract="WCFBook.Samples.IEchoClaims"
              binding="wsHttpBinding"
              bindingConfiguration="echoClaimsBinding"></endpoint>

    </service>
  </services>
```

2. Configure the `wsHttpBinding` to use message security with Windows authentication:

```
<bindings>
  <wsHttpBinding>
    <binding name="echoClaimsBinding">
      <security mode="Message">
        <message clientCredentialType="Windows"
                 negotiateServiceCredential="true"/>
```

```
            </security>
          </binding>
        </wsHttpBinding>
      </bindings>
```

The service credentials are automatically negotiated, so the client application does not need to manually configure the service SPN.

Step 3: Implement the Client Application

The client application is a basic console application that calls the service to obtain user claims. The client credentials are automatically negotiated from the current Windows logon session. (See Listing 8-11.)

LISTING 8-11: Client Application Implementation

```csharp
static void Main(string[] args)
{
    EchoClaimsReference.EchoClaimsClient client = new
    Client.EchoClaimsReference.EchoClaimsClient();

    try
    {
        string[] claims = client.Echo();

        foreach (string claim in claims)
        {
            Console.WriteLine(claim);
        }
    }
    catch (TimeoutException exception)
    {
        Console.WriteLine("Got {0}", exception.GetType());
        client.Abort();
    }
    catch (CommunicationException exception)
    {
        Console.WriteLine("Got {0}", exception.GetType());
        client.Abort();
    }
}
```

Step 4: Configure the Client with WsHttpBinding, Message Security, and Windows Authentication

The last step is to configure the client application to use the same security settings you configure on the service side. That is, a client endpoint that uses wsHttpBinding with Windows authentication over message security.

1. Add the client endpoint to the system.ServiceModel configuration section:

```xml
<client>
    <endpoint address="http://localhost:8000/EchoClaims"
        binding="wsHttpBinding"
```

```
              bindingConfiguration="echoClaimsBinding"
              contract="EchoClaimsReference.IEchoClaims"
              name="WSHttpBinding_IEchoClaims"
              behaviorConfiguration="echoClaimsBehavior">
        </endpoint>
    </client>
```

The endpoint identity is not required as it is automatically negotiated.

2. Configure the `wsHttpBinding` to use message security with Windows authentication:

```
<bindings>
  <wsHttpBinding>
    <binding name="echoClaimsBinding">
      <security mode="Message">
        <message
          clientCredentialType="Windows"
          negotiateServiceCredential="true"/>
      </security>
    </binding>
  </wsHttpBinding>
</bindings>
```

Claims Transformation and Security Context Initialization

As discussed in the previous "Claims-Based Identity Model" section, WCF converts every successfully authenticated security token into a set of claims that are passed to the service through the security context.

One of the problems with this approach is that services often require domain-specific claims about the business context where they are running — such as the user's e-mail address, purchase limits, and user's aliases. Technical claims about the authenticated security tokens are also included, such as the user's SID or the certificate's subject name.

The process of converting existing claims or creating new ones according to the service requirements often receive the name *claims transformation*. As the WCF operation should deal with claims only, it is easy enough to create new claim sets with the new information using the `ClaimSet` class. The only thing you need is some kind of extensibility point to perform that transformation before the claims are attached to the operation security context.

Fortunately, WCF provides an extensibility point for that purpose, which receives the name of authorization policies.

The authorization policies are executed by WCF after the internal claims generation is completed (based on the authenticated security tokens), and right before the service operation is executed. Therefore, all the claims associated with the client's credentials are also available in this extension.

A custom authorization policy can be created in WCF by implementing the interface `System` `.IdentityModel.Policy.IAuthorizationPolicy`:

```
public interface IAuthorizationPolicy
{
  string Id { get; }
```

```
  ClaimSet Issuer { get; }
  bool Evaluate(EvaluationContext evaluationContext, ref object state);
}
```

The Id property returns a unique identifier for the policy, which is usually a GUID. Issuer returns a claim set describing the issuer of the claims that the policy creates. The method Evaluate is where the concrete implementation of the policy goes. This last one receives an authorization context while it is still in the process of being built:

```
public class CustomAuthorizationPolicy : IAuthorizationPolicy
{
  string id = "Custom_" + Guid.NewGuid().ToString();

  public bool Evaluate(EvaluationContext evaluationContext, ref object state)
  {
    bool isFound = false;

    foreach (ClaimSet cs in evaluationContext.ClaimSets)
    {
      foreach (Claim claim in
cs.FindClaims(ClaimTypes.Name, Rights.PossessProperty))
      {
        if (claim.Resource.ToString()
.Equals("joe", StringComparison.InvariantCultureIgnoreCase))
        {
          isFound = true;
          break;
        }
      }
    }

    if (isFound)
    {
      evaluationContext.AddClaimSet(this,
        new DefaultClaimSet(this.Issuer,
            new Claim[] { new Claim("http://myClaimType", "I am joe",
Rights.PossessProperty)    }));
    }

    return true;
  }

  public ClaimSet Issuer
  {
    get { return ClaimSet.System; }
  }

  public string Id
  {
    get { return id; }
  }

}
```

The previous code shows a common implementation of an authorization policy. That authorization policy basically inspects the received evaluation context to find a specific claim that represents a username equal to "Joe." If the claim is found, a new claim set is added to the context with an application-specific claim `http://myClaimType`.

An authorization policy is also the right place to plug code into the service security context initialization. Setting a custom security principal in the security context is a good example of things that can be done in an authorization policy:

```
public class CustomAuthorizationPolicy : IAuthorizationPolicy
{
    string id = "Custom_" + Guid.NewGuid().ToString();

    public bool Evaluate(EvaluationContext evaluationContext, ref object state)
    {
        object obj;
        if (!evaluationContext.Properties.TryGetValue("Identities", out obj))
            return false;

        IList<IIdentity> identities = obj as IList<IIdentity>;
        if (obj == null || identities.Count <= 0)
            return false;

        evaluationContext.Properties["Principal"] =
new GenericPrincipal(identities[0], new string[]{});
        return true;

    }

    public ClaimSet Issuer
    {
        get { return ClaimSet.System; }
    }

    public string Id
    {
        get { return id; }
    }

}
```

The last thing you need to do is configure the authorization policies in the WCF configuration as part of the `<serviceAuthorization>` behavior so they are invoked when new requests arrive to the service. You can add one or more policies, and they are invoked in the same order as you add them:

```
<behaviors>
    <serviceBehaviors>
        <behavior name="echoClaimsBehavior">
            <serviceAuthorization>
                <authorizationPolicies>
                    <add policyType="Common.CustomAuthorizationPolicy, Common"/>
                </authorizationPolicies>
```

```
        </serviceAuthorization>
      </behavior>
    </serviceBehaviors>

  </behaviors>
```

Service Authorization

Now that you know how authentication works in WCF, and how the claims are transformed before they get to the service operation, it is a good moment to discuss another interesting aspect about security in WCF — authorization.

WCF provides two mechanisms for implementing authorization in services, a simple and easy-to-use schema based on user roles, and a more complex and powerful schema based on claims. As part of this section, we discuss both schemas in detail and how they can be used to implement robust service authorization.

Role-Based Authorization

Role-based authorization is not something new that WCF brings to the scene; it has been available since the beginning in the .NET platform. The idea is that you associate a list of roles with a user, and then at runtime, the service implementation can use that list to take authorization-related decisions. An application can get the roles assigned to the user from different places or stores (such as a database or Azman), or they can be inferred from the Windows groups where the user is a member.

In the .NET world, the user identity and the roles assigned to that identity in a specific context are represented by the interfaces System.Security.IIdentity and System.Security.IPrincipal respectively.

A System.Security.IIdentity implementation class provides information about the name of the user (Name), whether he was authenticated (IsAuthenticated), and how he was authenticated (AuthenticationType):

```
public interface IIdentity
{
  string AuthenticationType { get; }
  bool IsAuthenticated { get; }
  string Name { get; }
}
```

On the other hand, an implementation of the System.Security.IPrincipal class contains a reference to the user identity (IIdentity) and must provide a method to verify whether the user belongs to a specific role:

```
public interface IPrincipal
{
  bool IsInRole(string role);
  IIdentity Identity { get; }
}
```

Some implementations are provided out of the box in the .NET Framework; for example, you can find the System.Security.WindowsIdentity and System.Security.WindowsPrincipal implementations for representing a Windows user, or a more generic implementation for any purpose in the classes System.Security.GenericIdentity and System.Security.GenericPrincipal.

A security principal is typically attached to the currently executing thread in your application. This is through the static property CurrentPrincipal in the System.Threading.Thread class. One part of the application is responsible for initializing that property, so the rest of the application can grab it from there and use it to perform any authorization code.

WCF works in the same way — the <serviceAuthorization> behavior controls the creation of a System.Security.IPrincipal instance and associates it to the thread handling the current request. When the clients have been Windows authenticated, WCF tries to populate the Thread .CurrentPrincipal with a Windows principal. With other authentication types, you have a choice between getting the roles from an ASP.NET role provider and implementing a custom authorization policy to provide a principal implementation (a generic principal in most cases).

In addition to the method IsInRole available in the user principal to perform role-based security checks, there is an attribute PermissionAttribute that allows you to annotate your service operations with role requirements. When this attribute is set for a specific operation, the security subsystem in the .NET CLR checks whether the principal attached to the current thread meets the requirements specified in the attribute. If the requirements are not met, a SecurityException is thrown prior to executing the service operation. WCF catches and converts this exception into an Access Denied fault before returning a response to the client.

The following code snippets show authorization code using the PrincipalPermission attribute, and the equivalent version using the Principal.IsInRole method:

```
public class Service : IService
{
    [PrincipalPermission(SecurityAction.Demand, Role = "Administrators")]
    public string DoOperation() {
    {
        return ...;
    }
}
public class Service : IService
{
    public string DoOperation() {
    {
        if (Thread.CurrentPrincipal.IsInRole("Administrators"))
        {
            return ...
        }
        else
        {
            throw new SecurityException();
        }

    }
}
```

As you can see, the use of the `System.Security.PrincipalPermission` attribute requires that you hardcode any possible group names when the service operation is being developed.

Using an ASP.NET Role Provider

WCF provides the flexibility of using an existing ASP.NET role provider to retrieve the roles for a user when the principal instance is created. The strategy for using an ASP.NET role provider is very similar to what we saw for ASP.NET membership in authentication. You can use one of the built-in providers such as the role provider for SQL server (`System.Web.Security.SqlRoleProvider`), the role provider for Azman (`System.Web.Security.AuthorizationStoreRoleProvider`) or the Windows role provider (`System.Web.Security.WindowsTokenRoleProvider`), or develop your own provider by deriving from the base class `System.Web.Security.RoleProvider`.

When WCF is configured to use a role provider, the `<serviceAuthorization>` behavior attaches an instance of the class `System.ServiceModel.Security.RoleProviderPrincipal` to the executing thread. This class basically wraps an instance of the configured role provider, and forwards any call to the method `IsInRole` to the method `IsUserInRole` of the inner role provider.

Therefore, any role provider that you want to use with WCF must implement the method `IsUserInRole`:

```
public class MyCustomRoleProvider : RoleProvider
{
    public override string[] GetRolesForUser(string username)
    {
        if (username == "joe")
        {
            return new string[] { "administrators" };
        }
        else
        {
            return new string[] { "users" };
        }
    }

    public override bool IsUserInRole(string username, string roleName)
    {
        return GetRolesForUser(username).Contains(roleName);
    }

    #region Omitted
    #endregion

}
```

And the corresponding WCF configuration for using that custom role provider is shown here:

```
<behaviors>
    <serviceBehaviors>
        <behavior name="echoClaimsBehavior">
            <serviceAuthorization
                principalPermissionMode="UseAspNetRoles"
```

```
                rolePoviderName="MyRoleProvider"/>
            </behavior>
        </serviceBehaviors>
    </behaviors>
<system.web>
    <roleManager enabled="true">
        <providers>
            <add name="MyRoleProvider" type="Common.MyCustomRoleProvider, Common"/>
        </providers>
    </roleManager>
</system.web>
```

Using a Custom Principal

In case you decide to use a custom principal implementation, WCF gives you the chance to attach a custom principal in an authorization policy when the security context is initialized, as discussed in the "Claims Transformation and Security Context Initialization" section.

After you implement a custom authorization policy to attach the principal to the security context, the principalPermissionMode in the serviceAuthorization behavior has to be set to Custom to instruct WCF to load the principal into the Thread.CurrentPrincipal property as well:

```
<behaviors>
    <serviceBehaviors>
        <behavior name="echoClaimsBehavior">
            <serviceAuthorization
                principalPermissionMode="Custom">
            <authorizationPolicies>
                <add policyType="Common.CustomAuthorizationPolicy, Common"/>
            </authorizationPolicies>
            </serviceAuthorization>
        </behavior>
    </serviceBehaviors>

</behaviors>
```

Claim-Based Authorization and the Authorization Context

You know that WCF passes the claims associated to the authenticated credentials, and the claims created in the custom authorization policies as part of the security context to the operation. Therefore, you can use all the flexibility that claims provide to represent identity information or individual rights to implement authorization code in the service operations.

All the claim sets that were generated prior to the service operation execution are available in WCF through the authorization context.

WCF provides access to the authorization context via the thread-static ServiceSecurityContext, which represents a container for claim sets, authorization policies, and current user identities:

```
public class ServiceSecurityContext
{
    public AuthorizationContext AuthorizationContext { get; }
```

```
public ReadOnlyCollection<IAuthorizationPolicy> AuthorizationPolicies { get; }
public static ServiceSecurityContext Current { get; }
public bool IsAnonymous { get; }
public IIdentity PrimaryIdentity { get; }
public WindowsIdentity WindowsIdentity { get; }
}
```

The service operation can simply enumerate the claim sets received as part of the authorization context to verify whether the user has permissions to execute an action or not:

```
public class Service : IService
{
    public void DoAction()
    {
        bool isFound = false;

        foreach (ClaimSet cs in OperationContext
            .Current
            .ServiceSecurityContext
            .AuthorizationContext
            .ClaimSets)
        {
            foreach (Claim claim in cs.FindClaims("urn:Group",
Rights.PossessProperty))
            {
                if (claim.Resource.ToString().Equals("administrator",
StringComparison.InvariantCultureIgnoreCase))
                {
                    isFound = true;
                    break;
                }
            }
        }

        if (!isFound)
        {
            throw new SecurityException("You are not authorized");
        }

    }

}
```

In the previous example, the service operation looks for an specific claim `"urn:Group"` with a resource value equal to `"administrator"`. If that claim is not found, an exception is thrown as the user does not have permission to execute the operation.

Authorization Managers

You have seen so far how to use the user roles or claims in the service operation to implement authorization logic. However, in some cases, you might want to centralize all that authorization logic into one place and use it for every incoming request — without spreading it over all the service operations.

For that purpose, WCF provides a specific extensibility point known as the authorization manager. A service authorization manager is a class that derives from `System.ServiceModel` `.ServiceAuthorizationManager` and overrides the protected method `CheckAccessCore` to run custom authorization code for each request:

```
public class ServiceAuthorizationManager
{
    public virtual bool CheckAccess(OperationContext operationContext);
    public virtual bool CheckAccess(OperationContext operationContext,
ref Message message);

    protected virtual bool CheckAccessCore(OperationContext operationContext);

    protected virtual ReadOnlyCollection<IAuthorizationPolicy>
GetAuthorizationPolicies(OperationContext operationContext);
}
```

You can override any of the virtual methods in this class; however, WCF always calls the `CheckAccessCore` method.

That method receives the WCF operation context as an argument, so your authorization logic can either inspect the incoming message or the user authentication claims for enforcing authorization logic (or roles if you want to use role-based authorization logic). The result of the authorization logic is returned in that method, "true" when access is granted and "false" when it is denied.

The following code example uses the authentication claims to make an authorization decision:

```
public class MyAuthorizationManager : ServiceAuthorizationManager
{
    protected override bool CheckAccessCore(OperationContext operationContext)
    {
        bool isFound = false;

        foreach (ClaimSet cs in OperationContext
            .Current
            .ServiceSecurityContext
            .AuthorizationContext
            .ClaimSets)
        {
            foreach (Claim claim in
cs.FindClaims("urn:Group", Rights.PossessProperty))
            {
                if (claim.Resource.ToString().Equals("administrators",
StringComparison.InvariantCultureIgnoreCase))
                {
                    isFound = true;
                    break;
                }
            }
        }

        if (!isFound)
        {
```

```
            return false;
        }

        return true;
    }

}
```

A custom authorization manager implementation can be configured in WCF using the `serviceAuthorizationManagerType` attribute in the `<serviceAuthorization>` behavior:

```
<behaviors>
  <serviceBehaviors>
    <behavior name="serviceBehavior">
      <serviceAuthorization
            serviceAuthorizationManagerType=
"Common.MyAuthorizationManager, Common"/>
    </behavior>
  </serviceBehaviors>

</behaviors>
```

Although using some information in the message content (SOAP body) is not recommended for performance reasons, you should keep in mind that messages in WCF are always read once. That means that you have to create a copy first before reading the content. That can be accomplished using the following code (not recommended for large or streamed messages):

```
MessageBuffer buffer = operationContext
                .RequestContext
                .RequestMessage
                .CreateBufferedCopy(int.MaxValue);
```

9

Federated Authentication in WCF

WHAT'S IN THIS CHAPTER?

➤ Understanding the federated authentication principles

➤ Getting started with Windows Identify Foundation (WIF)

➤ Implementing a Security Token Service with WIF

➤ Implementing a Claim-Aware service

This chapter is exclusively dedicated to the integration between the Windows Identity Foundation framework and WCF, mainly focusing on how to negotiate claims from a secure token service and use it for security decisions in the services.

If you are not experienced with federated authentication, do not worry, as important aspects are discussed here about how this security model works under the scene in WCF.

FEDERATED AUTHENTICATION

Federated authentication is another example of Brokered Authentication, where services rely on a third party, a Security Token Service (STS), for authenticating callers and issuing security tokens that carry claims describing the caller.

An STS in this context provides a powerful mechanism to meet some of the following requirements:

➤ Decouple services from different authentication mechanisms or credential types so they can focus on authorizing or processing relevant claims.

➤ Support a federated architecture where clients authenticated in one domain are granted access to resources or services in another domain by establishing trust between each domain's STS.

➤ Transform claims into a relevant set of claims expected by the authorization code at services.

As you can see, it represents an excellent tool for consolidating the client authentication, and gets rid of the identity silos that have been created by different applications in the enterprise.

What Is a Security Token Service (STS)?

From a high level, a STS is service implementation that primarily follows the WS-Trust specification to issue security tokens. The WS-Trust is more than that, as it describes a contract with four operations — Issue, Validate, Renew, and Cancel. These operations are called by clients to request a new security token, to validate an existing token, to renew an expired token, or to cancel a token when it is no longer needed.

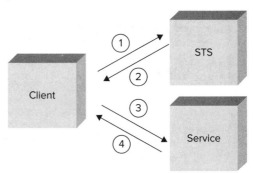

FIGURE 9-1: Security Token Service

Figure 9-1 summarizes the complete process for consuming a service that delegates the client authentication to a STS.

1. The client application sends a `RequestSecurityToken` message (RST), which is part of the WS-Trust specification, to request a new security token to the STS. This message contains client credentials, and it is protected with security settings previously agreed on between the client and the STS.

2. The STS receives the request message, authenticates the client, and verifies the message protection. If the client authentication and message protection verification give positive results, the STS uses information received in the message to create a session key and a new security token that includes an encrypted version of the session key (encrypted with a key that only the service possesses). The security token and the session key are attached to a `RequestSecurityTokenResponse` message (RSTR) and are sent back to the client.

3. The client receives the RSTR message and extracts the security token and the session key from that message. After that, it includes the security token as client credentials for the request message to service, and protects that message using the session key.

4. The service receives the request from the client, verifies that the security token used as client credentials is valid, and decrypts and extracts the session key from that token (using the same service key used by the STS). Finally, the session key is used to verify the message protection. If everything is okay, the service operation is executed and the results are sent back to the client.

Federation Authentication Between Multiple Domains

A simple STS works fine as long as all involved parties (clients, services, and the STS) live in the same trust boundary, which typically receives the name of domain or security realm.

The thing becomes complex when a client running in a specific domain wants to consume a service exposed in another domain. This problem is typically solved by establishing a trust relationship between the STSes running on each domain. (See Figure 9-2.)

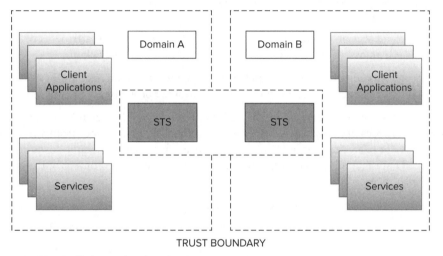

TRUST BOUNDARY

FIGURE 9-2: Federated authentication

In the way this works, a client in domain A should first obtain a security token from the STS in the same domain, and use it later for obtaining a security token from the STS running on domain B. Because there is a trust relationship between the STS running in both domains, the client should be able to get a security token from the domain B without problems, and use it for consuming any service exposed in that domain.

Everything is transparent for the client applications and the services. The client applications always authenticate against the first STS using the same credentials (which is usually known as Single Sign On or just SSO), and the services always receive a set of claims representing identity information about the clients.

The same example could be expanded to multiple domains by chaining multiple STSes to create a trust network.

Security Assertions Markup Language (SAML)

Discussed so far has been how a client application can obtain a security token from a STS to be used with a specific service. As you might notice, that security token is something abstract and it can be represented with any of the security tokens that we already know. These include usernames,

X509 certificates, or Kerberos. However, there is a security token that you haven't seen yet and it represents the best way to carry user claims in scenarios with federated authentication. Enter SAML to the scene.

SAML is the acronym for *Security Assertions Markup Language*, a vendor-neutral specification for exchanging units of security-related information called *assertions* — equivalent to an identity claim.

Four main factors have contributed in the adoption of SAML as a security token for federated authentication scenarios:

1. It is completely XML-based, and therefore assures interoperability between different platforms.

2. It contains a payload section totally extensible through the use of custom attributes or assertions. As said, an assertion can carry information about an identity claim.

3. It can carry cryptographic information to perform encryption or digital signature operations, which in essence are required for proving message protection.

4. It can carry a digital signature created by the issuer of the token. This signature is extremely useful for two purposes: it allows the services to verify that the token comes from a trusted party, and it has not been changed in transit. (Otherwise, the signature cannot be verified with unchanged data in a token. The signature cannot be verified if the content of the SAML token was changed.)

Nowadays, there are two available specifications for SAML; 1.1 and 2.0.

The following XML fragment illustrates how a SAML token 1.1 looks when it is included in a SOAP message:

```
<saml:Assertion MajorVersion="1" MinorVersion="1"
AssertionID="_5d1920bc-3efa-481a-99e2-1a9469f1a128"
Issuer="http://WCFBookSTS" IssueInstant="2009-08-13T14:00:37.716Z"
xmlsn:saml="urn:oasis:names:tc:SAML:1.0:assertion">
    <saml:Conditions NotBefore="2009-08-13T14:00:37.651Z"
NotOnOrAfter="2009-08-14T00:00:37.651Z">
      <saml:AudienceRestrictionCondition>
        <saml:Audience>http://localhost:8000/EchoClaims</saml:Audience>
      </saml:AudienceRestrictionCondition>
    </saml:Conditions>
    <saml:AttributeStatement>
      <saml:Subject>
        <saml:SubjectConfirmation>
          <saml:ConfirmationMethod>urn:oasis:names:tc:SAML:1.0:cm:holder-of-key
</saml:ConfirmationMethod>
          <KeyInfo xmlns="http://www.w3.org/2000/09/xmldsig#">
            <!-- Encrypted Session Key -->
          </KeyInfo>
        </saml:SubjectConfirmation>
      </saml:Subject>
      <saml:Attribute AttributeName="name"
AttributeNamespace="http://schemas.xmlsoap.org/ws/2005/05/identity/claims">
        <saml:AttributeValue>
          <!-- Attribute value -->
```

```
            </saml:AttributeValue>
          </saml:Attribute>
          <saml:Attribute AttributeName="AgeClaim"
 AttributeNamespace="http://WCFBookSamples/2008/05">
            <saml:AttributeValue>
              <!-- Attribute value -->
            </saml:AttributeValue>
          </saml:Attribute>
        </saml:AttributeStatement>
        <ds:Signature xmlns:ds="http://www.w3.org/2000/09/xmldsig#">
          <!-- Issuer Signature -->
        </ds:Signature>
      </saml:Assertion>
```

WINDOWS IDENTITY FOUNDATION (WIF)

The *Windows Identity Foundation (WIF) framework*, formerly called *Geneva framework*, is the name for the new framework for building claims-based applications and services, and for implementing federated security scenarios. Included among this framework's features is focusing on the development of a Security Token Service, and its close integration with WCF.

Claims-Based Model in WIF

Although WCF has native support for a claims-based security model, WIF enhances this experience by simplifying access to claims at runtime and providing a mechanism to support claims-based authorization using the role-based authorization principles already available in the .NET Framework. In other words, all the classes shipped as part of WCF to implement claims-based security, already discussed throughout this chapter, are no longer needed if you decide to develop your security authorization model on top of WIF.

> *All the classes discussed in the chapter are part of the WIF runtime. There is also an optional SDK that provides additional tools, documentation, and samples that are very useful for any person developing applications targeting the WIF runtime.*

A claim in WIF is represented by the class `Microsoft.IdentityModel.Claims.Claim`:

```
public class Claim
{
  public virtual string ClaimType { get; }
  public virtual string Issuer { get; }
  public virtual string OriginalIssuer { get; }
  public virtual IDictionary<string, string> Properties { get; }
  public virtual IClaimsIdentity Subject { get; }
  public virtual string Value { get; }
  public virtual string ValueType { get; }
}
```

The properties `ClaimType`, `Issuer`, and `OriginalIssuer` have the same meaning as we saw in the traditional WCF model. The property `Value`, on the other hand, presents a slight difference as it can only contain string values instead of an object reference that could point to any CLR type. So an integer value of 10 would be represented as `"10"`. The property `ValueType` has been added to figure out how to deserialize the value of the claim by telling you the format of the value. Some of the possible value types are available in the class `Microsoft.IdentityModel.Claims.ClaimValueTypes`:

```
public static class ClaimValueTypes
{
    public const string
        Base64Binary = "http://www.w3.org/2001/XMLSchema#base64Binary";
    public const string
        Boolean = "http://www.w3.org/2001/XMLSchema#boolean";
    public const string
        Date = "http://www.w3.org/2001/XMLSchema#date";
    public const string
        Datetime = "http://www.w3.org/2001/XMLSchema#dateTime";
    public const string
        DaytimeDuration = "http://www.w3.org/TR/2002/WD-xquery-operators-
20020816#dayTimeDuration";
    public const string
        Double = "http://www.w3.org/2001/XMLSchema#double";
    public const string
        DsaKeyValue = "http://www.w3.org/2000/09/xmldsig#DSAKeyValue";
    public const string
        HexBinary = "http://www.w3.org/2001/XMLSchema#hexBinary";
    public const string
        Integer = "http://www.w3.org/2001/XMLSchema#integer";

}
```

The property `Subject` references a valid instance of `Microsoft.IdentityModel.Claims.IClaimsIdentity`, a new interface derived from `System.Security.IIdentity` to represent the identity of the subject that owns the claim.

And finally, in case you want to include additional data about the claim that cannot be represented by any of the existing properties, you can use the `Properties` dictionary for that purpose. This dictionary is a generic property bag for storing key/value pairs.

The New IClaimsIdentity and IClaimsPrincipal Interfaces

WIF introduced two new interfaces for representing client identities and principals: `Microsoft.IdentityModel.Claims.IClaimsIdentity` and `Microsoft.IdentityModel.Claims.IClaimsPrincipal` respectively (and the corresponding implementations `ClaimsIdentity` and `ClaimsPrincipal`).

`IClaimsIdentity`, in addition to giving you information about the client identity, provides a Claims property to gain access to claims associated to that identity. This could be the name, whether it is authenticated, or the way the client was authenticated.

```
public interface IClaimsIdentity : IIdentity
{
  ClaimCollection Claims { get; }
}
```

Because you have a new identity interface, there is also a principal interface `IClaimsPrincipal`
with the corresponding implementation `ClaimsPrincipal`. This specific implementation wraps an
instance of `IClaimsIdentity` instance and implements the `IsInRole` method by checking into the
available claims:

```
public interface IClaimsPrincipal : IPrincipal
{
  ClaimsIdentityCollection Identities { get; }
}
```

Building an Active STS

Prior to WIF, building an active STS using WCF was a very complicated thing. All the documentation
and examples available were unofficial and spread across different blogs. WIF fulfills an important
missing piece in this area, providing all the necessary components and necessary classes to implement
a STS and introduce claims-based security in your applications.

The core functionality to build a custom STS in WCF is provided by the abstract class `Microsoft`
`.IdentityModel.SecurityTokenService.SecurityTokenService`.

A custom STS inherits this class and provides at least the following functionality:

1. A constructor that receives a `SecurityTokenServiceConfiguration` instance to configure
some specific features of the STS:

```
public class MySecurityTokenService : SecurityTokenService
{
  public MySecurityTokenService( SecurityTokenServiceConfiguration configuration )
    : base( configuration )
  {
  }
}
```

Security\Authentication\Federated\STS\MySecurityTokenService.cs

2. An implementation of the `GetScope` method to validate whether a security token can be
provided for the service that the client wants to consume, and to supply two appropriate
credentials for encrypting and signing the token:

```
protected override Scope GetScope( IClaimsPrincipal principal,
  RequestSecurityToken request )
{
    if (request.AppliesTo == null)
    {
        throw new InvalidRequestException("The appliesTo is null.");
    }

    if (!request.AppliesTo.Uri.Equals(new Uri("http://localhost:8000/EchoClaims")))
```

```
        {
            Console.WriteLine("The relying party address is not valid. ");
            throw new InvalidRequestException(String.Format(
                "The relying party address is not valid. Expected value is {0},
    the actual value is {1}.",
                "http://localhost:8000/EchoClaims",
                request.AppliesTo.Uri.AbsoluteUri));
        }
        X509Certificate2 serviceCertificate = CertificateUtil.GetCertificate(
            StoreName.My,
            StoreLocation.LocalMachine,
            "CN=WCFServer");

        X509EncryptingCredentials encryptingCredentials =
            new X509EncryptingCredentials(serviceCertificate);

        Scope scope = new Scope(request.AppliesTo.Uri.AbsoluteUri,
            SecurityTokenServiceConfiguration.SigningCredentials,
            encryptingCredentials );

        return scope;
    }
```

Security\Authentication\Federated\STS\MySecurityTokenService.cs

The previous code validates `AppliesTo` member of the request message, which identifies the
service that consumes the token (`http://localhost:8000/EchoClaims`), and provides a
certificate with a subject name equal to `"CN=WCFServer"` for encrypting the SAML token,
and a certificate available in the configuration for signing it.

3. An implementation of the `GetOutputClaimsIdentity` method to supply claims for the
resulting security token:

```
protected override IClaimsIdentity GetOutputClaimsIdentity(IClaimsPrincipal
    principal, RequestSecurityToken request, Scope scope)
{
    IClaimsIdentity callerIdentity = (IClaimsIdentity)principal.Identity;
    IClaimsIdentity outputIdentity = new ClaimsIdentity();

    Claim nameClaim = new Claim(ClaimTypes.Name, callerIdentity.Name);

    Claim ageClaim = new Claim(
            "http://WCFBookSamples/2008/05/AgeClaim",
            "25",
            ClaimValueTypes.Integer );

    outputIdentity.Claims.Add( nameClaim );
    outputIdentity.Claims.Add( ageClaim );

    return outputIdentity;
}
```

Security\Authentication\Federated\STS\MySecurityTokenService.cs

The methods `GetScope` and `GetOutputClaimsIdentity` receive as argument a valid instance of an
`IClaimsPrincipal` class that represents the authenticated caller's identity. This identity is typically

used to determine the appropriate class to grant the caller. In the previous example, two claims are added to the security token, a claim for representing the caller name, and another hard-coded claim for representing the age.

After you have the service implementation ready, you need to expose it with one or more endpoints as you normally would with a traditional WCF service. In the case of a STS, you need to expose one of the contracts provided by WIF, which mainly depends on the features and WS-Trust version that you want to support in the STS.

WIF includes four contracts in the `Microsoft.IdentityModel.Protocols.WSTrust` namespace: `IWSTrust13SyncContract` for exposing a WS-Trust endpoint with the latest version of the specification (1.3), `IWSTrustFeb2005SyncContract` for exposing an older version of the specification (February 2005), or the asynchronous versions of the same contracts `IWSTrust13AsyncContract` and `IWSTrustFeb2005AsyncContract`.

The service class that implements the four contracts, `WSTrustServiceContract`, is also available in the same namespace. The following example illustrates one possible configuration for exposing a WS-Trust endpoint (the sync version of a WS-Trust 1.3 specification) using this service implementation:

```
<services>
  <service name="Microsoft.IdentityModel.Protocols.WSTrust.WSTrustServiceContract"
          behaviorConfiguration="stsBehavior">
    <endpoint address="WCFBookSTS"
          contract=
            "Microsoft.IdentityModel.Protocols.WSTrust.IWSTrust13SyncContract"
          binding="ws2007HttpBinding"
          bindingConfiguration="stsBinding"/>

  </service>
</services>
```

You basically need to define as many endpoints as authentication types and WS-Trust features you want to support. The binding definition for the previous endpoint `"stsBinding"` could be the following if you want to support username authentication for that endpoint:

```
<bindings>
  <ws2007HttpBinding>
    <binding name="stsBinding">
      <security mode="Message">
        <message clientCredentialType="UserName"
                establishSecurityContext="false"
                negotiateServiceCredential="true"/>
      </security>
    </binding>
  </ws2007HttpBinding>
</bindings>
```

As you can see, the same security characteristics that were previously discussed for other WCF services also apply for a STS implemented with WIF.

The last step in the basic implementation of a STS is to host the service so it becomes available to be consumed by different client applications. A new service host type, `Microsoft.IdentityModel.Protocols.WSTrust.WSTrustServiceHost`, is provided for that purpose.

One of the constructors for this new service host receives as arguments the configuration for the STS, and the base addresses where the service will listen for incoming requests:

```
static void Main( string[] args )
{
    X509Certificate2 stsCertificate = CertificateUtil.GetCertificate(
        StoreName.My,
        StoreLocation.LocalMachine,
        "CN=WCFSTS");

    // Create and setup the configuration for our STS
    SigningCredentials signingCreds = new X509SigningCredentials(stsCertificate);
    SecurityTokenServiceConfiguration config =
        new SecurityTokenServiceConfiguration("http://WCFBookSTS", signingCreds);

    config.SecurityTokenHandlers.AddOrReplace(new CustomUsernameTokenHandler());
    // Set the STS implementation class type
    config.SecurityTokenService = typeof( MySecurityTokenService );

    // Create the WS-Trust service host with our STS configuration
    using ( WSTrustServiceHost host = new WSTrustServiceHost( config, new Uri(
     "http://localhost:6000" ) ) )
    {
        host.Open();
        Console.WriteLine( "WCFBookSTS started, press ENTER to stop ..." );
        Console.ReadLine();
        host.Close();
    }
}
```

Security\Authentication\Federated\Program.cs

The previous code initializes the STS configuration with the signing credentials that the STS will use to sign the issued SAML tokens, configure a custom security handler (discussed next), and finally create and open the service host using the configuration and the base address (http://localhost:6000).

Security Token Handlers

A security token handler in WIF represents a new way to plug in custom token handling functionality. By writing a token handler, you can add functionality to serialize, deserialize, authenticate, and create a specific kind of token.

WIF has basically replaced the core functionality that WCF provides to parse security tokens, and validate them using credential validators such as the UserNamePasswordValidator or the X509CertificateValidator. This infrastructure is still layered on top of the WCF service layer, but most of the functionality that you would write to extends the WCF built-in security token. Authenticators will not work with this new architecture.

The base class for creating a new token handler is Microsoft.IdentityModel.Tokens .SecurityTokenHandler:

```
public abstract class SecurityTokenHandler
{

    public virtual bool CanReadToken(XmlReader reader);
    public virtual SecurityToken ReadToken(XmlReader reader);
    public virtual ClaimsIdentityCollection ValidateToken(SecurityToken token);

    public virtual void WriteToken(XmlWriter writer, SecurityToken token);
    public virtual bool CanValidateToken { get; }
    public virtual bool CanWriteToken { get; }

    public abstract Type TokenType { get; }
}
```

You can derive this class, implement the abstract methods, and override some of the available virtual methods to customize the handlings of an existing security token or support new ones.

WIF ships with a set of built-in token handlers for some of the well-known tokens. These include KerberosSecurityTokenHandler (for Kerberos tokens), UserNameSecurityTokenHandler (for username tokens), X509SecurityTokenHandler (for X509 certificate tokens), Saml11SecurityTokenHandler (for SAML 1.1 security tokens), or Saml2SecurityTokenHandler (for SAML 2.0 security tokens).

For example, if you want to customize the way username tokens are authenticated, you need to derive the class UsernameSecurityTokenHandler and provide the implementation of the ValidateToken method:

```
public class CustomUsernameTokenHandler : UserNameSecurityTokenHandler
{
    public override bool CanValidateToken
    {
        get
        {
            return true;
        }
    }

    public override Microsoft.IdentityModel.Claims.ClaimsIdentityCollection
     ValidateToken(System.IdentityModel.Tokens.SecurityToken token)
    {
        UserNameSecurityToken userNameToken = token as UserNameSecurityToken;
        if (userNameToken.UserName != "joe" ||
            userNameToken.Password != "bar")
        {
            throw new SecurityTokenValidationException(
                "The user can not be authenticated");
        }

        return new ClaimsIdentityCollection(new IClaimsIdentity[] {
            new ClaimsIdentity(
            new Claim(System.IdentityModel.Claims.ClaimTypes.Name,
```

```
                            userNameToken.UserName), "CustomUsernameTokenHandler")});

    }

    public override SecurityTokenHandler Clone()
    {
        return new CustomUsernameTokenHandler();
    }
}
```

In this example, the handler is validating that the username and password are equal to `"Joe"` and `"bar"` respectively. Also, that method needs to provide the list of claims available in the parsed token (the `Name` claim in this case).

The security token handlers can either be configured through configuration or code using the STS configuration class, as is shown here:

```
SecurityTokenServiceConfiguration config =
        new SecurityTokenServiceConfiguration("http://WCFBookSTS", signingCreds);

    config.SecurityTokenHandlers.AddOrReplace(new CustomUsernameTokenHandler());
```

The `AddOrReplace` method replaces the built-in `UserNameSecurityTokenHandler`, which by default is `WindowsUserNameSecurityTokenHandler`, and validates the tokens using Windows authentication.

Configuring Federated Authentication in WCF

WCF provides a federation binding to support scenarios in which the services expect a token issued by an STS, which is typically a SAML token (although it could be any other). `WsFederationHttpBinding` is the original binding shipped in the first WCF release to support the issue token negotiation with an STS, and `Ws2007FederatedHttpBinding` is a new version that supports the latest WS-* protocol versions.

In this section, you use the `Ws2007FederationHttpBinding` to configure a WCF service that requires a SAML 1.1 token issued by a custom STS built with WIF. See Listing 9-1.

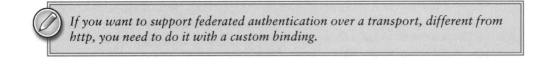

> *If you want to support federated authentication over a transport, different from http, you need to do it with a custom binding.*

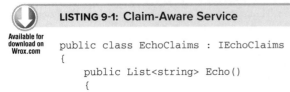

LISTING 9-1: Claim-Aware Service

Available for download on Wrox.com

```
public class EchoClaims : IEchoClaims
{
    public List<string> Echo()
    {
```

```
        List<string> claims = new List<string>();

        IClaimsPrincipal principal = Thread.CurrentPrincipal as IClaimsPrincipal;

        foreach (IClaimsIdentity identity in principal.Identities)
        {
            foreach (Claim claim in identity.Claims)
            {
                claims.Add(string.Format("{0} - {1}",
                    claim.ClaimType, claim.Value));
            }
        }

        return claims;
    }

}
```

The main difference is that the WCF authorization context is no longer needed to get access to the authentication claims. Instead, the `IClaimsPrincipal` instance available in the `Thread` `.CurrentPrincipal` property can be used to enumerate different `IClaimsIdentity` instances and its associated claims (as far as you use the built-in support, only one identity will be available in the principal, the primary identity).

The WCF configuration for that service using the `Ws2007FederationHttpBinding` is shown in Listing 9-2.

LISTING 9-2: Service Configuration

```xml
<services>
    <service name="WCFBook.Samples.EchoClaims"
             behaviorConfiguration="echoClaimsBehavior">
      <endpoint address="EchoClaims"
                contract="WCFBook.Samples.IEchoClaims"
                binding="ws2007FederationHttpBinding"
                bindingConfiguration="echoClaimsBinding"></endpoint>
      <endpoint address="mex"
                binding="mexHttpBinding"
                contract="IMetadataExchange" />
    </service>
  </services>
  <bindings>
    <ws2007FederationHttpBinding>
      <binding name="echoClaimsBinding" >
        <security mode="Message">
          <message negotiateServiceCredential="true">
            <claimTypeRequirements>
              <add claimType=
"http://schemas.xmlsoap.org/ws/2005/05/identity/claims/name"
isOptional="false"/>
              <add claimType="http://WCFBookSamples/2008/05/AgeClaim"
isOptional="false"/>
```

(continues)

LISTING 9-2 *(continued)*

```
          </claimTypeRequirements>
        </message>
      </security>
    </binding>
  </ws2007FederationHttpBinding>
</bindings>
<behaviors>
  <serviceBehaviors>
    <behavior name="echoClaimsBehavior">
      <serviceMetadata httpGetEnabled="true"/>
      <serviceCredentials>
        <issuedTokenAuthentication
          certificateValidationMode="None"
          revocationMode="NoCheck">
          <knownCertificates>
            <add
              findValue="CN=WCFSTS"
              storeLocation="LocalMachine"
              storeName="My"
              x509FindType="FindBySubjectDistinguishedName"/>
          </knownCertificates>
        </issuedTokenAuthentication>
        <serviceCertificate
          findValue="CN=WCFServer"
          storeLocation="LocalMachine"
          storeName="My"
          x509FindType="FindBySubjectDistinguishedName"/>
      </serviceCredentials>

    </behavior>
  </serviceBehaviors>
</behaviors>
</system.serviceModel>
```

The service binding and behavior configuration has some settings worth pointing out. Inside the binding configuration, the `<claimTypeRequirements>` element indicates the custom claims expected by the service. These claims are exposed by WCF in the service WS-Policy, so the client knows what claims must be negotiated with the STS.

Inside the `<serviceCredentials>` behavior, the `<issuedTokenAuthentication>` element indicates which X509 signature should be used to validate the SAML token signature. This section only instructs WCF to validate the signature, and it is still the responsibility of the service to check whether the token has been issued by a trusted issuer (WIF provides an extensibility point for performing these checks).

The `<serviceCertificate>` element specifies the X509 certificate that needs to be used to decrypt the SAML token or the session key included within the token. (It is the same certificate provided in the `GetScope` method of the STS implementation example.)

As happens with most of the examples in this chapter, the X509 certificate validations have been disabled to use test certificates. These validations should be activated before rolling out the services to production.

The code for hosting the service and enabling claims-based security with WIF also requires some modifications with respect to the traditional way that you would normally use:

```
static void Main(string[] args)
{
    ServiceHost host = new ServiceHost(typeof(EchoClaims),
        new Uri("http://localhost:8000"));
    try
    {
        ServiceConfiguration configuration = new
ServiceConfiguration("WCFBook.Samples.EchoClaims");
        configuration.IssuerNameRegistry = new CustomIssuerNameRegistry();

        FederatedServiceCredentials.ConfigureServiceHost(host, configuration);

        host.Open();

        Console.WriteLine("Service running....");
        Console.WriteLine("Press a key to quit");
        Console.ReadKey();
    }
    finally
    {
        host.Close();
    }
}
```

The method call `FederatedServiceCredentials.ConfigureServiceHost` injects and initializes the WCF service host with all the extensions required by the WIF infrastructure — this also includes the built-in security token handlers.

The code is also setting a custom class in the configuration property `IssuerNameRegistry`. As discussed previously, this is the extensibility point for performing validations against the token issuer.

A simple implementation of the base class `Microsoft.IdentityModel.Tokens.IssuerNameRegistry` is shown in Listing 9-3.

LISTING 9-3: IssuerNameRegistry Implementation

Available for
download on
Wrox.com

```
public class CustomIssuerNameRegistry : IssuerNameRegistry
{
    public override string GetIssuerName(System.IdentityModel.Tokens.SecurityToken
    securityToken)
    {
        X509SecurityToken token = securityToken as X509SecurityToken;
        if (token == null)
        {
            throw new SecurityTokenException("Token is not a X509 Security Token");
        }

        if (token.Certificate.SubjectName.Name != "CN=WCFSTS")
```

(continues)

LISTING 9-3 *(continued)*

```
        {
            throw new SecurityTokenException("STS not supported");
        }


        return "WCFSTS";
    }
}
```

As you might notice, this implementation is quite simple. It validates that the token was signed by the X509 certificate with subject name `CN=WCFSTS` (only the trusted STS should have this certificate private key). You probably need to perform more complex validations for production-ready services, as only checking the subject name is not safe in most scenarios (anyone can generate a valid certificate with the same subject name).

Listing 9-4 shows the corresponding configuration for consuming this service on the client side.

LISTING 9-4: Client Configuration

```xml
<system.serviceModel>
    <client>
        <endpoint address="http://localhost:8000/EchoClaims"
                  binding="ws2007FederationHttpBinding"
                  bindingConfiguration="echoClaimsBinding"
                  contract="EchoClaimsReference.IEchoClaims"
                  name="WSHttpBinding_IEchoClaims"
                  behaviorConfiguration="echoClaimsBehavior">
            <identity>
              <dns value="WCFServer"/>
            </identity>
        </endpoint>
    </client>
    <bindings>
      <ws2007FederationHttpBinding>
        <binding name="echoClaimsBinding">
          <security mode="Message">
            <message>
              <claimTypeRequirements>
                <add claimType=
"http://schemas.xmlsoap.org/ws/2005/05/identity/claims/name"
isOptional="false"/>
                <add claimType="http://WCFBookSamples/2008/05/AgeClaim"
isOptional="false"/>
              </claimTypeRequirements>
              <issuer address="http://localhost:6000/WCFBookSTS"
                      bindingConfiguration="stsBinding"
                      binding="ws2007HttpBinding">
                <identity>
                  <dns value="WCFSTS"/>
```

```
                    </identity>
                  </issuer>
                  <issuerMetadata
address="http://localhost:6000/WCFBookSTS/Mex"></issuerMetadata>
                </message>
              </security>
            </binding>
          </ws2007FederationHttpBinding>

          <ws2007HttpBinding>
              <binding name="stsBinding">
                <security mode="Message">
                  <message clientCredentialType="UserName"
                    establishSecurityContext="false"
                    negotiateServiceCredential="true"/>
                </security>
              </binding>
            </ws2007HttpBinding>
          </bindings>

          <behaviors>
            <endpointBehaviors>
              <behavior name="echoClaimsBehavior">
                <clientCredentials>
                  <serviceCertificate>
                    <defaultCertificate
                      findValue="CN=WCFSTS"
                      storeLocation="LocalMachine"
                      storeName="My"
                      x509FindType="FindBySubjectDistinguishedName"/>
                    <authentication
                      revocationMode="NoCheck"
                      certificateValidationMode="None"/>
                  </serviceCertificate>
                </clientCredentials>
              </behavior>
            </endpointBehaviors>
          </behaviors>
        </system.serviceModel>
```

The main difference with a traditional WCF endpoint is that two bindings are used, one for specifying the communication details with the final service, Ws2007FederatedBinding, and another for doing the same with the STS, Ws2007HttpBinding.

As you might notice, Ws2007FederatedBinding replicates the same configuration that you set on the service side with an extra element <issuer>. This specifies the issuer address a reference to the binding used for setting the communication details.

10

Windows Azure Platform AppFabric

WHAT'S IN THIS CHAPTER?

➤ Getting started with Windows Azure platform AppFabric

➤ Service Bus Integration

➤ Access Control Integration

The Windows Azure platform represents a radical change in the way applications can be built and managed. This platform provides an Internet-based cloud computing environment that anyone can use for hosting applications and storing the associated data. The platform in general comprises two core services that any cloud-based application can use: compute (e.g., executing an application) and storage (e.g., storing data on disk).

The compute service enables any application to run in the cloud. In essence, the applications are deployed in a highly scalable environment where they share computer processor time available in different virtual machines with Windows Server. These virtual machine instances are spread around the world in different Microsoft data centers.

The storage service, as its name clearly states, provides simple storage capabilities using different schemas such as BLOBs (binary objects), queues, or simple tables through a very easy-to-use REST API based on Http calls. In case an application requires richer querying capabilities for the storage (e.g., relational databases), an additional service, SQL Azure, is also provided by Microsoft in this platform.

In both cases, Windows Azure assures the availability and high scalability that any cloud-based application requires.

AppFabric extends the Windows Azure platform by providing two common building blocks, the Service Bus and Access Control, to make it easier to extend the reach of any .NET applications in this platform. They currently provide key functionality to support bi-directional connectivity and federated claims-based access control in any application trying to migrate to Windows Azure.

The primary feature of the Service Bus is to "route" messages from clients through the Windows Azure cloud to your software running on-premise, bypassing any NAT, firewalls, or other network obstacles that might be in the way. In addition to routing messages, the Service Bus can also help negotiate direct connections between applications. (See Figure 10-1.)

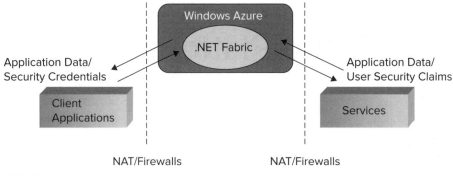

FIGURE 10-1

The primary feature of Access Control is to provide a claims-based access control mechanism for applications running on-premises or on the cloud. This makes federated authentication and authorization much easier to achieve, allowing third-party applications to trust identities provided by other systems.

Although each of these building blocks is available using open protocols and standards such as REST, Atom/AtomPub, and SOAP, Microsoft has also provided a SDK that simplifies the work for .NET developers by hiding many of the wire protocol complexities that they would otherwise experience when working with them directly. As part of this SDK, you can take advantage of some of the new WCF extensions. These include the relay bindings, to talk to the Service Bus, or custom authorization managers for parsing the security tokens generated by the Access Control.

In this chapter, introductory theory behind the AppFabric building blocks is discussed, as well as many of the available WCF extensions that you can use to integrate with your WCF services.

GETTING STARTED WITH THE SERVICE BUS AND ACCESS CONTROL

The first step to get started with the Service Bus and Access Control is to go to the Windows Azure platform portal at `http://www.microsoft.com/windowsazure/` to open a new account and download available tools and SDKs.

> *The SDK components can also be downloaded from the page opened on the Internet when any of the Visual Studio templates that target Windows Azure are opened.*

The SDK for Service Bus and Access Control is available as a separate link, just in case you are only interested in integrating your applications with these two services.

After you install the SDK, new assemblies will be available for taking advantage of the various Service Bus and Access Control features.

> *Users leveraging any of services in the Windows Azure platform have to pay for them. There are, however, sometimes exceptions to this rule, and which will ultimately benefit developers. Microsoft sometimes runs deals for MSDN subscribers, for example offering MSDN Premium subscribers Windows Azure for a total of eight months for free.*

An account is required to use the services, so you will probably have to register first. To create an account, log in to the portal using your Windows Live ID account. When you have successfully logged in, you can register for an account by creating a new project. A "project" in this context represents a container for all "service namespaces" that the Service Bus and Access Control services will use.

> *A service namespace is a container for a particular set of Service Bus endpoints and Access Control rules. For example, if you choose "WCFBook" as a service namespace for your Service Bus endpoints, the final address for getting access to them will be "sb://WCFBook.servicebus.windows.net". A service namespace must be globally unique across all accounts and it must be at least six characters long.*

In the future, all created projects will be associated with your Windows Live account. Figure 10-2 illustrates how the list of the projects looks in the Azure portal.

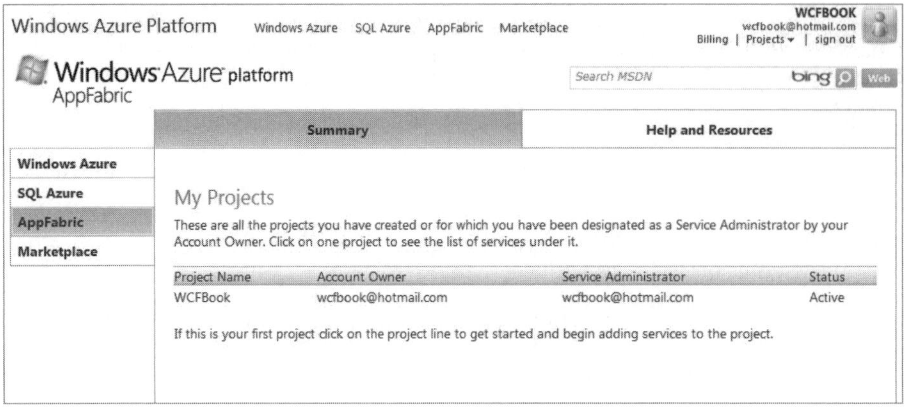

FIGURE 10-2

When you click one of the projects in the list, you will be redirected to a project-specific page that displays the project details and allows you to add new service namespaces. Figure 10-3 shows the details of a project "WCFBook" that already contains an associated service namespace with the same name.

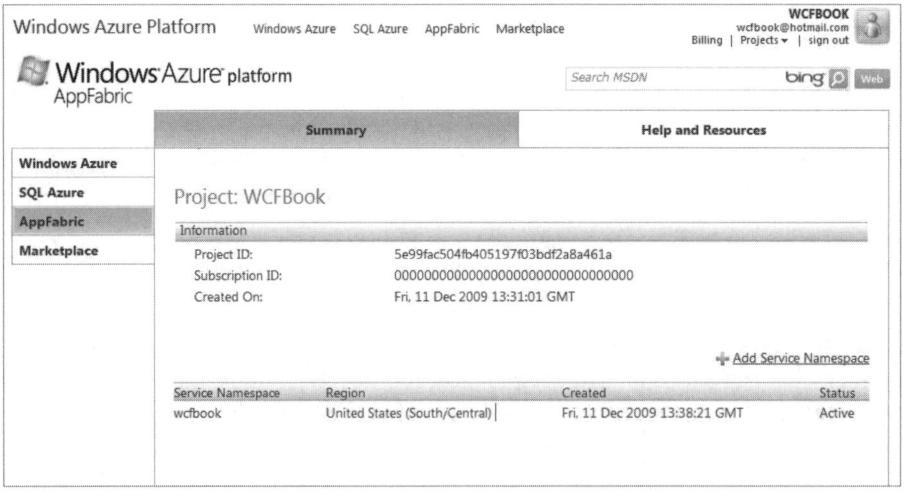

FIGURE 10-3

As a service namespace must be globally unique across all existing accounts, the screen for creating new namespaces provides a button for validating that the entered name is not in use by another account. After you create and associate a namespace to one of your projects, the Windows Azure infrastructure will execute the necessary steps to reserve and activate that address.

You can go to the service namespace details page by clicking on it. In that page, you can basically delete it or view all the important details around the service namespace such as the management key, the Service Bus endpoints, or the issuer name and key to name a few. Figure 10-4 shows the details of the "WCFBook" namespace.

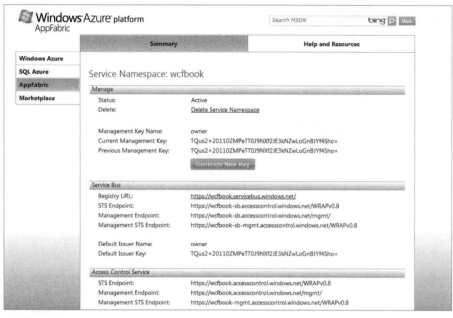

FIGURE 10-4

At this point, you should have the SDK installed. A new Service Bus and Access Control account with projects and service namespaces should also be added to start taking advantage of many of the Service Bus and Access Control features in your applications or services.

PLAYING WITH THE SERVICE BUS

The Service Bus in the Windows Azure platform AppFabric is a service running in Microsoft data centers. Its only purpose is to relay messages through the cloud to services running on-premises behind network obstacles of any kind, such as firewalls or NAT devices. The Service Bus secures all its endpoints by using the claim-based security model provided by the Access Control service.

Microsoft has decided to call this a *Service Bus* for all the similarities that can be found in its architecture compared to the architecture of many of the available products that try to address the famous Enterprise Service Bus (ESB) architectural pattern.

The ESB pattern in the real world refers to a model that integrates enterprise applications through a common messaging "bus." Figure 10-5 illustrates a possible architecture of an application that uses the ESB pattern for integrating several applications in different platforms. As you can see in this figure as well, the bus usually introduces a level of indirection between the client applications and the different services or applications through a publisher/subscriber architecture. That is, some applications subscribe to different events or messages in the bus, while others publish those events or messages into the bus. Other ESB environments also provide a service orchestration layer that provides a process flow engine for orchestrating the messaging interactions that make up a business process or workflow.

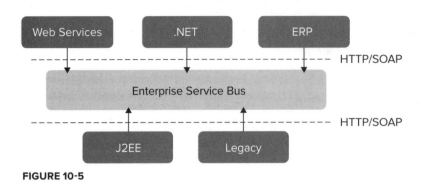

FIGURE 10-5

Today, there are a great number of technologies or products that can be used to implement an ESB, such as Active Directory, UDDI, MSQM, BizTalk, or WCF in the Windows platforms or many of the equivalent technologies available on other platforms too.

Going back to the Service Bus available as part of the Windows Azure platform AppFabric, this service provides different mechanisms such as a federated authentication and access control, a common service-naming mechanism, a common messaging fabric with a great variety of communication options, and a discoverable service registry that the applications trying to integrate with it can use. The main difference perhaps between this Service Bus and any other traditional enterprise Service Bus is that it makes it possible to integrate on-premises applications with services running in the cloud, or a variety of third-party services provided by Microsoft or other vendors.

The most important challenges that the Service Bus tries to address are the support for bidirectional communication at Internet scope and a centralized or federated schema for authentication and authorization.

The first one, a bidirectional communication, is not something trivial or easy to accomplish due to the reality we live today. The first and more important problem is the shortage of IPv4 addresses. The truth is that it is almost impossible to acquire a public IPv4 address anymore. For that reason, most Internet service providers (ISP), corporate networks, and wireless networks use dynamic IP address allocation and network address translation (NAT) techniques. A dynamic IP address is private within those networks and not publicly reachable from the outside.

The second challenge is also very important. In the way most enterprise environments work today, the on-premises software is completely shielded from the outside world by layers of firewalls and other protective network devices to keep everything secure. In most cases, the firewalls are configured to restrict the number of inbound connections, and only ports 80 and 443 are open for Http and Https connections. This aspect represents a big impediment for achieving a bidirectional communication between applications, which is a common scenario nowadays (e.g., instant messaging, file sharing, and online multiplayer games).

Creating Your First Service Bus Application

As previously discussed, you need to have a Service Bus account and some projects created within the Service Bus portal to start using this service.

Let's say you already have a project — the first step for hosting services in the Service Bus is to associate them to a service namespace. The service namespace is a unique name across all Service Bus accounts, and it acts as a container for a set of Service Bus endpoints. For example, if you created a service namespace "WCFBook," the base URI for all your endpoints within that namespace would be http://WCFBook.servicebus.windows.net. If you browse to that address, you will get an ATOM feed representing the Service Bus registry. The registry will basically contain an entry for each service hosted within that namespace.

Assuming that you already created the service namespace WCFBook, you use that for this first example. The service contract and implementation for the service to be exposed in the Service Bus is something simple that implements a classic HelloWorld operation. (See Listing 10-1.)

LISTING 10-1: Hello World Service Implementation

```
[ServiceContract]
public interface IHelloWorld
{
    [OperationContract]
    string Hello(string name);
}

public class HelloWorldService : IHelloWorld
{
    public string Hello(string name)
    {
        string message = string.Format("Hello {0}!", name);
        return message;
    }
}
```

This service can be hosted as any other regular WCF service. For the sake of simplicity, create a new instance of the ServiceHost class within a console application that reads all the service configuration details from the application configuration file. (See Listing 10-2.)

LISTING 10-2: Service Host Implementation

```
class Program
{
    static void Main(string[] args)
    {
        Console.WriteLine("Starting...");
        ServiceHost host = new ServiceHost(typeof(HelloWorldService));
        host.Open();
        Console.WriteLine("Press [Enter] to exit");
        Console.ReadLine();

        host.Close();
    }
}
```

Now it is time to configure the service host to listen on the Service Bus. To do that, the SDK already provides a set of built-in bindings that extends the underlying WCF infrastructure to listen on the cloud. For example, a `NetTcpRelayBinding` would be equivalent to the `NetTcpBinding`, but with a different transport channel for listening on the Service Bus. Relay bindings are discussed in more detail in the next section.

When using some of these bindings, you will also need to specify a valid Service Bus address for the endpoint. That address will reference one of the service namespaces already created in the Service Bus web portal. For instance, the final address for the namespace WCFBook and the endpoint `helloWorld` would be `sb://WCFBook.servicebus.windows.net/helloWorld`.

As you might notice, the protocol scheme was changed to use `sb`, which represents a special TCP-based protocol scheme used by the Service Bus. All the Service Bus endpoints, with exception of the HTTP endpoints, must use the `sb` protocol scheme.

The Service Bus somehow verifies that the application is allowed to listen within the chosen service namespace (e.g., WCFBook). This is accomplished through the Access Control Service. The application hosting the services needs to provide credentials to Access Control. This last one authenticates those credentials and issues a token that is presented to the Service Bus. The token indicates if the application is allowed to either "listen" on, "send" messages to, or "manage" the service namespace. In case you own the service namespace, the issue token will prove that you have full control over that namespace.

The client credentials can be supplied to Access Control through the use of the `<transportClientEndpointBehavior>` in configuration, or the equivalent class `TransportClientEndpointBehavior` in code. This behavior supports different types of client credentials today. Table 10-1 enumerates some of them.

TABLE 10-1: Client Credential Types

CREDENTIAL TYPE	DESCRIPTION
SharedSecret	Represents a shared secret automatically assigned to a service namespace when it is created.
SAML	A SAML token is used to authenticate the client. Access Control must trust the issuer of the SAML token to authenticate successfully.
SimpleWebToken	A Simple Web Token is used to authenticate the client. A Simple Web Token is a specific type of client credentials, which is more suitable for consuming RESTful services than SAML.
Unauthenticated	No client credentials provided.

The service configuration for this example uses a `"SharedSecret"`, which was automatically assigned to the namespace when it was created. It is available in the service namespace page in the web portal, under the Default Issuer Name and Default Issuer Key columns. You need to use those values in `issuerName` and `issuerSecret` attributes of the service configuration (see Listing 10-3).

LISTING 10-3: Service Configuration

```
<configuration>
  <system.serviceModel>
    <services>
      <service name="HelloWorld">
        <endpoint address=
            "sb://WCFBook.servicebus.windows.net/helloWorld"
            behaviorConfiguration="clientCredentials"
            binding="netTcpRelayBinding"
            contract="IHelloWorld" />
      </service>
    </services>
    <behaviors>
      <endpointBehaviors>
        <behavior name="clientCredentials">
          <transportClientEndpointBehavior credentialType="SharedSecret">
            <clientCredentials>
              <sharedSecret issuerName="issuer" issuerSecret="secret" />
            </clientCredentials>
          </transportClientEndpointBehavior>
        </behavior>
      </endpointBehaviors>
    </behaviors>
  </system.serviceModel>
</configuration>
```

The "SharedSecret" is sent to Access Control the first time the service host is opened in the console application to acquire a token for listening on the Service Bus.

After that, the application hosting the service tries to establish a TCP connection with the relay service by passing the recently acquired token. If the token does not contain the necessary claims for listening on the Service Bus, the application will of course receive a security exception. Otherwise, the Service Bus will create a listener for relaying messages to the service just created. In this way, the service will somehow be connected to the cloud.

Next, you can write a client application that invokes the service (see Listing 10-4). The code for this application is as straightforward as any other client application that consumes a WCF service. All the details about the Service Bus have been completely hidden by the relay binding.

LISTING 10-4: Client Application

```
class Program
{
    static void Main(string[] args)
    {
        ChannelFactory<IHelloServiceBus> channelFactory =
            new ChannelFactory<IHelloWord>();
        IHelloWorld channel = channelFactory.CreateChannel();

        string response = channel.Hello("The WCF Book");
```

continues

LISTING 10-4 *(continued)*

```
        Console.WriteLine(response);

        channelFactory.Close();
    }
}
```

The configuration for this application is very similar to the service one. You need to change the endpoint to use the NetTcpRelayBinding and the same Service Bus address that you configured our service to listen on. You also need to configure the client with credentials. As happens with services, Clients must also prove that they are allowed to send messages to a particular address on the Service Bus. They can prove that by acquiring a token from Access Control.

You will use the same "SharedSecret" used to configure the service application. Listing 10-5 shows the complete client-side configuration.

LISTING 10-5: Client Configuration

```xml
<configuration>
  <system.serviceModel>
    <client>
      <endpoint address=
        "sb://WCFBook.servicebus.windows.net/helloWorld"
        binding="netTcpRelayBinding"
        contract="IHelloWorld"
        behaviorConfiguration="clientCredentials"
        name="helloWorld" />
    </client>
    <behaviors>
      <endpointBehaviors>
        <behavior name="clientCredentials">
          <transportClientEndpointBehavior credentialType="SharedSecret">
            <clientCredentials>
              <sharedSecret issuerName="issuer" issuerSecret="secret" />
            </clientCredentials>
          </transportClientEndpointBehavior>
        </behavior>
      </endpointBehaviors>
    </behaviors>
  </system.serviceModel>
</configuration>
```

You are now ready to run the service host application followed by the client application to see how the communication is relayed through the Service Bus, making it possible to traverse different kinds of network obstacles in the way.

The following sections explore the relay service, which represents the core system of the Service Bus, and some of the built-in bindings that any application can use to connect to this service.

THE RELAY SERVICE

The relay service represents the core system that makes it possible to build applications capable of communicating through firewalls and other network obstacles using a variety of different messaging patterns.

This service supports traditional one-way, peer-to-peer, and request/response messaging patterns. It also supports two other interesting features, event distribution across Internet with a publisher/ subscriber architecture, and bidirectional communication between applications when possible.

An application that uses the relay service is basically delegating the transport-level listening responsibility to the relay service in the cloud. That means that any service that the application is hosting relies on the relay service for handling the specific transport communication details. This service will forward any incoming message to the on-premises services.

By using the SDK, you are connecting your on-premises services and the relay service via any of the built-in relay bindings. Those relay bindings make all the work of replacing the transport binding elements by some new ones that integrate with the Service Bus on the cloud. The transport binding elements that shipped as part of the SDK (that are integrated with the relay bindings) establish a bidirectional communication with the relay service. In that process, it also authenticates the application, specifies a name to listen on, and specifies what type of listener to establish.

Regarding the addresses you chose for the Service Bus endpoints in the relay service, you must be aware that only a single on-premises service can listen on a particular endpoint address, except when using the `NetEventRelayBinding`. It allows multiple services to listen on the same endpoint address.

However, in all other cases, you will get an exception when trying to use an address that is already being used by another service. What's more, if that address is within the URI scope of an address already used, it will also fail. For example, if your endpoint uses an address of `/WCFBook/MyService/HelloWorld` and there is another service listening on `/WCFBook/MyService`, the attempt to use that address will fail. The only valid point here is when you share the same base address for all the endpoints (e.g., `/WCFBook`).

The relay service routes messages using a specific algorithm that matches prefixes in the addresses, which is not necessarily an exact match. This makes it possible for the on-premises service to directly inspect the URI path segments and the query string to do custom processing, which is very useful for RESTful services.

The machine trying to connect to the relay service only requires a few outbound ports open in the firewall, which are ports 808, 818, 819, and 828. Port 808 is used for one-way TCP connections; port 828 for one-way TCP with SSL connections. Ports 818 and 819 are used for bidirectional TCP connections and some other advanced scenarios. The good thing is that the relay service does not require any inbound port open in the firewall or performing any kind of port mapping on any existing NAT/router devices that the machine uses.

There is also a special HTTP-based connectivity option that uses ports 80 (HTTP) and 443 (HTTPS) when the machine is operating in an environment where all the outbound socket connections are blocked.

It's time now to discuss all the details about the WCF relay bindings and show some examples of how to use them.

WCF RELAY BINDINGS

As previously discussed, WCF represents the primary programming model that works with the Service Bus on the .NET platform. The SDK provides a set of built-in bindings that facilitates the integration between WCF services and the service consumers through the relay service that is part of the Service Bus.

In most scenarios, you only need to replace the current WCF binding with one of the Service Bus relay bindings. As you can see in Table 10-2, most Relay bindings correspond to a built-in binding in WCF.

TABLE 10-2: Relay Bindings

RELAY BINDING	BUILT-IN WCF BINDING
WebHttpRelayBinding	WebHttpBinding
BasicHttpRelayBinding	BasicHttpBinding
Ws2007HttpRelayBinding	Ws2007HttpBinding
NetTcpRelayBinding	NetTcpBinding
NetOneWayRelayBinding	N/A
NetEventRelayBinding	N/A

As the table shows, only a few bindings do not have an equivalent WCF binding: NetOneWayRelayBinding and NetEventRelayBinding.

All these bindings work in the same way as built-in WCF bindings in most cases. They all support the same standard WCF features such as message versions, the different message security scenarios, reliable messaging, or the web programming model, to name a few.

They simply replace the WCF transport binding elements with a set of new binding elements to connect to the relay service. These new transport binding elements are RelayedHttpBindingElement and RelayedHttpsBindingElement for all Http-based bindings (WebHttpRelayBinding, BasicHttpBinding, and Ws2008HttpRelayBinding); TcpRelayTransportBindingElement for TCP-based bindings (NetTcpRelayBinding); and RelayedOneWayTransportBindingElement for the rest of the bindings (NetOneWayRelayBinding and NetEventRelayBinding).

In the following sections, the details of the main WCF relay bindings and some examples of how to use them are detailed.

NetOneWayRelayBinding

As its name states, this binding only supports one-way messaging, which means the client does not expect a reply message from the service. The default configuration for this binding is SOAP 1.2 over TCP with a binary encoder. All these settings can be customized through the standard binding configuration techniques. Only the sb protocol scheme can be used with this binding.

In the way this binding works with the default configuration, the WCF service tries to establish an outbound and secure connection (TCP/SSL) with the relay service through port 828. While the process for connecting to the relay service is performed, the WCF service also authenticates itself through the Access Control, specifies a name to listen on within the relay service, and establishes a type of service listener to create.

On the other hand, when the client uses the default configuration, it connects to the relay service through ports 808 (TCP) or 828 (TCP/SSL) depending on the binding configuration. The client also needs to authenticate against the Access Control first, and after it does, it can start sending one-way messages to the Service Bus that are later "relayed" to the on-premises service to listen on the Service Bus as well.

The architecture of the Service Bus is made up of two layers. In the top layer, you can find a farm of front-end nodes with a load-balancing schema that provides the necessary scalability required for this type of service. In the layer below, there is a backend system with the naming and routing fabric that basically forwards the messages from the front-end node that receives messages from the client to the front-end node where the service is attached. This means that clients and services are usually connected to different front-end nodes.

In case the client or service is using transport security, only the messages interchanged between the client or service and the relay service will be protected with SSL. The same messages will travel as plain text through the nodes in the relay service, so you need to use message security if you want to protect them all the way through the relay service.

As this binding works only to support one-way messaging, all the operations on the service contract must be marked as one-way with the IsOneWay attribute. The following code snippet illustrates the contract of service that can be used with this binding:

```
[ServiceContract()]
public interface IHelloWorld
{
    [OperationContract(IsOneWay = true)]
    void Hello(string name);
}
```

The implementation of this service can be configured in the host to use the NetOneWayRelayBinding with the following configuration:

```
<system.serviceModel>
    <behaviors>
        <endpointBehaviors>
            <behavior name="clientCredentials">
                <transportClientEndpointBehavior credentialType="SharedSecret">
                    <clientCredentials>
```

```
            <sharedSecret issuerName="ISSUER_NAME"
  issuerSecret="ISSUER_SECRET" />
            </clientCredentials>
          </transportClientEndpointBehavior>
        </behavior>
      </endpointBehaviors>
    </behaviors>
    <bindings>
      <netOnewayRelayBinding>
        <binding name="default" />
      </netOnewayRelayBinding>
    </bindings>
    <services>
      <service name="HelloWorldService">
        <endpoint address="" behaviorConfiguration="clientCredentials"
          binding="netOnewayRelayBinding" bindingConfiguration="default"
          name="RelayEndpoint" contract="IHelloWorld" />
      </service>
    </services>
  </system.serviceModel>
```

A single endpoint has been specified that uses a shared secret to authenticate against Access Control.

The client application for consuming this service should be configured with an equivalent endpoint configuration (also based on `NetOneWayRelayBinding`).

As discussed before, this binding always tries to connect to the relay service over TCP by default. When the service is hosted in a constrained environment where this connection cannot be made, you can opt for an alternative mode that uses the traditional Http and Https ports. The SDK provides a specific setting for changing this connectivity mode, which uses a very evident name, `ConnectivityMode`. This setting can basically take one of the following values: `TCP`, `Http`, or `AutoDetect`.

➤ `TCP` always tries to connect to the relay service via TCP through port 828.

➤ `Http` tries to connect to the relay service via Http to overcome any issue you would have to open the 828 port.

➤ `AutoDetect` is the default connectivity mode. It basically determines which is the best connectivity option based on a mechanism that probes whether either connectivity option is available for the current network environment.

You can change the connectivity mode through the static `ServiceBusEnvironment` class, which means that it is scoped at Application Domain level. This class contains a `SystemConnectivity` property that can be set with any of the values already discussed.

The following code snippet illustrates how to modify an application to use TCP connectivity mode:

```
ServiceBusEnvironment.SystemConnectivity.Mode = ConnectivityMode.Tcp;
ServiceHost host = new ServiceHost(typeof(HelloWorldService), address);
```

Although this setting has been discussed, it is valid for any of the other relay bindings as well.

NetEventRelayBinding

The `NetEventRelayBinding` is almost identical to the `NetOneWayRelayBinding` from the perspective of the implementation. They both support the same configuration defaults and security options and essentially have the same interaction with the relay service.

However, the scenario that this binding addresses is completely different allows multiple WCF services to register within the same Service Bus address. In this way, a type of subscriber/publisher architecture is generated, where the client is the publisher that sends a message to a specific service address in the Service Bus, and the relay service multicasts the message to all the WCF services currently subscribed to that address.

One thing to keep in mind is that this binding does not provide any assurances around message deliver or order, so it would be something equivalent to UDP multicasting with better error-handling support as the relay service relies on TCP for communication.

The following example shows an application that registers one WCF service for receiving messages using the NetEventRelayBinding, and a simple client application for consuming it.

> *Multiple instances of this application can be run at the same time because they all share the same address.*

Listing 10-6 shows the service contract and implementation of the WCF service. It actually does not do anything with the message; it only prints it in the Console output.

LISTING 10-6: Service Contract and Implementation

```
[ServiceContract()]
public interface ISubscriber
{
    [OperationContract(IsOneWay = true)]
    void ReceiveMessage(string message);
}

[ServiceBehavior()]
class SubscriberService : ISubscriber
{
    void ISubscriber.ReceiveMessage(string message)
    {
        Console.WriteLine("Receive " + message);
    }
}
```

For sake of simplicity, the client and service are both running on the same Console application. The Run method creates a new host for the SubscriberService, and after that, a client channel for consuming it. (See Listing 10-7.)

LISTING 10-7: Application Implementation

```
static void Main(string[] args)
{
  ServiceBusEnvironment.SystemConnectivity.Mode = ConnectivityMode.Tcp;

  Program programInstance = new Program();
  programInstance.Run();
}

private void Run()
{
  ServiceHost host = new ServiceHost(typeof(SubscriberService));
  host.Open();

  ChannelFactory<ISubscriberChannel> channelFactory =
new ChannelFactory<ISubscriberChannel>("RelayEndpoint");

  ISubscriberChannel channel = channelFactory.CreateChannel();
  channel.Open();

  Console.WriteLine("\nPress [Enter] to exit\n");

  channel.ReceiveMessage("This is a message!!!");

  channel.Close();
  channelFactory.Close();
  host.Close();
}
```

As the client and service run on the same application, the WCF configuration contains the configuration of both of them. As you can see, the NetEventRelayBinding has been configured for the client and service, and the authentication against Access Control is performed through a shared secret (see Listing 10-8).

LISTING 10-8: Client and Service Configuration

```
<system.serviceModel>

    <bindings>

      <netEventRelayBinding>
        <binding name="default" />
      </netEventRelayBinding>
    </bindings>
```

```
        <client>
          <endpoint name="RelayEndpoint"
                    contract="ISubscriber"
                    binding="netEventRelayBinding"
                    bindingConfiguration="default"
                    behaviorConfiguration="sharedSecret"

    address="sb://WCFBook.servicebus.windows.net/Subscriber" />
        </client>

        <services>

          <service name="SubscriberService">
            <endpoint name="RelayEndpoint"
                      contract="ISubscriber"
                      binding="netEventRelayBinding"
                      bindingConfiguration="default"
                      behaviorConfiguration="sharedSecret"
                      address="sb://WCFBook.servicebus.windows.net/Subscriber" />
          </service>
        </services>

        <behaviors>
          <endpointBehaviors>
            <behavior name="sharedSecret">
              <transportClientEndpointBehavior credentialType="SharedSecret">
                <clientCredentials>
                  <sharedSecret issuerName="[ISSUER]" issuerSecret="[SECRET]" />
                </clientCredentials>
              </transportClientEndpointBehavior>
            </behavior>
          </endpointBehaviors>
        </behaviors>

      </system.serviceModel>
```

NetTcpRelayBinding

The NetTcpRelayBinding is the binding Microsoft recommends you use when possible, because it provides two-way messaging semantics and it is closely aligned with the standard NetTcpBinding (the main difference is that the NetTcpRelayBinding creates a public address in the relay service).

This binding uses SOAP 1.2 over TCP by default, with a binary encoder for being more efficient with the network usage.

In addition, it supports two connection modes (see Table 10-3) that control how the client/service communicate with one another through the relay service.

TABLE 10-3: NetTcpRelayBinding Connectivity Modes

MODE	DESCRIPTION
Relayed	This is the default mode. All communication is relayed through the relay service. When the connection is established the relay service acts like a socket forwarder proxy relaying a bi-directional byte stream.
Hybrid	The initial communication is relayed through the relay service while the client and service tries to negotiate a direct socket connection between each other. All this negotiation is governed by the relay service. After a direct connection can be established, the existing connection is automatically upgraded to a direct connection without message or data loss. If the direct connection cannot be established, data will continue to flow through the relay service as usual.

When `Relayed` mode–the default mode — is enabled, any incoming message arriving on one of the front-end nodes generates a control message that is routed down to the on-premises WCF service with instructions to create a rendezvous connection back with the client's front-end node. When that happens, a direct socket-to-socket forwarder is established for relaying TCP messages.

On the other hand, the `Hybrid` mode instructs the relay service to do everything possible to establish a direct connection between the client and service applications, so the data no longer needs to go through the relay service. The name "hybrid" represents exactly how this binding works when the mode is enabled. It starts by relaying information through the relay while it attempts to upgrade to a direct connection. If the direct connection can be established, it will switch to this connection without any data loss. Otherwise, it will continue to use the relay service. This mode uses a special port prediction algorithm based on probing information from the client and service. The relay service looks at this probing information and tries to guess what ports are going to be open on their respective NAT devices. It can then provide that information to the client/service so that they can establish a direct connection with one another. If the information is correct, the connection will succeed; otherwise it will try again until it decides to give up and to stick with the relayed connection.

The following configuration shows how a WCF service is configured with a single `NetTcpRelayBinding` endpoint and the `Hybrid` mode:

```
<system.serviceModel>
    <behaviors>
      <endpointBehaviors>
        <behavior name="clientCredentials">
          <transportClientEndpointBehavior credentialType="SharedSecret">
            <clientCredentials>
              <sharedSecret issuerName="ISSUER_NAME"
issuerSecret="ISSUER_SECRET" />
            </clientCredentials>
          </transportClientEndpointBehavior>
        </behavior>
      </endpointBehaviors>
    </behaviors>
```

```
<bindings>
  <netTcpRelayBinding>
    <binding name="default" connectionMode="Hybrid">
      <security mode="None" />
    </binding>
  </netTcpRelayBinding>
</bindings>
<services>
  <service name="HelloWorldService">
    <endpoint address="sb://WCFBook.servicebus.windows.net/HelloWorld"
behaviorConfiguration="clientCredentials"
      binding="netTcpRelayBinding" bindingConfiguration="default"
      name="RelayEndpoint" contract="IHelloWorld" />
  </service>
</services>
</system.serviceModel>
```

The `Hybrid` mode also provides a property in the WCF client channel that the client application can use to subscribe events about connection status changes at runtime. The property is implemented in the type `IHybridConnectionStatus`, and it exposes a `ConnectionStateChanged` event where the client application can register an event handler. The following code snippet shows how a client application can subscribe to this event:

```
ChannelFactory<IHelloWorld> channelFactory = new
ChannelFactory<IHelloWorld>("RelayEndpoint");
IHelloWorld channel = channelFactory.CreateChannel();
channel.Open();

IHybridConnectionStatus hybridConnectionStatus =
    channel.GetProperty<IHybridConnectionStatus>();

hybridConnectionStatus.ConnectionStateChanged += ( o,e ) =>
{
  Console.WriteLine("Connection Upgraded!!!!");
};
```

You might also want to consider employing `WS-ReliableMessaging` with the `NetTcpRelayBinding`, as that will guarantee that the connections are reestablished on your behalf when any problem arises with the direct socket connections. This will give the impression that the direction connections are "reliable."

Http Relay Bindings

All the relay bindings discussed so far require clients to use WCF for consuming the on-premises services exposed on the Service Bus.

The Service Bus also comes with several HTTP bindings — `WebHttpRelayBinding`, `BasicHttpRelayBinding`, and `WS2007HttpRelayBinding` — to support scenarios where you need to integrate non-WCF clients. These bindings provide wider reach and more interoperability because they can support any client that knows how to use the standard protocols supported by each of these bindings.

Although WS2007HttpRelayBinding provides richer functionality through the support of the WS-* protocols, it requires the client to understand those protocols for the client and service to interoperate well. On the other hand, WebHttpRelayBinding and BasicHttpRelayBinding are based on simple Http/Rest and basic SOAP respectively, so interoperability is easier to accomplish.

No matter which Http relay binding you use, all of them work pretty much the same. The on-premises WCF service first connects to the relay service using either a TCP or Http connection depending on the chosen SystemConnectivityMode.

After that, clients start sending messages to the Http endpoint exposed by the relay service. They only need a simple Http or SOAP client library to consume the services.

The relay service can route any SOAP 1.1, SOAP 1.2, or plain Http messages. You only need to configure which message style or WS-* protocols you can to use for the services by employing one of the Http relay bindings. Let's go through the implementation of a simple RESTful Http service that is exposed in the Service Bus.

The on-premises WCF service exposes a simple RESTful service contract using the WCF 3.5 web programming model as shown in Listing 10-9.

LISTING 10-9: RESTful Service Implementation

```
[ServiceContract()]
public interface ICustomerManagement
{
    [OperationContract]
    [WebGet]
    string GetCustomerName(int customerId);
}

public class CustomerManagement : ICustomerManagement
{
    public string GetCustomerName(int customerId)
    {
        if (customerId > 5)
        {
            return "Foo";
        }

        return "Bar";
    }

}
```

The implementation of the GetCustomerName simply returns "Foo" or "Bar" according to the value received in the customerId argument.

The host application is configured with a single WebHttpRelayBinding endpoint (see Listing 10-10). The service endpoint is configured with a "SharedSecret" credential and the WebHttpRelayBinding has been configured to not require authentication from incoming clients. This means that clients will not have to authenticate with Access Control to use your endpoint.

LISTING 10-10: Service Configuration

```
<system.serviceModel>
    <bindings>
      <webHttpRelayBinding>
        <binding name="default">
          <security relayClientAuthenticationType="None" />
        </binding>
      </webHttpRelayBinding>
    </bindings>

    <services>
      <service name="CustomerManagement"
               behaviorConfiguration="default">
        <endpoint name="RelayEndpoint"
                  contract="ICustomerManagement"
                  binding="webHttpRelayBinding"
                  bindingConfiguration="default"
                  behaviorConfiguration="sharedSecretClientCredentials"
                  address="http://WCFBook.servicebus.windows.net/Customer" />
      </service>
    </services>

    <behaviors>
      <endpointBehaviors>
        <behavior name="sharedSecretClientCredentials">
          <transportClientEndpointBehavior credentialType="SharedSecret">
            <clientCredentials>
              <sharedSecret issuerName="ISSUER_NAME"
issuerSecret="ISSUER_SECRET" />
            </clientCredentials>
          </transportClientEndpointBehavior>
        </behavior>
      </endpointBehaviors>
      <serviceBehaviors>
        <behavior name="default">
          <serviceDebug httpHelpPageEnabled="false" httpsHelpPageEnabled="false" />
        </behavior>
      </serviceBehaviors>
    </behaviors>

  </system.serviceModel>
```

When the WCF service application is up and running, anyone can browse to
`http://WCFBook.servicebus.windows.net/CustomerManagement/GetCustomerName` with
a `customerId` in the query string (for example, `GetCustomerName?customerId=3`) to retrieve a
customer name.

PLAYING WITH THE ACCESS CONTROL SERVICE (ACS)

Access Control Service (ACS) is a cloud-based service that provides centralized authentication and
authorization for your application and on-premises services through a claim-based identity model.
You do not need to provide a custom code or have a user database for using it. ACS takes care of

all that. You can authorize access to both enterprise clients as well as simple clients with only a few lines of code. As more users start adopting ACS over time, more users of your applications will be able to authenticate or authorize without having to touch any code.

In the way ACS works, the user must obtain a security token (think SAML or Simple Web Token) from ACS to log into your service or application. This token is signed by ACS and contains a set of claims about the user's identity. ACS will not issue a token unless the user first authenticates successfully by presenting one of the supported client credentials (already discussed in Table 10-1, "Client Credential Types").

> *The current ACS version only issues Simple Web Tokens, and the main reason is that Microsoft has decided to target this first version to RESTful services only. At the same time, this kind of service has become popular in both web and enterprise developers. They believe a gap is emerging in the market for identity and access control technology. Developers are facing a lack of common patterns for managing identity and access control in a way that is compatible with the REST focus on simplicity. The main goal for ACS at this point is to fill in those gaps.*

You can find today three main pieces in ACS: a security token service, which issues security tokens; the administration portal; and an administration RESTful API for configuring the way generated tokens are constructed. The SDK also includes a command-line tool Access Control Management Tool (Acm.exe) that you can use to perform management operations (CREATE, GET, UPDATE, and DELETE) on the AppFabric Access Control entities (scopes, issuers, token policies, and rules). The Access Control entities are discussed in more detail in the next sections.

Service Namespaces

A service namespace in the context of ACS is nothing more than a container for the ACS entities. Basically the same thing seen in the Service Bus, but with entities specific to the ACS. A service namespace also has its own private STS and management endpoints.

Some of the entities found under a service namespace in Access Control are the rules. A rule determines what claims will be added in the tokens issued by the ACS STS. Each service namespace can have a completely different set of rules. The rules play a very important role because most applications are probably going to need different types of claims. One application might need to verify the user's full name, and would therefore expect a claim with the user's full name be included in the token issued by ACS. Another might need some other personal information. It is pretty clear that any application needs its own claims, and therefore its own set of rules so that ACS can generate those claims. This idea is so important that the request messages for getting a token from ACS must include an AppliesTo field, which is a URI identifying the logical destination for the token. ACS makes use of this by allowing you to assign a URI to each of your applications.

Figure 10-6 illustrates the structure of a service namespace in ACS. A service namespace WCFBook belongs to the Live ID account WCFBook@live.com and contains issuers, scopes, and rules.

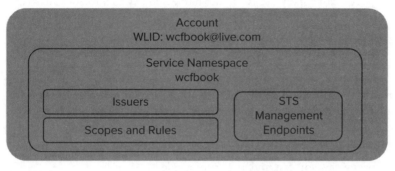

FIGURE 10-6

Scopes

Each application or service within an ACS service namespace must be assigned a unique URI. This represents the `AppliesTo` URI that was previously discussed. Although this can be technically any string representing a valid URI, most people find it convenient to use a URL associated with the application, for example, `http://localhost/MyService`. There are two obvious benefits to using an application URL as `AppliesTo`: it becomes immediately obvious what application the name refers to, and it is also hard to accidentally give the same URI to two different applications.

Each ACS service namespace can drive several applications, so each application should have its own scope with the settings and claims that make sense for that application.

A scope includes a set of rules that determine how ACS generates claims for the application, but also includes other important settings such as the key that ACS should use to sign the security tokens, and the lifetime for them (how long they will be valid).

The lifetime for a token is very important from the point of view of scalability and performance. After a token has been issued by ACS, it can be reused by the client until it expires, which reduces the number of times a client has to request a new token from an issuer, reducing latency for the client and load on the issuer.

As discussed in Chapter 9, this signature also plays an important role as it allows the services to verify that the token comes from a trusted party, and it has not been changed in transit.

These two settings can be found in ACS as part of a token policy. A token policy can be associated to multiple scopes.

Issuers

A service namespace also supports one or more issuers. An issuer in ACS basically represents a client that will be requesting tokens for consuming a service. Each issuer also includes a set of credentials including a key. You can simply use the issuer name and key to authenticate to that issuer and request a token, or you can go with other more complex alternatives that use existing tokens.

Rules

Rules play an important role in AC as they drive the token-issuing behavior. A rule is always associated with a scope and basically maps input claims to output claims. The input claims are generally created during the authentication process, and what a rule does is transform them to some other output claims that the service or application receiving the token is expecting.

Table 10-4 discusses all the properties you can find as part of a rule.

TABLE 10-4: Rule Properties

PROPERTY	DESCRIPTION
Name	A friendly name to identify a rule within a scope.
Type	Specifies the type of transformation the rule will apply over the input claims. The two possible values are `Simple` or `Pass-through`. A `Simple` transformation gets an input claim and creates a completely different output claim (different type and value). A `Pass-through` transformation simply changes the output claim type.
Input Claim - Issuer	Specifies the issuer of the input claim. The rule will only apply for input claims generated by this issuer.
Input Claim - Type	A string that represents the claim type. For example, `FullName` and `Email` are valid values for this property.
Input Claim - Value	A string representing the claim value. For example, for an `Email` claim type, a possible value could be "`foo@mail.com`".
Output Claim - Type	A string that represents the output claim type.
Output Claim - Value	A string representing the output claim value.

The ACS will execute all the rules for a given scope that matches the `Issuer`, `Type`, and `Value` in the input claims. The result will be a completely different set of output rules.

Let's say a service is expecting a set of claim of the type "action" that specifies all the actions the consumer is allowed to do on the service side. A rule can create all those claims based on the way the client was authenticated in ACS. For example, Table 10-5 illustrates a possible rule for this service.

TABLE 10-5: Rule Example

PROPERTY	VALUE
Name	ActionRule
Type	Simple
Input Claim – Issuer	MyClientApplication
Input Claim – Type	Issuer
Input Claim – Value	MyClientApplication
Output Claim – Type	Action
Output Claim – Value	DeleteCustomer

When the client application authenticates against the ACS using the name and password associated to the issuer MyClientApplication, ACS will automatically generate an input claim Issuer with that issuer name as value. That input claim will match the properties of this rule, and therefore an output claim Action with value DeleteCustomer will be added to the issue token. The claim type Issuer in this case is a built-in claim type that the ACS generates when the client authenticates with the issuer name and password.

Integrating Your First Service with Access Control

An introductory theory about what ACS, and how you can use it to secure your services, has so far been discussed. It is time now to see how this service works in action with a more concrete example.

For this first example, use the same namespace you created before for the Service Bus examples (for example, a service namespace WCFBook).

The service contract and implementation for the RESTful service you are going to expose in the Service Bus is something simple that implements a classic SayHello operation that returns a fixed string "Hello" (see Listing 10-11).

LISTING 10-11: Hello World Service Implementation

Available for
download on
Wrox.com

```
[ServiceContract]
public interface ISampleService
{
  [OperationContract]
  [WebGet(UriTemplate = "sayHello")]
  string SayHello();
}

public class SampleService : ISampleService
{
  public string SayHello()
  {
    return "Hello";
  }
}
```

As this service will rely on the ACS for receiving claims about the authenticated user, you will use a custom authorization manager that verifies the user permissions based on that evidence. The authorization manager will evaluate any of the received claims, and the client will execute the operation only when one of those claims matches of one of the expected claims. The expected claims are previously configured in the host when the authorization manager is initialized.

Therefore, the code you find in the console application, used as host, basically initializes the WCF service host with a `WebHttpBinding` for RESTful services, the custom authorization manager previously discussed, and a cryptographic key to verify the token signature.

Listing 10-12 shows the code required for hosting the service, and expecting some claims from ACS. As you can see, the authorization manager expects a token issued by ACS for the service "http://localhost/SampleService" (`AppliesTo`) that should contain at least one claim of type "action" with value "sayHello".

LISTING 10-12: Service Host Implementation

```
class Service
{
    static void Main(string[] args)
    {
        string acsHostName = "accesscontrol.windows.net";

        string trustedAudience = "http://localhost/SampleService";
        string requiredClaimType = "action";
        string requiredClaimValue = "sayHello";

        Console.WriteLine("Enter your service namespace, then press <ENTER>");
        string serviceNamespace = Console.ReadLine();

        Console.WriteLine("\nEnter your issuer key, then press <ENTER>");
        string trustedTokenPolicyKey = Console.ReadLine();

        WebHttpBinding binding = new WebHttpBinding(WebHttpSecurityMode.None);

        Uri address = new Uri("http://localhost/SampleService");

        WebServiceHost host = new WebServiceHost(typeof(SampleService));
        host.AddServiceEndpoint(typeof(ISampleService), binding, address);

        host.Authorization.ServiceAuthorizationManager = new ACSAuthorizationManager(
                acsHostName,
                serviceNamespace,
                trustedAudience,
                Convert.FromBase64String(trustedTokenPolicyKey),
                requiredClaimType,
                requiredClaimValue);

        host.Open();

        Console.WriteLine("The Sample Service is listening");
```

```
        Console.WriteLine("Press <ENTER> to exit");
        Console.ReadLine();
    }
}
```

The next step is to configure the rules and scopes within ACS so the claims expected for the service are generated. As part of the example, there is a batch file, setup.cmd, that automatically does all this for you using the command-line tool ACS.exe. There is also a cleanup.cmd file that does the opposite by removing all the previously created entities.

To see the results of this command execution in ACS, the SDK includes a very useful Windows application, AcmBrowser, that uses the administration API in the background to give you a visual representation of all the entities configured for a specific namespace. The sample can be found under the folder [SDK Folder]\Samples\AccessControl\ExploringFeatures\Management created during the SDK installation.

If you run this application, you need to provide a service namespace name and its management key (available in the web portal under the service namespace page) to get access to all the information stored in that namespace.

Figure 10-7 illustrates how the AcmBrowser shows all the entities the command batch created.

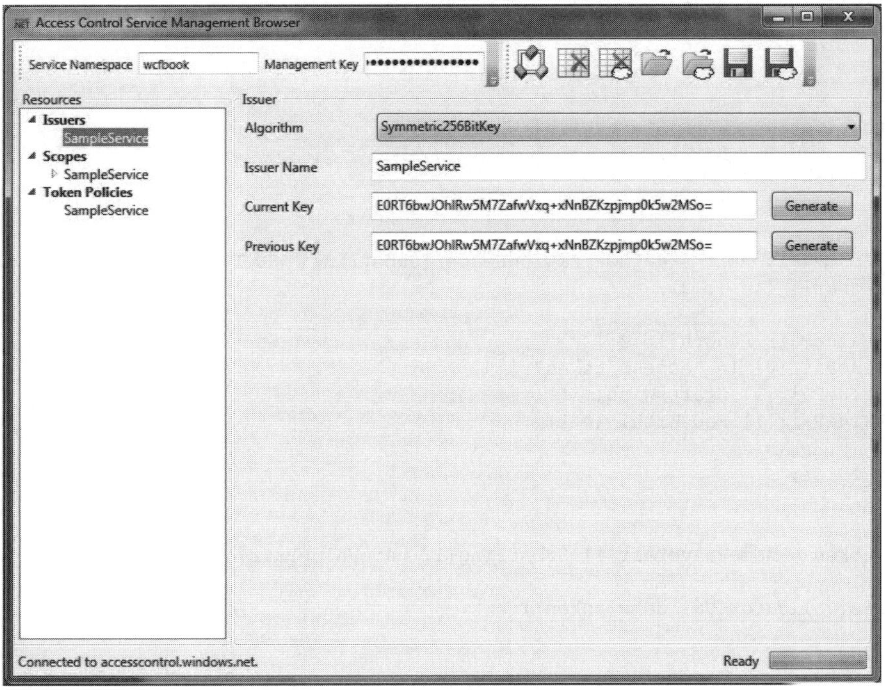

FIGURE 10-7

The batch file generated a new issuer, SampleService, with a key expressed in Base64 for requesting tokens, a new scope SampleService that applies to http://localhost/SampleService (the URI for identifying the service), and contains a simple rule to generate an output claim with the client permissions in the form of an "action" claim type. That scope is also associated with a token policy with the same name that provides the token lifetime and signing key.

You can generate all those entities manually by either using the command-line tool Acs.exe or the AcmBrowser, but that represents much more work on your side for preparing this example.

The authorization manager discussed previously implements all the logic for validating the Simple Web Token issued by ACS, and verifying that the token contains the claim expected by the service. In this example, the configured service expects a claim of type "action" and value "sayHello".

This authorization manager is mainly implemented in the ACSAuthorizationManager class (see Listing 10-13).

LISTING 10-13: WCF Authorization Manager Implementation

```
protected override bool CheckAccessCore(OperationContext operationContext)
{
    string authorizationHeader = WebOperationContext.Current.IncomingRequest.
Headers[HttpRequestHeader.Authorization];

    if (string.IsNullOrEmpty(authorizationHeader))
    {
      return false;
    }

    if (!authorizationHeader.StartsWith("WRAP "))
    {
      return false;
    }

    string[] nameValuePair = authorizationHeader.Substring("WRAP ".Length)
.Split(new char[] {'='}, 2);

    if (nameValuePair.Length != 2 ||
      nameValuePair[0] != "access_token" ||
      !nameValuePair[1].StartsWith("\"") ||
      !nameValuePair[1].EndsWith("\""))
    {
      return false;
     }

    string token = nameValuePair[1].Substring(1, nameValuePair[1].Length - 2);

    if (!this.validator.Validate(token))
    {
      return false;
    }
```

```
        Dictionary<string, string> claims = this.validator.GetNameValues(token);

        string actionClaimValue;
        if (!claims.TryGetValue(this.requiredClaimType, out actionClaimValue))
        {
          return false;
        }

        if (!actionClaimValue.Equals(this.requiredClaimValue))
        {
          return false;
        }

        return true;
    }
```

It basically gets the token from the Http Authorization headers, and performs a couple of validations to verify that it is a valid Simple Web Token using a helper class `TokenValidator`, which is also included as part of the example. In the last part of this method implementation, the claims are extracted from the token and compared against the claim expected by the service.

Finally, after you have all the service implementation and ACS configuration in place, it is time to implement a client application for consuming the service.

The implementation of the client application involves two main steps: the token negotiation with ACS, and the final execution of the service with the expected data and negotiated token.

To get a token from ACS, the client application needs to make an Http POST to the service including the following information:

➤   A `wrap_name` field representing the name of a configured issuer in ACS

➤   A `wrap_password` field representing the key assigned to the issuer

➤   A `wrap_scope` field representing the `AppliesTo` for a given scope in ACS

These three fields are only valid when the client is authenticated with the issuer name and password. The required fields vary according to the authentication method used against ACS.

Listing 10-14 shows how the token negotiation with ACS is handled.

LISTING 10-14: Token Negotiation with ACS

```
private static string GetTokenFromACS()
{
  WebClient client = new WebClient();
  client.BaseAddress = string.Format("https://{0}.{1}", serviceNamespace,
acsBaseAddress);

  NameValueCollection values = new NameValueCollection();
  values.Add("wrap_name", "SampleService");
  values.Add("wrap_password", issuerKey);
  values.Add("wrap_scope", "http://localhost/SampleService");
```

continues

LISTING 10-14 *(continued)*

```
        byte[] responseBytes = client.UploadValues("WRAPv0.9", "POST", values);

        string response = Encoding.UTF8.GetString(responseBytes);

        Console.WriteLine("\nreceived token from ACS: {0}\n", response);

        return response
                    .Split('&')
                    .Single(value => value.StartsWith("wrap_access_token=",
    StringComparison.OrdinalIgnoreCase))
                    .Split('=')[1];
    }
```

After the token is received, the client application can include it as part of the request message to the service as an HTTP Authorization header (the header that the authorization manager is expecting).

Listing 10-15 shows how service consumption is handled.

LISTING 10-15: Service Consumption

```
private static string SendMessageToService(string token)
{
    string message = null;

    WebHttpBinding binding = new WebHttpBinding(WebHttpSecurityMode.None);
    Uri address = new Uri(@"http://localhost/SampleService");

    WebChannelFactory<ISampleService> channelFactory = new
WebChannelFactory<ISampleService>(binding, address);

    ISampleService proxy = channelFactory.CreateChannel();

    using (new OperationContextScope(proxy as IContextChannel))
    {
        string authHeaderValue = string.Format("WRAP access_token=\"{0}\"",
        HttpUtility.UrlDecode(token));

        WebOperationContext.Current.OutgoingRequest.Headers.Add("authorization",
        authHeaderValue);

        message = proxy.SayHello();
    }

    ((IClientChannel)proxy).Close();

    channelFactory.Close();

    return message;
}
```

This method uses a WebChannelFactory for consuming the RESTful service, and therefore the authorization header can only be added through the OperationContextScope. This code might look different if you use a different Http client library.

11

Creating a SOA Case

WHAT'S IN THIS CHAPTER?

➤ Defining requirements for the case

➤ Developing the complete solution

➤ Testing the solution

This chapter is an interactive walkthrough of how to create a solution in SOA architecture with Visual Studio 2010 using WCF. It starts by defining requirements for a case and shows you how to develop the solution, step by step. At the end of this chapter you will have developed a number of services, hosts, and clients as part of the solution. This is a complete example — you can test the process and see it working in action.

THE REQUIREMENTS FOR THE CASE

You need to create services for a car rental company. The company needs a service for managing their fleet of cars, a service to register their customers, and a service to register the rentals.

These three services are considered internal and will be used by their own applications.

Besides these services, they also need an external service accessible by partners of the company that can insert a customer and register a rental with one call.

Operations for the `CarManagementService`:

➤ `InsertNewCar`: Receives the data for a car and inserts it into a database.

➤ `RemoveCar`: Receives the ID of a car and deletes it from the database.

➤ `UpdateMileage`: Receives the data for a car and updates the mileage for the car in the database.

➤   `ListCars`: Returns all cars with their data.

➤   `GetCarPicture`: Returns a picture for the car with a specified ID.

Operations in the `CustomerService`:

➤   `RegisterCustomer`: Receives the data for a customer and inserts it into a database.

Operations in the `RentalService`:

➤   `RegisterCarRental`: Receives all information to register the data for a rental.

➤   `RegisterCarRentalAsPaid`: Receives an ID of the rental and marks the rental as paid in the database.

➤   `StartRental`: Calls the method to indicate that the car was picked up at a given location where the rental starts.

➤   `StopCarRental`: Calls the method to indicate that the car was dropped off at a given location where the rental stops.

➤   `GetRentalRegistration`: Returns all data about the rental.

Operations for the `ExternalService`:

➤   `SubmitRentalContract`: Receives all the information for a new customer and all the information for the rental. It inserts the new customer and the rental data into a database.

Additional Requirements

Additional requirements for the `CarManagementService`:

➤   There is an enumerated field type for defining whether the car has a manual transmission or an automatic transmission.

➤   A number of car types are recognized by the company. Besides regular cars there are luxury cars and sports cars. Luxury cars have all the data elements of a car and a list of luxury items. Sports cars have all the data elements of a car and a horsepower value.

Additional requirements for the `RentalService`:

➤   Errors occurring in this service should be handled carefully. The data should be validated and when the data is not correctly filled in, the client must receive a well-structured message with a functional description of the validation rule.

➤   The code for the `RegisterCarRentalAsPaid` operation should be executed under the credentials of the client using the service.

Additional requirement for the `ExternalService`:

➤   The `SubmitRentalContract` calls operations in two other services (`CustomerService` and `RentalService`) in sequence to register the customer and to register the rental. It's clear that this has to happen in one transaction. The customer is not allowed to be inserted into the database without the rental being registered.

SETTING UP THE SOLUTION

You start by creating an empty Visual Studio solution. You will be creating every project needed in one solution. This makes it easy to test all applications at once and to have it checked in to the source control environment (see Figure 11-1).

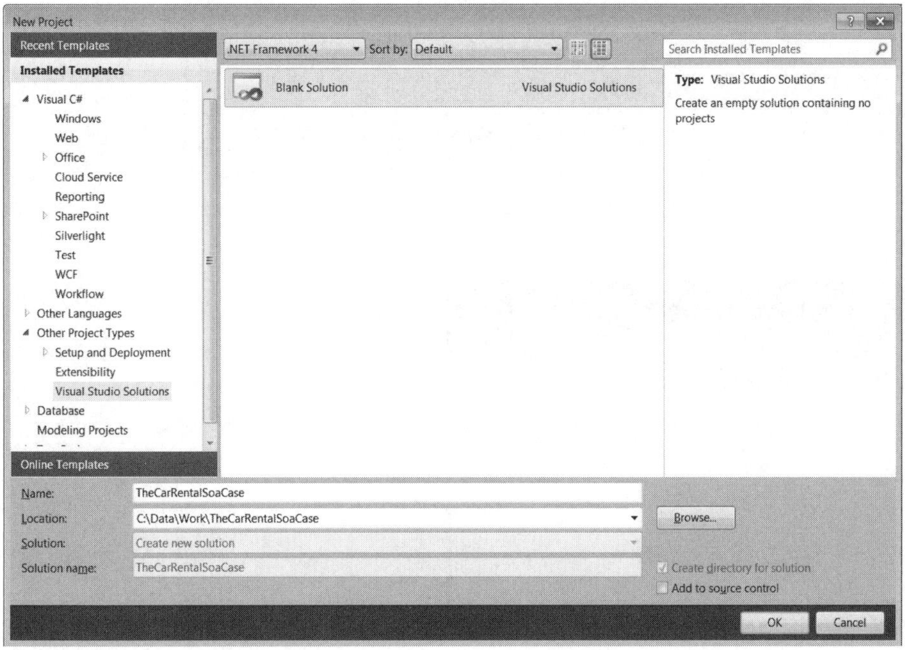

FIGURE 11-1

Name the solution TheCarRentalSOACase and place it in the directory C:\Data\Work\TheCarRentalSOACase.

Create a structure of solution folders to group projects together. Each folder will contain one or more projects. You can add a solution folder by right-clicking the solution and selecting Add ⇨ New Solution Folder. See Figure 11-2.

These solution folders are needed:

➤ Clients (foldername : Clients)

➤ Hosts (foldername : Hosts)

➤ Interfaces (foldername : Interfaces)

➤ Services (foldername : Services)

After adding the four solution folders, your solution should look like Figure 11-3.

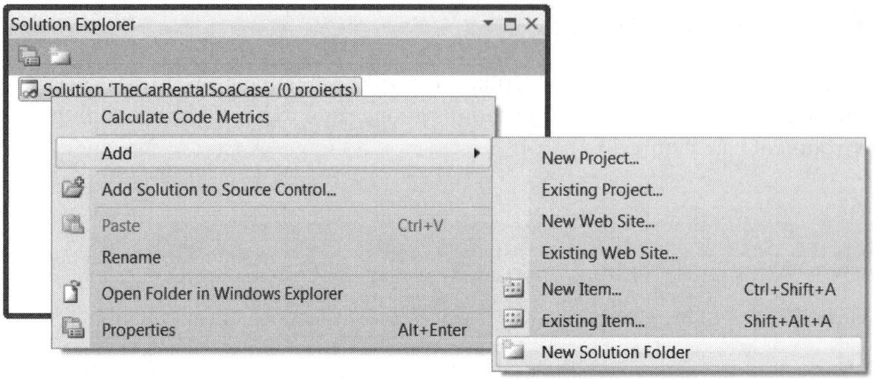

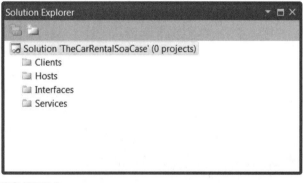

FIGURE 11-2

FIGURE 11-3

CREATING THE INTERFACES

Creating the interfaces first is the best approach and is typical for a SOA project. Start by creating the libraries to contain the interfaces. You need four libraries:

➤   CarManagementInterface

➤   CustomerInterface

➤   RentalInterface

➤   ExternalInterface

Do this by adding the four Class Libraries projects to the Interfaces folder in the solution. See Figure 11-4.

In the Add New Project dialog box, select Class Library from the list of templates. See Figure 11-5.

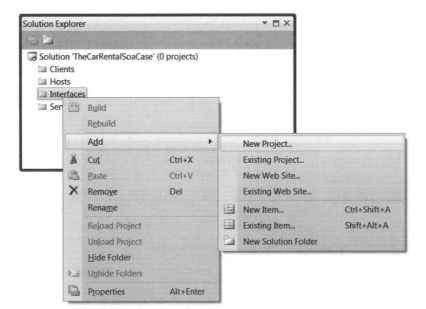

FIGURE 11-4

FIGURE 11-5

Do this for each of the four interfaces. Your solution should look like Figure 11-6.

Now you need to add references to the WCF libraries, System.ServiceModel and System .Runtime.Serialization. They contain the attributes needed for the contracts. Adding references is done by right-clicking References in a project in Solution Explorer. See Figure 11-7.

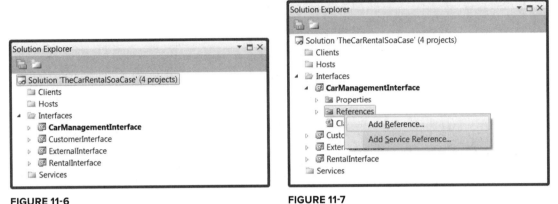

FIGURE 11-6

FIGURE 11-7

This opens the Add Reference dialog box. Select `System.ServiceModel` and `System.Runtime` `.Serialization` and click OK. See Figure 11-8.

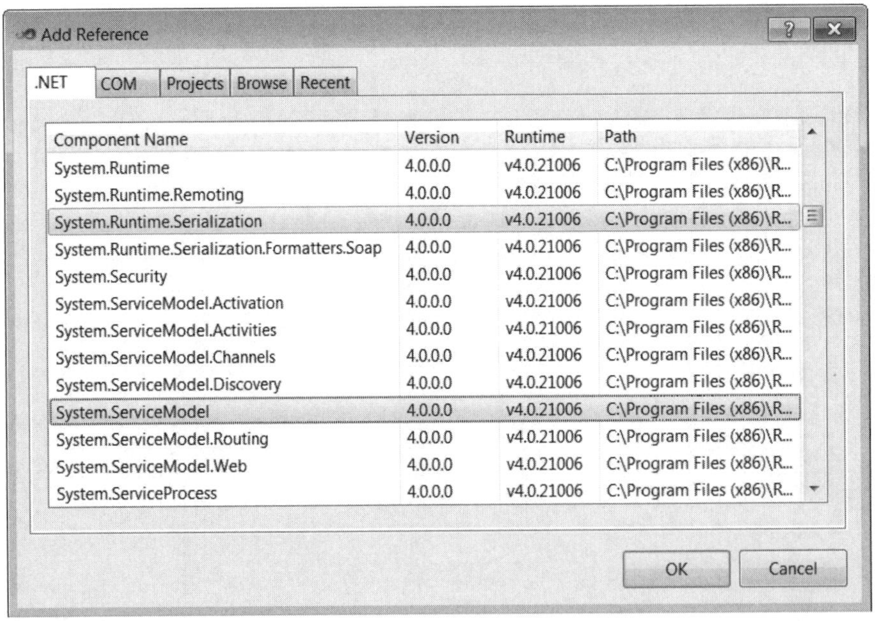

FIGURE 11-8

Repeat this step for the other three projects.

Because you selected Class Library as the template, Visual Studio has created a file called Class1.cs containing an empty class in the project. You don't need this file as you're creating interfaces. So you can delete the Class1.cs file in each of the four projects. See Figure 11-9.

Add an Interface file to each project (see Figure 11-10). The Interfaces are `ICarManagement`, `ICustomer`, `IRental`, and `IExternalInterface`.

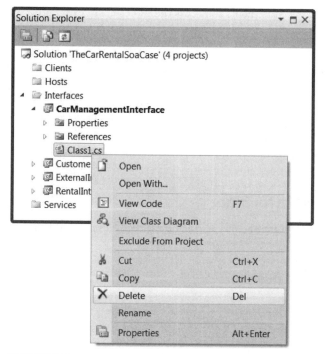

FIGURE 11-9

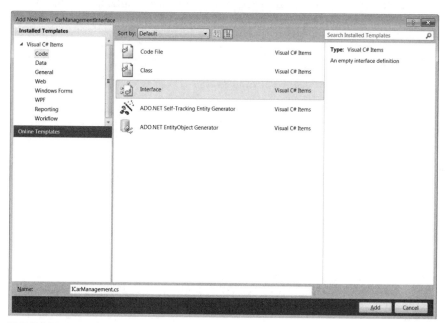

FIGURE 11-10

Open the interface and add the needed `using` statements to access the `System.ServiceModel` and `System.Runtime.Serialization` namespaces:

```
using System.ServiceModel;
using System.Runtime.Serialization;
```

Make the interface public by adding the public keyword to the interface declaration:

```
public interface ICarManagement
```

Repeat this for each of the interface projects.

Creating the CarManagement Interface

To support the requirement needed, an enumerated field type for the car transmission, add the following code:

```
[DataContract]
public enum TransmissionTypeEnum
{
    [EnumMember]
    Manual,
    [EnumMember]
    Automatic
}
```

This is a `public` enum called `TransmissionTypeEnum`. The enum must be attributed with the `DataContract` attribute and each choice in the enum must be attributed with the `EnumMember` attribute.

Now add code for the `Car` class:

```
[DataContract]
public class Car
{
    [DataMember]
    public string BrandName { get; set; }
    [DataMember]
    public string TypeName { get; set; }
    [DataMember]
    public TransmissionTypeEnum Transmission { get; set; }
    [DataMember]
    public int NumberOfDoors { get; set; }
    [DataMember]
    public int MaxNumberOfPersons { get; set; }
    [DataMember]
    public int LitersOfLuggage { get; set; }
}
```

This class is attributed with the `DataContract` attribute and each property is attributed as `DataMember`.

Now you can complete the interface containing the signatures of the service methods:

```
[ServiceContract]
interface ICarManagement
{
  [OperationContract]
  int InsertNewCar(Car car);

  [OperationContract]
  bool RemoveCar(Car car);

  [OperationContract]
  void UpdateMilage(Car car);

  [OperationContract]
  List<Car> ListCars();

  [OperationContract]
  byte[] GetCarPicture(string carID);
}
```

Fix any errors and then finish by compiling this class library.

Creating the Customer Interface

Add code to the `ICustomer` interface. This is the code for the `Customer` class and the signatures for the operation in the `CustomerService`:

```
[ServiceContract]
public interface ICustomer
{
  [OperationContract]
  int RegisterCustomer(Customer customer);
}

[DataContract]
public class Customer
{
  [DataMember]
  public string CustomerName { get; set; }
  [DataMember]
  public string CustomerFirstName { get; set; }
  [DataMember]
  public string CustomerMiddleLetter { get; set; }
  [DataMember]
  public DateTime CustomerBirthDate { get; set; }
}
```

Creating the Rental Interface

Add code to the `IRental` interface. This is the code for the `RentalRegistration` DataContract and the signatures for the operations in the `RentalService`:

```csharp
[ServiceContract]
public interface IRental
{
    [OperationContract]
    string RegisterCarRental(RentalRegistration rentalRegistration);

    [OperationContract]
    void RegisterCarRentalAsPaid(string rentalID);

    [OperationContract]
    void StartCarRental(string rentalID);

    [OperationContract]
    void StopCarRental(string rentalID);

    [OperationContract]
    RentalRegistration GetRentalRegistration(string rentalID);
}

[DataContract]
public class RentalRegistration
{
    [DataMember]
    public int CustomerID { get; set; }
    [DataMember]
    public string CarID { get; set; }
    [DataMember]
    public int PickUpLocation { get; set; }
    [DataMember]
    public int DropOffLocation { get; set; }
    [DataMember]
    public DateTime PickUpDateTime { get; set; }
    [DataMember]
    public DateTime DropOffDateTime { get; set; }
    [DataMember]
    public PaymentStatusEnum PaymentStatus { get; set; }
    [DataMember]
    public string Comments { get; set; }
}

[DataContract]
public enum PaymentStatusEnum
{
    [EnumMember(Value = "PUV")]
    PaidUpFrontByVoucher,
    [EnumMember(Value = "PUC")]
    PaidUpFrontByCreditCard,
    [EnumMember(Value = "TPP")]
    ToBePaidAtPickUp,
```

```
      [EnumMember(Value = "INV")]
      ToBePaidByInvoice
    }

    [DataContract]
    public enum IncludedInsurance
    {
      [EnumMember]
      LiabilityInsurance = 1,
      [EnumMember]
      FireInsurance = 2,
      [EnumMember]
      TheftProtection = 4,
      [EnumMember]
      AllRiskInsurance = 1 + 2 + 4
    }
```

Code snippet CreatingaSOACase.zip

Creating the External Interface

The External Interface project reuses the Customer contract and the Rental contract and thus needs a reference to both libraries. Open the Add Reference dialog box and switch to the Projects tab. Select both `CustomerInterface` and `RentalInterface`. See Figure 11-11.

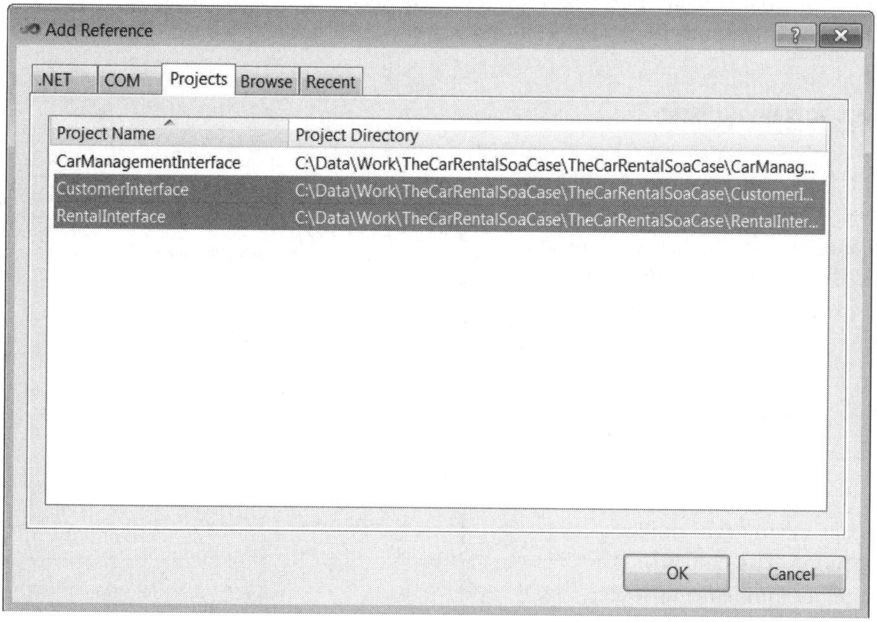

FIGURE 11-11

Besides adding using statements for the two system libraries, add using statements for RentalInterface and CustomerInterface:

```
using RentalInterface;
using CustomerInterface;
```

The following is code for the ExternalInterface:

```
[ServiceContract]
public interface IExternalInterface
{
  [OperationContract]
  void SubmitRentalContract(RentalContract rentalContract);
}

[DataContract]
public class RentalContract
{
  [DataMember]
  public string Company { get; set; }
  [DataMember]
  public string CompanyReferenceID { get; set; }
  [DataMember]
  public RentalRegistration RentalRegistration { get; set; }
  [DataMember]
  public Customer Customer { get; set; }
}
```

The ExternalInterface has one method that receives a parameter. It is structured by a DataContract which has properties for a RentalRegistration and a Customer.

CREATING THE SERVICES

In the solution, add four projects as a class library, one for each service. These projects reference the interface projects and contain the implementation of the logic. Name them CarManagementService, CustomerService, ExternalInterfaceFacade, and RentalService. Your solution should now look like Figure 11-12.

Add the assemblies, System.ServiceModel and System.Runtime.Serialization, to each of the projects.

Rename the Class1.cs file in each project to the appropriate name. The names of the files are CarManagementImplementation.cs, CustomerServiceImplementation.cs, RentalServiceImplementation.cs, and ExternalInterfaceFacadeImplementation.cs.

FIGURE 11-12

Visual Studio asks you if you would like to rename the code element 'Class1'. Click Yes. See Figure 11-13.

The result is seen in Figure 11-14.

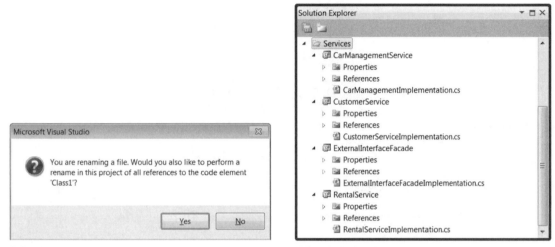

FIGURE 11-13

FIGURE 11-14

Add the `using` statements needed to each of the files:

```
using System.Runtime.Serialization;
using System.ServiceModel;
```

For each project, add a reference to the corresponding project containing the interface. Then add a corresponding `using` statement in each class to access its interface:

```
using CarManagementInterface;
```

Implement the interface in the class by adding a column and the name of the interface after the class declarations:

```
public class CarManagementImplementation : ICarManagement
{
}
```

Implementing all methods in an interface can be done quickly by right-clicking the name of the interface you just typed in the source code editor and selecting Implement Interface. See Figure 11-15.

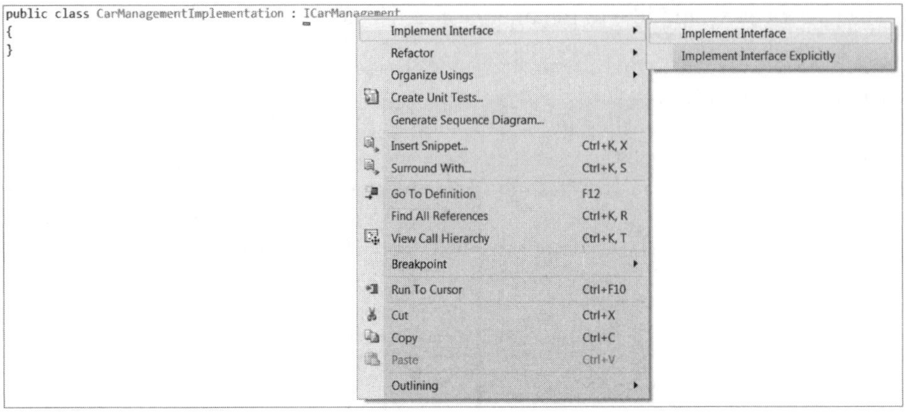

FIGURE 11-15

For the CarManagement Interface, the result should look like this:

```
public int InsertNewCar(Car car)
{
  throw new NotImplementedException();
}

public bool RemoveCar(Car car)
{
  throw new NotImplementedException();
}

public void UpdateMilage(Car car)
{
  throw new NotImplementedException();
}

public List<Car> ListCars()
{
  throw new NotImplementedException();
}

public byte[] GetCarPicture(string carID)
{
  throw new NotImplementedException();
}
```

Do this for the other three services, making sure to use the corresponding interface for each implementation library, and then build the solution.

CREATING THE HOST

Start by creating a console application as host. This is more convenient for testing and debugging. Later you can create a Windows service which will host the services.

Add a Console application to the solution in the host solution folder. See Figure 11-16.

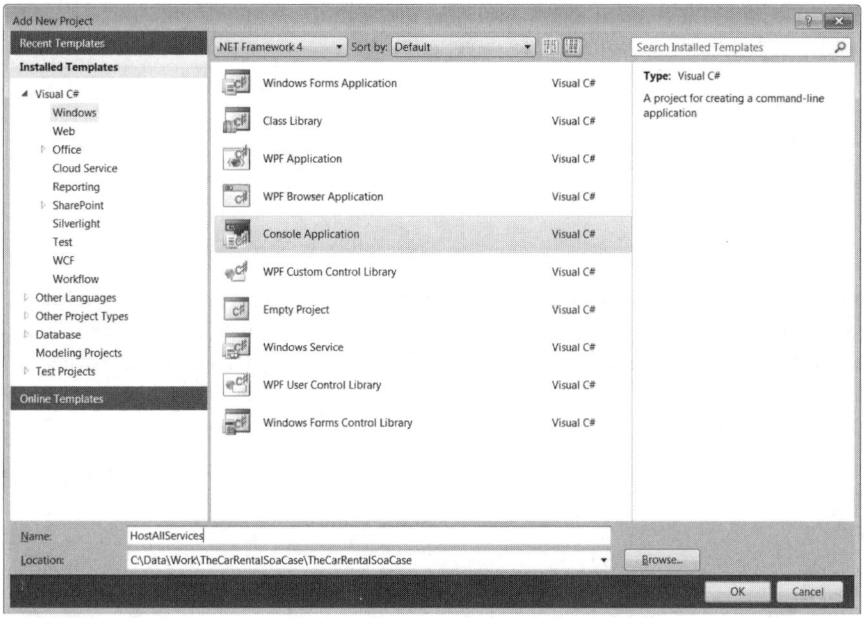

FIGURE 11-16

Next you add the needed WCF libraries and all the interface and implementation libraries. Add the `System.ServiceModel` and `System.Runtime.Serialization` assemblies. Then add all four Interface Projects together with the Implementation Projects. See Figure 11-17.

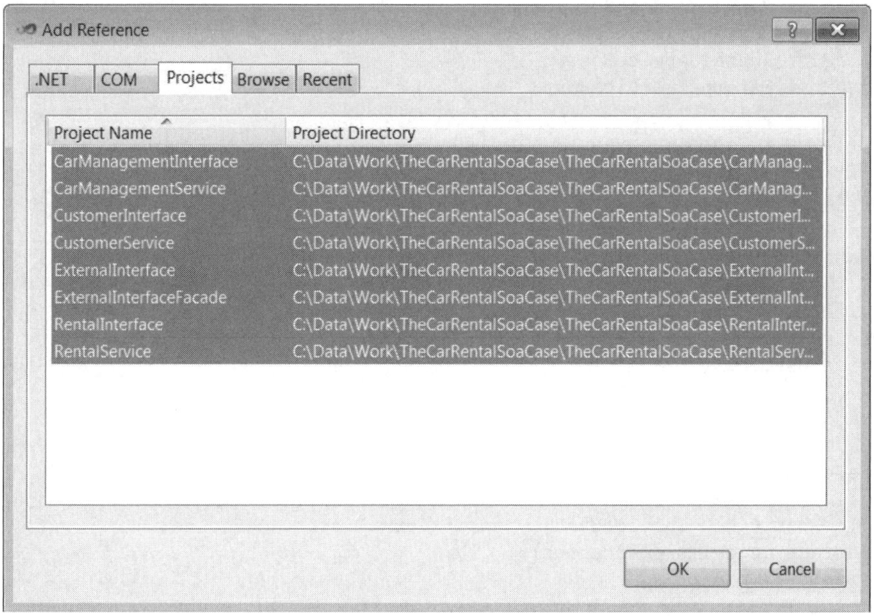

FIGURE 11-17

To the code of program.cs, add the needed `using` statements. Both the system namespaces and the four namespaces of the implementation projects are needed:

```
using System.ServiceModel;
using System.Runtime.Serialization;
using CarManagementService;
using RentalService;
using CustomerService;
using ExternalInterfaceFacade;
```

Add code to the main method for an exception handler together with statements that write the status of the service to the console. The last line is a console.readkey operation. It is there to make sure the host application keeps running after the services are opened so clients can access them:

```
Console.WriteLine("ServiceHost");
try
{

  //Open hosts here

}
catch (Exception ex)
{
  Console.WriteLine(ex.Message);
}
Console.WriteLine("Started");
Console.ReadKey();
```

You need four service hosts. Declare a reference variable for each of the hosts in the program class:

```
static ServiceHost CarManagementServiceHost;
static ServiceHost CustomerServiceHost;
static ServiceHost RentalServiceHost;
static ServiceHost ExternalServiceHost;
```

Write the code to instantiate and open each host in the `try-catch` block of the main method:

```
CarManagementServiceHost = new ServiceHost(typeof(CarManagementService.
 CarManagementImplementation));
CarManagementServiceHost.Open();

CustomerServiceHost = new ServiceHost(typeof(CustomerService.
 CustomerServiceImplementation));
CustomerServiceHost.Open();

RentalServiceHost = new ServiceHost(typeof(RentalService.
RentalServiceImplementation));
RentalServiceHost.Open();

ExternalServiceHost = new ServiceHost(typeof(ExternalInterfaceFacade.
 ExternalInterfaceFacadeImplementation));
ExternalServiceHost.Open();
```

Add an application configuration file to the project. Do this by using the Add New Item dialog box. Select Application Configuration File and use the default name, which is App.config. See Figure 11-18.

FIGURE 11-18

Build all solutions. It's important that the host is built correctly. The build will copy the assemblies for the interfaces and the implementations to the bin directory of this project. The binaries are needed as the WCF Configuration Editor needs to have access to them while configuring them.

Right-click the App.config file and select Edit WCF Configuration. See Figures 11-19 and 11-20.

In the WCF Configuration Editor, click Create a New Service. See Figure 11-21.

FIGURE 11-19

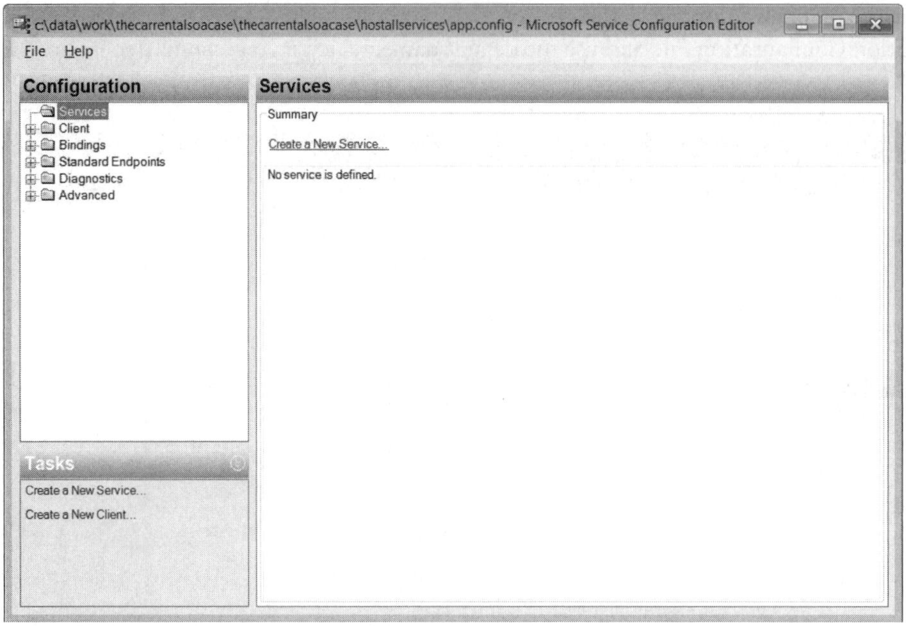

FIGURE 11-20

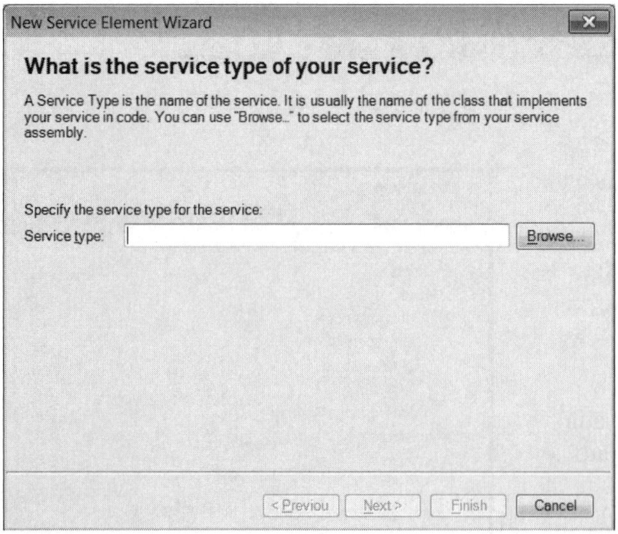

FIGURE 11-21

Click Browse to open the Type Browser dialog box. Navigate into the bin directory and then into the debug directory. The dialog box shows a number of assemblies. Select the CarManagamentService.dll assembly and click Open. See Figure 11-22.

This will show you the implementation class in this assembly. Click CarManagamentService. CarManagementImplementation and click Open. See Figure 11-23.

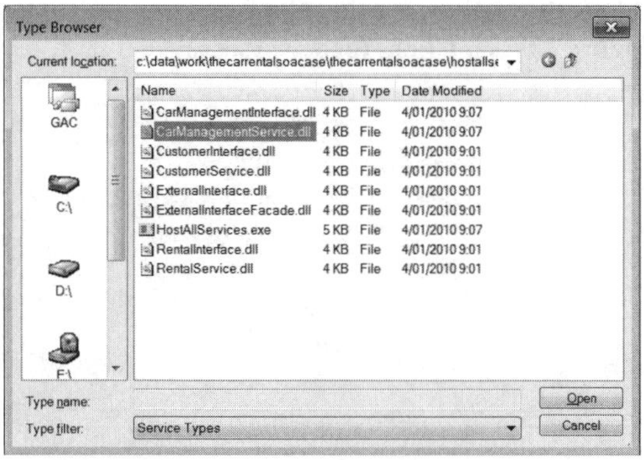

FIGURE 11-22

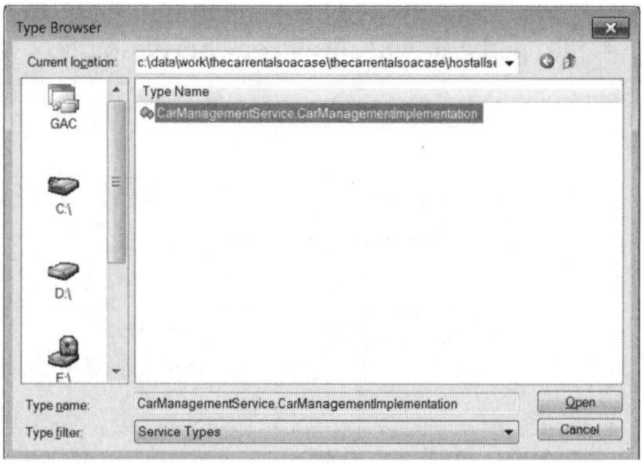

FIGURE 11-23

The Add Service wizard proposes the name of the implementation in the dialog box. Click Next.

The wizard decides what the name of the contract is. Do not change this. Click Next.

The wizard now asks you for the communication mode the service is using. Leave the selection on HTTP (see Figure 11-24). Click Next.

The wizard now asks for the method of interoperability, as shown in Figure 11-25. Select Advanced Web Services interoperability and leave the Simplex Communication button selected. Click Next.

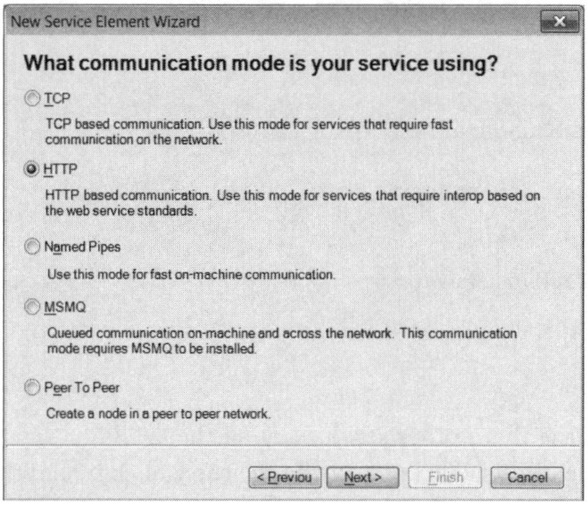

FIGURE 11-24

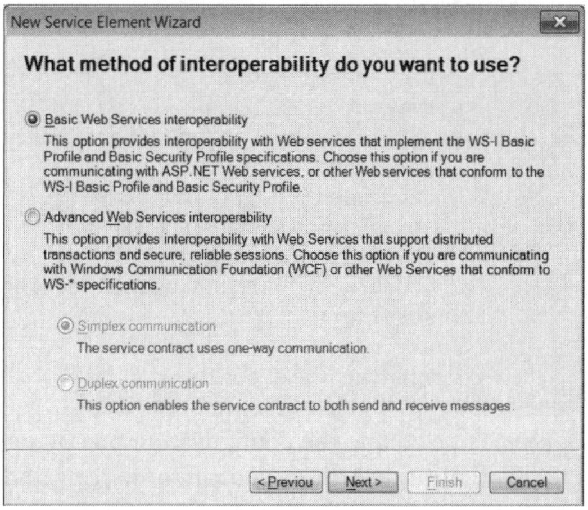

FIGURE 11-25

The wizard asks for the address of your endpoint: `http://localhost:9876/CarManagementService`. See Figure 11-26.

Click Next and Finish. Save the configuration (File, Save) and exit the WCF Configuration Editor.

If the App.config file was open in an editor, Visual Studio will detect that the App.config file has changed and will show you this dialog box (see Figure 11-27). Click Yes.

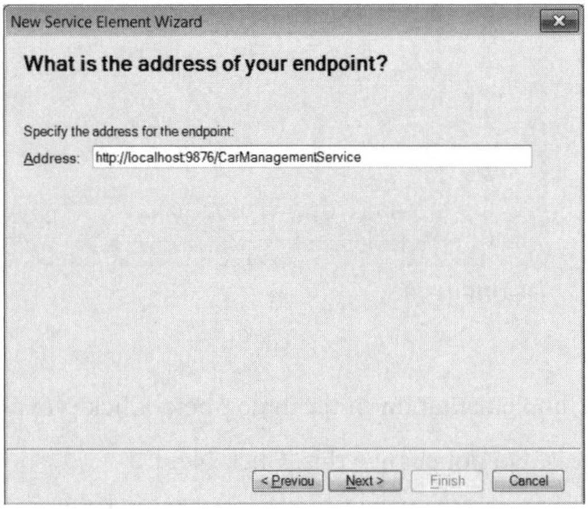

FIGURE 11-26 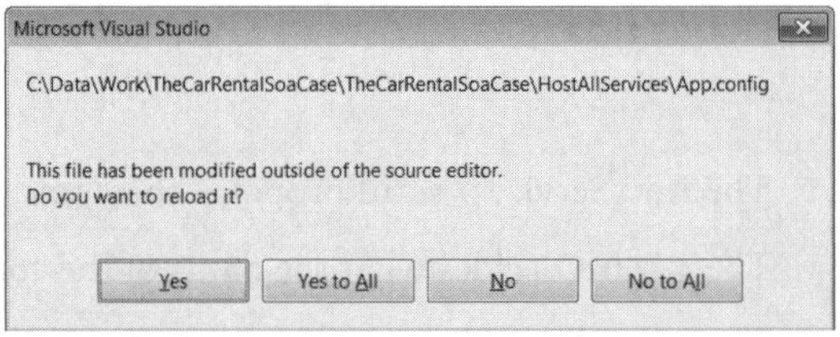   **FIGURE 11-27**

Check the configuration created. The wizard has configured `ws2007HttpBinding` as binding for the endpoint. Change this to `wsHttpBinding`. Be careful, this value is case sensitive. The result should look like this:

```
<system.serviceModel>
  <services>
   <service name="CarManagementService.CarManagementImplementation">
    <endpoint
      address="http://localhost:9876/CarManagementService"
      binding="wsHttpBinding"
      bindingConfiguration=""
      contract="CarManagementInterface.ICarManagement" />
   </service>
  </services>
</system.serviceModel>
```

Instead of doing the configuration one by one for the three other services using the WCF Configuration Editor, you can now copy and paste the service tag and change the values by hand. Use the following addresses for the other services:

➤ http://localhost:9876/CustomerService

➤ http://localhost:9876/RentalService

➤ http://localhost:9876/ExternalInterfaceService

Make sure you change the name and the contract correctly. The result should look like this:

```
<system.serviceModel>
    <services>
      <service name="CarManagementService.CarManagementImplementation">
        <endpoint
          address="http://localhost:9876/CarManagementService"
          binding="wsHttpBinding"
          bindingConfiguration=""
          contract="CarManagementInterface.ICarManagement" />
      </service>
      <service name="CustomerService.CustomerServiceImplementation">
        <endpoint
          address="http://localhost:9876/CustomerService"
          binding="wsHttpBinding"
          bindingConfiguration=""
          contract="CustomerInterface.ICustomer" />
      </service>
      <service name="RentalService.RentalServiceImplementation">
        <endpoint
          address="http://localhost:9876/RentalService"
          binding="wsHttpBinding"
          bindingConfiguration=""
          contract="RentalInterface.IRental" />
      </service>
      <service
       name="ExternalInterfaceFacade.ExternalInterfaceFacadeImplementation">
        <endpoint
          address="http://localhost:9876/ExternalInterfaceService"
          binding="wsHttpBinding"
          bindingConfiguration=""
          contract="ExternalInterface.IExternalInterface" />
      </service>
    </services>
</system.serviceModel>
```

Code snippet CreatingaSOACase.zip

Set HostAllServices as the startup project. Do this by right-clicking the HostAllServices project and selecting Set as StartUp Project. See Figure 11-28.

Now you can run the application. This application exposes the services you created. See Figure 11-29.

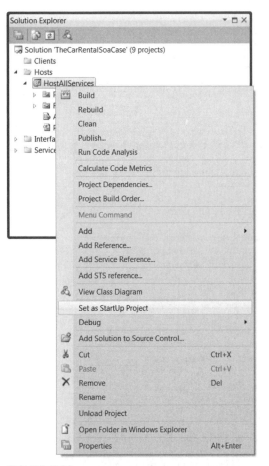

FIGURE 11-28

FIGURE 11-29

CREATING THE DATABASE

Open Server Explorer in Visual Studio and create a new SQL Server Database (see Figure 11-30). Name the database RentalCarCaseDB.

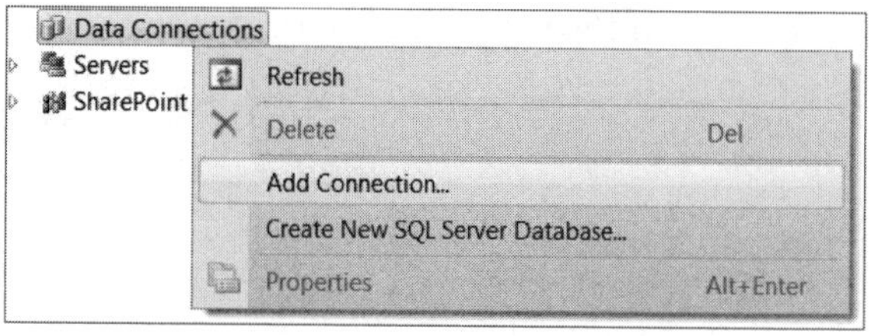

Add two tables to the database. You can do this by executing this SQL statement or by adding the tables manually:

FIGURE 11-30

```
CREATE DATABASE [CarRentalCaseDB]
GO
USE [CarRentalCaseDB]
GO
CREATE TABLE [dbo].[Rental]
(
   [RentalID] [int] IDENTITY(1,1) NOT NULL,
   [CustomerID] [int] NULL,
   [CarID] [nvarchar](50) NULL,
   [PickUpLocation] [int] NULL,
   [DropOffLocation] [int] NULL,
   [PickUpDateTime] [datetime] NULL,
   [DropOffDateTime] [datetime] NULL,
   [PaymentStatus] [char](3) NULL,
   [Comments] [nvarchar](1000) NULL,
 CONSTRAINT [PK_Rental] PRIMARY KEY CLUSTERED
 ([RentalID] ASC))
GO
CREATE TABLE [dbo].[Customer](
   [CustomerID] [int] IDENTITY(1,1) NOT NULL,
   [CustomerName] [nvarchar](50) NULL,
   [CustomerFirstName] [nvarchar](50) NULL,
 CONSTRAINT [PK_Customer] PRIMARY KEY CLUSTERED
([CustomerID] ASC))
GO
```

IMPLEMENTING THE SERVICE

Now you'll add code to the implementation to make your services work.

This is not the complete business logic behind the services as this book is focusing on WCF only. Instead you'll write temporary code so the operations can return meaningful answers to clients. For the implementation of InsertCustomer and RegisterCarRental, use a LINQ to SQL model to insert the data into a database.

Creating Database Access for the CustomerService and the RentalService

Add a LINQ to SQL Classes file to both the CustomerService and the RentalService (see Figure 11-31). Both CustomerService and RentalService access the same database in this case.

In a real production environment these would probably be two different databases, but using one database is more convenient for this walkthrough. At `CustomerService`, add a LINQ to SQL Classes and name it DataClassesCustomer.dbml (see Figure 11-32).

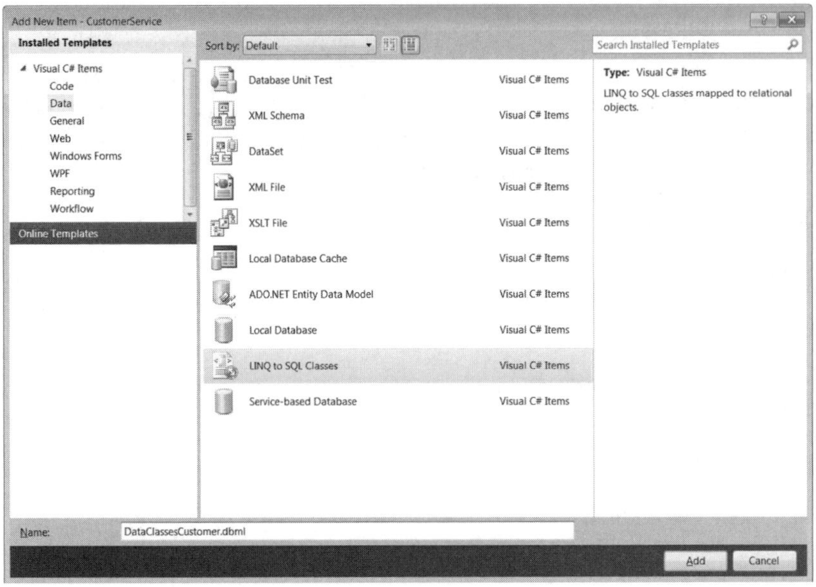

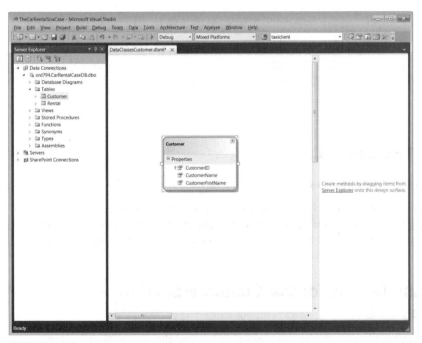

FIGURE 11-31

FIGURE 11-32

Drag and drop the Customer table into the designer.

Do this also for the `RentalService`. Create a LINQ to SQL model named DataClassesRental.dbml and drag and drop the Rental Table into it.

Now you can add the implementation code to the `CustomerService`. Open the CustomerServiceImplementation.cs file. In the code for the `RegisterCustomer` method, delete the throw statement and replace it with the following code:

```
using (DataClassesCustomerDataContext ctx = new DataClassesCustomerDataContext())
{
  Customer customerToInsert;
  customerToInsert = new Customer();
  customerToInsert.CustomerName = customer.CustomerName;
  customerToInsert.CustomerFirstName = customer.CustomerFirstName;
  ctx.Customers.InsertOnSubmit(customerToInsert);
  ctx.SubmitChanges();
  return customerToInsert.CustomerID;
}
```

This code opens the LINQ to SQL DataContext, creates a new customer, and inserts and submits the customer to the database.

Add similar code to insert a rental into the database in the implementation of the `RentalService`. Open RentalServiceImplementation.cs and replace the throw statement with the following code:

```
Console.WriteLine("RegisterCarRental");
using (DataClassesRentalDataContext ctx = new DataClassesRentalDataContext())
{
  Rental rentalToInsert;
  rentalToInsert = new Rental();
  rentalToInsert.CustomerID = rentalRegistration.CustomerID;
  rentalToInsert.CarID = rentalRegistration.CarID;
  rentalToInsert.Comments = rentalRegistration.Comments;
  ctx.Rentals.InsertOnSubmit(rentalToInsert);
  ctx.SubmitChanges();
}

return "OK";
```

Creating the CarManagement Service

Here you add code to the `CarManagementService`. Start by adding a `using` statement for the system.IO namespace. You need this namespace to read an image from a file:

```
using System.IO;
```

Implement the operations with the following code. Make sure you use a path that refers to a file that exists in the GetCarPicture operation:

```
public int InsertNewCar(Car car)
{
  Console.WriteLine("InsertNewCar " + car.BrandName + " " + car.TypeName);
  return 1;
}

public bool RemoveCar(Car car)
{
  Console.WriteLine("RemoveCar " + car.BrandName + " " + car.TypeName);
  return true;
}

public void UpdateMilage(Car car)
{
  Console.WriteLine("UpdateMilage " + car.BrandName + " " + car.TypeName);
}

public List<Car> ListCars()
{
  Console.WriteLine("ListCars");
  List<Car> listCars;
  listCars = new List<Car>();
  listCars.Add(new Car {
      BrandName = "XXX",
      Transmission = TransmissionTypeEnum.Automatic,
      TypeName = "YYY" });
  listCars.Add(new Car {
      BrandName = "XXX",
      Transmission = TransmissionTypeEnum.Automatic,
      TypeName = "YYY" });

  return listCars;
}

public byte[] GetCarPicture(string carID)
{
  Console.WriteLine("GetCarPicture");

  byte[] buff;

  string pathToPicture;
  pathToPicture = @"C:\Data\WCFBook\Code\SOACase\Pics\CarExample.jpg";

  FileStream fileStream =
   new FileStream(pathToPicture, FileMode.Open,FileAccess.Read);
  BinaryReader binaryReader = new BinaryReader(fileStream);

  buff = binaryReader.ReadBytes((int)fileStream.Length);
  return buff;
}
```

In this implementation the `InsertCar`, `RemoveCar`, and `UpdateMileage` operations do not interact with a database. They just write a status line to the console. The `ListCars` operation creates and returns a hardcoded list of cars. The `GetCarPicture` operation reads the image in a file and returns this as an array of bytes. It's up to the client to transform these bytes to an image again.

EXPOSING METADATA

Now you're able to host the service by adding configuration to expose the metadata. Exposing metadata allows Visual Studio to download the WSDL file to create the needed proxies. Allowing a service to expose its metadata can be done by configuration.

You'll do this for the `CarManagementService` only. You'll see other ways to create proxies for the other services in this chapter.

Open the App.config of the `HostAllServices` applications with the WCF Configuration Editor. Look for the Service Behaviors node and click the New Service Behavior Configuration link. See Figure 11-33.

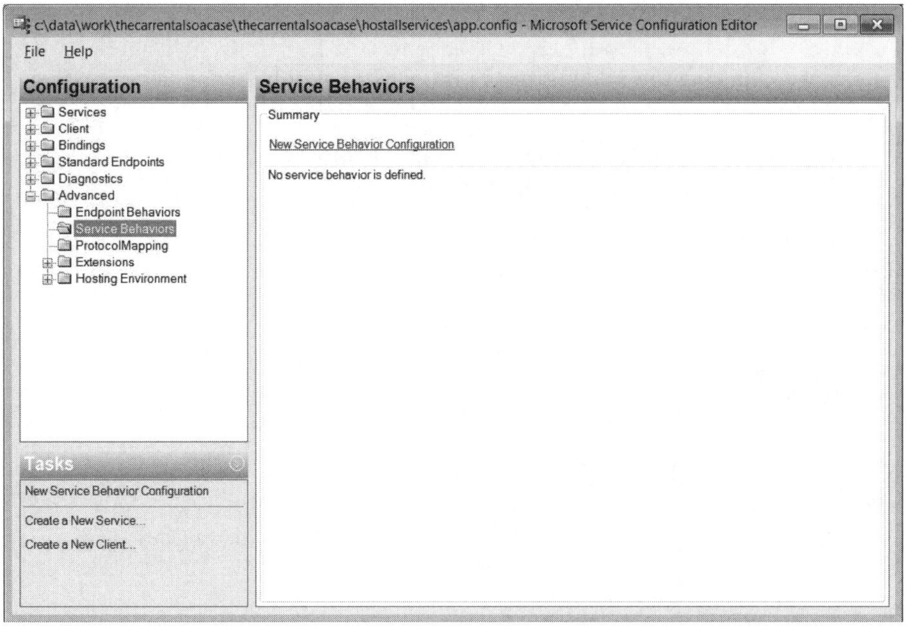

FIGURE 11-33

Name the behavior `ExposeMetaDataBehavior`. See Figure 11-34.

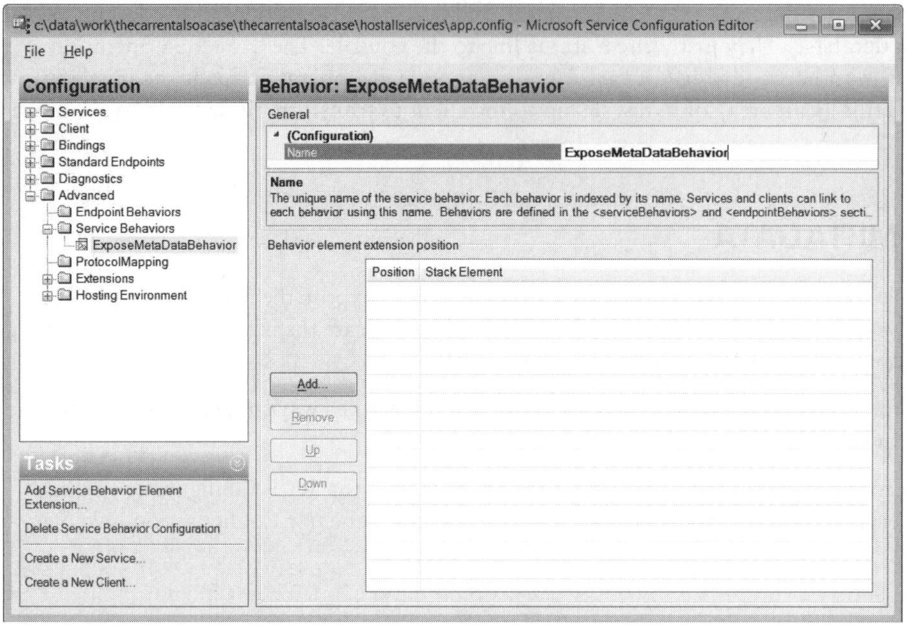

FIGURE 11-34

Add a behavior element by clicking the Add button. This opens a list of behavior elements. See Figure 11-35.

Select the serviceMetadata element and click Add. Notice the element is now added to the ExposeMetaDataBehavior node in the treeview on the right.

Click this new node and edit the serviceMetadata attributes. Enter `http://localhost:9876/ CarManagement/MEX` as the HttpGetUrl and set the `HttpGetEnabled` property to `True`. See Figure 11-36.

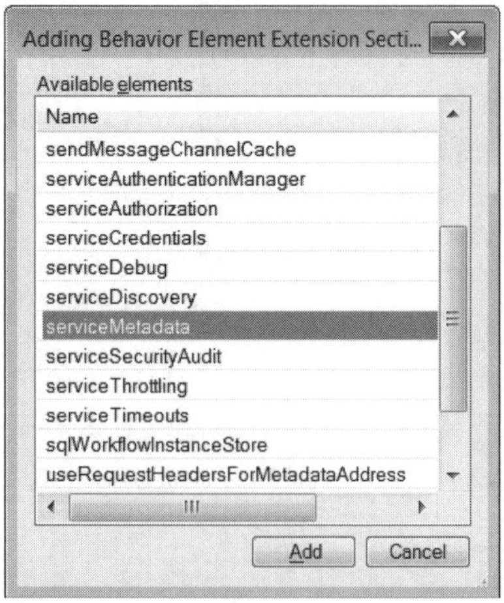

FIGURE 11-35

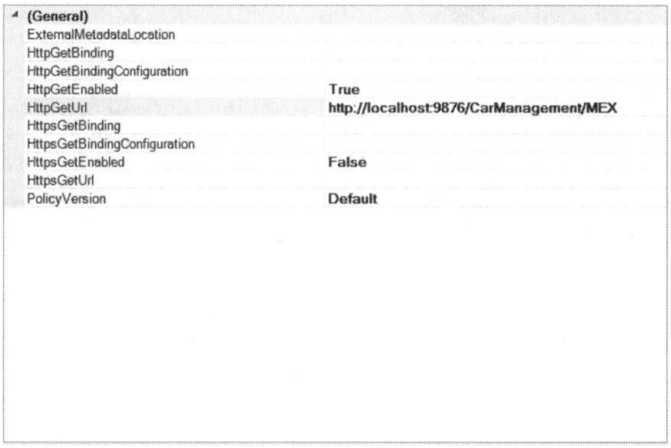

FIGURE 11-36

Now refer CarManagementService to this new behavior. Click CarManagementService in the tree and set the BehaviorConfiguration to ExposeMetaDataBehavior. See Figure 11-37.

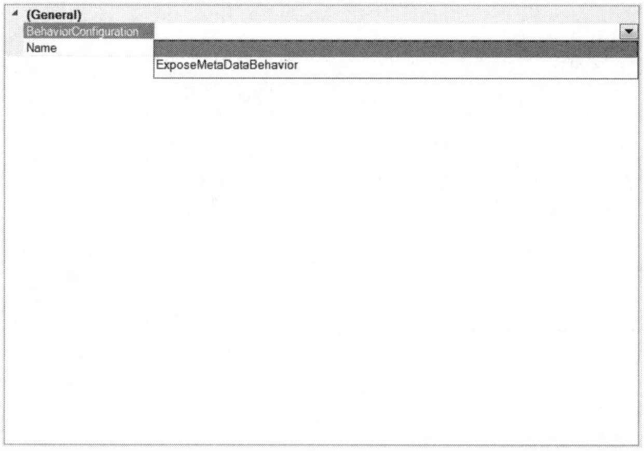

FIGURE 11-37

Save the configuration, close the WCF Configuration Editor, and reload the App.config file.

The configuration in the App.config should now include a serviceBehavior tag like this:

```
<behaviors>
  <serviceBehaviors>
    <behavior name="ExposeMetaDataBehavior">
      <serviceMetadata
        httpGetEnabled="true"
        httpGetUrl="http://localhost:9876/CarManagement/MEX" />
    </behavior>
  </serviceBehaviors>
</behaviors>
```

The configuration of the CarManagementService should now look like the following — notice the behaviorConfiguration attribute of the service tag:

```
<service
 behaviorConfiguration="ExposeMetaDataBehavior"
 name="CarManagementService.CarManagementImplementation">
  <endpoint
    address="http://localhost:9876/CarManagementService"
    binding="wsHttpBinding"
    bindingConfiguration=""
    contract="CarManagementInterface.ICarManagement" />
</service>
```

Now you can test the metadata endpoint. Start the `HostAllServices` application and start a browser. After the `HostAllServices` application is up, browse to `http://localhost:9876/CarManagement/MEX`. The browser should show you the WSDL file, as in Figure 11-38.

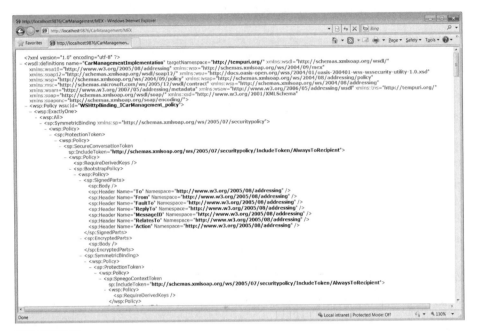

FIGURE 11-38

CREATING THE CARMANAGEMENT CLIENT

Add a `WindowsForms` application to the Client solution folder called `CarApplication`. This application uses the `CarService`.

Start the `HostAllServices` application outside Visual Studio instead of running it from within Visual Studio. You can do this by navigating to the bin\debug directory of the project and starting HostAllServices.exe.

In Visual Studio, click Add Service Reference in the `CarManagementClient` application. Type the address of the metadata endpoint in the Add Service Reference dialog box: `http://localhost:9876/CarManagement/MEX`.

Set the namespace of the service reference to CarService and click the Go button. Visual Studio downloads the WSDL and shows the available operations. See Figure 11-39.

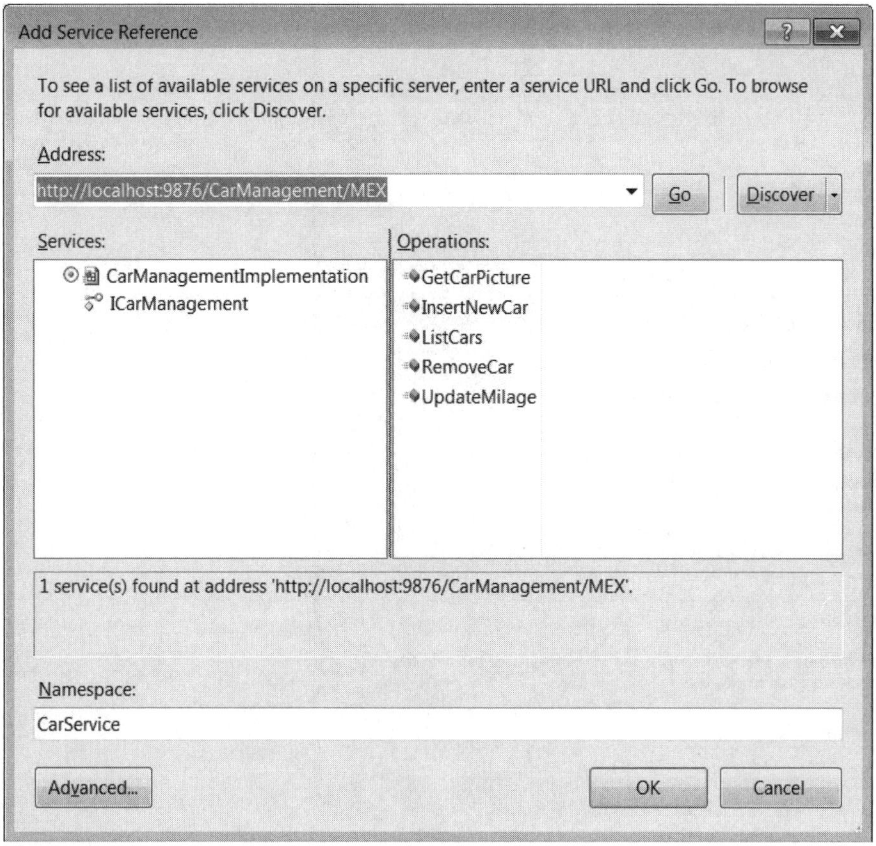

FIGURE 11-39

Click the Advanced button to access the Service Reference Settings dialog box. Set the Collection type to System.Collections.Generic.LinkedList. See Figure 11-40. This is needed for Visual Studio to generate generic lists instead of arrays in the proxies for all collection types found in the contract.

Click OK twice. The code for the proxies and the configuration for the client endpoints are now generated. You can check this by clicking the Show All Files button in Solution Explorer. See Figure 11-41.

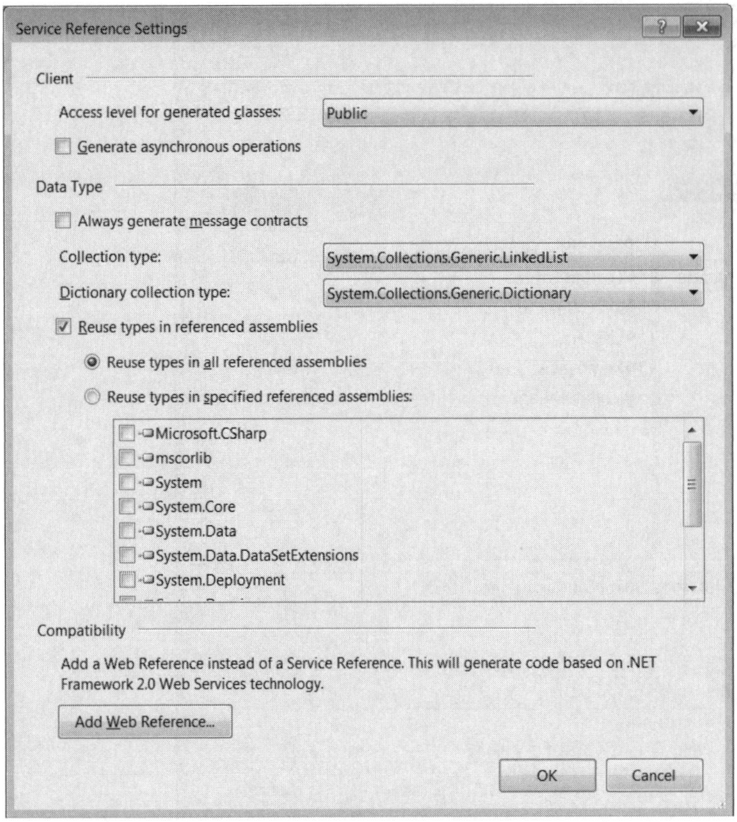

FIGURE 11-40

FIGURE 11-41

Now you can close the `HostAllServices` application and check the result in Visual Studio. Open the App.config file and look up the configuration for the client endpoint. For testing purposes, remark the `<identity>` tag for the generated client endpoint. The result should look like this:

```
<client>
    <endpoint address="http://localhost:9876/CarManagementService"
        binding="wsHttpBinding" bindingConfiguration="WSHttpBinding_ICarManagement"
        contract="CarService.ICarManagement" name="WSHttpBinding_ICarManagement">
        <!--<identity>
            <userPrincipalName value="XXX\YYY" />
        </identity>-->
    </endpoint>
</client>
```

Continue creating the application by adding user interface components to the form. For this walkthrough you need to add three buttons: a listbox, a textbox with the multiline property set to true, and a picturebox. It should look like Figure 11-42.

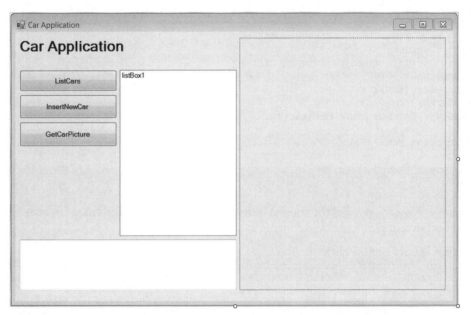

FIGURE 11-42

The three buttons will call the `ListCars` operation, the `InsertNewCar` operation, and the `GetCarPicture` operation. The listbox is used to show the results; the picturebox is there to show the picture of the car; and the textbox is there to show error messages, should they occur.

Add the following code for the ListCars button:

```
try
{
    CarService.CarManagementClient client;
```

```
      client = new CarService.CarManagementClient();
      List<CarService.Car> listCars;
      listCars = client.ListCars();
      foreach (CarService.Car car in listCars)
      {
         listBox1.Items.Add(car.BrandName + " " + car.TypeName);
      }
   }
   catch (Exception ex)
   {
      textBox1.Text = ex.Message;
   }
```

This code instantiates the proxy called `CarManagementClient`, calls the `ListCars` operation, and adds all cars returned to the listbox.

Add code for the `InsertNewCar` button:

```
   try
   {
      CarService.CarManagementClient client;
      client = new CarService.CarManagementClient();
      CarService.Car car;
      car = new CarApplication.CarService.Car();
      car.BrandName = "BMW";
      car.TypeName = "320d"
      int newCarID;
      newCarID = client.InsertNewCar(car);
   }
   catch (Exception ex)
   {
      textBox1.Text = ex.Message;
   }
```

This code creates a new car, specifies the content of its properties, and calls the `InsertNewCar` operation in the service.

Add code for the `GetCarPicture` button:

```
   try
   {
      CarService.CarManagementClient client;
      client = new CarService.CarManagementClient();
      byte[] buff;
      buff = client.GetCarPicture("C67872");
      TypeConverter typeConverter;
      typeConverter = TypeDescriptor.GetConverter(typeof(Bitmap));
      Bitmap bitmap = (Bitmap)typeConverter.ConvertFrom(buff);
      pictureBox1.Image = bitmap;
   }
```

```
catch (Exception ex)
{
  textBox1.Text = ex.Message;
}
```

This code calls the `GetCarPicture` operation, receives the array of bytes, converts them to a bitmap, and shows the bitmap in the picturebox.

You need to make changes to the configuration of the host to allow receiving the pictures correctly. To get a picture from the service with a size bigger than the default, you need to add a binding specification in the App.config file of the `HostAllServices` application and specify the `maxReceivedMessageSize` property for the binding.

Open the App.config file and add the following code in the `system.serviceModel` tag:

```
<system.serviceModel>
  <bindings>
    <wsHttpBinding>
      <binding name="AllowBigMessageSize" maxReceivedMessageSize="999999">
      </binding>
    </wsHttpBinding>
  </bindings>

</system.serviceModel>
```

This adds a binding configuration called `AllowBigMessageSize`. Use this binding configuration in the endpoint configuration of the `CarManagementService`. See the configuration code here:

```
<service
  behaviorConfiguration="ExposeMetaDataBehavior"
  name=
   "CarManagementService.CarManagementImplementation">
<endpoint
  address="http://localhost:9876/CarManagementService"
  binding="wsHttpBinding"
  bindingConfiguration="AllowBigMessageSize"
  contract="CarManagementInterface.ICarManagement" />
</service>
```

Also change the configuration of the client so it accepts large messages. Open the App.config of the `CarApplication` and set the `maxReceivedMessageSize` of the `WsHttpBinding` to `999999` and also set the `maxArrayLength` of the `readerQuotas` to `999999`. This should be enough for all images:

```
<wsHttpBinding>
    <binding name="WSHttpBinding_ICarManagement" closeTimeout="00:01:00"
        openTimeout="00:01:00" receiveTimeout="00:10:00" sendTimeout="00:01:00"
        bypassProxyOnLocal="false" transactionFlow="false"
        hostNameComparisonMode="StrongWildcard"
        maxBufferPoolSize="524288" maxReceivedMessageSize="999999"
```

```
        messageEncoding="Text" textEncoding="utf-8" useDefaultWebProxy="true"
        allowCookies="false">
        <readerQuotas maxDepth="32" maxStringContentLength="8192"
            maxArrayLength="999999"
            maxBytesPerRead="4096"
            maxNameTableCharCount="16384" />
        <reliableSession ordered="true" inactivityTimeout="00:10:00"
            enabled="false" />
        <security mode="Message">
            <transport clientCredentialType="Windows" proxyCredentialType="None"
                realm="" />
            <message clientCredentialType="Windows"
                negotiateServiceCredential="true"
                algorithmSuite="Default" establishSecurityContext="true" />
        </security>
    </binding>
</wsHttpBinding>
```

Now you can test both client and service. To make sure Visual Studio starts both projects, change the properties of the solution so it has multiple startup projects. Right-click the solution and select Properties. See Figure 11-43. Select Multiple startup projects and set the Actions of the CarApplication and the HostAllServices to Start.

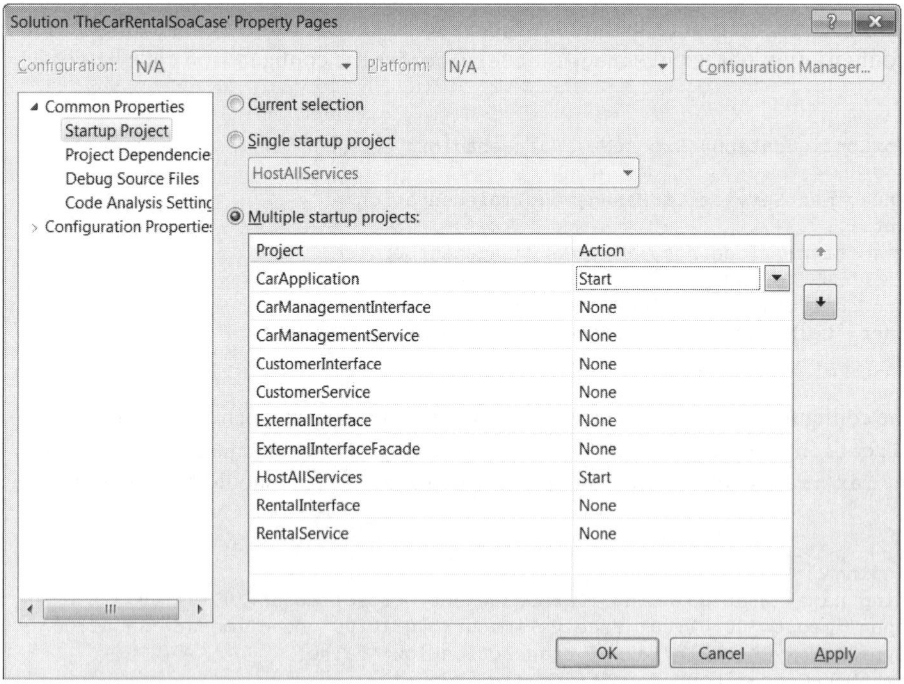

FIGURE 11-43

Start the application by running the solution and executing the operations by clicking the buttons. See Figure 11-44. Watch the console of the ServiceHost to see if the operations are called correctly.

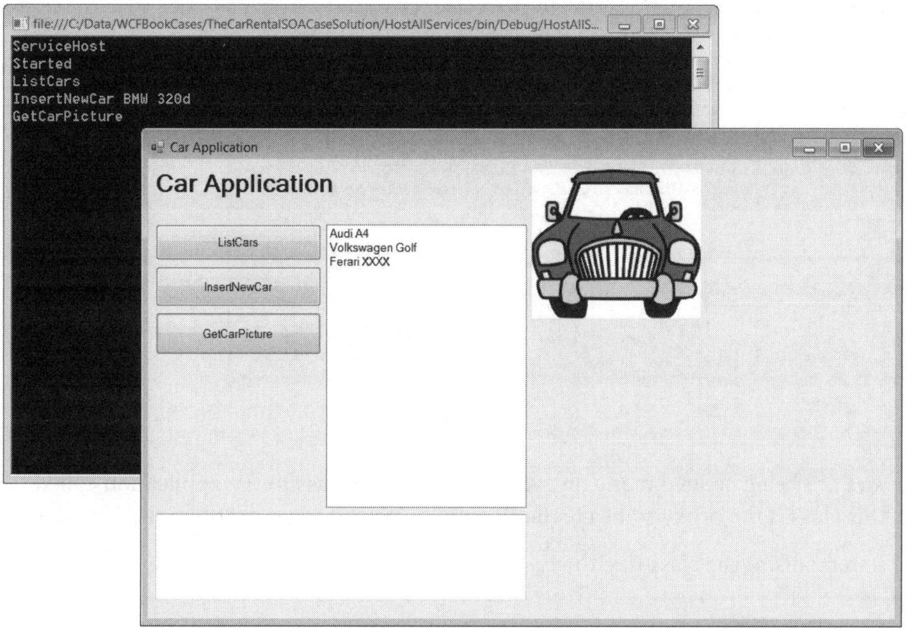

FIGURE 11-44

CREATING THE RENTALAPPLICATION

In the client solution folder, add a Windows form application called RentalApplication. Add the System.ServiceModel and System.Runtime.Serialization assemblies to this application.

For this client you will not create the proxies by adding a service reference referring to a WSDL. Instead you'll refer to the RentalInterface project itself as this project also has all the necessary metadata in the form of WCF attributes. This approach is easier and more flexible but only valid if the client is also a .NET environment. With non-.NET clients you need the WSDL file.

Add a reference to the RentalInterface to the application. See Figure 11-45.

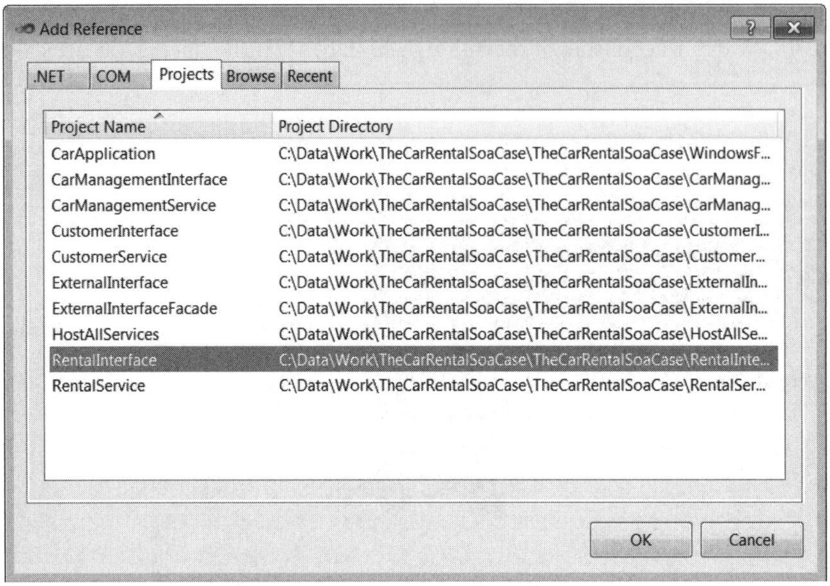

FIGURE 11-45

Because the proxies are being created manually, you need to add a class to the application called `RentalProxy`. This class is the proxy to be created manually instead of generating it by Visual Studio.

Add the `using` statements to the class like this:

```
using System.ServiceModel;
using System.Runtime.Serialization;
```

Also add a `using` statement to the namespace of the referenced `RentalInterface`:

```
using RentalInterface;
```

Make the class public, make it inherit from `ClientBase<RentalInterface.IRental>`, and let it implement the `IRental` interface. The code should look like this:

```
public class RentalProxy : ClientBase<IRental>,IRental
{
  #region IRental Members

  public string RegisterCarRental(RentalRegistration rentalRegistration)
  {
    throw new NotImplementedException();
  }

  public void RegisterCarRentalAsPaid(string rentalID)
  {
    throw new NotImplementedException();
  }

  public void StartCarRental(string rentalID)
```

```
  {
    throw new NotImplementedException();
  }

  public void StopCarRental(string rentalID)
  {
    throw new NotImplementedException();
  }

  public RentalInterface.RentalRegistration GetRentalRegistration(string rentalID)
  {
    throw new NotImplementedException();
  }

  #endregion
}
```

Now create a constructor for the class that calls the constructor of the base class with a string as parameter. This string is the name of an endpoint in the configuration file. You will create this endpoint later.

```
public RentalProxy()
  : base("RentalServiceEndpoint")
{

}
```

Implement each method with code that calls the corresponding method on the channel property. The channel property is a protected member in the ClientBase<T> class with a generic type used in the class declaration. As it is protected, it is only accessible in classes that inherit from the class where it is declared. In your case, it is the IRental interface. This results in the channel having the same methods as the implementation class. As you see, a proxy is simply a class at the client side with the same methods as the class at the service side. Therefore it implements the interface. The proxy's responsibility is simply to pass the parameters it gets from its caller to the channel and return the output from the channel back to the caller.

After implementing the interface, delete the throw statement for each method and replace it as follows:

```
public string RegisterCarRental(RentalRegistration rental)
{
  return Channel.RegisterCarRental(rental);
}

public void RegisterCarRentalAsPaid(string rentalID)
{
  Channel.RegisterCarRentalAsPaid(rentalID);
}

public void StartCarRental(string rentalID)
{
  Channel.StartCarRental(rentalID);
}

public void StopCarRental(string rentalID)
```

```
{
    Channel.StopCarRental(rentalID);
}

public RentalRegistration GetRentalRegistration(string rentalID)
{
    return Channel.GetRentalRegistration(rentalID);
}
```

As you're not taking the add service reference approach, you need to add and configure the App.config file yourself. Add an App.config file to the application and edit the file with the WCF Configuration Editor. See Figure 11-46.

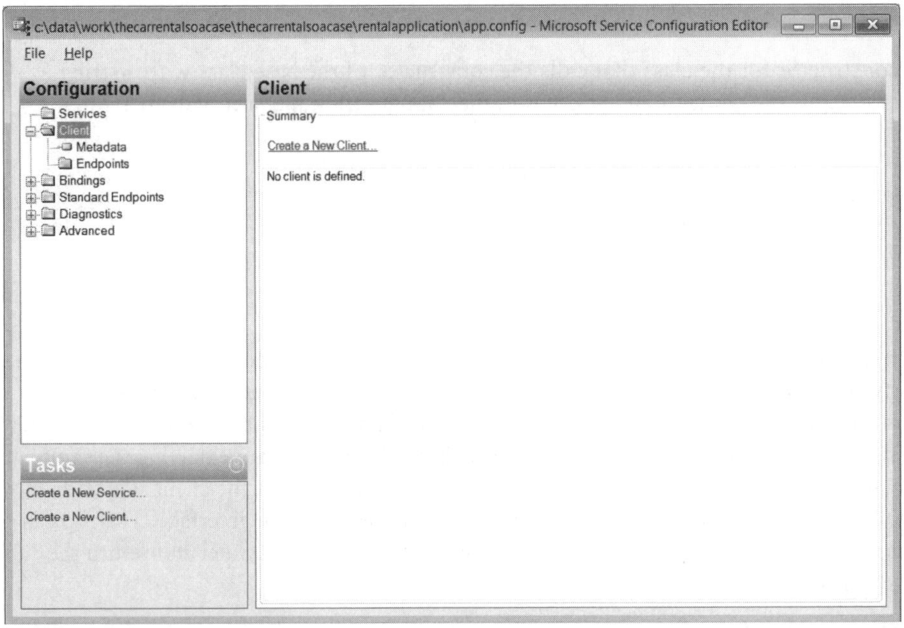

FIGURE 11-46

Add the client configuration by clicking the Create a New Client link. A wizard starts up asking how to create the configuration. See Figure 11-47.

Select the From Service Config option and browse to the App.config file of the `HostAllServices` application. This is C:\Data\Work\TheCarRentalSOACase\TheCarRentalSOACase\HostAllServices\app.config.

Select the endpoint to which the client will talk. In the drop-down you'll find all four endpoints. See Figure 11-48. Select the `RentalService` endpoint.

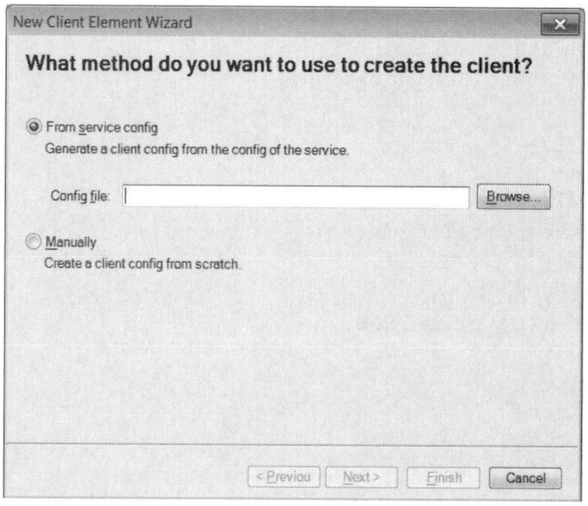

FIGURE 11-47

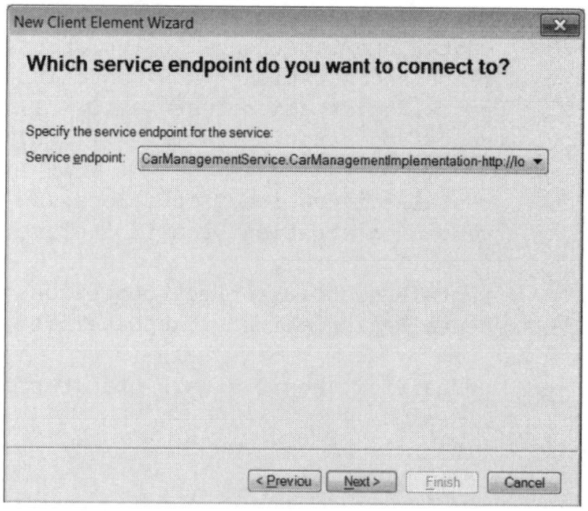

FIGURE 11-48

The wizard now asks you for a name to identify your client configuration. This name is `RentalServiceEnpoint`. See Figure 11-49. This is the string you specified in the constructor of the proxy. This is how WCF knows where to look for the configuration when the proxy is instantiated.

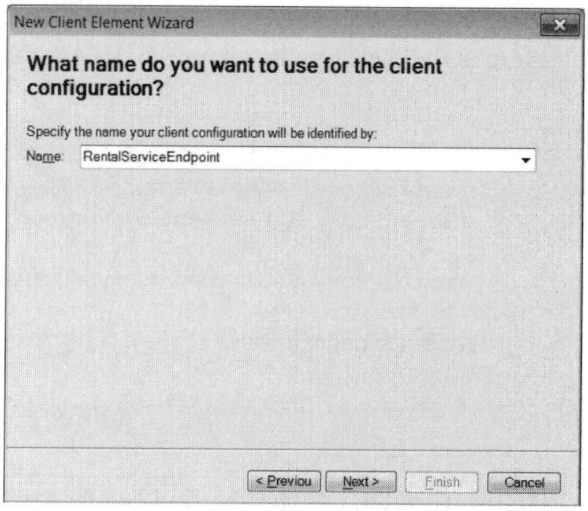

Click Next, click Finish, save the configuration, and close the WCF Configuration Editor. Reload the App.config file in Visual Studio.

For testing purposes, delete the `<identity>` tag in the generated configuration. The configuration should look like this:

FIGURE 11-49

```
<system.serviceModel>
  <client>
    <endpoint
        address="http://localhost:9876/RentalService" binding="wsHttpBinding"
        bindingConfiguration=""
        contract="RentalInterface.IRental"
        name="RentalServiceEndpoint">
    </endpoint>
  </client>
</system.serviceModel>
```

For the user interface of the application, add two buttons to the form. See Figure 11-50. These buttons will execute the code to call to the proxy.

Following is the code for the `RegisterCarRental` application:

```
try
{
  RentalProxy rentalProxy;
```

FIGURE 11-50

```
  rentalProxy = new RentalProxy();
  RentalInterface.RentalRegistration rentalRegistration;
  rentalRegistration = new RentalInterface.RentalRegistration();
  rentalRegistration.CustomerID = 1;
  rentalRegistration.CarID = "123767";

  rentalRegistration.DropOffLocation = 1327;
  rentalRegistration.DropOffDateTime = System.DateTime.Now;

  rentalRegistration.PickUpLocation = 7633;
  rentalRegistration.PickUpDateTime = System.DateTime.Now;

  rentalProxy.RegisterCarRental(rentalRegistration);

}
catch (Exception ex)
{
  MessageBox.Show(ex.Message);
}
```

Here is the code for the `RegisterCarRentalAsPaid` button:

```
try
{
  RentalProxy rentalProxy;
  rentalProxy = new RentalProxy();

  rentalProxy.RegisterCarRentalAsPaid("1876893");
}
catch (Exception ex)
{
  MessageBox.Show(ex.Message);
}
```

To test this, change the solution properties, and set the `RentalApplication` and the `HostAllServices` as startup. Run the applications, call the operations by clicking the buttons, and check the database to verify records are correctly inserted.

ADDING CORRECT ERROR HANDLING

At this moment the applications have no correct error handling. A good error-handling strategy starts with defining fault contracts in the interfaces.

Open the IRental.cs file and add a `DataContract` for the faults:

```
[DataContract(Name = "RentalRegisterFault",
              Namespace = "FaultContracts/RentalRegisterFault")]
public class RentalRegisterFault
{
  [DataMember]
  public string FaultDescription { get; set; }
```

```
    [DataMember]
    public int FaultID { get; set; }
}
```

Now add the `FaultContract` attribute to every method in the `IRental` interface. The interface now looks like this:

```
[ServiceContract]
public interface IRental
{
  [OperationContract]
  [FaultContract(typeof(RentalRegisterFault))]
  string RegisterCarRental(RentalRegistration rentalRegistration);

  [OperationContract]
  [FaultContract(typeof(RentalRegisterFault))]
  void RegisterCarRentalAsPaid(string rentalID);

  [OperationContract]
  [FaultContract(typeof(RentalRegisterFault))]
  void StartCarRental(string rentalID);

  [OperationContract]
  [FaultContract(typeof(RentalRegisterFault))]
  void StopCarRental(string rentalID);

  [OperationContract]
  [FaultContract(typeof(RentalRegisterFault))]
  RentalRegistration GetRentalRegistration(string rentalID);
}
```

The next step is to add the logic to detect exceptions in the service implementation. This is done at two levels. The first level is checking the incoming parameter to determine whether it's a null value or not. In case of a null value, you're throwing a `FaultException` of type `RentalRegisterFault`. Then you surround the code to insert the rental registration with a `try...catch`. When an error occurs, you're also throwing a `FaultException` of type `RentalRegisterFault` in the catch handler.

The changed code for the implementation is as follows:

```
public string RegisterCarRental(RentalRegistration rentalRegistration)
{
  Console.WriteLine("RegisterCarRental");

  if (rentalRegistration == null)
  {
    RentalRegisterFault fault;
    fault = new RentalRegisterFault();
    fault.FaultID = 1;
    fault.FaultDescription = "Input is not valid, got null value";
    throw new FaultException<RentalRegisterFault>(fault, "");
  }

  try
```

```
  {
    using (DataClassesRentalDataContext ctx = new DataClassesRentalDataContext())
    {
      Rental rentalToInsert;
      rentalToInsert = new Rental();
      rentalToInsert.CustomerID = rentalRegistration.CustomerID;
      rentalToInsert.CarID = rentalRegistration.CarID;
      rentalToInsert.Comments = rentalRegistration.Comments;
      ctx.Rentals.InsertOnSubmit(rentalToInsert);
      ctx.SubmitChanges();
      return "OK";
    }
  }
  catch (Exception ex)
  {
    RentalRegisterFault fault;
    fault = new RentalRegisterFault();
    fault.FaultID = 123;
    fault.FaultDescription = "An error occurred while inserting the registration";
    throw new FaultException<RentalRegisterFault>(fault, "");
  }
}
```

Code snippet CreatingaSOACase.zip

At the client side, it's advisable to catch on four types of exceptions:

➤ A `FaultException` of type `RentalRegisterFault`

➤ The generic `FaultException`

➤ The `EndpointNotFoundException`

➤ The `CommunicationException`

The changed code for the button in the client application is shown here:

```
try
{
  RentalProxy rentalProxy;
  rentalProxy = new RentalProxy();

  RentalInterface.RentalRegistration rentalRegistration;
  rentalRegistration = new RentalInterface.RentalRegistration();
  rentalRegistration.CustomerID = 1;
  rentalRegistration.CarID = "123767";

  rentalRegistration.DropOffLocation = 1327;
  rentalRegistration.DropOffDateTime = System.DateTime.Now;

  rentalRegistration.PickUpLocation = 7633;
  rentalRegistration.PickUpDateTime = System.DateTime.Now;

  rentalProxy.RegisterCarRental(rentalRegistration);

}
```

```
catch (FaultException<RentalInterface.RentalRegisterFault> rentalRegisterFault)
{
  MessageBox.Show("rentalRegisterFault " + rentalRegisterFault.Message);
}
catch (FaultException faultException)
{
  MessageBox.Show("faultException " + faultException.Message);
}
catch (EndpointNotFoundException endpointNotFoundException)
{
  MessageBox.Show("endpointNotFoundExc " + endpointNotFoundException.Message);
}
catch (CommunicationException communicationException)
{
  MessageBox.Show("communicationException" + communicationException.Message);
}
```

Code snippet CreatingaSOACase.zip

IMPERSONATING THE CLIENT

Another requirement was that the call to the `RegisterCarRentalAsPaid` method in the `RentalService` needs to be impersonated. This means the implementation code in the service should run under the credentials of the user behind the client application.

To do this, open the RentalServiceImplementation.cs file. Add a `using` statement to the `System.Security.Principal` namespace. This makes the `WindowsIdentity` class available. The `WindowsIdentity` class is useful to get the name of the user running the code. In this way you can test if the impersonation is really happening:

```
using System.Security.Principal;
```

You need to add an `OperationBehavior` attribute at the `RegisterCarRentalAsPaid` method in the implementation and set the impersonation parameter of the attribute to `Required`:

```
[OperationBehavior(Impersonation = ImpersonationOption.Required)]
```

The complete method becomes this:

```
[OperationBehavior(Impersonation = ImpersonationOption.Required)]
public void RegisterCarRentalAsPaid(string rentalID)
{
  Console.WriteLine("RegisterCarRentalAsPaid " + rentalID);
  Console.WriteLine("  WindowsIdentity : {0} ", WindowsIdentity.GetCurrent().Name);
}
```

Testing this can be done by starting the `RentalApplication` at the command prompt with the runas tool. With the runas tool you can specify that another user besides the one logged in is running the application. Open a command prompt and navigate to the directory where the `RentalApplication` is present. Execute the following command:

```
runas /user:UserX RentalApplication.exe
```

Here you specify that RentalApplication.exe runs under the credentials of a user called UserX. You can use any username in your domain for which you know the password. The `runas` tool asks you for this password and then starts the application.

EXTENDING THE CARMANAGEMENT INTERFACE TO ACCEPT THE SUBTYPES OF CARS

Another requirement allows that operations can exchange subclasses of the car class. Add two classes that inherit from car to the `ICarManagement` interface like this:

```
[DataContract]
public class LuxuryCar : Car
{
  [DataMember]
  List<LuxuryItems> LuxuryItemsList { get; set; }
}

[DataContract]
public class LuxuryItems
{
  [DataMember]
  public string ItemName { get; set; }
  [DataMember]
  public string ItemDescription { get; set; }
}

[DataContract]
public class SportsCar : Car
{
  [DataMember]
  public int HorsePower { get; set; }
}
```

Specify the `KnownType` attribute at the `Car` class for each possible subclass. Using this attribute allows that the `returnvalues` for the `ListCars` method can be of types that inherit from the class `Car`. In our case these are types `LuxuryCar` and `SportsCar`:

```
[DataContract]
[KnownType(typeof(LuxuryCar))]
[KnownType(typeof(SportsCar))]
public class Car
{
  [DataMember]
  public string BrandName { get; set; }
  [DataMember]
```

```
    public string TypeName { get; set; }
    [DataMember]
    public TransmissionTypeEnum Transmission { get; set; }
    [DataMember]
    public int NumberOfDoors { get; set; }
    [DataMember]
    public int MaxNumberOfPersons { get; set; }
    [DataMember]
    public int LitersOfLuggage { get; set; }
}
```

You can now change the implementation of the `ListCars` method so it also includes a `SportsCar` in the list as return, like here:

```
public List<Car> ListCars()
{
  Console.WriteLine("ListCars");
  List<Car> listCars;
  listCars = new List<Car>();
  listCars.Add(new Car {
              BrandName = "Audi",
              Transmission = TransmissionTypeEnum.Automatic,
              TypeName = "A4" });
  listCars.Add(new Car {
              BrandName = "Volkswagen",
              Transmission = TransmissionTypeEnum.Automatic,
              TypeName = "Golf" });
  listCars.Add(new SportsCar {
              BrandName = "Ferrari",
              Transmission = TransmissionTypeEnum.Automatic,
              TypeName = "XXXX", HorsePower= 600 });

    return listCars;
}
```

Using the `KnownType` attribute results in a new version of the contract, so there is a new version of the WSDL file. This new WSDL file now also includes the structure of the two types inheriting from the `Car` type. You need to update the clients using this contract.

To update the service reference in the `CarApplication`, start the `HostAllServices` application outside Visual Studio again. Right-click the existing CarService service reference and select Update Service Reference. See Figure 11-51.

This generates the proxies again and the two subtypes will now be known in the client.

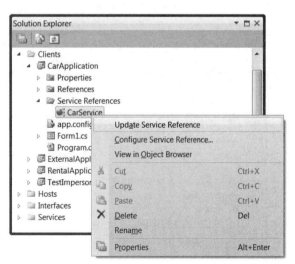

FIGURE 11-51

To test this, close the `HostAllServices` application and change the startup projects in the solution to the `CarApplication` and the `HostAllServices` applications. Try to get the list of cars again. The result should now also include cars of one of the subtypes.

IMPLEMENTING THE EXTERNALINTERFACEFACADE

The implementation of the `ExternalInterface` has one method. This method is called `SubmitRentalContract` and receives a parameter that has the data for a new customer and the rental registration. The purpose of the `SubmitRentalContract` method is to insert the new customer and register a rental for it in one single transaction. The method calls the `RegisterCustomer` method in the `CustomerService` and the `RegisterCarRental` method in the `RentalService`.

Using the ExternalInterfaceFacade

The `ExternalInterfaceFacade` calls to these two services by using the named pipes binding. This can be done by creating a channel to the services with a `ChannelFactory` and specifying the type of binding and its address in code instead of configuration. This is yet another way of creating proxies. Instead of adding a service reference or creating a proxy inheriting from the `ClientBase` class manually, you're now using the `ChannelFactory` which can create proxies dynamically at runtime based on an interface.

Defining the scope of the transaction is done by a `using` block in which you instantiate a `TransactionScope`. After calling both methods you flag the scope as being complete.

In the ExternalInterfaceFacade project, add a reference to `System.Transactions`. See Figure 11-52.

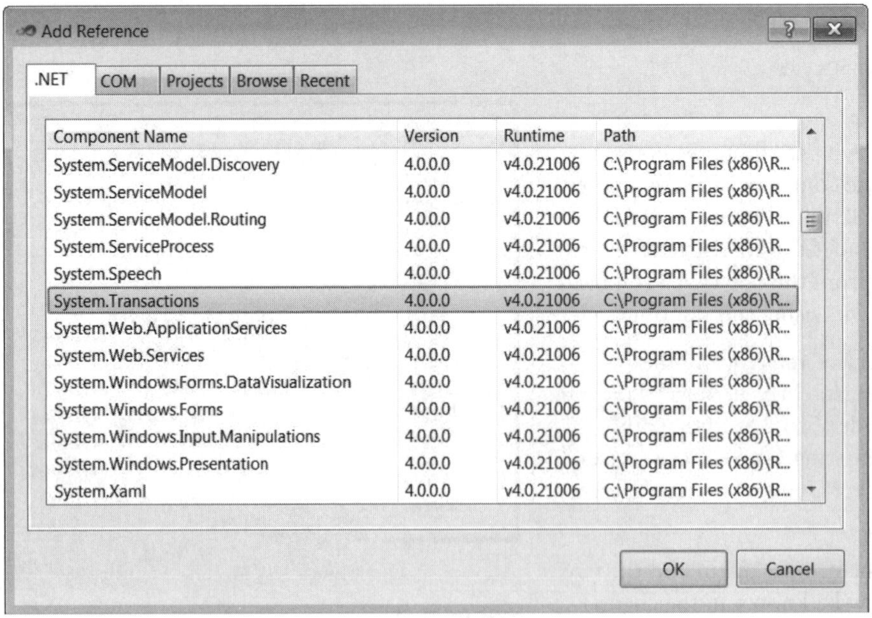

FIGURE 11-52

Open the ExternalInterfaceFacadeImplementation.cs file and add a `using` statement to the System. Transactions namespace:

```
using System.Transactions;
```

Add a reference to both the `CustomerInterface` and the `RentalInterface` libraries in the `ExternalInterfaceFacade` project. See Figure 11-53.

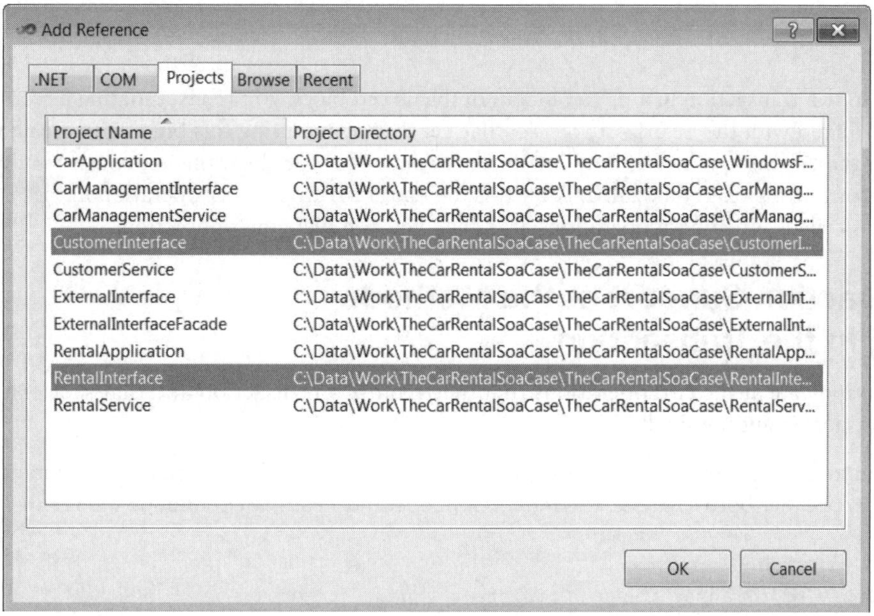

FIGURE 11-53

Add this code to the implementation of the `SubmitRentalContract` method:

```
using (TransactionScope scope =
        new TransactionScope(TransactionScopeOption.RequiresNew))
{

  NetNamedPipeBinding netNamedPipeBinding;
  netNamedPipeBinding = new NetNamedPipeBinding();
  netNamedPipeBinding.TransactionFlow = true;

  CustomerInterface.ICustomer customerServiceChannel;
  customerServiceChannel = ChannelFactory<CustomerInterface.ICustomer>.
   CreateChannel(netNamedPipeBinding, new
   EndpointAddress("net.pipe://localhost/customerservice"));

  int newCustomerID;
  newCustomerID =
  customerServiceChannel.RegisterCustomer(rentalContract.Customer);
```

```
    rentalContract.RentalRegistration.CustomerID = newCustomerID;

    RentalInterface.IRental rentalServiceChannel;
    rentalServiceChannel = ChannelFactory<RentalInterface.IRental>.
     CreateChannel(netNamedPipeBinding, new
     EndpointAddress("net.pipe://localhost/rentalservice"));

    rentalServiceChannel.RegisterCarRental(rentalContract.RentalRegistration);

    scope.Complete();

  }
```

In this code you start a transaction in a `using` block. In the `using` block you're instantiating a `netNamedPipeBinding` with the `transactionFlow` flag set to true and using this binding to create two channels, one for the `CustomerService` and one for the `RentalService`. First the `RegisterCustomer` operation in the `CustomerService` is called. After this the `RegisterCarRental` operation in the `RentalService` is called. When both operations are called you complete the transaction.

Setting Transaction Support at the Methods Participating in the Transaction

Now you need to indicate at the two operations that they require a transaction and that they can complete the transaction automatically.

Add a `OperationBehavior` attribute to the `RegisterCustomer` method in the implementation of the `CustomerService`. Set both `TransactionAutoComplete` and `TransactionScopeRequired` to true:

```
    [OperationBehavior( TransactionAutoComplete = true,
                        TransactionScopeRequired = true)]
    public int RegisterCustomer(CustomerInterface.Customer customer)
    {
      //...
    }
```

Add an `OperationBehavior` attribute to the `RegisterCustomer` method in the implementation of the `CustomerService`. Set both `TransactionAutoComplete` and `TransactionScopeRequired` to true:

```
    [OperationBehavior( TransactionAutoComplete = true,
                        TransactionScopeRequired = true)]
    public string RegisterCarRental(RentalRegistration rentalRegistration)
    {
      //...
    }
```

Configuring Additional Endpoints for the servicehost

Add a `netNamedPipeBinding` endpoint to the `CustomerService` in the App.config of the `HostAllServices` application:

```xml
<service name="CustomerService.CustomerServiceImplementation">
...
  <endpoint
    address="net.pipe://localhost/customerservice"
    binding="netNamedPipeBinding"
    bindingConfiguration=" SupportTransactionsNetNamedBinding"
    contract="CustomerInterface.ICustomer" />
</service>
```

Do this also for the RentalService:

```xml
<service name="RentalService.RentalServiceImplementation">
...
  <endpoint
    address="net.pipe://localhost/rentalservice"
    binding="netNamedPipeBinding"
    bindingConfiguration="SupportTransactionsNetNamedBinding"
    contract="RentalInterface.IRental" />
</service>
```

These endpoints refer to a bindingConfiguration called SupportTransactionsNetNamedBinding. You need to configure the binding as follows:

```xml
<bindings>
  <netNamedPipeBinding>
    <binding name="supportTransactionsNetNamedBinding" transactionFlow="true">
    </binding>
  </netNamedPipeBinding>
</bindings>
```

Back in the code, add a TransactionFlow attribute on the RegisterCarRental operation of the IRental interface with the transactionFlowOption set to Allowed:

```csharp
[OperationContract]
[FaultContract(typeof(RentalRegisterFault))]
[TransactionFlow(TransactionFlowOption.Allowed)]
string RegisterCarRental(RentalRegistration rentalRegistration);
```

Do this also for the RegisterCustomer method in the ICustomer interface:

```csharp
[OperationContract]
[TransactionFlow(TransactionFlowOption.Allowed)]
int RegisterCustomer(Customer customer);
```

12

Creating the Communication and Integration Case

This chapter is an interactive walkthrough about how to create a communication and integration case in Visual Studio 2010 using WCF. It starts with defining requirements for a case and shows how to develop the solution step by step. At the end of this chapter, you will have developed interfaces, hosts, and clients that interact with each other. This is a complete example — you test the process and see it working in action.

DEFINING THE REQUIREMENTS

A global U.S.-based company sells its products to customers worldwide. Orders are entered in the U.S. headquarters but the products are shipped out of warehouses all over the world (Belgium, Argentina, and so on). The company has to integrate existing applications into different branches worldwide for order entry, order tracking, and local delivery management where different types of clients and services (legacy and new) communicate to fulfill the order.

An order is created at the U.S. headquarters using an existing order entry application. This application is not using WCF as it was developed before WCF was available. It uses queued messaging based on MSMQ to send a message containing the data for the order to other applications.

This data has to be picked up by a service running at the U.S. headquarters which is responsible for first checking the validity of the order. This validation is a functionality that cannot be implemented in the legacy order entry client. An order is invalid if the products that are ordered are not available for the country where the order has to be delivered. This service figures out which products are available by calling another service for each country.

Another responsibility of this service is to add information to the message. As the order entry application was developed before the company started doing business on a global scale, the format of the ID of the product does not support a global business. The service has to add a prefix to these IDs, indicating the country where the product is in the warehouse.

Checking if the product is available for the country is done by yet another service. This service is an existing ASMX .NET 2.0 service that searches for the information on a small SQL Server-based database.

The service also has to add a localized description for each ordered product. This is done by calling a service which is on the intranet but does not act as a SOAP-enabled service. It's a REST-based service which answers with XML containing the localized description.

After the data is valid and complete it has to be sent to services at the correct local branch. This needs to be done via a routing service to quickly allow new branches in other countries to receive orders. In each branch the services have the same interface but they can use different protocols of communicating. Currently the branch in Argentina is using a wsHttpBinding and the branch in Belgium is using netTcpBinding. This is due to an internal firewall configuration aspect where the Argentina branch is not allowed to use the netTCP as protocol.

There is another application that wants to monitor the number of orders for each country. This application is always running and must show these metrics in real-time as in kiosk mode at the desktop of the CEO of the company. The CEO considers this a business activity that monitors and wants to see these metrics without clicking buttons. This application subscribes to events coming from the OrderEntry service.

See Figure 12-1 for a complete overview of the case.

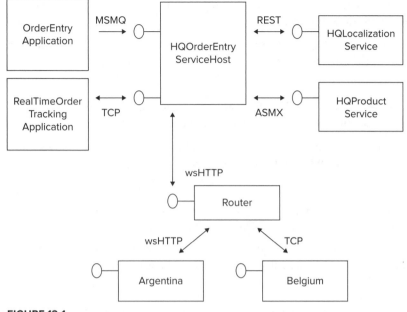

FIGURE 12-1

SETTING UP THE SOLUTION

The complete solution consists of 13 projects. These projects are divided into 5 groups. This results in the following list of projects.

1. Services

➤ HQOrderEntryServiceHost: A console application as host for the OrderEntry service running at the headquarters.

➤ HQOrderEntryImplementation: A class library containing the implementation of the operations for receiving orders; also to subscribe to the tracking information.

➤ HQLocalizationService: A console application that hosts the localization service which is responsible for translating product descriptions. In this application the host, the interface, and the implementation of it are present together.

➤ HQProductServiceASMX: A classic .NET 2.0 ASMX web service responsible for checking whether a product is available for a country.

➤ RouterHost: A console application that exposes a service acting as the router.

2. Service Interfaces

➤ HQOrderEntryServiceInterface: A class library containing the interface describing the operation to receive the order.

➤ `LocalOrderEntryInterface`: A class library containing the interface for the order entry services at the branches.

➤ `RealTimeOrderTrackingCallBackContract`: A library containing a contract for the calls from the `HQOrderEntryServiceHost` to the tracking application.

3. Clients

➤ `OrderEntryApplication`: A Windows application for entering orders. This application sends the order as a message on a queue.

➤ `RealTimeOrderTrackingApplication`: A Windows application that shows the number of orders for each country in real-time.

4. Branches

➤ `BelgiumHost`: A console application as host exposing the implementation of the `LocalOrderEntryInterface` for Belgium on a `netTcpBinding`.

➤ `ArgentinaHost`: A console application as host exposing the implementation of the `LocalOrderEntryInterface` for Belgium on a `wsHttpBinding`.

5. HelperLib

➤ `HelperLib`: A class library containing functions for serialization and deserialization.

Start by creating a blank solution named `CommunicationAndIntegrationCase` and add five solution folders to the project (see Figure 12-2).

FIGURE 12-2

These solution folders are listed in Figure 12-3.

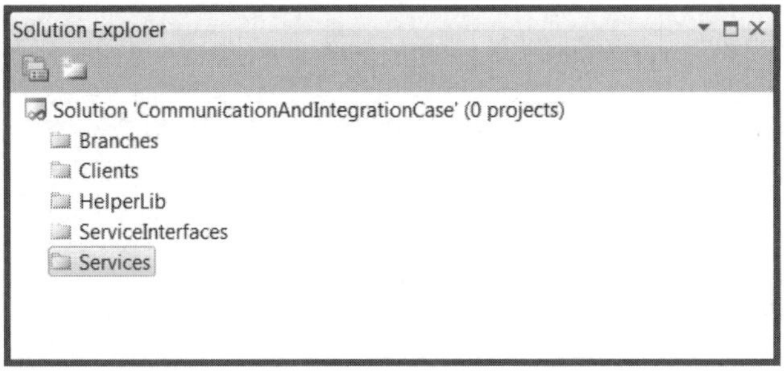

FIGURE 12-3

CREATING THE HQORDERENTRYINTERFACE

The interface for receiving an order is a WCF `ServiceContract`. You create this interface in a separate class library so it can be referenced from multiple applications.

Add a class library project to the solution folder called `HQOrderEntryServiceInterface`. Add reference to the System.ServiceModel and `System.Runtime.Serialization` libraries.

Add a class called `HQOrderEntry`. This class defines the structure of the order as a WCF service contract.

Add a `using` statement to make the attributes in the `System.Runtime.Serialization` namespace available.

```
using System.Runtime.Serialization;
```

Add the following code to the `OrderEntry` class:

```
[DataContract]
public class HQOrderEntry
{
    [DataMember]
    public String OrderEntryID { get; set; }
    [DataMember]
    public DateTime OrderEntryDate { get; set; }
    [DataMember]
    public Customer OrderCustomer { get; set; }
    [DataMember]
    public List<OrderedProducts> OrderOrderedProducts { get; set; }

}
[DataContract]
public class Customer
{
    [DataMember]
```

```
    public string CustomerName { get; set; }
    [DataMember]
    public string CustomerAddressLine1 { get; set; }
    [DataMember]
    public string CustomerAddressLine2 { get; set; }
    [DataMember]
    public string CustomerCountryCode { get; set; }
}
[DataContract]
public class OrderedProducts
{
    [DataMember]
    public string ProductID { get; set; }
    [DataMember]
    public int Quantity { get; set; }
    [DataMember]
    public string ProductName { get; set; }
}
```

Add an interface to the project called `IOrderEntryService` and add the following `using` statements:

```
using System.ServiceModel;
using System.Runtime.Serialization;
```

Define the interface as follows:

```
[ServiceContract]
[ServiceKnownType(typeof(HQOrderEntryServiceInterface.HQOrderEntry))]
public interface IOrderEntryService
{
    [OperationContract(IsOneWay = true, Action = "*")]
    void SendOrderEntry(System.ServiceModel.MsmqIntegration.MsmqMessage
            <HQOrderEntryServiceInterface.HQOrderEntry> orderEntry);
}
```

This defines a method that will receive a MSMQ message and that message contains an `OrderEntry`. It also specifies that it's a one-way operation which is needed when working with queues. With the `serviceKnownType`, indicate that data can be expected in the message that can be serialized to an `OrderEntry` class.

CREATING THE HELPERLIB

Before continuing with the solution, you need to create a library with some general functions that are useful throughout the project. The `HelperLib` is a class library that is used from multiple projects. It has a static class called `GenericSerializer` with methods to serialize objects into strings and deserialize strings back into objects.

There are two ways to serialize and deserialize. The first way is to do this with the `XmlSerializer` which does not rely on WCF. This is needed for the `OrderEntry` application. The second way is using the `DataContractSerializer` part of WCF. You need code for both approaches.

First reference the `System.Runtime.Serialization` library from this project. Add a class called `GenericSerializer.cs` to the `HelpLib` project and add the following code.

The needed `using` statements are shown here:

```
using System.Xml;
using System.Xml.Serialization;
using System.IO;

using System.Runtime.Serialization;
```

The code for the functions is shown here:

```
public static class GenericSerializer<T>
{
    public static string Serialize(T p)
    {
        XmlSerializer ser = new XmlSerializer(typeof(T));
        StringWriter sw = new StringWriter();
        ser.Serialize(sw, p);

        return sw.ToString();
    }

    public static T Deserialize(string xml)
    {
        XmlSerializer ser = new XmlSerializer(typeof(T));
        StringReader sr = new StringReader(xml);

        return (T)ser.Deserialize(sr);
    }

    static public string SerializeDC(T o)
    {
        DataContractSerializer dataContractSerializer =
                new DataContractSerializer(typeof(T));

        StringWriter stringWriter = new StringWriter();

        XmlWriter xmlWriter = XmlWriter.Create(stringWriter);

        dataContractSerializer.WriteObject(xmlWriter, o);
        xmlWriter.Close();

        return (stringWriter.ToString());
    }

    static public T DeserializeDC(string Xml)
    {
        DataContractSerializer dataContractSerializer =
                new DataContractSerializer(typeof(T));

        StringReader stringReader = new StringReader(Xml);
```

```
            XmlReader xmlReader = XmlReader.Create(stringReader);

            T obj = (T)dataContractSerializer.ReadObject(xmlReader);

            return obj;
        }
    }
```

Code snippet CreatingtheCommunicationandIntegrationCase.zip

CREATING THE ORDERENTRYIMPLEMENTATION

Add a class library to the Services solution folder named `HQOrderEntryImplementation`. This library contains the implementation of the `OrderEntryServiceInterface` and will process the incoming messages on the queue. It will read the messages using the `msmqIntegrationBinding` which will be configured later when the `HQOrderEntryServiceHost` is created.

This class library needs references to the `HQOrderEntryServiceInterface`, the `HelperLib`, `System.Runtimte.Serialization`, and `System.ServiceModel`.

Add a class and name it `HQOrderEntryService.cs`. This class needs to implement the `IOrderEntryService` in the `HQOrderEntryServiceInterface` namespace. See the following code:

```
public class HQOrderEntryService : HQOrderEntryServiceInterface.IOrderEntryService
{

    public void SendOrderEntry
       (MsmqMessage<HQOrderEntryServiceInterface.HQOrderEntry> orderEntryMsg)
    {
        //Add code later
    }
}
```

CREATING THE HQORDERENTRYSERVICEHOST

This application hosts the `OrderEntryService`. Add a console application to the Service solution folder and name it `HQOrderEntryServiceHost`. This project needs references to the `HQOrderEntryImplementation` library and the `OrderEntryServiceInterface` library. It also needs references to `System.ServiceModel` and `System.Runtime.Serialization`.

In the program class, add the following `using` statements:

```
using System.Runtime.Serialization;
using System.ServiceModel;
```

In the main method, add a `try catch` handler and some console writeline statements to indicate the status of the service host. The last line is a readkey operation to make sure the host application stays open to process the messages.

```
Console.WriteLine("Started");
try
{
    //Add code later
    Console.WriteLine("OK");
}
catch (Exception ex)
{
    Console.WriteLine(ex.Message);
    if (ex.InnerException != null)
    {
        Console.WriteLine(ex.InnerException.Message);
    }
}
Console.ReadKey();
```

In the `try` block declare a variable of type `ServiceHost`, instantiate it referring to the `HQOrderEntryService` implementation, and open the host.

```
ServiceHost serviceHostOrderEntryService;
serviceHostOrderEntryService = newServiceHost(
       typeof(HQOrderEntryImplementation.HQOrderEntryService));
serviceHostOrderEntryService.Open();
```

Add an application configuration file to the project. In this configuration you need to add a service with the name set to `HQOrderEntryImplementation.HQOrderEntryService`.

The service has one endpoint with the following Address-Binding-Contract properties:

➤ Address: `msmq.formatname:DIRECT=OS:.\private$\OrderEntryQueue`

➤ Binding: `MsmqIntegrationBinding`

➤ Contract: `HQOrderEntryServiceInterface.IOrderEntryService`

You also need to specify more detailed properties about the `msmqIntegrationBinding`. Set the `exactlyOnce` to false as a nontransactional queue will be used. For testing purposes, set the security mode to none so you do not need to activate the Active Directory integration. The app.config file should look like this:

```
<?xml version="1.0"?>
<configuration>
  <system.serviceModel>

    <services>
      <service name="HQOrderEntryImplementation.HQOrderEntryService">
        <endpoint
          address="msmq.formatname:DIRECT=OS:.\private$\OrderEntryQueue"
          binding="msmqIntegrationBinding"
          contract="HQOrderEntryServiceInterface.IOrderEntryService"
          bindingConfiguration="BindingMSMQ"/>
      </service>

    <bindings>
```

```
        <msmqIntegrationBinding>
          <binding name="BindingMSMQ" exactlyOnce="false">
            <security mode="None"/>
          </binding>
        </msmqIntegrationBinding>
      </bindings>

    </system.serviceModel>

</configuration>
```

CREATING THE ORDERENTRYAPPLICATION

For the OrderEntryApplication, add a Windows forms application to the solution under the Client solution folder. Name it OrderEntryApplication.

This project needs references to the HelperLib, the HQOrderEntryInterface, and System.Messaging. System.Messaging contains the API to send a message to a MSMQ queue.

In the form, add a method called SendMessage with the following code. This method takes a string as parameter and sends this data to the queue. It instantiates a MessageQueue object for the OrderEntryQueue, instantiates a message, and constructs an XMLDocument. The InnerXML property of the XMLDocument is set to the data and the Body property of the message is set to this XMLDocument. After this the messageQueue sends the message.

```
private static void SendMessage(string data)
{
    MessageQueue messageQueue;
    messageQueue = new MessageQueue(@".\Private$\OrderEntryQueue");

    System.Messaging.Message message;
    message = new System.Messaging.Message();

    System.Xml.XmlDocument xmlDocument;
    xmlDocument = new XmlDocument();

    xmlDocument.InnerXml = data;

    message.Body = xmlDocument;
    messageQueue.Send(message);
}
```

This method needs to receive data in an XML format which contains the serialization of the message. To create this XML, add a function called GetXMLForOrderEntry. The function looks like this:

```
private static string GetXMLForOrderEntry ()
{
    string tmp;

    HQOrderEntryServiceInterface.HQOrderEntry test;
```

```
test = new HQOrderEntryServiceInterface.HQOrderEntry();

test.OrderEntryID = "00000001";
test.OrderEntryDate = System.DateTime.Now;
test.OrderCustomer = new HQOrderEntryServiceInterface.Customer();
test.OrderCustomer.CustomerName = "WROX";
test.OrderCustomer.CustomerAddressLine1 = "CustomerAddressLine1";
test.OrderCustomer.CustomerAddressLine2 = "CustomerAddressLine2";
test.OrderCustomer.CustomerCountryCode = "BE";
test.OrderOrderedProducts =
  new List<HQOrderEntryServiceInterface.OrderedProducts>();
test.OrderOrderedProducts.Add(
  new HQOrderEntryServiceInterface.OrderedProducts()
  );
test.OrderOrderedProducts[0].ProductID = "P08872";
test.OrderOrderedProducts[0].Quantity = 5;
test.OrderOrderedProducts[0].ProductName = "Car";
test.OrderOrderedProducts.Add(
  new HQOrderEntryServiceInterface.OrderedProducts()
  );
test.OrderOrderedProducts[1].ProductID = "P02287";
test.OrderOrderedProducts[1].ProductName = "Bike";
test.OrderOrderedProducts[1].Quantity = 5;

tmp = HelperLib.GenericSerializer<HQOrderEntryServiceInterface.HQOrderEntry>
                .Serialize(test);

return tmp;
}
```

The function instantiates an `OrderEntry` class, sets the values of the members of this class to some meaningful values, and then uses the Serialize function in the `HelperLib` to obtain the XML.

Now you can add a button to the form which will execute the following code:

```
SendMessage(GetXMLForOrderEntry());
```

You can also experiment with more buttons sending messages with other content to the queue.

CREATING THE LOCALORDERENTRYINTERFACE

Add a class library project. Name it `LocalOrderEntryInterface` and add an interface called `IReceiveOrderEntryLocalBranch`. This interface contains the service contract for the local OrderEntry services at the different branches and defines the datacontract for the local OrderEntry.

First add a reference to the `System.ServiceModel` and `System.Runtime.Serialization` libraries.

Add an interface to this project called `IReceiveOrderEntryLocalBranch.cs`.

In this file, add the needed `using` statements:

```
using System.Runtime.Serialization;
using System.ServiceModel;
```

Add the following code:

```
[ServiceContract]
public interface IReceiveOrderEntryLocalBranch
{
    [OperationContract]
    int SendLocalOrderEntry(LocalOrderEntry localOrderEntry);
}

[DataContract]
public class LocalOrderEntry
{
    [DataMember]
    public String OrderEntryID { get; set; }
    [DataMember]
    public DateTime OrderEntryDate { get; set; }
    [DataMember]
    public string CustomerName { get; set; }
    [DataMember]
    public string CustomerAddressLine1 { get; set; }
    [DataMember]
    public string CustomerAddressLine2 { get; set; }
    [DataMember]
    public string CustomerCountryCode { get; set; }
    [DataMember]
    public List<OrderedProducts> OrderOrderedProducts { get; set; }
}

[DataContract]
public class OrderedProducts
{
    [DataMember]
    public string ProductID { get; set; }
    [DataMember]
    public int Quantity { get; set; }
    [DataMember]
    public string LocalizedDescription { get; set; }
}
```

Code snippet CreatingtheCommunicationandIntegrationCase.zip

CONTINUING THE ORDERENTRYIMPLEMENTATION

You need to implement the flow of the process for an order received by the SendOrderEntry
method. When the message is received it is checked to see if the order is valid. If considered valid,
it is converted to the localOrderEntry structure. This conversion will also take care of the
translation of the product descriptions. When the order is not valid it is sent back to a queue.

The OrderEntryService library needs references to the HelperLib, the LocalOrderEntryInterface,
the OrderEntryInterface, System.ServiceModel, System.Runtime.Serialization, and
System.Transactions.

Add the following method stubs to the `HQOrderEntryService.cs` file in the `OrderEntryImplementation` project. These will be stubs for now; later you will add the needed code. You need method stubs for checking whether the order is valid, converting the schema, routing the order entry, and sending the order entry to the invalid queue.

```
private bool CheckIfOrderIsValid
            (HQOrderEntryServiceInterface.HQOrderEntryorderEntry)
{
    //Add code later
    return true;
}

private LocalOrderEntryInterface.LocalOrderEntry
    ConvertOrderEntrySchema(HQOrderEntryServiceInterface.HQOrderEntry orderEntry)
{
    //Add code later
    return null;
}

private void RouteOrderEntry
            (LocalOrderEntryInterface.LocalOrderEntry localOrderEntry)
{
    //Add code later
}

private void SendToInvalidOrderQueue
            (MsmqMessage<HQOrderEntryServiceInterface.HQOrderEntry> orderEntryMsg)
{
    //Add code later
}

private string TranslateProductDescription(string productID, string languageCode)
{
    //Add code later
    return "";
}
```

After creating these stubs you can write the process flow in the `SendOrderEntry` method:

```
public void SendOrderEntry(
            MsmqMessage<HQOrderEntryServiceInterface.HQOrderEntry> orderEntryMsg)
{
    try
    {
        if (CheckIfOrderIsValid(orderEntryMsg.Body))
        {
            RouteOrderEntry(ConvertOrderEntrySchema(orderEntryMsg.Body));
        }
        else
        {
            SendToInvalidOrderQueue(orderEntryMsg);
        }
    }
```

```
        catch (Exception ex)
        {
            Console.WriteLine(ex.Message);
        }
    }
```

CREATING THE HQPRODUCTSERVICEASMX

There are several things you need to do to create the HQProductServiceASMX. First you must create the web service. Then you need to add it as a service reference to the implementation. Finally you need to create the `CheckIfOrderIsValid`, `TranslateProductDescription`, and `ConvertOrderEntrySchema` methods.

Creating the Web Service

The order is valid if all ordered products can be delivered to the country of the customer. This check is done by an ASMX web service based on the `productId` and the `countryCode` of the customer.

Add a new web site to the Services solution folder. You can do this by right-clicking the solution folder and selecting Add . . . New Website. In the Add New Web Site dialog box, select ASP.NET Web Service. See Figure 12-4.

FIGURE 12-4

Rename the file called Service.asmx in ProductService.asmx and open the Service.cs file in the App_Code directory. In this file, delete the HelloWorld method and add code for a method called IsProductAvailableForCountry. This method takes a productID and a countryCode as parameters and returns a Boolean.

```
[WebMethod]
public bool IsProductAvailableForCountry(string productID, string countryCode)
{
}
```

A hardcoded approach is needed to implement this method. Instead of checking whether the database of the product is deliverable for the country, you return true or false based on the country. If the countryCode is BE or AR, consider it valid. Otherwise, it is not valid. You can implement the method like this:

```
[WebMethod]
public bool IsProductAvailableForCountry(string productID, string countryCode)
{

    if ((countryCode == "BE") || (countryCode == "AR") || (countryCode == "AT"))
    {
        return true;
    }
    else
    {
        return false;
    }
}
```

You need to configure this web site to not use dynamic ports but use a static port number. Use port number 8081 for this. Open the Properties window of the web site. You can do this by pressing F4 on the projectname. Set Use Dynamic Ports to False and set the Port Number to 8081. See Figure 12-5.

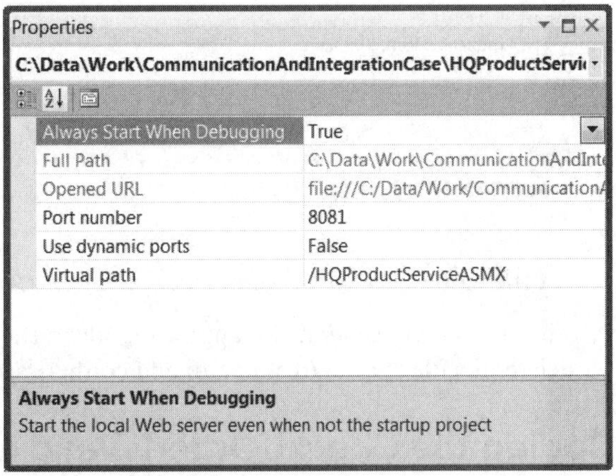

FIGURE 12-5

Adding the HQProductServiceASMX as Service Reference to the OrderEntryServiceImplementation

Add a service reference in the HQOrderEntryImplementation project.

Right-click the references and select Add Service Reference. This opens the Add Service Reference dialog box. Click the Discover button. You should see the operation in HQProductService. See Figure 12-6.

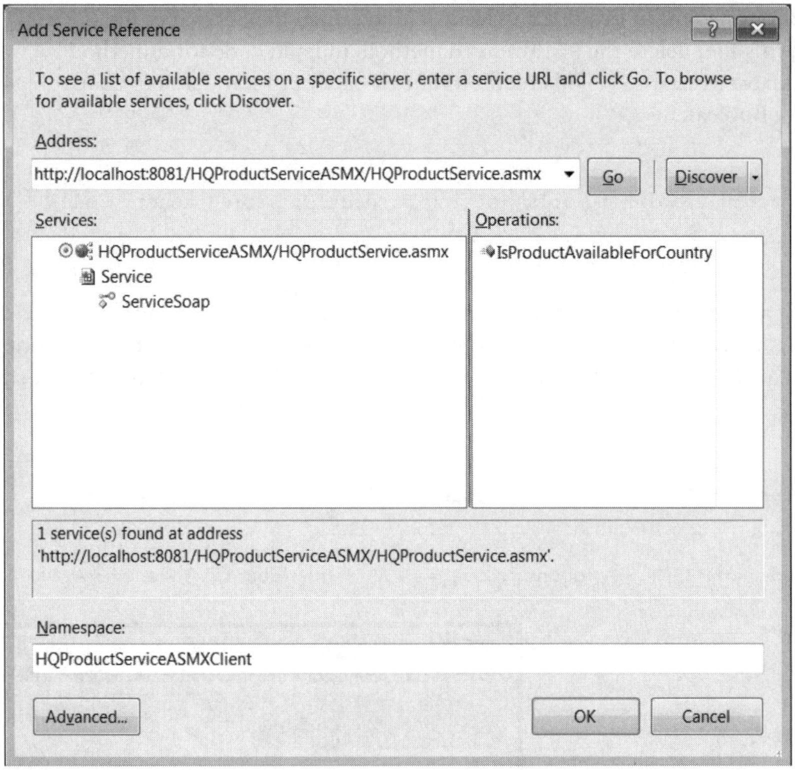

FIGURE 12-6

Set the namespace to `HQProductServiceASMXClient` and click OK.

This action will generate an app.config file in the `HQOrderEntryImplementation` project. You can delete this file as you are going to add configuration to the `HQOrderEntryServiceHost`.

Coding the CheckIfOrderIsValid Method

Now the `HQProductService` is added as a reference so you can develop the `CheckIfOrderIsValid` method like this:

```
private bool CheckIfOrderIsValid
                (HQOrderEntryServiceInterface.HQOrderEntry orderEntry)
{

    HQProductServiceASMXClient.ServiceSoapClient client;
    client = new HQProductServiceASMXClient.ServiceSoapClient();

    bool orderIsValid;
    orderIsValid = true;

    foreach (var item in orderEntry.OrderOrderedProducts)
```

```
    {
        orderIsValid = client.IsProductAvailableForCountry(
                                item.ProductID,
                                orderEntry.OrderCustomer.CustomerCountryCode);
    }
    return orderIsValid;
}
```

Coding the TranslateProductDescription Method

For accessing the TranslateProductDescription service via REST there's no need to add a service reference or to create proxies. You need to use an HttpWebRequest and specify the languageCode and productID as part of the URL to reach the service. The service responds with a string, serialized as a WCF datacontract containing the translation. You need to deserialize this with the DeserializeDC method from the HelperLib.

```
private string TranslateProductDescription(string productID, string languageCode)
{
    System.Net.HttpWebRequest webrequest;
    webrequest = (System.Net.HttpWebRequest)System.Net.HttpWebRequest.Create(
                    string.Format
                    (@"http://localhost:8081/HQLocalizationService/
                      TranslateProductDescriptions/{0}/{1}",
                      languageCode,
                      productID));
    webrequest.ContentLength = 0;

    System.Net.HttpWebResponse webresponse;

    webresponse = (System.Net.HttpWebResponse)webrequest.GetResponse();

    Encoding enc = System.Text.Encoding.GetEncoding(1252);
    System.IO.StreamReader loResponseStream = new
            System.IO.StreamReader(webresponse.GetResponseStream(), enc);

    string response = loResponseStream.ReadToEnd();

    string answer;
    answer = GenericSerializer<string>.DeserializeDC(response);

    return answer;

}
```

Coding the ConvertOrderEntrySchema Method

This method takes an HQOrderEntry as input and results in a LocalOrderEntry. The method creates a new LocalOrderEntry and fills it with the data from the HQOrderEntry. It loops through all the products in the order, calls the TranslateProductDescription for each product, and adds it together with the country prefix to the local order.

To have access to the `LocalOrderEntry` class, you need to add a reference to `LocalOrderEntryInterface` project first.

```
private LocalOrderEntryInterface.LocalOrderEntry
        ConvertOrderEntrySchema(
            HQOrderEntryServiceInterface.HQOrderEntry orderEntry)
{

    LocalOrderEntryInterface.LocalOrderEntry localOrderEntry;
    localOrderEntry = new LocalOrderEntryInterface.LocalOrderEntry();

    localOrderEntry.CustomerName =
            orderEntry.OrderCustomer.CustomerName;
    localOrderEntry.CustomerAddressLine1 =
            orderEntry.OrderCustomer.CustomerAddressLine1;
    localOrderEntry.CustomerAddressLine2 =
            orderEntry.OrderCustomer.CustomerAddressLine2;
    localOrderEntry.CustomerCountryCode =
            orderEntry.OrderCustomer.CustomerCountryCode;

    localOrderEntry.OrderOrderedProducts =
            new List<LocalOrderEntryInterface.OrderedProducts>();

    foreach (var item in orderEntry.OrderOrderedProducts)
    {
        string translation;
        translation = TranslateProductDescription(item.ProductID,
                    orderEntry.OrderCustomer.CustomerCountryCode);

        localOrderEntry.OrderOrderedProducts.Add(
                new LocalOrderEntryInterface.OrderedProducts
                { ProductID = orderEntry.OrderCustomer.CustomerCountryCode
                            + "/"
                            + item.ProductID, Quantity = item.Quantity,
                    LocalizedDescription = translation });
    }
    return localOrderEntry;

}
```

Code snippet CreatingtheCommunicationandIntegrationCase.zip

CREATING THE HQLOCALIZATIONSERVICE

This service is a REST service exposed by WCF and is hosted in a console application. This means you are not using the standard WCF ServiceHost or IIS as host. Instead, use the `WebServiceHost`. You will not separate the interfaces, implementation, and host in three projects. As you are using a REST approach there is no reason to have the interfaces used by any other applications than the service itself.

Add a console application to the solution in the Services solution folder and give it references to `System.Runtime.Serialization`, `System.ServiceModel`, and `System.ServiceModel.Web`.

Add an interface called ITranslateProductDescriptions.cs. This file needs a using statement for the System.ServiceModel.Web namespace and has the following code:

```
[ServiceContract]
public interface ITranslateProductDescriptions
{
    [OperationContract]
    [WebGet(UriTemplate = @"/{languageCode}/{productID}")]
    string GetProductDescription(string productID, string languageCode);
}
```

Here you define a method called GetProductDescription which takes the two needed parameters to answer with a translation. On top of this method you should place a WebGet attribute indicating the URI template. This template will map the data found in the URL to the input parameters of the method.

Add a class for the implementation of this interface. For now this code will not really do the translation but will simply return a hardcode string:

```
public class TranslateProductDescriptions : ITranslateProductDescriptions
{

    public string GetProductDescription(string productID, string languageCode)
    {
        return "Translated";
    }
}
```

To start this host and open the URL you need to add the following code to the main method of the console application:

```
Console.WriteLine("TranslateProductDescriptions");
WebServiceHost webServiceHost;
webServiceHost = new WebServiceHost(typeof(TranslateProductDescriptions));
webServiceHost.Open();

Console.ReadKey();
```

You also need a using statement for System.ServiceModel.Web. Configure this host as follows:

```
<?xml version="1.0"?>
<configuration>
  <system.serviceModel>
    <services>
      <service name="TranslateProductDescriptions">
        <endpoint
            address=
        "http://localhost:8082/HQLocalizationService/TranslateProductDescriptions"
            binding="webHttpBinding"
            contract="ITranslateProductDescriptions" />
      </service>
    </services>
  </system.serviceModel>
</configuration>
```

Here you use the webHttpBinding as binding for the service.

CODING THE ROUTERORDERENTRY METHOD

Now that you have the method to convert the order entry schema to the local order entry ready, you can develop the method to route the order entry further to the destination. For this you need to first create a proxy for the IReceiveOrderEntryLocalBranch interface. Add a file called LocalOrderEntryProxy.cs to the HQOrderEntryImplementation project and add the needed include statements for System.ServiceModel. Insert the following code :

```
public class LocalOrderEntryProxy :
            ClientBase<LocalOrderEntryInterface.IReceiveOrderEntryLocalBranch>,
            LocalOrderEntryInterface.IReceiveOrderEntryLocalBranch
{
    public LocalOrderEntryProxy()
        : base("LocalOrderEntryEndpoint")
    {

    }
    public int SendLocalOrderEntry(
            LocalOrderEntryInterface.LocalOrderEntry localOrderEntry)
    {
        return Channel.SendLocalOrderEntry(localOrderEntry);
    }
}
```

This proxy is a class inheriting from ClientBase<T> and is implementing the IReceiveOrderEntryLocalBranch interface. This interface is also the generic type for the base class. The constructor of the class gets a string that is the name of the endpoint name in the configuration. The SendLocalOrderEntry method is just sending the localOrderEntry data to the channel by calling the method with the same name of the channel property of ClientBase.

With this proxy in place, you can now change the RouteOrderEntry method to HQOrderEntryService.cs like this :

```
private void RouteOrderEntry
            (LocalOrderEntryInterface.LocalOrderEntry localOrderEntry)
{
    try
    {
        LocalOrderEntryProxy localOrderEntryProxy;
        localOrderEntryProxy = new LocalOrderEntryProxy();
        int a;
        a = localOrderEntryProxy.SendLocalOrderEntry(localOrderEntry);
    }
    catch (Exception ex)
    {
        Console.WriteLine(ex.Message);
    }
}
```

CREATING THE REALTIMEORDERTRACKINGAPPLICATION

The `RealTimeOrderTrackingApplication` is an application that receives a signal for every order that was processed by the `HQOrderEntry` service. It displays the number of orders for each country it receives. To realize this you use a pub-sub pattern. The application subscribes itself to publications coming from the `HQOrderEntryService`. Subscribing is done by calling an operation that is exposed by a subscription service hosted by the `HQServiceHost`. When this operation is called the service remembers the caller. It does this by storing the reference to the callback channel in a list in memory at the service. When an order is placed the service calls a method on this callback channel. This method is part of a callback interface that is known by the service and is implemented at the caller. This means that at the moment of publication, the `OrderEntry` Service is acting as client and sends data to a service which is implemented at the tracking application.

First defined is the callback contract which is placed in a separate project.

Add a new class library called `RealTimeOrderTrackingCallBackContract` to the solution in the `ServiceIntefaces` solution folder. Add the `System.ServiceModel` library as reference and add an interface called `IOrderTracking` with the following code:

```
[ServiceContract]
    public interface IOrderTracking
    {
        [OperationContract]
        void NewOrderForCountry(string countryID);
    }
```

Coding the RealTimeOrderTrackingApplication Method

This application will be a Windows application. Add this application called `RealTimeOrderTrackingApplication` to the solution in the Clients solution folder. The application needs a reference to `System.ServiceModel` and to the `RealTimeOrderTrackingCallBackContract`.

You create the implementation of the `RealTimeOrderTrackingCallBackContract` by adding a class called `CallBackImplementation`. Create the class like this:

```
public class CallBackImplementation :
                  RealTimeOrderTrackingCallBackContract.IOrderTracking
{
    Dictionary<string,int> NumberOfOrderEntries;

    public CallBackImplementation()
    {
        NumberOfOrderEntries = new Dictionary<string, int>();

    }

    public void NewOrderForCountry(string countryID)
    {
    }
}
```

The constructor of this class instantiates a dictionary of string and int. This is needed to store the numbers of orders for each country. In this generic list the string is the country code and the int is the number of orders.

In the NewOrderForCountry method, you could show the number of order entries on a listbox on the form or update a chart. As this is more of a UI aspect, it is not included in the code for this book.

Adding the ISubscribeToOrderTrackingInfo Interface

For the subscription to the order tracking signal you need to have an interface with methods to subscribe and unsubscribe. This interface is placed in the HQOrderEntryServiceInterface project. This interface must also be aware of the CallbackContract, so first add a reference to the RealTimeOrderTrackingCallBackContract to the HQOrderEntryServiceInterface project.

Add an interface called ISubscribeToOrderTrackingInfo and add the needed namespaces:

```
using System.ServiceModel;
using System.Runtime.Serialization;
```

The interface looks like this:

```
[ServiceContract(CallbackContract =
                 typeof(RealTimeOrderTrackingCallBackContract.IOrderTracking))]
public interface ISubscribeToOrderTrackingInfo
{
    [OperationContract]
    void Subscribe();

    [OperationContract]
    void UnSubscribe();
}
```

This interface is like a regular service contract and uses the CallBackContract parameter of the ServiceContract attribute to refer to the callback contract.

Implementing the SubscribeService Method

The implementation of this service goes into the HQOrderEntryServiceImplementation project. Switch to this project and add a reference to the RealTimeOrderTrackingCallBackContract library. Next add a class called SubscribeService and let this class implement the ISubscribeToOrderTrackingInfo interface. The implementation looks like this:

Available for
download on
Wrox.com

```
[ServiceBehavior(InstanceContextMode = InstanceContextMode.Single)]
public class SubscribeService :
                OrderEntryServiceInterface.ISubscribeToOrderTrackingInfo
{

    List<RealTimeOrderTrackingCallBackContract.IOrderTracking> callBacks;

    public SubscribeService()
```

```
    {
        callBacks =
          new List<RealTimeOrderTrackingCallBackContract.IOrderTracking>();
    }
    public void Subscribe()
    {
        Console.WriteLine("**Someone Subscribed");
        callBacks.Add(
                System.ServiceModel.OperationContext.Current
                 .GetCallbackChannel
                    <RealTimeOrderTrackingCallBackContract.IOrderTracking>());
    }

    public void PublishOrderEntrySignal(string countryID)
    {
        foreach (var item in callBacks)
        {
            item.NewOrderForCountry(countryID);
        }
    }

    public void UnSubscribe()
    {
        Console.WriteLine("**Someone UnSubscribed");
        callBacks.Remove(
                System.ServiceModel.OperationContext.Current.
                GetCallbackChannel
                    <RealTimeOrderTrackingCallBackContract.IOrderTracking>());
    }
}
```

Code snippet CreatingtheCommunicationandIntegrationCase.zip

Here you see that the service is going to run in the Single `InstanceContextMode`. This means there will be only one instantiation at the service and that this instantiation will be there before the first call and will be kept in memory after this call. This is needed because you want to remember the list of callback channels.

The list of subscribers is a list of references to the callback interface (`IOrderTracking`). When the subscribe method is called WCF, you have access to the callbackchannel by using the `OperationContext` class. This class is a static one and can get you the callback channel. This callback channel is of type `IOrderTracking` and is added to the list. Unsubscribing is just a matter of removing it from the list.

You also have a function called `PublishOrderEntrySignal` which takes the country ID as parameter and loops through all subscribed callback channels, and calls the `NewOrderForCountry` method.

Calling the Subscribers When the Order Is Processed

When an order entry is processed, you need to call all the callback channels. This can be done by calling the `PublishOrderEntrySignal` in the `SubscribeService`. Therefore you need access to the `SubscribeService` from within the implementation of the `SendOrderEntry` operation. To do this you need to use another class with a static reference to the `SubscribeService`. Add a class called `SubscriberSingleton` with the following code:

```
public class SubscriberServiceSingleton
{
    private static SubscribeService instance;
    private static readonly object singletonLock = new object();


    public static SubscribeService GetInstance()
    {
        if (instance == null)
        {
            lock (singletonLock)
            {
                if (instance == null)
                {
                    instance = new SubscribeService();
                }
            }
        }
        return instance;
    }
}
```

This class has a method to get the instance of the `SubscribeService`. When this method is called, it instantiates the `SubscribeService` if needed, and returns the instance.

As the `GetInstance` method is public and static it can be called from the `HQOrderEntry` service. Now you can add the call to publish the signal to the implementation of the `SendOrderEntry` method, like this:

```
if (CheckIfOrderIsValid(orderEntryMsg.Body))
{
    Console.WriteLine("Order Is VALID");
    RouteOrderEntry(ConvertOrderEntrySchema(orderEntryMsg.Body));
    HQOrderEntryImplementation.SubscriberServiceSingleton
    .GetInstance().PublishOrderEntrySignal(
            orderEntryMsg.Body.OrderCustomer.CustomerCountryCode);
}
else
{
    Console.WriteLine("Order Is not VALID");
    SendToInvalidOrderQueue(orderEntryMsg);
}
```

Opening the SubscribeService

You need to open this service in the main method of the `HQOrderEntryServiceHost`. In this code you instantiate the `SubscribeService` by using the `SubscribeServiceSingleton` class. The reference to the service is given to the service host at construction time. This results in the `SubscribeService` being available in all services hosted by this application:

```
ServiceHost serviceHostSubscribeService;
OrderEntryServiceImplementation.SubscribeService subscribeService;
subscribeService = HQOrderEntryImplementation.SubscriberServiceSingleton.
GetInstance();
serviceHostSubscribeService = new ServiceHost(subscribeService);
serviceHostSubscribeService.Open();
```

Subscribing from the RealTimeOrderTrackingApplication

This application needs a reference to the `HQOrderEntryServiceInterface`.

Add a button on the form that will start the subscription. The code behind this button is instantiating the `CallBackImplementation` class and wraps it into an `InstanceContext`:

```
CallBackImplementation callBack;
callBack = new CallBackImplementation();
InstanceContext instanceContext = new InstanceContext(callBack);
```

Then use a `ChannelFactory` of the `ISubscribeToOrderTrackingInfo` interface. This is done by using the `DuplexChannelFactory`, which takes the `instanceContext` wrapping the `callbackimplementation` as a parameter together with a `NetTcpBinding`:

```
ChannelFactory<OrderEntryServiceInterface.ISubscribeToOrderTrackingInfo> cf
    = new DuplexChannelFactory
            <OrderEntryServiceInterface.ISubscribeToOrderTrackingInfo>
               (instanceContext, new System.ServiceModel.NetTcpBinding());
HQOrderEntryServiceInterface.ISubscribeToOrderTrackingInfo subscriber
    = cf.CreateChannel(new EndpointAddress("net.tcp://localhost:9875"));
subscriber.Subscribe();
```

After the channel is created using the correct address you can call the subscribe method.

Configuring the HQOrderEntryServiceHost

The `HQOrderEntryServiceHost` is now hosting two services and has one client endpoint. The complete configuration becomes the following:

```
<configuration>
  <system.serviceModel>

    <services>
      <service name="HQOrderEntryImplementation.HQOrderEntryService">
        <endpoint
          address="msmq.formatname:DIRECT=OS:.\private$\OrderEntryQueue"
          binding="msmqIntegrationBinding"
          contract="HQOrderEntryServiceInterface.IOrderEntryService"
          bindingConfiguration="BindingMSMQ"/>


      </service>
      <service name="HQOrderEntryImplementation.SubscribeService">
```

```
        <endpoint
          address="net.tcp://localhost:9875"
          binding="netTcpBinding"
          contract="HQOrderEntryServiceInterface.ISubscribeToOrderTrackingInfo"/>
      </service>
    </services>

    <bindings>
      <msmqIntegrationBinding>
        <binding name="BindingMSMQ" exactlyOnce="false">
          <security mode="None"/>
        </binding>
      </msmqIntegrationBinding>
    </bindings>
    <client>

      <endpoint
        address="http://localhost:8081/HQProductServiceASMX/HQProductService.asmx"
        binding="basicHttpBinding"
        contract="HQProductServiceASMXClient.ServiceSoap"
        name="ServiceSoap" />

    </client>

  </system.serviceModel>

</configuration>
```

Code snippet CreatingtheCommunicationandIntegrationCase.zip

CREATING THE ROUTER

For the router you need another service host application. This host will not implement a functional interface but rather a technical interface which is part of the WCF `ServiceModel.Routing` namespace. Instead of executing code, the router will send the incoming message to another service based on filters defined in the configuration.

Add a console application named `RouterHost` to the services solution folder and give it references to `System.ServiceModel` and `System.ServiceModel.Routing`.

The code in the main method for opening the router is this:

```
try
{
    Console.WriteLine("RoutingService");
    ServiceHost serviceHost;
    serviceHost = new ServiceHost
        (typeof(System.ServiceModel.Routing.RoutingService));
    serviceHost.Open();
    Console.WriteLine("Started");
}
```

```
catch (Exception ex)
{
    Console.WriteLine(ex.Message);
}
```

Instead of giving the type of an implementation you just give the type of `System.ServiceModel`
`.Routing.RoutingService`.

All the magic happens in configuration. First add a service like this:

```
<services>
  <service
      behaviorConfiguration="RoutingServiceBehavior"
      name="System.ServiceModel.Routing.RoutingService">
    <endpoint
      address="http://localhost:9874/Router"
      binding="wsHttpBinding"
      name="RoutingServiceEndpoint"
      contract="System.ServiceModel.Routing.IRequestReplyRouter" />
  </service>
</services>
```

Here you specify that the service you are hosting is called `System.ServiceModel.Routing`
`.RoutingService` with `System.ServiceModel.Routing.IRequestReplyRouter` as contract.
You also specify the address and the binding.

This service has a `behaviorConfiguration` called `RoutingServiceBehavior` where there is a
routing element referring to a `filterTableName` called `routingRules`.

```
<behaviors>
  <serviceBehaviors>
    <behavior name="RoutingServiceBehavior">
      <serviceDebug includeExceptionDetailInFaults="true" />
      <routing filterTableName="routingRules" routeOnHeadersOnly="false" />
    </behavior>
  </serviceBehaviors>
</behaviors>
```

This `filterTableName` refers to another section in the configuration where two filters are defined.
Both filters are defined as XPath. The first one filters out the messages where the text of the country
code is AR. The second one filters out the message for BE. Both filters have a name which refers
back to the `routingRules` where the two names of the filters are mapped to endpoints:

```
<routing>
  <filters>
    <filter name="Filter_CustomerCountryCode_AR"
            filterType="XPath"
            filterData=
              "boolean(//*[local-name()= 'CustomerCountryCode']/text() = 'AR')"
      />
    <filter name="Filter_CustomerCountryCode_BE"
            filterType="XPath"
```

```
                    filterData=
                     "boolean(//*[local-name()= 'CustomerCountryCode']/text() = 'BE')"
     />
  </filters>
  <filterTables>
    <filterTable name="routingRules">
      <add filterName="Filter_CustomerCountryCode_AR"
           endpointName="ArgentinaEndpoint"/>
      <add filterName="Filter_CustomerCountryCode_BE"
           endpointName="BelgiumEndpoint"/>
    </filterTable>
  </filterTables>

</routing>
```

The endpoints are normal endpoints and have their addresses, bindings, and contracts:

```
<client>
  <endpoint
      binding="wsHttpBinding"
      bindingConfiguration=""
      contract="*"
      address="http://localhost:9874/ArgentinaHost"
      name="ArgentinaEndpoint" kind=""
      endpointConfiguration="">

  </endpoint>
  <endpoint
      binding="netTcpBinding"
      bindingConfiguration=""
      contract="*"
      address="net.tcp://localhost:9871/BelgiumBranch"
      name="BelgiumEndpoint" kind=""
      endpointConfiguration="">

  </endpoint>

</client>
```

CONFIGURING THE HQORDERENTRYSERVICEHOST

To make the complete solution work you need to take care of the correct configuration of the `HQOrderEntryServiceHost`. This configuration has two services: one for receiving order entries from the queue and one for the subscription service. There are also two clients: one to reach the ASMX service to check the availability of the order for a country, and another to reach the router.

This is the complete configuration:

Available for
download on
Wrox.com

```
<configuration>
  <system.serviceModel>

    <services>
```

```xml
      <service name="HQOrderEntryImplementation.HQOrderEntryService">
        <endpoint
          address="msmq.formatname:DIRECT=OS:.\private$\OrderEntryQueue"
          binding="msmqIntegrationBinding"
          contract="HQOrderEntryServiceInterface.IOrderEntryService"
          bindingConfiguration="BindingMSMQ"/>


      </service>
      <service name="HQOrderEntryImplementation.SubscribeService">
        <endpoint
          address="net.tcp://localhost:9875"
          binding="netTcpBinding"
          contract="HQOrderEntryServiceInterface.ISubscribeToOrderTrackingInfo"/>
      </service>
    </services>

    <bindings>
      <msmqIntegrationBinding>
        <binding name="BindingMSMQ" exactlyOnce="false">
          <security mode="None"/>
        </binding>
      </msmqIntegrationBinding>
    </bindings>
    <client>

      <endpoint
          address=
           "http://localhost:8081/HQProductServiceASMX/HQProductService.asmx"
          binding="basicHttpBinding"
          contract="HQProductServiceASMXClient.ServiceSoap"
          name="ServiceSoap" />
      <endpoint
        name="LocalOrderEntryEndpoint"
        address="http://localhost:9874/Router"
        binding="wsHttpBinding"
        contract="LocalOrderEntryInterface.IReceiveOrderEntryLocalBranch" />
    </client>

  </system.serviceModel>
</configuration>
```

Code snippet CreatingtheCommunicationandIntegrationCase.zip

Creating the Business Process

This chapter is an interactive walkthrough on how to create a business process in Visual Studio 2010 using WCF and workflow services. It starts with defining requirements for a case and shows how to develop the solution step by step. At the end of this chapter, you will have developed the business process, a host for the process, the clients, and other services that interact with this process. This is a complete example so you can test the process and see it in action.

DEFINING THE REQUIREMENTS

Let's take a simple process (see Figure 13-1). This should be a kind of proof-of-concept to learn how to develop workflow processes. It's a classic example of a business process that deals with holiday requests.

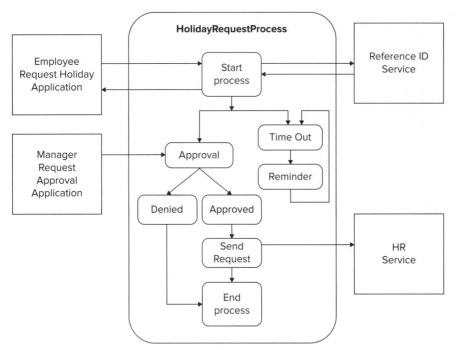

FIGURE 13-1: The holiday request process

A company wants to expose a workflow as a service that receives a holiday request from its employees, waits for approval from a manager, and sends the request to the HR service.

This workflow is started by the request from the employee and the requester receives a reference ID for further reference. The reference ID is unique and is calculated by another service. The employee can use this reference ID to check the status of the request later. When the process starts it calls out to this service to obtain the ID and sends it as the answer to the requester. After this step the process waits for the approval (or denial) for this holiday request by a manager. The process only waits for this approval for a configurable amount of time. The manager uses another application where he/she needs to input this reference ID and approve or deny the holiday request. This action results in a call to the same instance of the already running process as a signal that it can continue. When this signal arrives at the process, it continues and sends the holiday request to another service as part of the HR application that is expecting only approved requests. This step completes the process and the employee can take his holiday. When the manager does not approve or deny the request within one week, the process sends an e-mail as a reminder and waits again for the approval or denial from the manager. This can be repeated three times. If the manager does not approve or deny within three weeks, the process ends.

SETTING UP THE SOLUTION

For this solution you need to create multiple projects in one solution. Start by creating a solution called `TheHolidayRequestProcessSolution`.

In this solution you need to add the following eight projects:

➤ `HolidayRequestDataContracts`: A class library which contains the WCF data contracts needed for this solution.

➤ `HolidayRequestProcess`: This is a workflow activity library. It contains the definition of the process for the holiday request declared as XAML. You can select this template in the workflow section of the installed templates.

➤ `EmployeeHolidayRequestApplication`: A Windows forms application. This application is used by the employee to request the holiday and start the process.

➤ `CalculateReferenceIDService`: A WCF service application. This web service calculates the reference ID. You can find the template in the web sections of the installed templates.

➤ `ManagersHolidayRequestApprovalApplication`: A Windows forms application that allows approving or denying the holiday requests by filling in the reference ID.

➤ `HolidayRequestProcessHost`: A console application that hosts the process and exposes the complete process as a service.

➤ `HolidayRequestActivityLibrary`: Another workflow activity library that contains a reference to other services and has workflow activities for the calls to the methods in these services. These activities are used in the `HolidayRequestProcess` activity library.

➤ `ReceiveApprovedHolidayRequestsService`: A console application that hosts a service that receives the approved request. This is a simulation of a real web service in the HR department.

The complete solution should look like Figure 13-2.

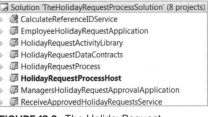

FIGURE 13-2: The HolidayRequest ProcessSolution

CREATING THE DATA CONTRACTS

Every solution that uses WCF starts with defining the data contracts. This is the base for defining the other parts of the solution. It's clear you need a stable set of data contracts before continuing with the rest of the development. You will create a class file in the `HolidayRequestDataContracts` project that contains all the needed contracts.

Four data contracts in this case are recognized:

➤ A contract as input for the holiday request containing the `EmployeeID`, the start date, and end date of the requested holiday.

➤ A contract as the return for this request containing the reference ID calculated by the external service.

➤ A contract for the approval or denial of the holiday request by the manager containing the employee ID of this manager, the reference ID of the holiday request being approved, and a flag indicating whether the request was approved or denied.

➤ A contract as the return for this approval. For this case it contains the start date and the end date again.

First you need to add a reference to the `System.Runtime.Serialization` library to the `HolidayRequestDataContracts` project. This allows you to use the attributes to declare classes as WCF data contracts:

Add a class file to the project, name it `HolidayRequestDataContract.cs` and write following code in this file.

```
[DataContract]
public class HolidayRequestDataContract_Input
{
    [DataMember]
    public int EmployeeID { get; set; }
    [DataMember]
    public DateTime HolidayStartDate { get; set; }
    [DataMember]
    public DateTime HolidayEndDate { get; set; }
}

[DataContract]
public class HolidayRequestDataContract_Output
{
    [DataMember]
    public int ReferenceID { get; set; }
}

[DataContract]
public class HolidayApprovalDataContract_Input
{
    [DataMember]
    public int ManagerID { get; set; }
    [DataMember]
    public int ReferenceID { get; set; }
    [DataMember]
    public ApprovedOrDeniedEnum ApprovedOrDenied { get; set; }
}

[DataContract]
public enum ApprovedOrDeniedEnum
{
    [EnumMember]
    Approved,
    [EnumMember]
    Denied
}

[DataContract]
public class HolidayApprovalDataContract_Output
{
    [DataMember]
    public int EmployeeID { get; set; }
    [DataMember]
    public DateTime HolidayStartDate { get; set; }
    [DataMember]
    public DateTime HolidayEndDate { get; set; }
}
```

Code snippet CreatingtheBusinessProcess.zip

CREATING THE CALCULATEREFERENCEIDSERVICE

This external service calculates the reference ID for the holiday request. Visual Studio added a service named Service1.svc, a code-behind file named Service1.svc.cs, and an interface IService1.cs. You can delete these three files by doing the following:

➤ Add a new WCF service named CalculateReferenceIDService.svc (see Figure 13-3).

➤ In the ICalculateReferenceIDService.cs, delete the `DoWork` operation generated by the template together with the `OperationContract` attribute.

➤ Replace it with a signature for your `GetNewReferenceID` method.

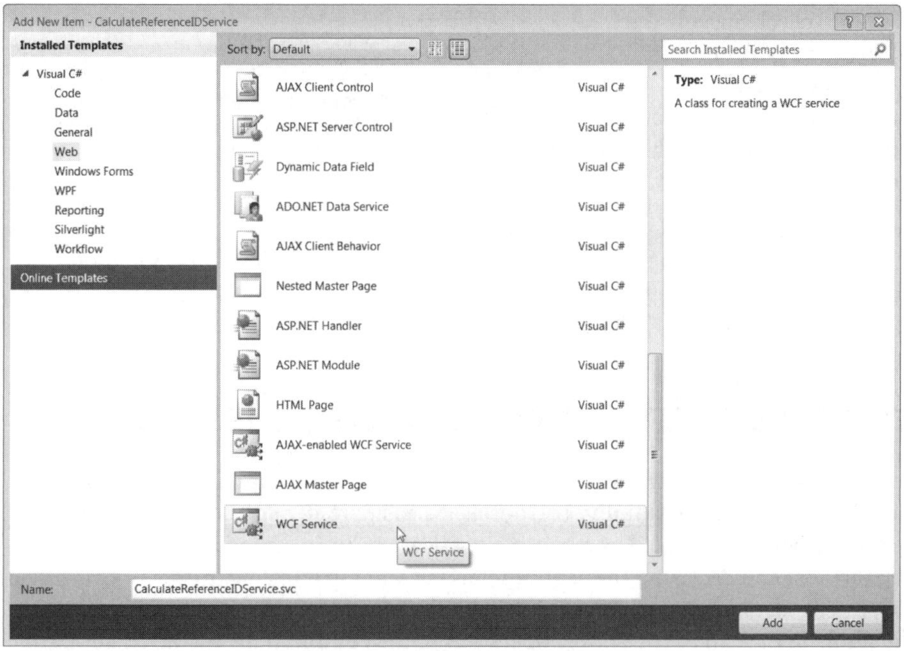

FIGURE 13-3: Creating the CalculateReferenceIDservice

```
[ServiceContract]
public interface ICalculateReferenceIDService
{
    [OperationContract]
    int GetNewReferenceID();
}
```

In the CalculateReferenceIDService.svc.cs you can also delete the `DoWork` method and replace it with the implementation for your `GetNewReferenceID` method:

For this implementation as proof-of-concept for this chapter we will not add complex logic to calculate a unique reference ID now. To make the process work we just return an integer in a somewhat hardcoded way. This allows testing the process soon. Later on you need to add the behavior to calculate a unique reference ID. This could be done based on a table in a database with an identity field.

```
public int GetNewReferenceID()
{
    return 42;
}
```

Configure the properties of this project so the service will run on a specific port instead of an auto-assigned port. This allows the service to be found by the process on exactly the same port.

Open the properties of the `CalculateReferenceIDService` project, switch to the Web tab, check Specific port, and enter the **9876** as the port number (see Figure 13-4). You can test if this service is exposing its metadata correctly.

| Use Visual Studio Development Server |
| Auto-assign Port |
| Specific port | 9876 |

FIGURE 13-4: Configuring the port

In solution explorer, right-click the CalculateReferenceIDService.svc file and select the View in Browser menu option.

This opens a browser to CalculateReferenceIDService.svc. Click the link `http://localhost:9876/CalculateReferenceIDService.svc?wsdl`. Now you should see the WSDL for this service. Should the browser only show the directory listing, you need to click on the link to CalculateReferenceIDService.svc first.

CREATING THE RECEIVEAPPROVEDHOLIDAYREQUESTSSERVICE

You created the `ReceiveApprovedHolidayRequestService` as a console application instead of a web application. This is done for testability reasons as it's easier to debug and show results to the tester of the service when it's created as a console application. In this console application, the code for opening the host and declaring the service interface and the implementation of this service interface will be present together. This makes it a self-service host. The reason you use a self-service host is to see the result of the call to the service operation in the console. This is convenient in this proof-of-concept stage but in production this could change to an IIS serviced service with the same contract and configuration.

Add the references to the `System.ServiceModel` and `System.Runtime.Serialization` libraries.

Add a class file called `ReceiveApprovedHolidayRequestService.cs` and add the following code:

```
[ServiceContract]
public interface IReceiveApprovedHolidayRequestService
{
    [OperationContract]
    void ReceiveApprovedHolidayRequest(ApprovedHolidayData approvedHolidayData);
}

public class ReceiveApprovedHolidayRequestService :
        IReceiveApprovedHolidayRequestService
```

```
{
    public void ReceiveApprovedHolidayRequest
                    (ApprovedHolidayData approvedHolidayData)
    {
      Console.WriteLine("Got Approved Holiday Request");
      Console.WriteLine(
        string.Format(" by employee {0}, approved by {1}, from  {2} to {3}",
        approvedHolidayData.EmployeeID.ToString(),
        approvedHolidayData.ApprovedByManagerID.ToString(),
        approvedHolidayData.HolidayStartDate.ToShortTimeString(),
        approvedHolidayData.HolidayEndDate.ToShortTimeString()));
    }
}

[DataContract]
public class ApprovedHolidayData
{
    [DataMember]
    public int EmployeeID { get; set; }
    [DataMember]
    public int ApprovedByManagerID { get; set; }
    [DataMember]
    public DateTime HolidayStartDate { get; set; }
    [DataMember]
    public DateTime HolidayEndDate { get; set; }
}
```

Code snippet CreatingtheBusinessProcess.zip

This file now contains the data contract, the service contract, and the implementation of the operation together.

Add an application configuration file to the project. This app.config file should contain following configuration:

Available for
download on
Wrox.com

```
<system.serviceModel>
<behaviors>
 <serviceBehaviors>
  <behavior name="ExposeMetadata">
   <serviceMetadata
     httpGetEnabled="true"
     httpGetUrl=
       "http://localhost:9875/ReceiveApprovedHolidayRequestsService/MEX"/>
   </behavior>
  </serviceBehaviors>
 </behaviors>
 <services>
  <service
    name=
      "ReceiveApprovedHolidayRequestsService.ReceiveApprovedHolidayRequestService"
    behaviorConfiguration="ExposeMetadata">
    <endpoint
      address="http://localhost:9875/ReceiveApprovedHolidayRequestsService"
      binding="basicHttpBinding"
```

```
        bindingConfiguration=""
        contract=
         "ReceiveApprovedHolidayRequestsService.
            IReceiveApprovedHolidayRequestService" />
      </service>
    </services>
  </system.serviceModel>
```

Code snippet CreatingtheBusinessProcess.zip

To host the service, add this code to the main method in the program.cs file:

```
try
{
    Console.WriteLine("HOST : ReceiveApprovedHolidayRequestsService");
    ServiceHost serviceHost;
    serviceHost = new ServiceHost(typeof(ReceiveApprovedHolidayRequestService));
    serviceHost.Open();
    Console.WriteLine("started");
}
catch (Exception ex)
{
    Console.WriteLine(ex.Message);
}
Console.ReadKey();
```

You can now test that this console application is exposing the WSDL file correctly. First build and then start this application outside Visual Studio. You need to start as administrator. Browse to the directory where the executable is placed, right-click it and select the Run As Administrator option.

Now open a browser and type in the URL configured in the serviceMetaData behavior of the configuration file, which is `http://localhost:9875/ReceiveApprovedHolidayRequests Service/MEX`.

You should see the WSDL in the browser.

ADDING SERVICE REFERENCES TO THE HOLIDAYREQUESTACTIVITYLIBRARY PROJECT

The `HolidayRequestActivityLibrary` project will only contain two service references to the services you just created. It will not contain anything else. So you can delete the Activity1.xaml file.

Adding service references to a workflow activity library results in the creation of reusable activities to call operations in these services. These activities become visible in the workflow designer of other workflow activity libraries that reference this project, such as your `HolidayRequestProcess` project. This is a good design approach and separates the activities as wrappers to service calls from the workflow itself.

This leads to reusability of activities in other business processes.

Adding service references here also generates the configuration for client endpoints in the app.config file. This configuration has no use here as this project is a library. You will see later that you need to copy this configuration to the project which is hosting the workflow process.

Adding the CalculateReferenceIDService

To add a reference to the `CalculateReferenceIDService`, right-click References and select Add Service Reference (see Figure 13-5). This opens the Add Service Reference dialog box.

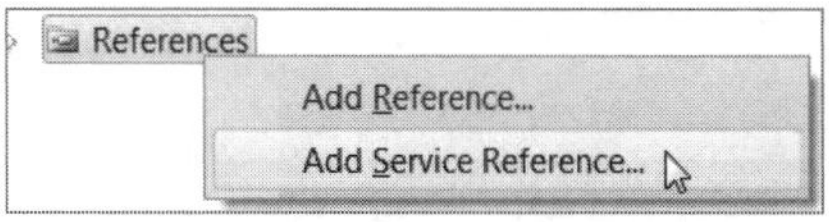

FIGURE 13-5: Adding a service reference

Now click the Discover button and select Services in Solution (see Figure 13-6). This results in an overview of the interface containing the operations in this service.

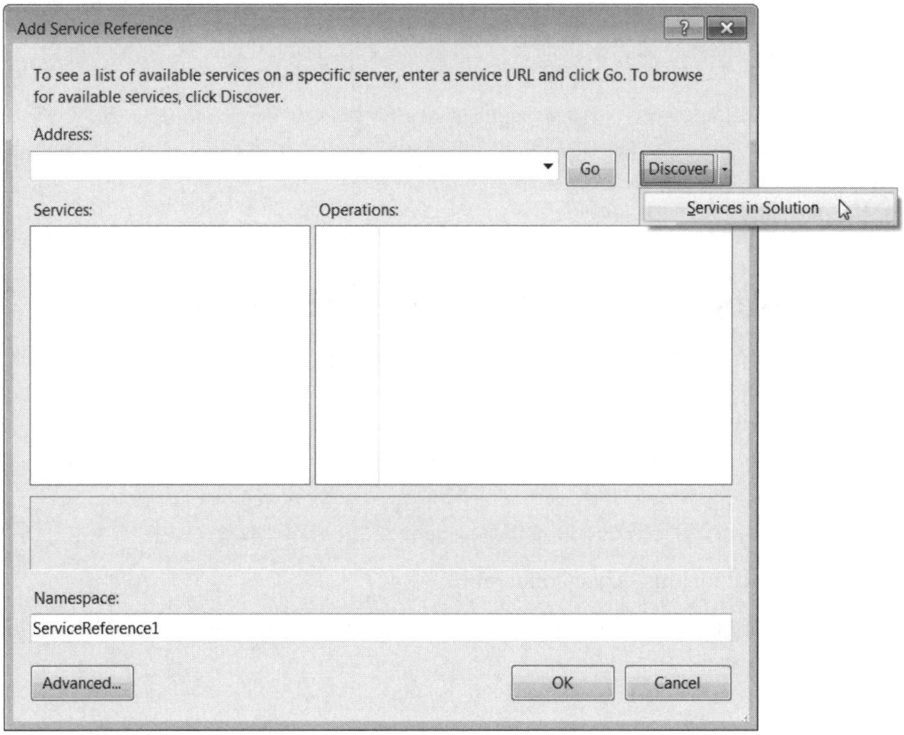

FIGURE 13-6: Discover the services in the solution

You should see the `GetNewReferenceID` operation (see Figure 13-7). Set the namespace to `CalcIDService`.

Click OK and Visual Studio now generates the proxies and adds an endpoint to the configuration file.

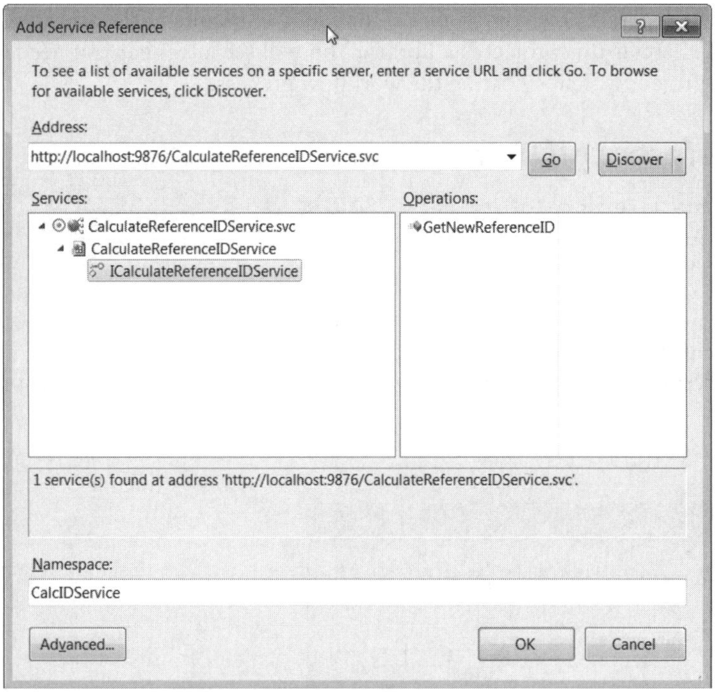

FIGURE 13-7: Set the namespace to CalcIDService

Adding the ReceiveApprovedHolidayRequestsService

Add a second service reference to the `ReceiveApprovedHolidayRequestsService`. Visual Studio cannot detect the WSDL from the solution as this is a self-hosted service. You have to start the `ReceiveApprovedHolidayRequestsService` outside Visual Studio. Remember to do this as administrator.

The address for this service is

```
http://localhost:9875/ReceiveApprovedHolidayRequestsService/MEX.
```

Use `HRService` as a namespace for this service reference.

Now have a look at the app.config file of the `HolidayRequestActivityLibrary` project. It should contain two endpoints like this:

```
<endpoint
    address="http://localhost:9876/CalculateReferenceIDService.svc"
    binding="basicHttpBinding"
    bindingConfiguration="BasicHttpBinding_ICalculateReferenceIDService"
    contract="ICalculateReferenceIDService"
    name="BasicHttpBinding_ICalculateReferenceIDService" />
<endpoint
    address="http://localhost:9875/ReceiveApprovedHolidayRequestsService"
    binding="basicHttpBinding"
```

```
bindingConfiguration="BasicHttpBinding_IReceiveApprovedHolidayRequestService"
contract="IReceiveApprovedHolidayRequestService"
name="BasicHttpBinding_IReceiveApprovedHolidayRequestService" />
```

It's okay to now to close the console application hosting the ReceiveApprovedHolidayRequestsService.

Developing the HolidayRequestProcess

The HolidayRequestProcess contains the definition of workflow and needs references to a number of system libraries: System.Activities, System.Runtime.Serialization, System.ServiceModel, and System.ServiceModel.Activities.

This project also needs a reference to the HolidayRequestActivityLibrary library and the HolidayRequestDataContracts library. This is needed as the first one contains the activities to call the operation in the external services (CalcIDService and HRService) and the HolidayRequestDataContracts contains the data contracts that define the input parameters and output parameters for the service operations you develop in the workflow.

In this workflow service you create two service operations, RequestHoliday and ApproveRequest, by dropping activities to the workflow designer. This is a workflow-first approach and allows you to define the service contract while developing the business process.

Adding the Workflow

Add a workflow activity to the project. You can select the template in the workflow part of the installed templates in the Add New Item dialog box (see Figure 13-8). Name this workflow activity HolidayRequestProcessDefinition.xaml.

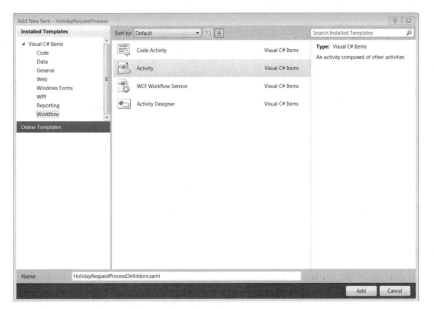

FIGURE 13-8: Add a workflow activity to the project

Now to build the complete solution, open the activity, and make the toolbox visible. This toolbox should now contain two activities as wrappers to the operations in the two services — see Figure 13-9. At this moment the designer canvas is empty. Add a `ReceiveAndSendReply` activity from the toolbox to the designer.

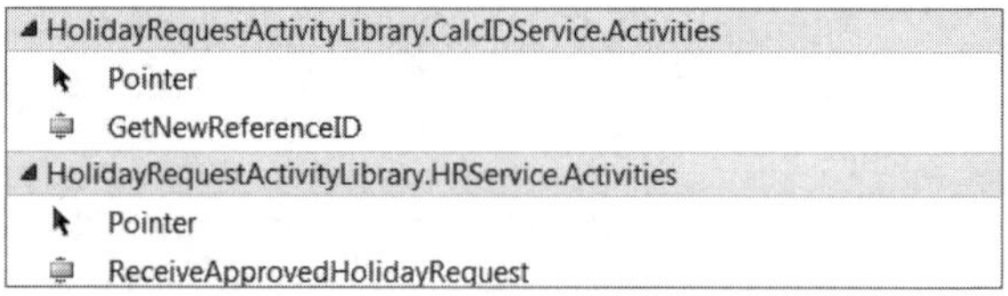

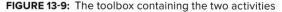

FIGURE 13-9: The toolbox containing the two activities

You can find this activity in the Messaging section of the Toolbox. See Figure 13-10. Simply drag the activity into Drop Activity Here.

This results in two separate activities — see Figure 13-11.

➤ The first one is a `Receive` activity that defines the incoming parameters for the operation.

➤ The second one is a `SendReply` activity that defines the return type for the operation.

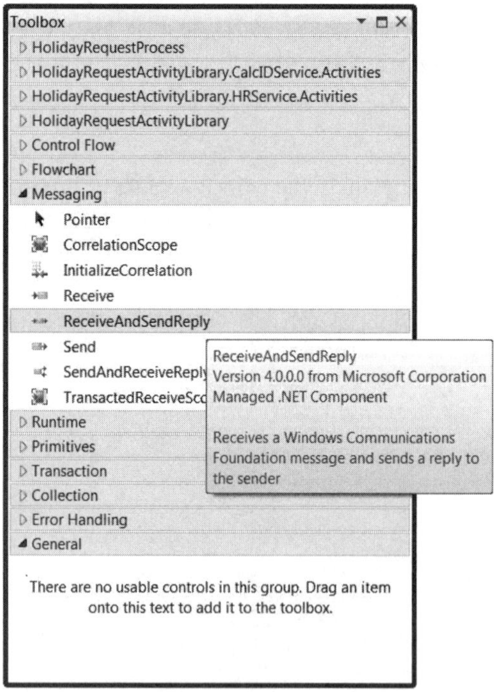

FIGURE 13-10: The ReceiveAndSendReply activity

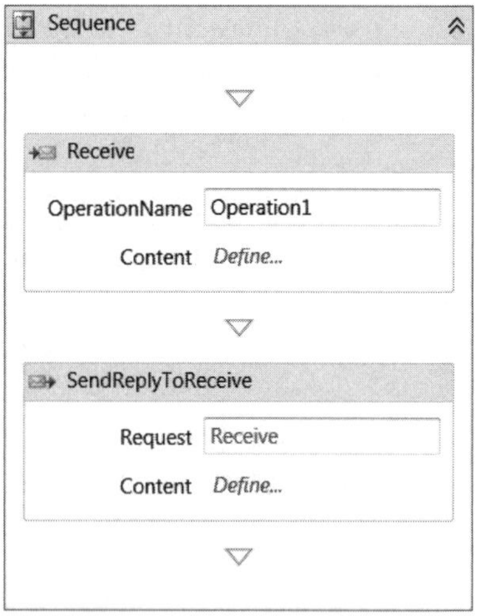

FIGURE 13-11: The activities in the designer

Creating Variables

Before configuring the activities in detail for the workflow, you need to create variables to contain the data you are getting as input from the activities and to contain the data you are sending back as answers.

A variable is also needed to contain the reference ID obtained from the external service. You also need a variable to contain the number of iterations waiting for the timeout that has been executed.

Add six variables — to create those variables, click the sequence activity to set the scope and click the Variables button in the lower-left part of the designer, as seen in Figure 13-12. Every variable needs a type. These types are either defined in the `HolidayRequestDataContracts` library, a type generated by the proxies in the `HolidayRequestActivityLibrary` library, or simply an integer for the reference ID and `retryCounter`.

Selecting a type for the variable is done in the Browse and Select a .NET Type dialog box. This dialog box can be opened by selecting the Browse for Types option in the Variable type column in the variables list — see Figure 13-13.

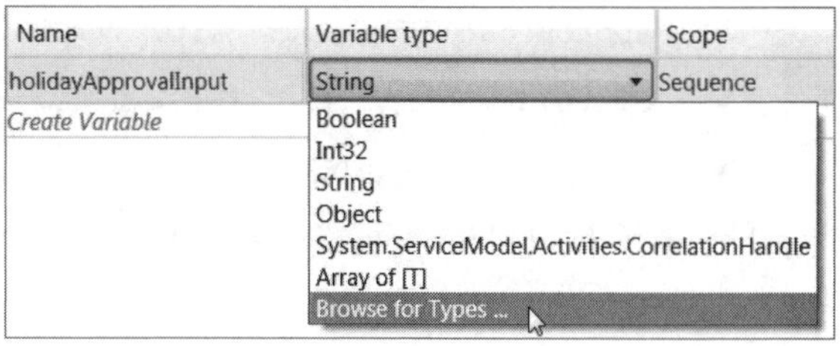

Create the variables named `holidayApprovalInput`, `holidayApprovalOutput`, `holidayRequestInput`, `holidayRequestOutput`, `approvedHolidayInput`, `referenceID`, and `retryCounter`. Select the appropriate type in the dialog box (see Figure 13-14).

FIGURE 13-12: The variables tab

FIGURE 13-13: Browse for Types

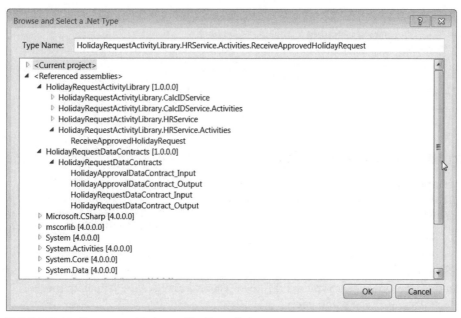

FIGURE 13-14: Browse and Select a .Net Type dialog

The variables and their types are shown here:

➤ holidayApprovalInput: HolidayApprovalDataContract_Input

➤ holidayApprovalOutput: HolidayApprovalDataContract_Output

➤ holidayRequestInput: HolidayRequestDataContract_Input

➤ holidayRequestOutput: HolidayRequestDataContract_Output

➤ referenceID: Int32

➤ approvedHolidayInput: ApprovedHolidayData

➤ correlationHandle: CorrelationHandle

➤ retryCounter: Int32

The result should look like Figure 13-15.

Name	Variable type	Scope
holidayApprovalInput	HolidayApprovalDataContract_Input	Sequence
holidayApprovalOutput	HolidayApprovalDataContract_Output	Sequence
holidayRequestInput	HolidayRequestDataContract_Input	Sequence
holidayRequestOutput	HolidayRequestDataContract_Output	Sequence
referenceID	Int32	Sequence
approvedHolidayInput	ApprovedHolidayData	Sequence
correlationHandle	CorrelationHandle	Sequence
retryCounter	Int32	Sequence

FIGURE 13-15: All variables

Configuring the Receive Activity

Change the Operation Name to RequestHoliday — see
Figure 13-16. To define the parameters for this operation,
click the Define box.

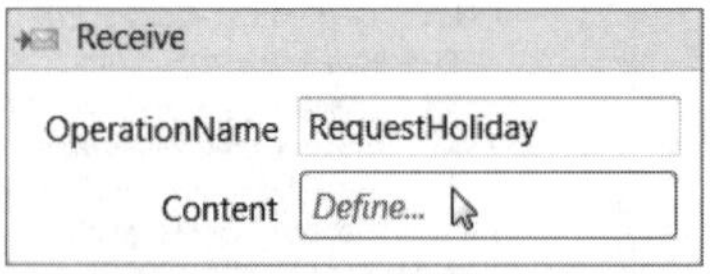

FIGURE 13-16: The Receive activity

This opens the Content Definition dialog box. Check
the Parameters radio button. Click the Add New Parameter link. Name the parameter
inputparam_holidayRequest. To define the type of the parameter, select the Browse for
Types option in the drop-down. The type is HolidayRequestDataContract_Input in the
HolidayRequestDataContracts namespace.

Back in the Content Definition dialog box, type the name of the variable for this incoming data. The
name of the variable is holidayRequestInput (see Figure 13-17).

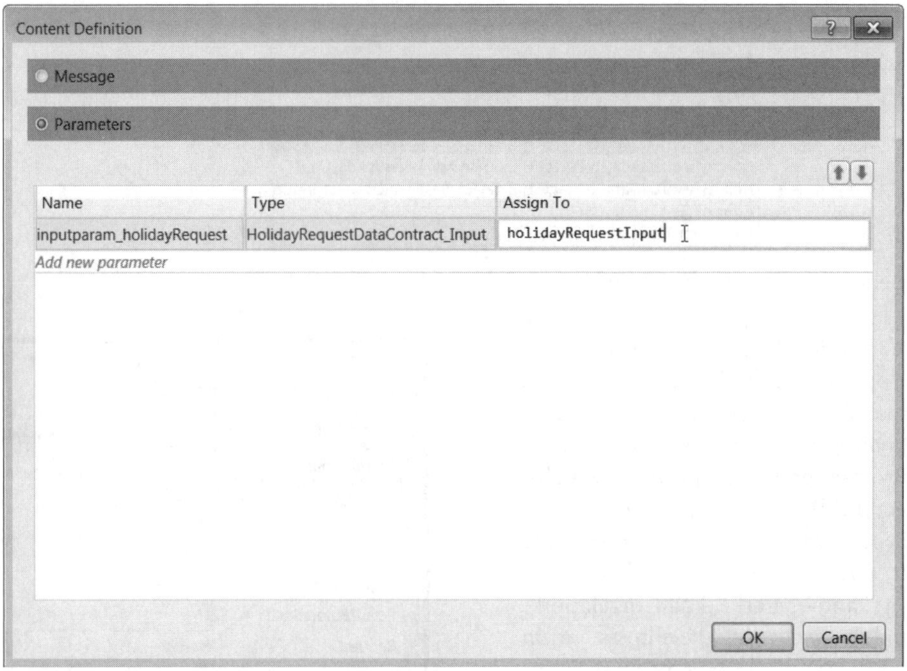

FIGURE 13-17: Content Definition dialog box

Notice that this input box supports intellisense and lets you find the name of the variable easily.

Close the Content Definition dialog box.

Back in the designer, open the property window of the Receive activity and check the CanCreateInstance property. This indicates that calling this operation creates a new instance of the workflow. See Figure 13-18.

Configuring the Send Activity

Before configuring the Send activity, you need to add a correlation variable. This variable is used in the configuration of the SendReply activity and later in the Receive activity for the ApproveRequest operation. In the designer, activate the sequence again to set the scope and open the variables list.

FIGURE 13-18: Check the CanCreateInstance flag

Add a variable called correlationHandle and set the type to CorrelationHandle. See Figure 13-19. Now click the define link in the Content input box of the Send activity.

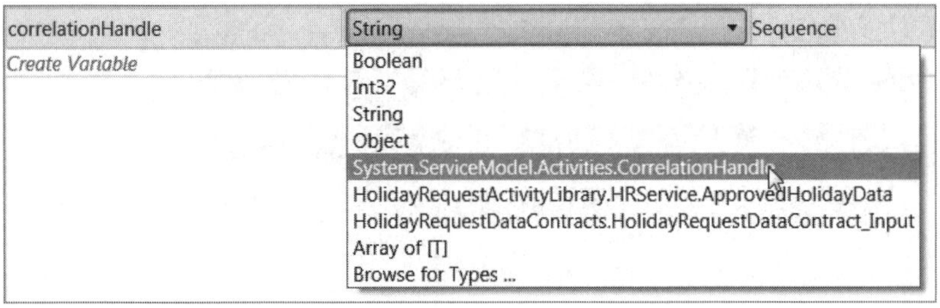

FIGURE 13-19: Select correlationHandle as type

This opens the Content Definition window. In this window select parameters, add a new parameter called `outputparam_holidayRequest`, and set the type to `HolidayRequestDataContract_Output` by using the Browse for Types option — which opens the Select a .NET Type dialog box. Set the value to the `holidayRequestOutput` variable. In the designer, open the property window of the `Send` activity, and open the Add Correlation Initializers window by clicking the ellipsis button of the `CorrelationInitializers` property (see Figure 13-20).

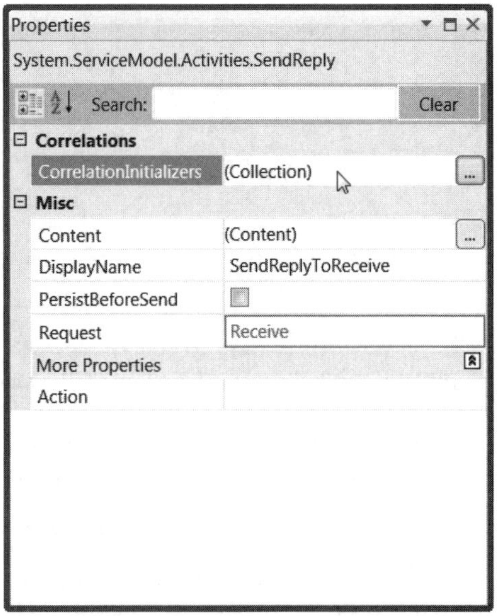

In this dialog box, click the Add Initializer link and type in **correlationHandler**. This is the name of the variable you created to correlate the `Send` activity to the `Receive` activity of the `ApproveRequest` operation. Leave the drop-down list on Query correlation initializer and open the drop-down under XPATH Queries. In this drop-down, select `ReferenceID` from the `outputparam_holidayRequest` parameter. See Figure 13-21. Call to the `CalcIDService`.

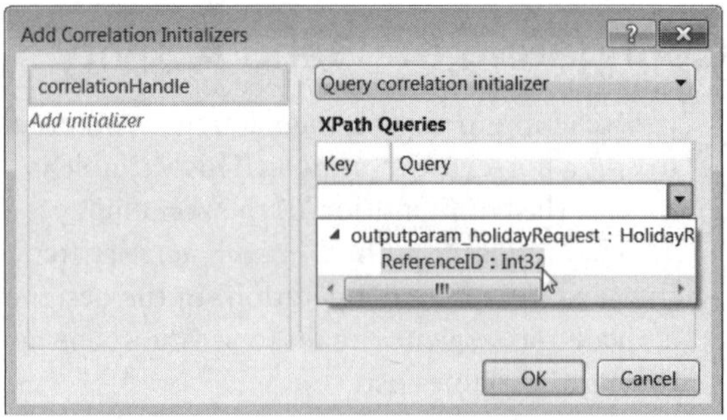

Between the Receive and the Send Activities, you need to call the `CalcIDService` to obtain the reference ID and you need to assign the value of it to the return value of the operation.

Drag and drop the `GetNewReferenceID` activity from the toolbox between the Receive and the Send Activities.

Open the property window of this activity and click the ellipsis button of the `GetNewReferenceIDResult` property. This

FIGURE 13-20: The SendReply properties

FIGURE 13-21: The correlation initializer

opens the Expression Editor. In this editor, enter `referenceID`. This is the name of the variable that holds the value of the `referenceID` — see Figure 13-22. Now you need to assign the obtained `referenceID` to the output parameter for the `Send` activity. For this you need to drop two `Assign` activities between the `GetNewReferenceID` and the `SendActivity` activities. The `Assign` activity can be found in the toolbox in the Primitives part. The first `Assign` activity instantiates the variable `holidayRequestOutput` and the second `Assign` activity sets the `referenceID` to the output value of the `GetNewReferenceID` activity.

Open the Properties window of the first `Assign` activity and configure these properties (see Figure 13-23):

➤ To: `holidayRequestOutput`

➤ Value: `New HolidayRequestDataContract_Output()`

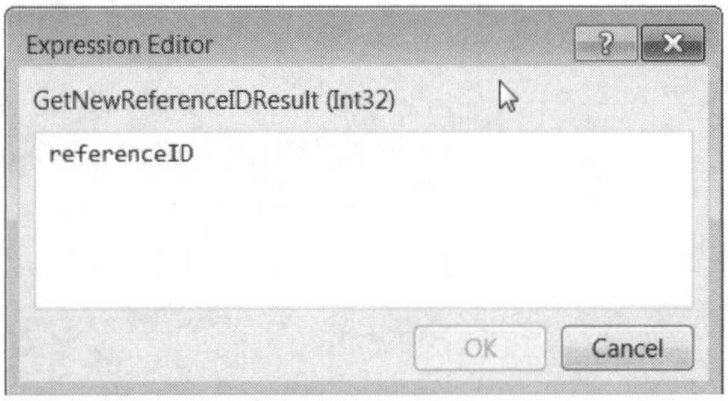

FIGURE 13-22: Expression Editor

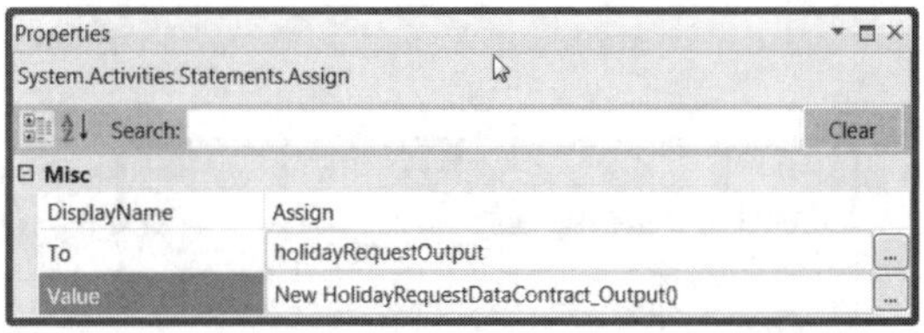

FIGURE 13-23: Properties of the Assign activity

Open the Properties window for the second Assign activity and configure these (see Figure 13-24):

➤ To: `holidayRequestOutput.ReferenceID`

➤ Value: `referenceID`

We add a `WriteLine` activity after the `Send` activity to see when the `RequestHoliday` operation is called and what the `referenceID` from the service is. You can drag the `WriteLine` activity from the Primitives part in the toolbox — see Figure 13-25.

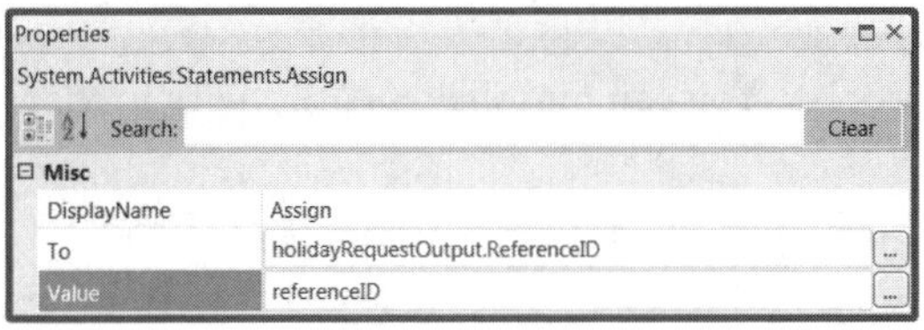

FIGURE 13-24: Properties of the Assign activity

FIGURE 13-25: The WriteLine activity in the toolbox

This `WriteLine` activity is here for testing purposes. The activity writes a string of data to the console application which is hosting this workflow service. You can delete this activity when the workflow is compiled for production.

Open the Properties of this activity and configure the text so it contains a formatted string displaying the obtained `referenceID`. You can configure the text in the Expression Editor after clicking the ellipsis button of the text property. Add this code in the editor — see Figure 13-26.

```
String.Format("Received Request {0}", referenceID)
```

The sequence should now look like Figure 13-27.

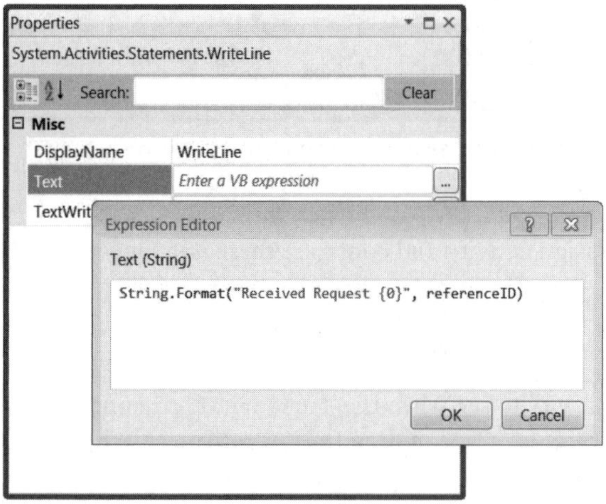

FIGURE 13-26: The expression editor

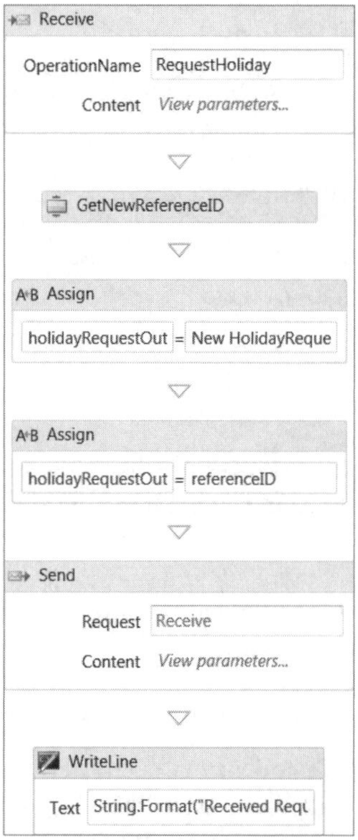

FIGURE 13-27: The Complete sequence

Now add a `while` activity as the next step in the process. You can find the `while` activity in the Control Flow part of the toolbox.

This `while` activity allows the steps to be defined and repeated while a condition is true. This condition is based on the `retryCounter` variable. Only if the `retryCounter` is less than three, will the steps be repeated. The `retryCounter` will be incremented or changed by the activities in the `while` activities.

Open the Properties of the `while` activity and set the value of the condition property to a Boolean Condition. Specify that the `retryCounter` should be less than 5 (see Figure 13-28).

Use this condition:

```
retryCounter < 3
```

The next step is to add a `Pick` activity in the body of the `while` activity. A `Pick` activity allows the process to wait for a trigger before continuing. In this case the process needs to wait for either a timeout configured by a `Delay` activity or the received approval or denial of the holiday request from the managers.

This `Pick` activity can be found in the Control Flow section of the toolbar.

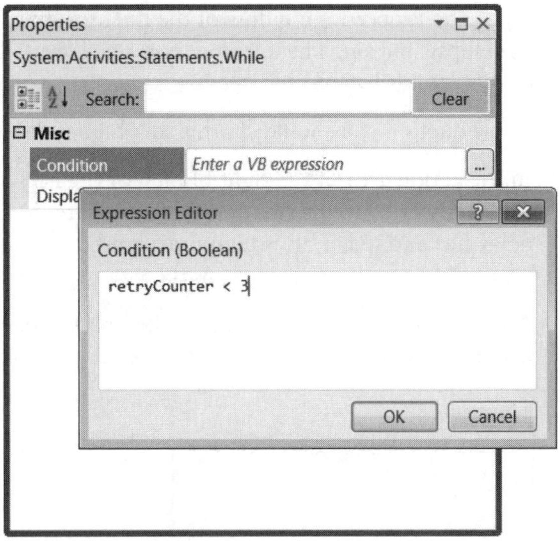

Properties

System.Activities.Statements.While

Search: _____ Clear

Misc

Condition   *Enter a VB expression*   ...

Displa

Expression Editor

Condition (Boolean)

retryCounter < 3

OK   Cancel

FIGURE 13-28: The condition

Now drag a `Delay` activity to the Trigger area in the left branch of this `Pick` activity (see Figure 13-29).

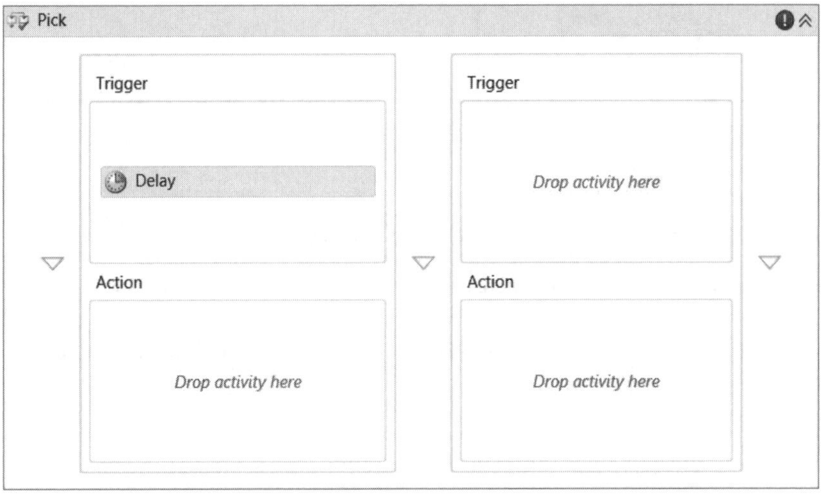

Pick

Trigger	Trigger
Delay	*Drop activity here*
Action	Action
Drop activity here	*Drop activity here*

FIGURE 13-29: The Pick activity in the designer

Open the Properties window of the `Delay` activity and configure the duration property by clicking the ellipsis button. The duration is defined as a VB.NET expression. For the first test, use a duration of 30 seconds by entering `System.TimeSpan.FromSeconds(30)`.

In production you should set this to a higher delay expressed in weeks — see Figure 13-30.

In the action area of the right branch of the `Pick` activity, below the delay, add a `Sequence` activity. This activity contains two activities. The first is a `WriteLine` activity to write the console that the delay has expired. This is temporary and only there to see how the delay works. The second one is an `Assign` activity to increment the `retryCounter` variable.

Add a `WriteLine` activity and set the text to delayed. Add an `Assign` activity and set the `To` property to `retryCounter` and the `Value` property to `retryCounter+1`. See Figure 13-31.

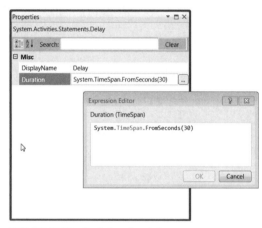

FIGURE 13-30: Defining the delay   **FIGURE 13-31:** Properties of the Assign activity

Configuring the ApproveRequest ReceiveAndSendReply Activity

In the Trigger area of the sequence in the right branch of the `Pick` activity, drop another `ReceiveAndSendReply` activity. See Figure 13-32. This will create the second operation in the workflow service and will receive the approval or denial of the holiday request. This operation is called by the `ManagersHolidayRequestApproval` application.

Now set the `OperationName` to `ApproveRequest`. Click the Define link to set the content of the `Receive` activity. In the Content Definition window, check the Parameters radio button. Add a parameter called `inputparam_holidayApproval`, set the type to `HolidayRequestDataContract_input`, and assign this parameter to the `holidayApprovalInput` variable. See Figure 13-33.

Configure the correlation by setting the `CorrelatesWith` to `correlationHandle`.

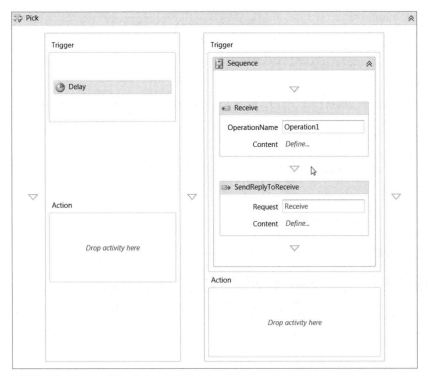

FIGURE 13-32: How the Pick activity looks now

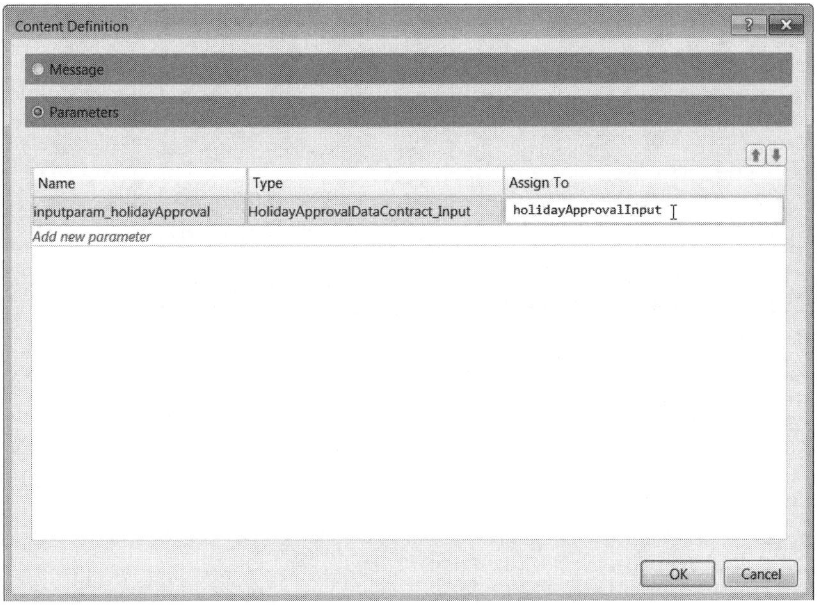

FIGURE 13-33: Assign the parameter

Open the `CorrelatesOn` Definition window by clicking the ellipsis button of the `CorrelatesOn` property. In the XPath Queries drop-down, select `ReferenceID` as the parameter to correlate. See Figure 13-34.

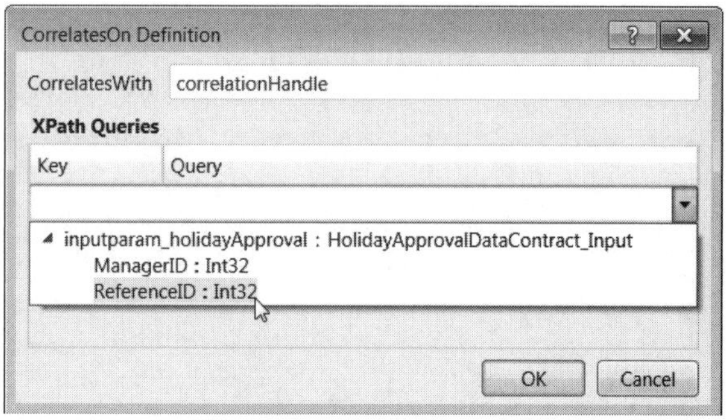

Configure the `SendReply` activity. Open the `Content` Definition window, select Parameters, and add a parameter called `outputparam_holidayApproval`. Set the type to `HolidayApprovalDataContract_Output`, found in the `HolidayRequest DataContracts`, and assign this to the `holidayApprovalOutput` variable. See Figure 13-35.

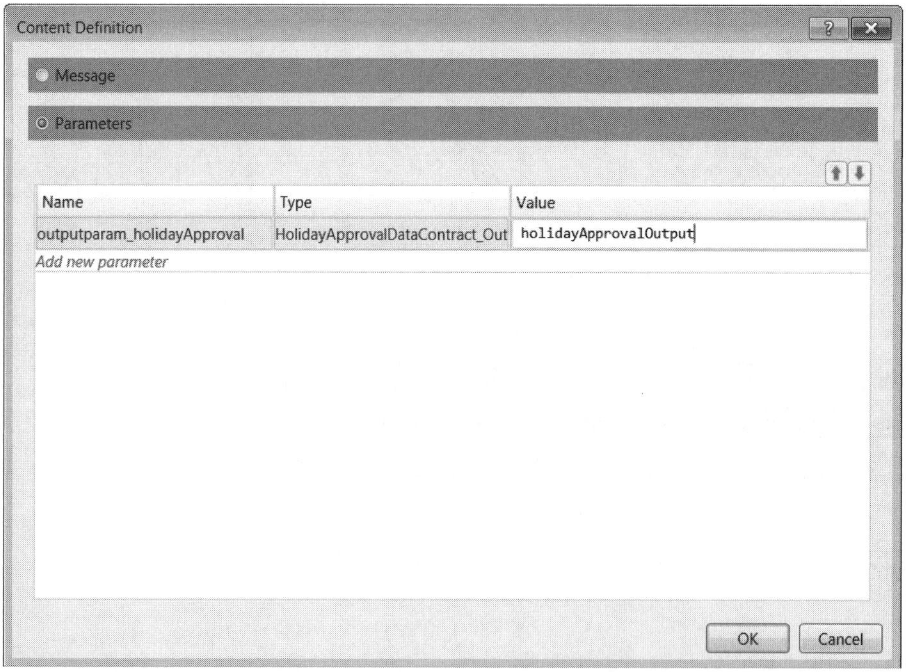

FIGURE 13-34: Configuring the correlation

FIGURE 13-35: Content definition window

In-between the `Receive` activity and the `SendReply` activity, drop two `Assign` activities. The first `Assign` activity instantiates the output variable. The second `Assign` activity sets the `EmployeeID` as a property of this variable. It is set to the `EmployeeID` which is received as input for the approval request:

```
holidayApprovalOutput               New HolidayApprovalDataContract_Output()
holidayApprovalOutput.EmployeeID    holidayRequestInput.EmployeeID
```

After the `SendReply` activity, add an `Assign` activity that sets the `retryCounter` variable to 99. The result should look like Figure 13-36.

This is a value higher than the value used in the condition of the `while` activity and will stop the `while` activity (see Figure 13-37). In the Action part of the right branch of the `Pick` activity, add an `If` activity. You can find this in the Control Flow Section of the toolbox. This activity will check the `holidayApprovalInput` variable to see whether it was approved or denied.

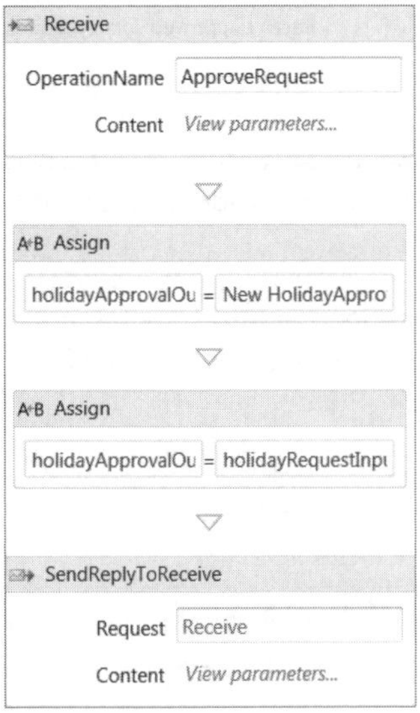

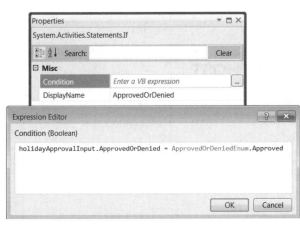

FIGURE 13-36: The assign statements

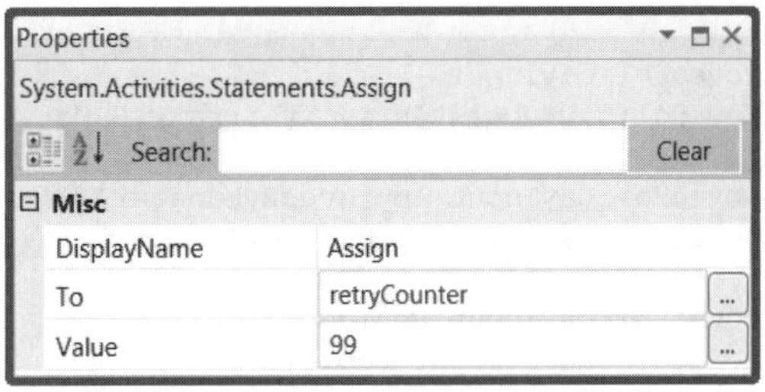

FIGURE 13-37: Set the retryCounter

Change the `DisplayName` to `ApprovedOrDenied`. Edit the condition and enter the following condition:

```
holidayApprovalInput.ApprovedOrDenied = ApprovedOrDeniedEnum.Approved
```

See Figure 13-38 for the result.

FIGURE 13-38: The condition in the Expression Editor

In the `Then` branch of the `If` activity, drop a `Sequence` activity to group all needed activities when the holiday request is approved. Also drop a `Sequence` activity in the Else branch.

Add the `ReceiveApprovedHolidayRequest` activity from the toolbox to the left `Sequence`. The call to the `HRService` only executes when the holiday request is approved.

Set the `approvedHolidayData` property of this activity to the `approvedHolidayInput` variable. See Figure 13-39.

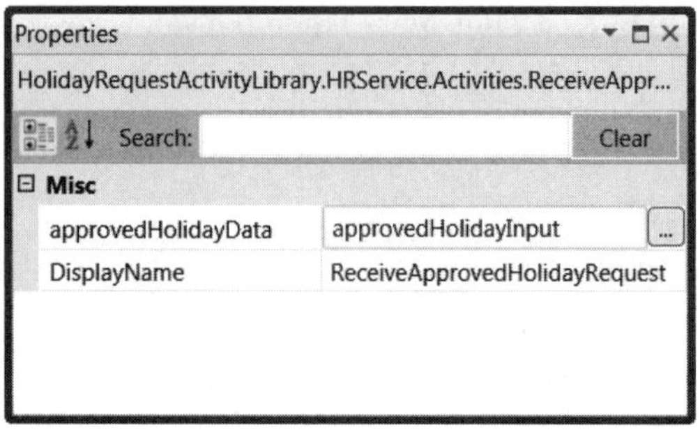

FIGURE 13-39: Set the approvedHoliday property

Add these five assigned activities to the action part before the `ReceiveApprovedHolidayRequest` activity. These activities construct the `approvedHolidayInput` variable. Configure the `To` and `Value` properties for these activities as follows:

```
To: approvedHolidayInput
Value: New HolidayRequestActivityLibrary.HRService.ApprovedHolidayData

To: approvedHolidayInput.ApprovedByManagerID
Value: holidayApprovalInput.ManagerID

To: approvedHolidayInput.EmployeeID
Value: holidayRequestInput.EmployeeID

To: approvedHolidayInput.HolidayStartDate
Value: holidayRequestInput.HolidayStartDate

To: approvedHolidayInput.HolidayEndDate
Value: holidayRequestInput.HolidayEndDate
```

See Figure 13-40.

Add a `WriteLine` activity to each of the branches indicating what the result of the managers is to the console screen.

DEVELOPING THE HOLIDAYREQUESTHOST

In the `HolidayRequestHost`, add references to `HolidayRequestActivityLibrary`, `HolidayDataContracts`, and `HolidayRequestProcess`.

FIGURE 13-40: The assign statements

The console application also needs references to `System`
`.Activities`, `System.ServiceModel`, `System.Runtime`
`.Serialization`, `System.ServiceModel.Activities`, and
`System.ServiceProcess` (see Figure 13-41).

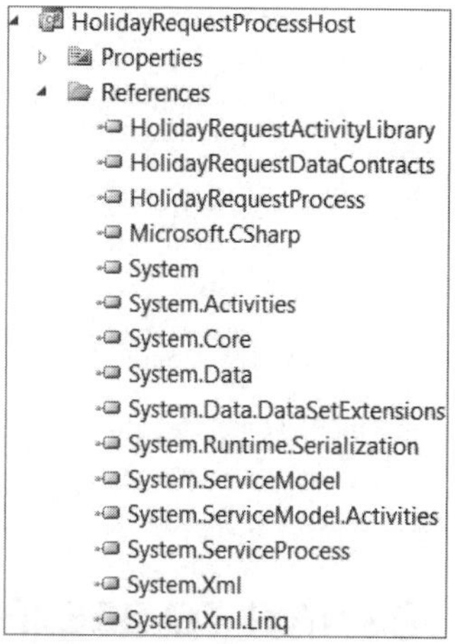

Add an application configuration file to the project.
Copy/Paste the complete content of the app.config file of
the `HolidayRequestActivityLibrary` project into this
configuration file.

In the program.cs file, add code to the main
method to instantiate a `WorkflowServiceHost`;
add a `SqlWorkflowInstanceStoreBehavior` to the
`WorkflowServiceHost`; add `ServiceMetadataBehavior`;
and then set the `timeToUnload` interval to 0 seconds:

FIGURE 13-41: The references
needed for the Host

```
try
{
    WorkflowServiceHost workflowServiceHost;
    workflowServiceHost = new WorkflowServiceHost(
        new HolidayRequestProcess.HolidayRequestProcessDefinition(),
        new Uri(@"http://localhost:9874/HolidayRequestProcess"));

    workflowServiceHost.Description.Behaviors.Add(
        new SqlWorkflowInstanceStoreBehavior(
            "Data Source=.;
             Initial Catalog=SqlWorkflowInstanceStore;Integrated Security=True"));

    ServiceMetadataBehavior serviceMetadataBehavior;
    serviceMetadataBehavior = new ServiceMetadataBehavior();
    serviceMetadataBehavior.HttpGetEnabled = true;
    workflowServiceHost.Description.Behaviors.Add(serviceMetadataBehavior);

    WorkflowIdleBehavior workflowIdleBehavior = new WorkflowIdleBehavior()
    {
        TimeToUnload = TimeSpan.FromSeconds(0)
    };
    workflowServiceHost.Description.Behaviors.Add(workflowIdleBehavior);

    workflowServiceHost.Description.Behaviors.Find<ServiceDebugBehavior>().
      IncludeExceptionDetailInFaults = true;

    workflowServiceHost.Open();

    Console.WriteLine("WorkflowServiceHost started.");

}
```

```
catch (Exception ex)
{
  Console.WriteLine(ex.Message);
  if (ex.InnerException != null)
  {
    Console.WriteLine(ex.InnerException.Message);
  }
}

Console.ReadKey();
```

Code snippet CreatingtheBusinessProcess.zip

TESTING TO SEE IF THIS SERVICE HOST EXPOSES THE METADATA CORRECTLY

Start the `HolidayRequestProcessHost` application outside Visual Studio. Make sure you start it as administrator. Open a browser and browse to `http://localhost:9874/HolidayRequestProcess`. This should show a page with a link to `http://localhost:9874/HolidayRequestProcess?wsdl`. See Figure 13-42. Develop the `EmployeeHolidayRequestApplication` application.

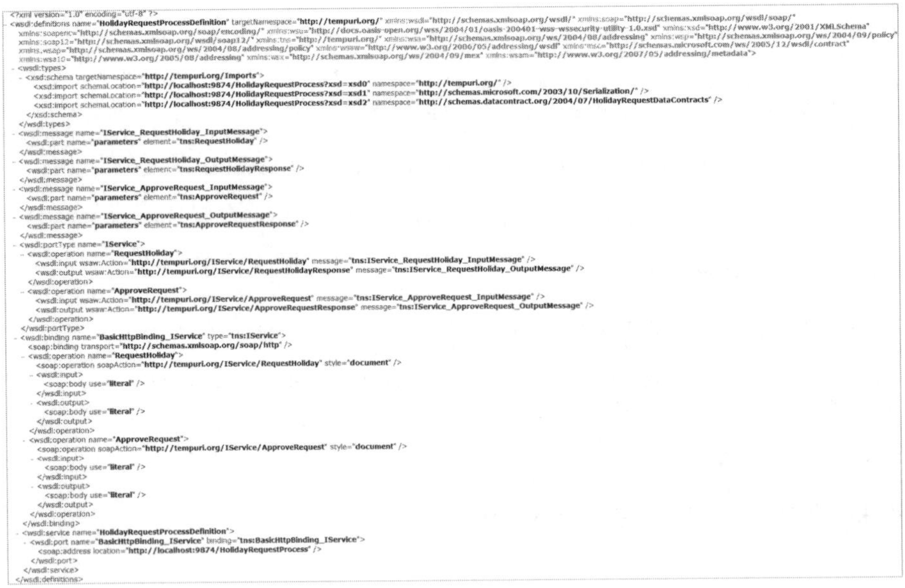


```
<?xml version="1.0" encoding="utf-8" ?>
- <wsdl:definitions name="HolidayRequestProcessDefinition" targetNamespace="http://tempuri.org/" xmlns:wsdl="http://schemas.xmlsoap.org/wsdl/" xmlns:soap="http://schemas.xmlsoap.org/wsdl/soap/"
  xmlns:soapenc="http://schemas.xmlsoap.org/soap/encoding/" xmlns:wsu="http://docs.oasis-open.org/wss/2004/01/oasis-200401-wss-wssecurity-utility-1.0.xsd" xmlns:xsd="http://www.w3.org/2001/XMLSchema"
  xmlns:soap12="http://schemas.xmlsoap.org/wsdl/soap12/" xmlns:tns="http://tempuri.org/" xmlns:wsa="http://schemas.xmlsoap.org/ws/2004/08/addressing" xmlns:wsp="http://schemas.xmlsoap.org/ws/2004/09/policy"
  xmlns:wsap="http://schemas.xmlsoap.org/ws/2004/08/addressing/policy" xmlns:wsaw="http://www.w3.org/2006/05/addressing/wsdl" xmlns:msc="http://schemas.microsoft.com/ws/2005/12/wsdl/contract"
  xmlns:wsa10="http://www.w3.org/2005/08/addressing" xmlns:wsx="http://schemas.xmlsoap.org/ws/2004/09/mex" xmlns:wsam="http://www.w3.org/2007/05/addressing/metadata">
 - <wsdl:types>
  - <xsd:schema targetNamespace="http://tempuri.org/Imports">
     <xsd:import schemaLocation="http://localhost:9874/HolidayRequestProcess?xsd=xsd0" namespace="http://tempuri.org/" />
     <xsd:import schemaLocation="http://localhost:9874/HolidayRequestProcess?xsd=xsd1" namespace="http://schemas.microsoft.com/2003/10/Serialization/" />
     <xsd:import schemaLocation="http://localhost:9874/HolidayRequestProcess?xsd=xsd2" namespace="http://schemas.datacontract.org/2004/07/HolidayRequestDataContracts" />
    </xsd:schema>
  </wsdl:types>
 - <wsdl:message name="IService_RequestHoliday_InputMessage">
    <wsdl:part name="parameters" element="tns:RequestHoliday" />
  </wsdl:message>
 - <wsdl:message name="IService_RequestHoliday_OutputMessage">
    <wsdl:part name="parameters" element="tns:RequestHolidayResponse" />
  </wsdl:message>
 - <wsdl:message name="IService_ApproveRequest_InputMessage">
    <wsdl:part name="parameters" element="tns:ApproveRequest" />
  </wsdl:message>
 - <wsdl:message name="IService_ApproveRequest_OutputMessage">
    <wsdl:part name="parameters" element="tns:ApproveRequestResponse" />
  </wsdl:message>
 - <wsdl:portType name="IService">
  - <wsdl:operation name="RequestHoliday">
     <wsdl:input wsaw:Action="http://tempuri.org/IService/RequestHoliday" message="tns:IService_RequestHoliday_InputMessage" />
     <wsdl:output wsaw:Action="http://tempuri.org/IService/RequestHolidayResponse" message="tns:IService_RequestHoliday_OutputMessage" />
    </wsdl:operation>
  - <wsdl:operation name="ApproveRequest">
     <wsdl:input wsaw:Action="http://tempuri.org/IService/ApproveRequest" message="tns:IService_ApproveRequest_InputMessage" />
     <wsdl:output wsaw:Action="http://tempuri.org/IService/ApproveRequestResponse" message="tns:IService_ApproveRequest_OutputMessage" />
    </wsdl:operation>
  </wsdl:portType>
 - <wsdl:binding name="BasicHttpBinding_IService" type="tns:IService">
    <soap:binding transport="http://schemas.xmlsoap.org/soap/http" />
  - <wsdl:operation name="RequestHoliday">
     <soap:operation soapAction="http://tempuri.org/IService/RequestHoliday" style="document" />
   - <wsdl:input>
      <soap:body use="literal" />
     </wsdl:input>
   - <wsdl:output>
      <soap:body use="literal" />
     </wsdl:output>
    </wsdl:operation>
  - <wsdl:operation name="ApproveRequest">
     <soap:operation soapAction="http://tempuri.org/IService/ApproveRequest" style="document" />
   - <wsdl:input>
      <soap:body use="literal" />
     </wsdl:input>
   - <wsdl:output>
      <soap:body use="literal" />
     </wsdl:output>
    </wsdl:operation>
  </wsdl:binding>
 - <wsdl:service name="HolidayRequestProcessDefinition">
  - <wsdl:port name="BasicHttpBinding_IService" binding="tns:BasicHttpBinding_IService">
     <soap:address location="http://localhost:9874/HolidayRequestProcess" />
    </wsdl:port>
  </wsdl:service>
</wsdl:definitions>
```


FIGURE 13-42: The WSDL of the HolidayRequestProcess

While the `HolidayRequestProcessHost` is running outside Visual Studio, open the `EmployeeHolidayRequestApplication` and add a service reference to the `HolidayRequestProcess` service. In the Add Service Reference window, set the address to `http://localhost:9874/HolidayRequestProcess?wsdl` and set the namespace to `HolidayRequestService`. See Figure 13-43.

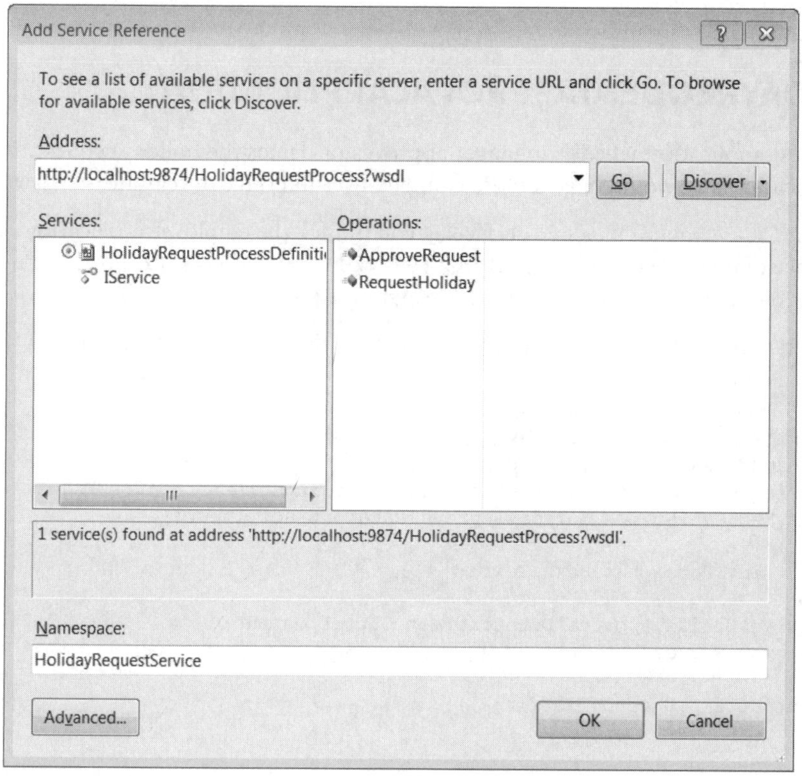

FIGURE 13-43: Adding a service reference to the HolidayRequestProcess service

Add a button to the form and write the following code as code-behind:

```
HolidayRequestService.ServiceClient client;
client = new HolidayRequestService.ServiceClient();
HolidayRequestService.HolidayRequestDataContract_Output output;
output = client.RequestHoliday(
  new HolidayRequestService.HolidayRequestDataContract_Input()
    { EmployeeID = 101,
      HolidayEndDate = System.DateTime.Now,
      HolidayStartDate = System.DateTime.Now
    });
MessageBox.Show(output.ReferenceID.ToString());
```

This is not really the final code, just a test client as part of the proof-of-concept. In real life, the `EmployeeHolidayRequestApplication` would have a more complex interface. But this application allows us to test the workflow. The code just calls the `RequestHoliday` method of the proxy which starts the workflow you developed and is hosted by the `workflowservicehost` in the `HolidayRequestProcessHost`. The result of the call, the received `EmployeeID`, is shown in a message box.

DEVELOPING THE MANAGERSHOLIDAYREQUESTAPPROVALAPPLICATION

This application is the test application where a manager approves or denies the holiday request. Again this is a test application and would have a more complex user interface in real life.

Add a reference to the `HolidayRequestProcess` service as you did for the employee application. In the Add Service Reference dialog, use `http://localhost:9874/HolidayRequestProcess` as the address and type in `HolidayRequestService` as the namespace for the service.

Add a button and a textbox to the form. The textbox is needed for the `referenceID`. For the button, add the following code:

```
HolidayRequestService.ServiceClient client;
client = new HolidayRequestService.ServiceClient();
HolidayRequestService.HolidayApprovalDataContract_Input input;
input = new HolidayRequestService.HolidayApprovalDataContract_Input();
input.ManagerID = 1;
input.ReferenceID = int.Parse(textBox2.Text);

HolidayRequestService.HolidayApprovalDataContract_Output output;
output = client.ApproveRequest(input);

MessageBox.Show(output.EmployeeID.ToString());
```

CREATING THE SQLWORKFLOWINSTANCESTORE

You need to create a SQL database to store the state of the process. This SQL database can be running under SQL Express or SQL Server. This database needs to contain the appropriate tables and stored procedures so the `workflowservicehost` can store and retrieve the state of the process. The name of the database must be specified in the `connectionstring` you gave to the `SqlWorkflowInstanceStoreBehavior` you added to the `WorkflowServiceHost`.

To create the needed tables and stored procedures, you need to run two scripts on the database, which can be found in the C:\Windows\Microsoft.NET\Framework\v4.0.30128\SQL\en. directory. The scripts are SqlWorkflowInstanceStoreLogic.sql and SqlWorkflowInstanceStoreSchema.sql.

14

Hosting

WCF is a great and powerful platform to develop service. But after you have developed your service, how can you make it available to the world? You need a host process to run your service. The host process creates the various configuration settings that enable the service execution. It prepares the environment, creates the endpoints, starts the listening processes, and manages the service lifecycle.

The role of the host process is very important, and should be chosen carefully. There are two main options for hosting your service:

➤ Self-hosting

   ➤ Console application

   ➤ Windows application

   ➤ Windows services

➤ IIS

   ➤ IIS 6 only for Http protocol

   ➤ Windows Activation Service (WAS)

   ➤ Windows Server AppFabric

The self-hosting option allows you to host a service directly in your application. If you want to enable a Windows application to receive messages, or if you want to enable communication between different processes, you can use this option. This makes your application totally independent from the configuration of the machine. You don't need to install third-party software to host your services. Therefore, you have to manage the service lifetime. For example, if the host process stops unexpectedly, your service becomes unavailable.

Using IIS is a robust and efficient hosting option. This is the best choice if you are in a distribute environment and your service is deployed in dedicated servers. IIS manages for you application recycling, availability, reliability, and manageability.

A service requires a process and at least one Application Domain to be executed. An Application Domain in .NET Framework provides a great level of isolation where the managed code is executed. As shown in Figure 14-1, a single Windows process is able to run multiple Application Domains.

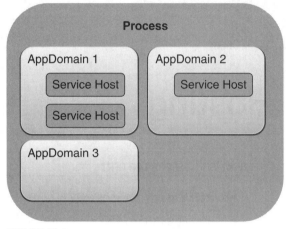

FIGURE 14-1

SELF-HOSTING APPLICATIONS

As described in the previous section, you can host your service in any kind of .NET application. A typical example is an application that runs in the background and captures requests because it has to enqueue messages and process them afterward. In this scenario, the background application could implement and self-host a service, open a channel, and listen for incoming messages.

A self-host solution needs to be executed in a Windows process. It inherits all the settings, such as security, from the hosting process. It is your responsibility to manage the hosting environment. You have to control the host (and the service) lifecycle. A self-host solution is useful when you want to enable communication with the various components of your application, typically in a local environment where the number of clients or the number of transactions is very limited.

Implementing the self-host is the simplest way to host your services. Exploring how to do this is explained next.

The ServiceHost and the ServiceHostBase

To host your service in a .NET application you need to use a specific class: `ServiceHost`. The `ServiceHost` class allows you to set the execution environment of your services. As shown in Listing 14-1, you can set the service settings programmatically by using the configuration file or also with a combination of the two.

LISTING 14-1: Using the ServiceHost

```
using Wrox.CarRentalService.Implementations.Europe;
...

ServiceHost carRentalHost = new ServiceHost(typeof(CarRentalService));
carRentalHost.Open();
```

Listing 14-1 creates an instance of the ServiceHost related to the service implementation
Wrox.CarRentalService.Implementations.Europe.CarRentalService. One important thing is
that each ServiceHost instance can host only one service type at a time. Note that there aren't any
ServiceEndpoint added to the host. In this case, when the Open method is called, the ServiceHost
tries to find the settings in the current configuration file (Web.config or App.config).

Starting from WCF version 4.0, if a configuration section is not found, the ServiceHost can use the
default endpoints settings, as explained in Chapter 3. In a self-hosted scenario, you need to provide
the list of base endpoint addresses that the ServiceHost will use, and then explicitly call the
AddDefaultEndpoints() method to create the endpoints. Listing 14-2 shows the complete code.

LISTING 14-2: Using the ServiceHost to Add Default Endpoints

```
...

Uri[] baseAddresses = new Uri[]
{
    new Uri("http://localhost:10101/CarRentalService"),
    new Uri("net.tcp://localhost:10102/CarRentalService")
};

ServiceHost host = new ServiceHost(typeof(CarRentalService), baseAddresses);
host.AddDefaultEndpoints();
try
{
    host.Open();

    Console.WriteLine("The car rental service is up and listening on the
    endpoints:");
    foreach (var endpoint in host.Description.Endpoints)
    {
        Console.WriteLine("\t" + endpoint.Address.Uri.ToString());
    }
    Console.ReadLine();

    host.Close();
}
catch (CommunicationException ex)
{
    host.Abort();
}
catch (TimeoutException ex)
{
```

continues

LISTING 14-2 *(continued)*

```
        host.Abort();
    }
    catch (Exception ex)
    {
        host.Abort();
        throw;
    }
```

> ⊗ *Listing 14-2 shows how you can create an instance of* ServiceHost *and open the channels to start listening to receive messages. Note the usage of a* try... catch *block and the usage of the* Close() *method. This is the best way you have to manage the* ServiceHost *state. You have to call the* Close() *method only if your application flow is successfully completed. Otherwise, when an exception is thrown, you have to call the* Abort() *method to make sure that each channel is immediately terminated and closed. All the connected clients receive a* CommunicationException. *Though* ServiceHost *implements* IDisposable, *don't use the* using *block because it causes a call to the* Dispose *method and then, internally, to the* Close *method even when an exception is thrown. This will cause an unpredictable exception since the Close method waits for completion of current work while the ServiceHost is in an inconsistent state.*

The output of this code is shown in Figure 14-2.

Although you can use one ServiceHost per service implementation, you can expose multiple interfaces and then multiple endpoints. In the same process, you can create more than one ServiceHost instance to host different service types or host the same service type.

Calling the methods Open and Close, you allow the service to listen on a preconfigured address and ready it to receive messages. As

FIGURE 14-2

shown in Listing 14-3, you can also use the asynchronous methods BeginOpen/EndOpen and BeginClose/EndClose.

Available for download on Wrox.com

LISTING 14-3: ServiceHost Opened Asynchronously

```
using Wrox.CarRentalService.Implementations.Europe;
...

Uri[] baseAddresses = new Uri[]
{
    new Uri("http://localhost:10101/CarRentalService"),
    new Uri("net.tcp://localhost:10102/CarRentalService")
};
```

```
ServiceHost host = new ServiceHost(typeof(CarRentalService), baseAddresses);
host.AddDefaultEndpoints();
IAsyncResult result = host.BeginOpen(
    new AsyncCallback(ServiceHostOpenCallback), null);
```

The `ServiceHostOpenCallback` method is invoked when the `BeginOpen` method ends its execution. In this method, which matches the `System.AsyncCallback` delegate, you can place action to execute in this stage. See Listing 14-4.

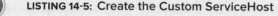

LISTING 14-4: ServiceHost Callback Handler

Available for
download on
Wrox.com

```
ServiceHost cachedHost;
public void ServiceHostOpenCallback(IAsyncResult result)
{
    ...
}
```

Implementing a Custom ServiceHost

Some situations may require reusing the same `ServiceHost` with the same settings, in a different place. For example, you could create a `ServiceHost` to programmatically handle service configuration or a part of the service configuration. In this case, extend the `ServiceHost` and write a custom implementation.

The `ServiceHost` inherits from an abstract base class: the `ServiceHostBase`. You can extend the `ServiceHostBase` or the `ServiceHost` class, which only adds four `AddServiceEndpoint` overloads and manages the service instance creation for singleton services.

The .NET Framework also has specific host implementations:

➤   `System.ServiceModel.Web.WebServiceHost`, available in the `System.ServiceModel.Web` assembly, extends the `ServiceHost` and automatically sets the `WebHttpBinding` and the `WebHttpBehavior` to handle the creation of an environment to execute a REST-based service.

➤   `System.ServiceModel.WorkflowServiceHost`, available in the `System.WorkflowServices` assembly, extends the `ServiceHostBase` class. It initializes the workflow context and adds the `WorkflowRuntimeBehavior` to the host instance.

Both host implementations are a simplified way to create a host instance. You can do the same by using the `ServiceHost`, but in this case you'll write a lot of code every time you use it.

As shown in Listing 14-5, inheriting from the `ServiceHost` only requires the explicit implementation of the `ApplyConfiguration` abstract method to apply the specific host logic.

LISTING 14-5: Create the Custom ServiceHost

Available for
download on
Wrox.com

```
public class CustomServiceHost : ServiceHost
{
    public CustomServiceHost(Type serviceType, params Uri[] baseAddresses)
        : base(serviceType, baseAddresses)
```

continues

LISTING 14-5 *(continued)*

```
        {
        }

        protected override void ApplyConfiguration()
        {
            base.ApplyConfiguration();
            // custom logic here
        }
    }
```

The `ApplyConfiguration` method is invoked from the `InitializeDescription` method of the `ServiceHostBase` class that you can also override. In most cases, the `InitializeDescription` is invoked from the class constructor. If you don't call the base constructor, you have to invoke the `InitializeDescription` directly; otherwise your custom implementation may not work correctly.

Using the `ApplyConfiguration` allows you to change the settings only after they have been read from the configuration file. If you want to change the configuration load logic, you don't have to call the base implementation but write your custom logic directly.

Another trick is to apply the custom host logic as late as possible and after all configurations and programmatic settings are already applied, as shown in Listing 14-6. Thus your settings cannot be changed after the host instance is created. You can do it in the `Opening` event, before the `Open` process is complete.

LISTING 14-6: Programmatically Configure the Custom ServiceHost

```
public class CustomServiceHost : ServiceHost
{
    public CustomServiceHost(Type serviceType, params Uri[] baseAddresses)
        : base(serviceType, baseAddresses)
    {
        this.Opening += new EventHandler(CustomServiceHost_Opening);
    }

    void CustomServiceHost_Opening(object sender, EventArgs e)
    {
        MyCustomBehavior behavior =
                this.Description.Behaviors.Find<MyCustomBehavior>();
        if (behavior == null)
        {
            this.Description.Behaviors.Add(new MyCustomBehavior());
        }
    }
}
```

Extending the `ServiceHost` is the easiest way to create a custom host implementation and it is valid in most scenarios. If your host differs from the "classic" WCF programming model, such as the `WorkflowServiceHost`, you may consider extending the `ServiceHostBase`. This is because the `ServiceHostBase` has the abstract method `CreateDescription` that allows creating the service description and defines the implemented contracts. The `ServiceHost` uses this method to create the service description based on the WCF programming model and the usage of its attributes such as the `ServiceContractAttribute`, the `OperationContractAttribute`, and the `ServiceBehaviorAttribute`. If you want to create your own programming model to build services, then you have to inherit from `ServiceHostBase`. This is done by the `WorkflowServiceHost`, but inheriting from `ServiceHost` is the right choice in the other case.

IIS HOSTING

When you have to address complex scenarios where your service is exposed in a distributed environment, you need to use a very robust and efficient managed hosting. Indeed, your services need to be reliable and always running to serve the various client requests. In this case the solution is offered by the Internet Information Services (IIS) web server.

Hosting in IIS, also known as managed hosting, offers you a set of important features:

➤ Recycling process—Limits the memory leak problem.

➤ Application pool concept—Enables application isolation (you can also recycle the single application).

➤ Isolated worker process—For each application pool, a separate worker process exists to provide scalability features and performance, as well as crash isolation.

➤ Message-based activation—Allows creating the instance and opens the host when a new incoming message is received. The host is subject to a pool of instance and then reused when a new request arrives.

➤ Process monitoring—Ensures the availability of a process to handle the incoming requests. If no worker process is available, a new one is initialized and started.

The WCF service hosting feature in IIS is built on top of the ASP.NET Http pipeline. This means that this kind of host only supports the Http/Https transport protocol. The ASP.NET Http pipeline has the concept of Http Handlers and Http Module. Although the Http Module is a special class that you can use to intercept and manipulate the incoming and outgoing messages, the Http Handler is the class responsible for processing the specific message. An Http Handler is activated by mapping an extension to a class that implements the `IHttpHandler` interface. In the case of WCF, .svc is the file extension used to identify services.

In Visual Studio you can select a new project and create a web site application by using the WCF Service template, as shown in Listing 14-7. The generated project contains the configuration file, a sample service contract and implementation, and a .svc file that references the service implementation.

Available for download on Wrox.com

LISTING 14-7: The Template-Generated .svc File

```
<%@ ServiceHost Language="C#" Debug="true"
Service="Service" CodeBehind="~/App_Code/Service.cs" %>
```

If you browse the .svc file, you can view the help page, shown in Figure 14-3. It has a link that points to the WSDL (see Figure 14-4), if the display metadata option is enabled, as in the default setting.

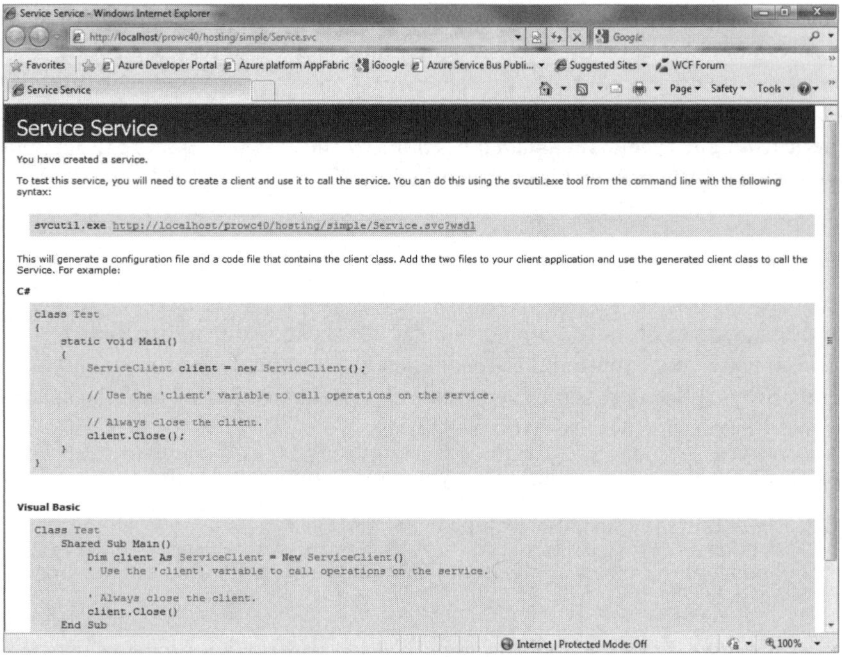

FIGURE 14-3

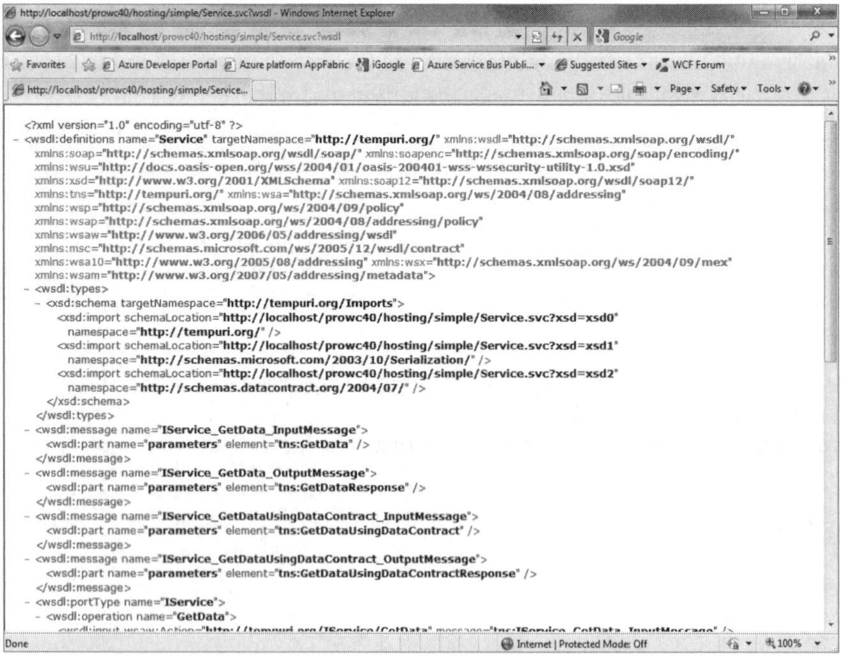

FIGURE 14-4

The ServiceHost class, described in the self-hosting section, is used even in managed hosting. But this time another component is needed to successfully create the host instance: ServiceHostFactory.

The ServiceHostFactory and the ServiceHostFactoryBase

Similar to ServiceHostBase and ServiceHost classes, WCF has the ServiceHostFactoryBase and the ServiceHostFactory. These two classes provide factory methods to create the host instance in managed environments that support the dynamic activation. As you have seen, the WCF extensibility model allows you to create your own ServiceHost implementation. But in this case, different from the self-host scenario, a managed environment such as IIS doesn't know anything about your custom host. In this case, the IIS host needs to use the factory class as an entry point to create the host instance. The default factory called from the IIS is the ServiceHostFactory, but you can also create your own.

The CreateServiceHost method is the most important method you have to override. It first accepts a parameter string called constructorString that represents anything useful to retrieve the correct service to host. In the ServiceHostFactory implementation, it must to be the full name of the service type (for example, CarRentalService.Implementations.Europe.CarRentalService). The second parameter is a list of base addresses inherited from the host.

To use the ServiceHostFactory (or the ServiceHostFactoryBase) class, you have to add a reference to the System.ServiceModel.Activation assembly. Listing 14-8 shows a simple implementation for your CustomServiceHost.

LISTING 14-8: Create the Custom ServiceHostFactory

```
public class CustomServiceHostFactory : ServiceHostFactory
{
    public override ServiceHostBase CreateServiceHost(
        string constructorString, Uri[] baseAddresses)
    {
        return new CustomServiceHost(Type.GetType(constructorString),
                                     baseAddresses);
    }

    protected override ServiceHost CreateServiceHost(
        Type serviceType, Uri[] baseAddresses)
    {
        return new CustomServiceHost(serviceType, baseAddresses);
    }
}
```

The logic in the factory must remain simple. To grant the code reusability you have to move all the logic into the custom host. It is good practice to extend and use the ServiceHostFactoryBase when you inherit from the ServiceHostBase, and to extend and use the ServiceHostFactory when you inherit from the ServiceHost.

Use the CustomServiceHostFactory

As previously seen, to host services in IIS you need to use a .svc file in a web site project. To use the `CustomServiceHostFactory`, simply specify it in the `Factory` property of the `@ServiceHost` directive in the .svc file. See Listing 14-9.

LISTING 14-9: Declare the Custom Factory

```
<%@ ServiceHost Language="C#" Service="Service"
Factory="CustomServiceHostFactory" %>
```

The `Factory` property defines the `ServiceHostFactory` implementation that IIS must instantiate and invoke. The value of the `Service` property is passed as a `constructorString` in the `CreateServiceHost` call. In your custom host/factory, the value of the `constructorString` could be anything useful for the recovery of the service to host—for example, a key to retrieve the service type from a shared storage like a database or an XML file.

With IIS 7.0 and WAS, explained in the next section in more depth, you are able to handle multiple site binding. The list of the base addresses that are passed to the `ServiceHostFactory` from IIS include all the host names that the server could accept. In most cases this means that addresses such as `http://localhost` and `http://machinename` are passed to the ServiceHost and an exception is thrown like this: `System.ArgumentException: This collection already contains an address with scheme Http. There can be at most one address per scheme in this collection.`

With the WCF 4.0, you can finally handle this scenario and allow the usage of multiple bindings. In the configuration file you need to add the setting in Listing 14-10.

LISTING 14-10: Enable Multiple Bindings

```
<system.serviceModel>
  <serviceHostingEnvironment multipleSiteBindingsEnabled="true" />
</system.serviceModel>
```

The SVC File-less Activation

You have seen how you can host a service in IIS\WAS using the .svc file. Based on the .svc extension, the runtime that handles the specific request calling is the relative `HttpHandler`. This is pre-configured in the base Web.config located in the .NET Framework folder with the configuration in Listing 14-11.

LISTING 14-11: The Configured HttpHandler for .svc

```
<httpHandlers>
  [...]
  <add path="*.svc" verb="*"
```

```
    type="System.ServiceModel.Activation.HttpHandler,
    System.ServiceModel.Activation, Version=4.0.0.0, Culture=neutral,
    PublicKeyToken=31bf3856ad364e35" validate="False" />
  [...]
</httpHandlers>
```

In the new WCF 4, a combined feature with IIS allows you to create a service without the need to specify the .svc file. How? Simply by using the configuration file, as shown in Listing 14-12.

LISTING 14-12: File-less Activation

```
<system.serviceModel>
  [...]
<serviceHostingEnvironment multipleSiteBindingsEnabled="true">
    <serviceActivations>
        <add relativeAddress="CarRentalService.svc"
service="Wrox.CarRentalService.Implementations.Europe.CarRentalService"/>
    </serviceActivations>
</serviceHostingEnvironment>
  [...]
<services>
  <service name="Wrox.CarRentalService.Implementations.Europe.CarRentalService">
  <endpoint address=""
            binding="basicHttpBinding"
            contract="Wrox.CarRentalService.Contracts.ICarRentalService" />
  </service>
</services>
</system.serviceModel>
```

With this configuration you are able to browse to the `CarRentalService.svc` and see the service help page like a real .svc file.

Windows Activation Services

WCF allows you to create services independently from the used transport protocol. But with IIS 6 you can only use and expose services on the Http protocol by using the ASP.NET Http Pipeline. This is a big limit when you gain advantages from the WCF architecture that, as was already described, could manage a wide range of protocols. To enable the usage of the complete list of the WCF-supported protocols, such as net.tcp, net.pipe, net.msmq, and msmq.formatname, you can use the platform named Windows Activation Services (WAS).

WAS listens in on the specific protocol and routes the received message to the worker process to handle the request. The WAS architecture defines the following components:

➤ Listener adapter—Used to receive messages on a particular protocol and route it to the specific worker process.

➤ Protocol-specific handler—Runs in the worker process and is responsible for receiving and sending messages from and to the listener adapter.

In IIS, a preconfigured set of bindings is created that defines the hostname, the port, the IP address, and some binding information that each binding has to use, as in Figure 14-5. Each website has its own configuration.

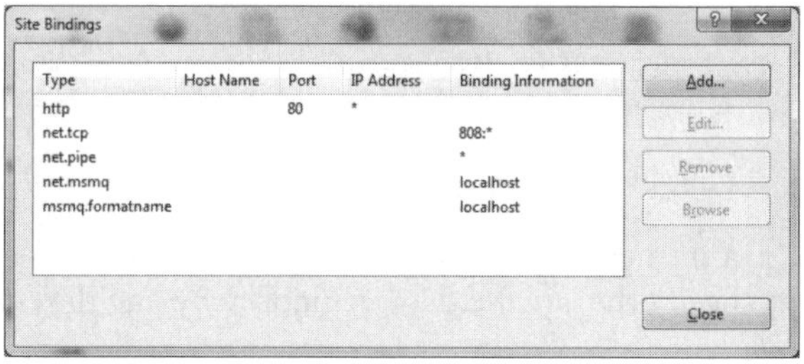

Enabling the usage of a specific protocol is very simple. First, ensure that the binding relative to the desired non-HTTP protocol is configured for the web site (for example, net.

FIGURE 14-5

tcp in the default web site). Second, enable the usage of protocol in the virtual dir Advanced Settings by adding, for example, the net.tcp protocol to the list of enabled protocols, as in Figure 14-6.

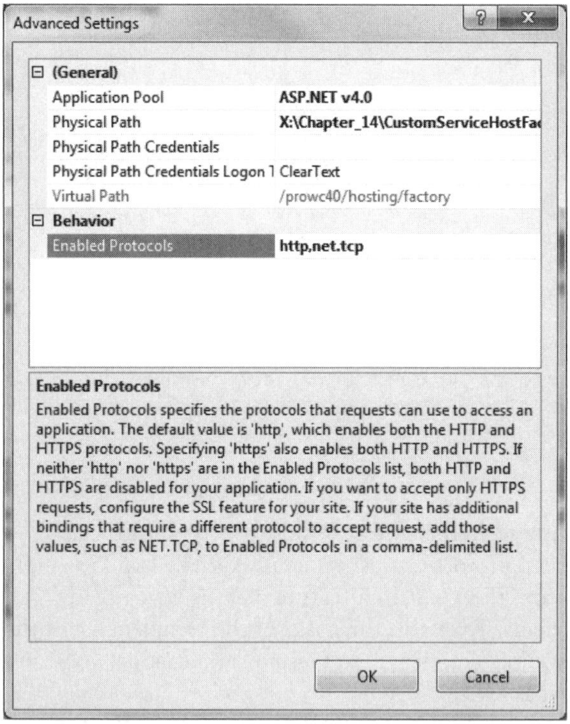

FIGURE 14-6

You can also enable the use of a non-Http protocol by using the `appcmd.exe` command-line tool:

```
appcmd.exe set site "Default Web Site"
-+bindings.[protocol='net.tcp',bindingInformation='808:*']
```

You can still use the Http protocol, but now you are also able to use the net.tcp. Both the UI and the appcmd.exe updates the content of the applicationHost.config file located in the `%windir%\system32\inetsrv\config` folder, as shown in Listing 14-13.

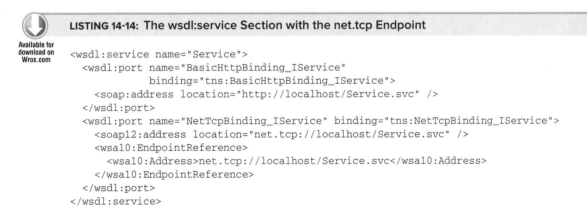

LISTING 14-13: The applicationHost.config

```
<sites>
  <site name="Default Web Site" id="1">
    <application path="/prowc40/hosting" applicationPool="DefaultAppPool">
      <virtualDirectory path="/"
                        physicalPath="C:\inetpub\wwwroot\prowc40\hosting" />
    </application>
    <bindings>
      <binding protocol="http" bindingInformation="*:80:" />
      <binding protocol="net.tcp" bindingInformation="808:*" />
      <binding protocol="net.pipe" bindingInformation="*" />
      <binding protocol="net.msmq" bindingInformation="localhost" />
      <binding protocol="msmq.formatname" bindingInformation="localhost" />
    </bindings>
  </site>
</sites>
```

The net.tcp protocol is now a part of the base address list provided from the IIS-managed host. In WCF 4.0, with the introduction of the default endpoints, it is not necessary to define the endpoint in the configuration file. The service is exposed with two addresses, one for each protocol: Http and net.tcp.

Now, if you check the produced WSDL, you'll see the correct net.tcp port element in the `wsdl:service` section. The XML in Listing 14-14 is part of the generated WSDL (the location of the service depends on your specific configuration).

LISTING 14-14: The wsdl:service Section with the net.tcp Endpoint

```
<wsdl:service name="Service">
  <wsdl:port name="BasicHttpBinding_IService"
             binding="tns:BasicHttpBinding_IService">
    <soap:address location="http://localhost/Service.svc" />
  </wsdl:port>
  <wsdl:port name="NetTcpBinding_IService" binding="tns:NetTcpBinding_IService">
    <soap12:address location="net.tcp://localhost/Service.svc" />
    <wsa10:EndpointReference>
      <wsa10:Address>net.tcp://localhost/Service.svc</wsa10:Address>
    </wsa10:EndpointReference>
  </wsdl:port>
</wsdl:service>
```

However, if you want to modify the default endpoint settings, you can do so, as in Listing 14-15.

LISTING 14-15: Setting the Custom net.tcp Configuration

```
<system.serviceModel>
  <services>
    <service name="Service">
      <endpoint address=""
```

continues

LISTING 14-15 *(continued)*

```
                binding="netTcpBinding"
                bindingConfiguration="ServiceNetTcp"
                contract="IService">
        </endpoint>
      </service>
    </services>
    <bindings>
      <netTcpBinding>
        <binding name="ServiceNetTcp">
          <security mode="TransportWithMessageCredential"/>
        </binding>
      </netTcpBinding>
    </bindings>
  </system.serviceModel>
```

Because the only defined endpoint is for the net.tcp protocol, the endpoint for the Http protocol is no longer available. The service listens only with the `net.tcp://localhost/Service.svc` address.

MANAGING AND TRACKING ENDPOINTS WITH WINDOWS APPFABRIC

WAS is only the first step in making IIS a complete application server. In fact, some other features that real distributed environments need are actually missing. Deploy your services, configure them, and check the health state—monitoring and troubleshooting are not covered in IIS/WAS.

To bridge this gap, Microsoft has released Windows Server AppFabric, already known as *Dublin*—an extension for WAS that introduces a set of new and very important enhancements for the hosted WCF services and workflows. With AppFabric you have a very simple way of monitoring what services and workflows are running and their performance.

Windows Server AppFabric provides the following:

➤ Deploy: A simplified approach to deploy services. You can create and deploy your package from Visual Studio 2010, but you can also export/import installer packages from existing applications.

➤ Configuration: An integrated interface with IIS that allows you to configure application autostart, performance, the database connection for durable workflow, the service certificate, and some other features that an administrator can change without manually modifying the configuration file.

➤ Monitoring: Windows Server AppFabric for .NET 4 introduces new monitoring tools to check the state, exceptions, and the number of completed and failed calls in end-to-end scenarios.

➤ Hosting: A reliable hosting for workflow enabling the use of a robust, sharable state-persistent database based on SQL Server. This allows you to resume long-running workflows if a server crashes or restarts.

➤ Distributed Cache: Already known as Microsoft Velocity, you can use this feature to cache items and reuse them from any servers in your web farm.

The powerful interface totally integrated into the IIS Manager and enabled it to configure applications in a simpler manner. With Windows Server AppFabric, an administrator could update the default services settings without change and recompile the code or, worse, manually modify the web.config file. Figure 14-7 shows how the Windows Server AppFabric Architecture is totally integrated in IIS.

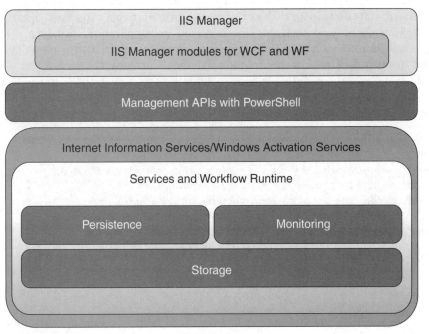

FIGURE 14-7

The IIS integrated set of tools, which in the past was also called Windows Application Server Extensions for .NET 4.0, allow you to do the following:

➤ Configure monitoring, persistence, availability, and autostart; and then performance and security at the Web Application, Web Site, or Service levels.

➤ List and configure the endpoints of a specific service.

➤ Manage the connection and the initialization or the upgrade of a Monitoring Database Configuration.

➤ Manage the connection and the initialization or the upgrade of a Persistence Database Configuration.

➤ Perform a real-time check of services and workflows for health state by monitoring completed, faulted, or failed calls for services, and active, idle, or suspended instances for workflows.

In addition, a set of PowerShell commands were also released and allow you to do all the same actions of the previous extensions.

Navigating from one to another is a very simple thing because the extensions allow you, for example, to retrieve the list of endpoints for a service, or to obtain the service of a selected endpoint.

Furthermore, the Web Deployment tool, another IIS extension installed with Visual Studio 2010 but also available as a separate download, enables you to export/import application packages directly from the IIS Manager. You are then able to export your web application, including settings, and import it in another server of your server farm. Visual Studio 2010 also allows the creation of the same installer package from the Solution Explorer. Currently, the deployment process lacks the WCF and now the Web Deployment tool offers a very simple and powerful way to deploy your services.

> *Microsoft has also released Windows Azure platform AppFabric. Windows Azure platform AppFabric allows users to easily develop solutions in the cloud while Windows Server AppFabric is for "classic" environments (also called on-premises). Windows Azure platform AppFabric, unlike Windows Server AppFabric, provides a Service Bus solution to facilitate communication between services and an Access Control Service (ACS) to create security tokens for federated authorization. Windows Azure platform AppFabric is discussed later in this chapter.*

In the following sections you'll see how to configure and use the Windows Server AppFabric tools to monitor WCF and WF services.

Setting Up Windows Server AppFabric

Windows Server AppFabric is available as a different install package downloadable from the Microsoft official site: `http://msdn.microsoft.com/en-us/windowsserver/ee695849.aspx`. Windows Server AppFabric runs only on Windows Vista, Windows 7, or Windows Server 2008 and Windows Server 2008 R2. Some features, such as autostart, are run only in Windows 7 and in Windows Server 2008 R2. SQL Server is not a requirement to install Windows Server AppFabric, but some features like monitoring, persistence, or caching are not enabled if it is missing. You could also use SQL Server 2008, but SQL Server 2005 is not supported. It is also possible to use other databases or data stores, particularly for persistence and cache.

After the installer process has finished, as shown in Figure 14-8, you can start the configuration wizard to create and initialize the monitoring database and the persistence database.

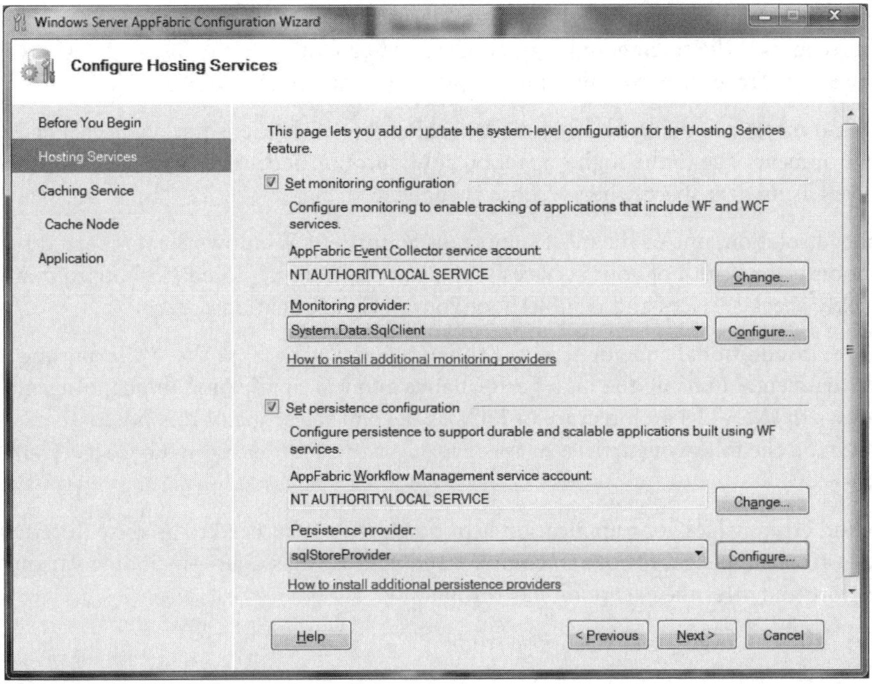

FIGURE 14-8

By clicking the Configure button you can initialize or simply reference the already created database (see Figure 14-9).

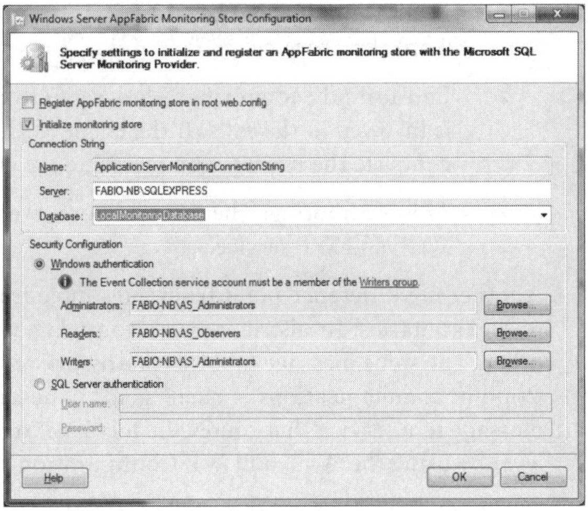

If you want to configure this setting later, you can execute the Windows Server AppFabric Configuration Wizard by accessing All Programs ⇨ Windows Server AppFabric ⇨ Configure AppFabric.

At the end of the wizard, you'll see new sections in the IIS interface that allow you to access to the AppFabric features.

Monitoring Services with AppFabric

FIGURE 14-9

Troubleshooting in running services is not so simple. Actually, the only way to find application exception or stack trace is by enabling WCF Diagnostic Tracing and Message Logging. In much of this scenario it is not so simple to change the configuration file, and it writes a lot of settings to enable the environment. After this, you have to be able to reproduce the step that generates the service failure, get the tracing files, and then disable the tracing because it has a great impact on application performance because they append strings on a text file. After you have the tracing and logging files, you can analyze it by using the Microsoft Service Trace Viewer (SvcTraceView.exe) distributed with the Microsoft Windows SDK.

Using the tracing and message logging files is not a bad thing, but their use is not recommended in production environments due to the high impact on configuration settings and application performance, as well as on disk space when verbose is enabled.

To offer an enhanced solution, one of the most important features of Windows Server AppFabric is the ability to monitor the health of your services with a simple and integrated Dashboard that allows you to quickly check services and troubleshoot your WCF applications.

You don't need to write additional code or change configuration files because the WCF runtime in the .NET 4.0 is instrumental in using the high performance and low application impact of Event Tracing for Windows (ETW). The architecture of ETW is beyond the scope of this book. To get more info about it, read the following article: `http://msdn.microsoft.com/en-us/magazine/cc163437.aspx`.

When you try to find errors while your application is in production, you need to analyze different levels of messages—from simple exceptions to complex and verbose messages—including various steps occurring before and after the exception has thrown.

AppFabric handles different levels you can choose from:

➤ Off: The monitor is completely disabled.

➤ Errors Only: Tracks data only when an exception or a warning event occurs.

➤ Health Monitoring: Default level that allows you to display WCF and WF service health on AppFabric tooling.

➤ End-to-End Monitoring: Allows you to track the message flow when more than one service is involved in the calls. If the client calls a service and that service calls another service to complete the process of a message, the entire flow is reconstructed and tracked.

➤ Troubleshooting: The most verbose level that must be enabled to diagnose issues with your WCF and WF service.

Another big difference point from the simple tracing is the capacity to track message flow in end-to-end scenarios. In distributed environments you have more services that communicate with each other. The same message might be across more than one service before it is processed. In point-to-point communications, a client sends a message to a service; in end-to-end, a client sends a message to a service that routes the message to another service, and so on. You can configure the level by using the WCF and WF Configuration tool installed with AppFabric.

The AppFabric monitoring correlates the WCF traces allowing you to see what happens to the message from the client to the final service and back. If you handle more than one server, as in a web farm, using a common and shared SQL Server database to collect the event collection enables the message correlation across servers.

To start using monitoring you don't need to change any part of your source code. By simply right-clicking your web application node in IIS, you can select the .NET WCF and WF item and then the Configure button to open the Configure WCF and WF for Application tool. As you see in Figure 14-10, the Configuration tool allows setting the Health Monitoring Level for your WCF or WF service application.

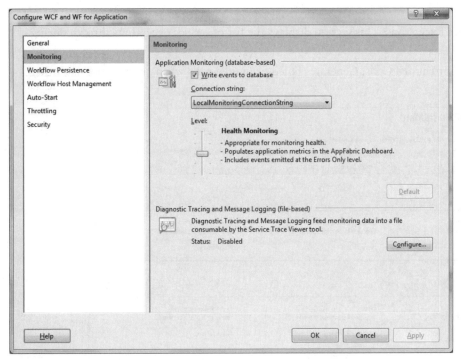

FIGURE 14-10

This tool also allows enabling the Diagnostic Tracing and Message Logging feature in a few simple steps, without using the WCF Service Configuration Editor that has an interface often difficult and less intuitive to use. Especially for system administrators, AppFabric simplifies the configuration process.

Now that your service is running, hosted in IIS, and the Health Monitoring Level is enabled, you can monitor your service by using the Fabric Dashboard, shown in Figure 14-11. A Windows service named *AppFabric Event Collection Service* "collects events from an ETW session and writes them to a monitoring database."

FIGURE 14-11

Accessing the Dashboard allows you to get info about the current running requests, the completed requests, and get details about failed requests. As you can see in Figure 14-12, there are three sections:

➤ Completed Calls: Displays the list of successfully completed calls, with a row for each address.

➤ Service Exceptions: This section displays the list of service exceptions thrown during execution.

➤ Failed or Faulted Calls: Generates failed or faulted calls when an exception is thrown.

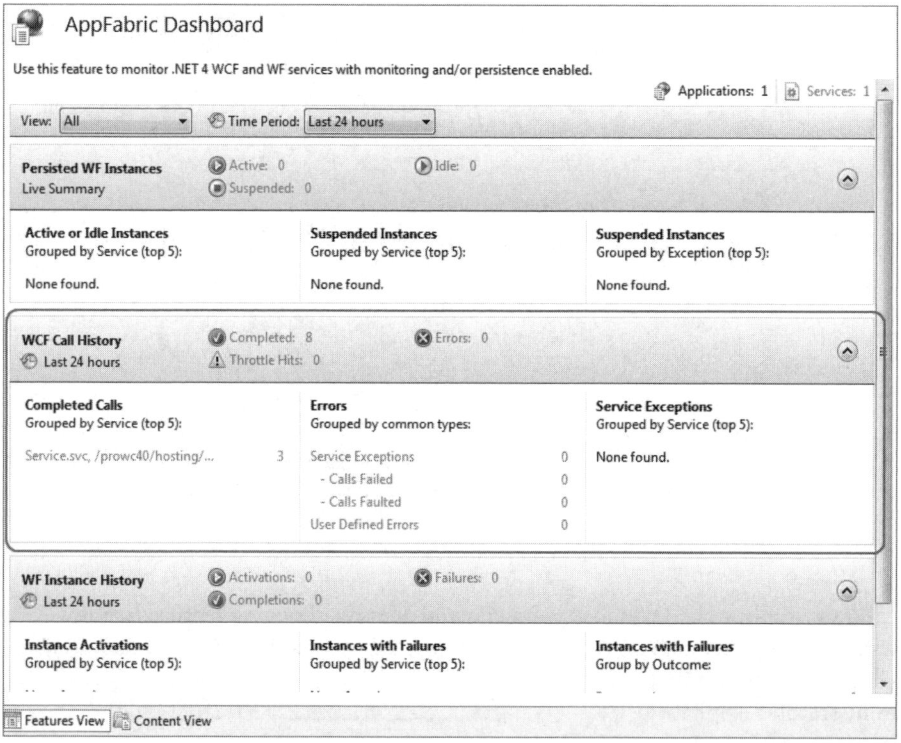

FIGURE 14-12

By clicking one of the rows displayed, a query on tracked data is generated and the result is a list of collected events filtered by the passed input parameters. You can also change the input parameters to restrict the resultset.

In Figure 14-13, the list of real-time collected events are displayed. You will also see, if activated, the E2EActivityId that displays the correlation event ID for end-to-end scenarios.

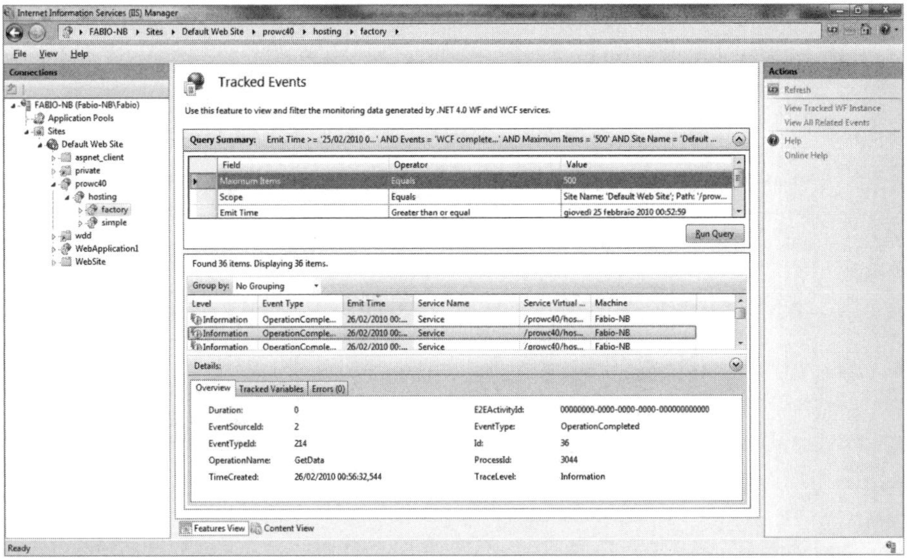

FIGURE 14-13

You can also display the list of service exceptions. Figure 14-14 displays the service exception and the related error details with stack trace.

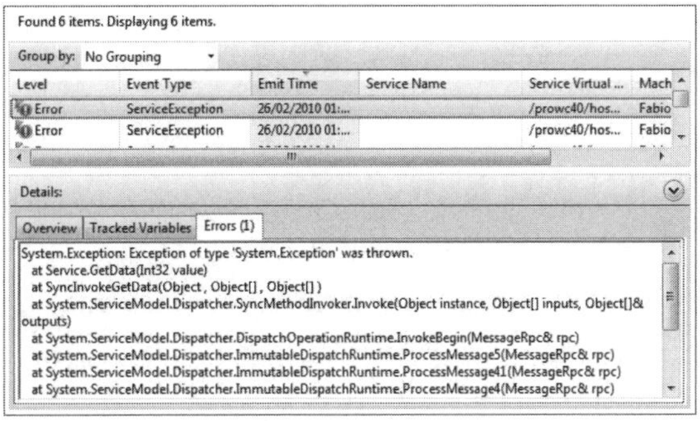

Enabling the Event Viewer

Troubleshooting applications, especially service, is sometimes a very difficult activity. As previously said, until WCF 3.5 Service Pack 1, you could enable the Diagnostic Trace and Message Logging, a really valid tool but sometimes difficult to read and find problems.

FIGURE 14-14

With WCF 4 and AppFabric, you can also gain advantage from the usage of ETW infrastructure. This is disabled by default. To enable, open the Event Viewer, then select Application and Services Logs, Microsoft, Windows and then right-click Application Server-Applications node. Select View, Show Analytic and Debug Logs if not already checked. Under the Application Server-Applications node, select Analytic and then click Enable Log Item in the Actions pane.

Now if you call your service, the events appear in the Analytic log, as you can see in Figure 14-15.

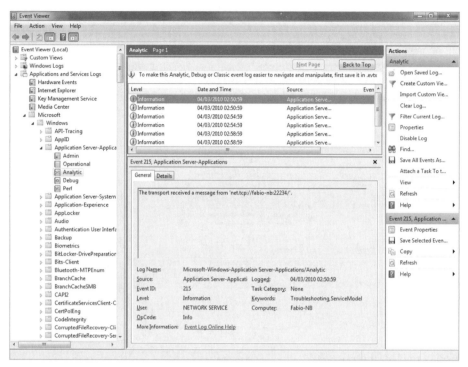

FIGURE 14-15

ROUTING SERVICES

By developing distributed applications, you may need to create a frontend service that acts as a bridge between your internal services, such as a protected internal network. With the WCF 4.0, a new service has been released: the `RoutingService`. This allows you to create a front-end service that accepts the requests and routes messages to the internal set of services deployed into your private network, maybe beyond a firewall.

Some of the features include the following:

➤ Content-based routing

➤ Protocol and security bridging

➤ Error handling

The `RoutingService` acts as an intermediate between the client and the service. It receives the message from the client and, based on the filters you have applied, routes the message to the designated service.

Content-Based Routing

The principal role of a routing service is to route messages received from a client to backend services that could process it. How can it retrieve the correct service endpoint that has to be invoked? The routing service doesn't know the backend services directly, but it knows the message and applies to it a set of configured filters to individuate the endpoint services to invoke.

A set of predefined filters are already available in WCF 4.0 and ready to use. You could apply a filter based on the message's action or as a result of an applied XPath query. Table 14-1 summarizes the various filter types and describes how to use them.

TABLE 14-1: Routing Service Filters

FILTER TYPE	DESCRIPTION
Action	This filter is based on the message action specified in the filterData attribute. Example: `<filter name="actionFilter" filterType="Action" filterData="http://wrox/CarRentalService/2009/10/RentalService/CalculatePrice"/>`
And	This filter is used to indicate the names of two other filters, with results that have to be combined and evaluated to true. Example: `<filter name="andFilter" filterType="And" filter1="firstFilter" filter2="secondFilter"/>`
EndpointAddress	This filter is based on the messages To header value. Example: `<filter name="endpointAddressFilter" filterType="EndpointAddress" filterData=" http://localhost:10101/CarRentalService" />`
EndpointAddressPrefix	Similar to the `EndpointAddressFilter`, this filter matches the beginning of the messages To header value. Example: `<filter name="endpointAddressPrefixFilter" filterType="EndpointAddress" filterData="http://localhost:10101" />`
EndpointName	This filter matches the name of one of the service endpoints exposed on the routing service. Example: `<filter name="endpointNameFilter" filterType="EndpointName" filterData="routingEndpoint1" />`
Custom	This filter allows defining a custom filter type. Example: `<filter name="customFilter" filterType="Custom" customType="MatchVersionMessageFilter" filterData="Soap11" />`

continues

TABLE 14-1 *(continued)*

FILTER TYPE	DESCRIPTION
MatchAll	This filter matches all incoming messages. Example: `<filter name="matchAllFilter" filterType="MatchAll" />`
XPath	Applies an XPath expression to the incoming messages. Example: `<filter name="xPathFilter" filterType="XPath" filterData="//*/location" />`

As seen in Table 14-1, with the type `Custom` you can implement your own filter simply by extending the abstract `MessageFilter` class.

The routing service is implemented as a WCF service that you can find in the `System. ServiceModel.Routing` assembly. The architecture of the service is composed of the following components:

➤ A set of contracts: `IDuplexSessionRouter`, `IRequestReplyRouter`, `ISimplexDatagramRouter`, and `ISimplexSessionRouter`.

➤ RoutingService: A service that implements the available routing contracts.

➤ Service behavior: Allows you to define the filter table that the routing service must use.

➤ Routing configuration setting: Allows you to define the filters to apply to the client endpoints to calls, and the service backup list to handle exceptions.

Each defined contract allows you to process messages using different message-exchange patterns. You have to choose the correct message pattern based on what your internal services implement. In fact, different message patterns might not work properly. What does it mean if a request-reply pattern, for example Http, waits for a response message that it never receives from a one-way communication?

As shown in Listing 14-16, configuring the routing service is really simple because it is very similar to any other service in WCF. Using the configuration file, you have to create the service section.

LISTING 14-16: Configuring the Routing Service

```
<system.serviceModel>
    <services>
      <service behaviorConfiguration="routingBehavior"
          name="System.ServiceModel.Routing.RoutingService">
        <host>
          <baseAddresses>
            <add baseAddress="http://localhost:9001/routing"/>
          </baseAddresses>
        </host>

        <endpoint address=""
```

```
                   binding="basicHttpBinding"
                   name="requestReplyEndpoint"
                   contract="System.ServiceModel.Routing.IRequestReplyRouter" />
        </service>
      </services>
   <system.serviceModel>
```

As shown in Listing 14-17, the service behavior `routingBehavior` simply defines the name of the routing table that the service must use.

LISTING 14-17: Configuring the Service Behavior

```
<behaviors>
  <serviceBehaviors>
    <behavior name="routingBehavior">
      <routing filterTableName="routingTable" />
    </behavior>
  </serviceBehaviors>
</behaviors>
```

Now you have to configure the list of the endpoints that the routing service, acting as a client, should invoke. See Listing 14-18.

LISTING 14-18: Configuring the client endpoints

```
<client>
    <endpoint name="HospitalServiceEndpoint"
              address="net.tcp://localhost:9050/hospitalservice"
              binding="netTcpBinding"
              contract="*" />
    <endpoint name="LabServiceEndpoint"
              address="net.tcp://localhost:9051/labservice"
              binding="netTcpBinding"
              contract="*" />
</client>
```

Finally, to allow the correct execution of the routing service, it is necessary to configure the routing rules. As shown in Listing 14-19, you can do it using the `routing` configuration section.

LISTING 14-19: Configuring the Routing Rules

```
<routing>

    <filters>
      <filter name="LabFilter"
              filterType="Action"
              filterData="http://healthcare/lab" />
      <filter name="HospitalFilter"
              filterType="Action"
```

continues

LISTING 14-19 *(continued)*

```
                filterData="http://healthcare/hospital" />
    </filters>

    <filterTables>
      <filterTable name="routingTable">
        <add filterName="HospitalFilter"
            endpointName="HospitalServiceEndpoint"/>
        <add filterName="LabFilter"
            endpointName="LabServiceEndpoint" />
      </filterTable>
    </filterTables>
  </routing>
```

In this section, you have created and named two filters with each one based on the message action. In the `filterTable` you configure the endpoint that must be used when one of the filters is applied to the incoming message.

As previously said, by extending the abstract `MessageFilter` class, you can also use a custom filter to change the standard message filtering. See Listing 14-20.

LISTING 14-20: Creating the Custom Message Filter

```
class VersionBasedMessageFilter : MessageFilter
{
    private string MessageVersion;

    public VersionBasedMessageFilter(object filterData)
    {
        this.MessageVersion = filterData as string;
    }

    public override bool Match(System.ServiceModel.Channels.Message message)
    {
        return this.InnerMatch(message);
    }

    public override bool Match(System.ServiceModel.Channels.MessageBuffer buffer)
    {
        bool response;
        Message message = buffer.CreateMessage();
        try
        {
            response = this.InnerMatch(message);
        }
        finally
        {
            message.Close();
        }

        return (response);
```

```
    }

    private bool InnerMatch(System.ServiceModel.Channels.Message message)
    {
        return (message.Version.Envelope.ToString == this.MessageVersion);
    }
}
```

To use the custom filter, simply set up the configuration file, as shown in Listing 14-21.

LISTING 14-21: Enable the Usage of the Custom Message Filter

```
<routing>
  <filters>
    <filter
      name="LabFilter"
      filterType="Custom"
      customType="HealthRoutingService.Description.VersionBasedMessageFilter,
          HealthRoutingService" filterData="http://healthcare/lab" />
  </filters>
</routing>
```

Protocol and Security Bridging

This feature allows the service to receive messages from the client in any kind of protocol (e.g., Http) or message encoding (Soap 1.1) and call the internal services by using a totally different protocol (e.g., net.tcp with Soap 1.2), as shown in Figure 14-16.

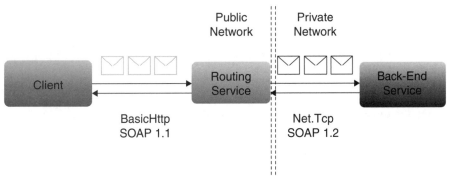

FIGURE 14-16

You can use different bindings for the communication between the client and the routing service, and another binding for the communication between the routing service and the backend services. This is a useful behavior when you need to enable or adapt communications with legacy clients, which could use only a simple Http version, and the new version of service that uses the high performance net.tcp protocol.

As for the protocol, you can use a kind of security mechanism for the routing service that is totally different from the backend service by separating the credentials used by the client from the internal management of the identity.

Error Handling

Another feature of the routing service is the ability to manage the exceptions. Sometimes, although your application runs, a service may become unreachable. In this case, you can configure the routing service to try a list of back-up services.

First, you have to configure the list of the client endpoints that the routing services use, as shown in Listing 14-22.

LISTING 14-22: Setting the Custom net.tcp Configuration

```xml
<client>
    <endpoint name="LabServiceEndpoint"
              address="net.tcp://localhost:9052/labservice"
              binding="netTcpBinding"
              contract="*"  />
    <endpoint name="LabServiceBackupEndpoint"
              address="http://server1/labservice"
              binding="basicHttpBinding"
              contract="*" />
    <endpoint name="LabServiceBackupEndpoint"
              address="net.tcp://server2:9052/labservice"
              binding="netTcpBinding"
              contract="*" />
</client>
```

After you have configured the list of endpoints and the list of filters you want to apply, omitted in Listing 14-23, you have to configure the `filterTables` to define the endpoint that the routing service must use when the filter is applied. In this element, you can specify the name of the backup list to find the sequence of endpoints that the routing service must call if the first endpoint throws an exception.

LISTING 14-23: Define the Filter Table and the Name of the Backup List

```xml
<filterTables>
    <filterTable name="routingTable">
      <add filterName="LabFilter"
           endpointName="LabServiceEndpoint"
           backupList="labBackupList"/>
    </filterTable>
</filterTables>
```

Finally, you can configure the list of the backup service endpoints that must refer to an existing client endpoint defined in the configuration file. See Listing 14-24.

LISTING 14-24: Define the Endpoints in the Backup List

```
<backupLists>
    <backupList name="labBackupList">
      <add endpointName=" LabServiceBackupEndpoint "/>
      <add endpointName=" LabServiceBackup2Endpoint "/>
    </backupList>
  </backupLists>
</routing>
```

CLOUD-BASED HOSTING

In this chapter, hosting services in a "classic" distributed environment was discussed. In this scenario, most times you are the owner of the servers where the solution will be deployed or you at least directly know the hardware infrastructure. The hardware is then sized based on your solution requirements. Therefore, when you have to scale up your server farm, you need to buy new hardware.

In cloud computing, instead, the details about the hardware are totally abstracted from the user (or rather the developer) point of view. The developer doesn't need to know anything about the infrastructure. The concept is to allow scaling up or down the solutions when necessary, requiring resources on-demand with a pay-per-use mode. If your solution, during the start-up, requires fewer hardware resources to run, you'll pay only the consumed storage, the amount of data in transactions, and the hour of computing to make your application available. This dramatically reduces the cost of start-up, because you don't need to invest in hardware and the effort of IT management.

The entire infrastructure is then totally scalable and has the capacity to manage large-volume data and storage. In addition, the cloud computing also has the support for reliability that makes your solution available 24/7. Furthermore, a replication system of nodes allows starting a backup node if the first stops unexpectedly.

It is clear that the applications that take advantage of cloud computing are mainly web applications. You can deploy a web application that exposes your service and obtains all the cloud computing benefits previously discussed. An application hosted in a cloud computing infrastructure is also called *in-the-cloud*, while a classic application is called *on-premises*. Windows Azure is the Microsoft solution for the applications in-the-cloud. In the following sections the options to expose a WCF service using the cloud infrastructure are explored.

Hosting WCF Services in Windows Azure

Windows Azure is a set of technologies for the cloud computing. It allows you to deploy web applications, as previously mentioned, but it also provides cloud storage to handle data such as Tables, BLOBS, or Queues, and a SQL Azure Database that is the cloud version of SQL Server. Another option offered by Azure is the support to applications and services connections across networks by providing a Service Bus, and an Access Control Service that issues tokens for federated authorization. These two options are grouped in a technology called Windows Azure platform AppFabric. It is different from the already discussed Windows Server AppFabric and should not be confused. Azure platform AppFabric is discussed in more depth in the next section.

Windows Azure Computing allows you to deploy your application in-the-cloud. You don't know anything about the hardware of the servers (or nodes) when deploying your application. You don't know its location in the web farm, its IP, and you can't access the local resource (drive C: or similar). You simply develop your solution and deploy it in-the-cloud.

With Azure, you have two application-type options, also called roles:

➤ Web role: For frontend solutions such as a web application.

➤ Worker role: Comparable to a Windows service. It is designed to perform background operations.

These two roles enable the decoupling between the frontend interface and the related backend operations. In a typical scenario, a web role enqueues a message that a worker role processes. It is important to note that you don't know if a worker role runs in the same node of a web role. In this way, decoupling contributes to load balance and scales up your solution.

If you want to host your WCF service in Windows Azure, using the web role is the best solution. From the developer point of view, there is no big difference between an on-premise and an in-the-cloud web application. By using Visual Studio 2010, you could create a WCF Azure Service by using the Web Cloud Service template and then add your services and endpoints like any other web project. Then finally build your solution and deploy it using the generated packages.

The Azure AppFabric Service Bus

There are particular scenarios where your endpoints could be difficult to reach due to dynamic IP assignment, firewalls, or NAT boundaries. To accomplish this scenario, the AppFabric Service Bus provides a way to make this connection. Any service that wants to receive messages simply registers its address in the AppFabric Service Bus. Any application that wants to send messages to a registered service simply refers to the exposed and well-known Service Bus endpoint, as you can see in Figure 14-17.

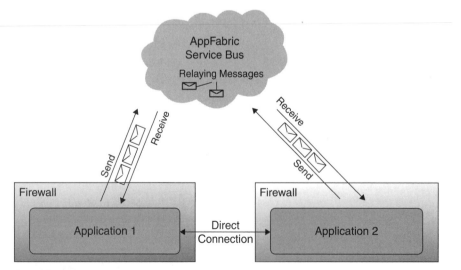

FIGURE 14-17

The connection between the client and service starts using the relayed mode through the relay service. The relay service tries to communicate the connection information of the service to the client and of the client to the service. If it succeeds, the connection continues using direct mode. Otherwise the connection continues using relayed mode.

Relaying Through the Cloud

To use the AppFabric Service Bus with WCF you don't need to know a different programming model. You can define contracts and create a host environment in exactly the same way as with WCF, as already seen in Chapter 2. The only difference is related to the listening address (the target address if you are on client side), and the binding used. Indeed, you need to use a specific binding that uses one of the bindings that supports the relay transport protocol. Table 14-2 describes the new bindings now available and installed with the .NET Services SDK.

TABLE 14-2: Bindings in .NET Services

BINDING NAME	DESCRIPTION
BasicHttpRelayBinding	The ServiceBus version of the BasicHttpBinding.
NetEventRelayBinding	This binding enables the Publish&Subscribe mode. By using this binding, a message can be relayed to zero, or to one or more listening services.
NetOnewayRelayBinding	Corresponds to the one-way mode of a NetTcpBinding connection.
NetTcpRelayBinding	This binding is based to the NetTcpBinding and allows establishing TCP connections through the cloud.
WebHttpRelayBinding	This binding is based to the WebHttpBinding and allows establishing RESTful-style communications.
WS2007HttpRelayBinding	This binding is based to the WS2007HttpBinding and allows the usage of most recent versions of WS-* standard specifications in cloud communications.
WSHttpRelayBinding	This binding is based to the WSHttpBinding and allows the usage of WS-* standard specifications in cloud communications.

All these bindings are available in the Microsoft.ServiceBus assembly. With the November 2009 CTP of the Microsoft .NET Services SDK, you can find the assembly in the %programfiles%\ Microsoft .NET Services SDK (Nov 2009 CTP)\Assemblies.

As previously said, you have to create the specific address to enable communications. As shown in Listing 14-25, the ServiceBusEnvironment class helps you create the specific address by using the CreateServiceUri static method.

LISTING 14-25: Build the Listening Address for the Service Bus

```
Uri address = ServiceBusEnvironment.CreateServiceUri("sb", "carrental",
                "CarRentalRelayService");
```

The previous code produces the following URI: `sb://carrental.servicebus.windows.net/CarRentalRelayService/`. The first parameter specifies the URI schema that must be used to build the address. The second parameter specifies the name of the AppFabric solution. Finally, the third parameter defines the relative address of your service.

With one of the relaying bindings, the address is then used to build the endpoint address. Finally, you also need to authenticate your connection, providing credentials by choosing one of the options in Table 14-3.

TABLE 14-3: Available Credentials

MEMBER NAME	DESCRIPTION
SAML	A SAML (Security Assertion Markup Language) token is used to authenticate with the Service Bus.
SharedSecret	A Shared Secret is used to authenticate with the AppFabric Service Bus.
SimpleWebToken	A Simple Web Token is used to authenticate with the AppFabric Service Bus.
Unauthenticated	A client doesn't provide any kind of credential.

A SAML token is a type of credential used in a federated scenario, as explained in Chapter 9, and in this case it enables the reuse of the existing infrastructure. The `SharedSecret` credential is a token based on a shared secret, such as a password or an array of bytes, known both to the client and to the service and used to secure the communication. A `SimpleWebToken`, instead, is a really compact key/value encrypted token secured by signature and mostly used in RESTful architectures.

In the following code you can create a new `ServiceHost` that handles the cloud relayed version of `CarRentalService`.

LISTING 14-26: Hosting a Cloud-Relayed Service

```
ServiceBusEnvironment.SystemConnectivity.Mode = ConnectivityMode.Tcp;
Uri address = ServiceBusEnvironment.CreateServiceUri("sb", "carrental",
                "CarRentalRelayService");

NetTcpRelayBinding binding = new NetTcpRelayBinding();
binding.Security.Mode = EndToEndSecurityMode.None;

ServiceHost host = new ServiceHost(typeof(CarRentalService));
```

```
ServiceEndpoint endpoint =
    host.AddServiceEndpoint(typeof(ICarRentalService), binding, address);

TransportClientEndpointBehavior sharedSecretServiceBusCredential =
            new TransportClientEndpointBehavior();
sharedSecretServiceBusCredential.CredentialType =
            TransportClientCredentialType.SharedSecret;
sharedSecretServiceBusCredential.Credentials.SharedSecret.IssuerName = "owner";
sharedSecretServiceBusCredential.Credentials.SharedSecret.IssuerSecret =
            "4+X1iL29uQ4kJiDMBTQ9Sz9n8T16RTgL9SIpyGWKryc=";

endpoint.Behaviors.Add(sharedSecretServiceBusCredential);

host.Open();

Console.WriteLine("Waiting for incoming messages...");
Console.ReadLine();

host.Close();
```

You have used a `SharedSecret` credential type that needs an IssuerName and an IssuerSecret to authenticate the connection to the specified Azure AppFabric application. The `TransportClientEndpointBehavior` is used to hold the credentials and must be assigned to the service endpoint.

On client side, the code is similar (as shown in Listing 14-27).

LISTING 14-27: Call a Cloud-Relayed Service from client

```
ServiceBusEnvironment.SystemConnectivity.Mode = ConnectivityMode.Http;

Uri address = ServiceBusEnvironment.CreateServiceUri("sb", "carrental",
            "CarRentalRelayService");

NetTcpRelayBinding binding = new NetTcpRelayBinding();
binding.Security.Mode = EndToEndSecurityMode.None;

TransportClientEndpointBehavior sharedSecretServiceBusCredential =
            new TransportClientEndpointBehavior();
sharedSecretServiceBusCredential.CredentialType =
            TransportClientCredentialType.SharedSecret;
sharedSecretServiceBusCredential.Credentials.SharedSecret.IssuerName = "owner";
sharedSecretServiceBusCredential.Credentials.SharedSecret.IssuerSecret =
            "4+X1iL29uQ4kJiDMBTQ9Sz9n8T16RTgL9SIpyGWKryc=";

ServiceEndpoint endpoint = new ServiceEndpoint(
        ContractDescription.GetContract(typeof (ICarRentalService)),
        binding,
        new EndpointAddress(address));
```

continues

LISTING 14-27 *(continued)*

```
    endpoint.Behaviors.Add(sharedSecretServiceBusCredential);

ChannelFactory<ICarRentalService> channelFactory =
    new ChannelFactory<ICarRentalService>(endpoint);
ICarRentalService ps = channelFactory.CreateChannel();
```

You might note the usage of the `ServiceBusEnvironment.SystemConnectivity.Mode = ConnectivityMode.Http` setting. This is because you can set a different protocol connection for both the sender service and for the receiver service.

INDEX

X